Flash 8 Cookbook™

Other resources from O'Reilly

Related titles

Flash 8 Cookbook™

Flash 8: Projects for Learning Animation and Interactivity

ActionScript 3.0 Cookbook™

ActionScript 3.0 Pocket Reference

ActionScript 3.0: The Definitive Guide

Flash Remoting: The Definitive Guide

Programming Flash Communication Server

Flash Hacks

Essential ActionScript 2.0

Essential ActionScript 3

Flash 8: The Missing Manual

oreilly.com

oreilly.com is more than a complete catalog of O'Reilly books. You'll also find links to news, events, articles, weblogs, sample chapters, and code examples.

oreillynet.com is the essential portal for developers interested in open and emerging technologies, including new platforms, programming languages, and operating systems.

Conferences

O'Reilly brings diverse innovators together to nurture the ideas that spark revolutionary industries. We specialize in documenting the latest tools and systems, translating the innovator's knowledge into useful skills for those in the trenches. Visit *conferences.oreilly.com* for our upcoming events.

Safari Bookshelf (*safari.oreilly.com*) is the premier online reference library for programmers and IT professionals. Conduct searches across more than 1,000 books. Subscribers can zero in on answers to time-critical questions in a matter of seconds. Read the books on your Bookshelf from cover to cover or simply flip to the page you need. Try it today for free.

Flash 8 Cookbook™

Joey Lott

with *Jeffrey Bardzell, Ezra Freedman,*
Kris Honeycutt, and Robert Reinhardt

O'REILLY®

Beijing · Cambridge · Farnham · Köln · Paris · Sebastopol · Taipei · Tokyo

Flash 8 Cookbook™
by Joey Lott with Jeffrey Bardzell, Ezra Freedman, Kris Honeycutt, and Robert Reinhardt

Published by O'Reilly Media, Inc., 1005 Gravenstein Highway North, Sebastopol, CA 95472.

O'Reilly books may be purchased for educational, business, or sales promotional use. Online editions are also available for most titles (*safari.oreilly.com*). For more information, contact our corporate/institutional sales department: (800) 998-9938 or *corporate@oreilly.com*.

Editor: Steve Weiss
Developmental Editor: Elise Walter
Production Editor: Darren Kelly
Copyeditor: Nancy Kotary
Proofreader: Chris Downey

Indexer: Johnna VanHoose Dinse
Cover Designer: Karen Montgomery
Interior Designer: David Futato
Illustrators: Robert Romano, Jessamyn Read, and Lesley Borash

Printing History:

April 2006:   First Edition.

 This book uses RepKover™, a durable

ISBN: 0-596-10240-2
[M]

Table of Contents

Preface

Flash began as a technology for building and deploying vector animations. Since that time, Flash has developed into a platform of technologies with Flash Player at the core. The Flash Platform consists of the Flash IDE (the Flash authoring application) as well as server-side technologies, including Flash Remoting and Flash Media Server. In recent years, the Flash Platform has expanded to also include new technologies for building Flash content, such as Flex.

Clearly, the Flash Platform is a large subject. This book focuses primarily on how to use the Flash IDE to build Flash animations and applications, but additional Flash Platform technologies are discussed when deemed appropriate and within the scope of the book.

Audience

This book is intended for anyone who wants to learn solutions to specific tasks using Flash. Whether you are a Flash beginner or a Flash expert, this book can help.

Assumptions This Book Makes

This book is not a typical reference book or training guide. We necessarily assume that you are already familiar with the basics of Flash.

We also assume that if you are reading this book, you are most interested in Flash-based, authoring time, non-ActionScript solutions. For example, it is technically possible to animate programmatically with ActionScript; however, the non-ActionScript timeline tween solution is emphasized in this book. It's possible that an ActionScript solution is either necessary or better in some circumstances, and, in those cases, we provide the ActionScript solution either by itself or in addition to a non-ActionScript solution. If you are looking for a book that focuses on ActionScript solutions, you may want to consider a different book.

Conventions Used in This Book

The following typographical conventions are used in this book:

Plain text

Indicates menu titles, menu options, menu buttons, and keyboard accelerators (such as Alt and Ctrl).

Italic

Indicates new terms, URLs, email addresses, methods, filenames, file extensions, pathnames, directories, and Unix utilities.

`Constant width`

Indicates commands, options, switches, variables, attributes, keys, functions, types, classes, namespaces, modules, properties, parameters, values, objects, events, event handlers, XML tags, HTML tags, macros, the contents of files, or the output from commands.

`Constant width bold`

Shows commands or other text that should be typed literally by the user.

`Constant width italic`

Shows text that should be replaced with user-supplied values.

 Indicates a tip, suggestion, or general note.

 Indicates a tip, suggestion, or general note.

Using Code Examples

This book is here to help you get your job done. In general, you may use the code in this book in your programs and documentation. You do not need to contact us for permission unless you're reproducing a significant portion of the code. For example, writing a program that uses several chunks of code from this book does not require permission. Selling or distributing a CD-ROM of examples from O'Reilly books does require permission. Answering a question by citing this book and quoting example code does not require permission. Incorporating a significant amount of example code from this book into your product's documentation does require permission.

We appreciate, but do not require, attribution. An attribution usually includes the title, author, publisher, and ISBN. For example: "*Flash 8 Cookbook* by Joey Lott. Copyright 2006 O'Reilly Media, Inc., 0-596-10240-2."

If you feel your use of code examples falls outside fair use or the permission given above, feel free to contact us at *permissions@oreilly.com*.

How to Contact Us

Please address comments and questions concerning this book to the publisher:

> O'Reilly Media, Inc.
> 1005 Gravenstein Highway North
> Sebastopol, CA 95472
> (800) 998-9938 (in the United States or Canada)
> (707) 829-0515 (international or local)
> (707) 829-0104 (fax)

We have a web page for this book, where we list errata, examples, and any additional information. You can access this page at:

> *http://www.oreilly.com/catalog/flash8ckbk*

To comment or ask technical questions about this book, send email to:

> *bookquestions@oreilly.com*

For more information about our books, conferences, Resource Centers, and the O'Reilly Network, see our web site at:

> *http://www.oreilly.com*

Safari® Enabled

 When you see a Safari® Enabled icon on the cover of your favorite technology book, it means the book is available online through the O'Reilly Network Safari Bookshelf.

Safari offers a solution that's better than e-books. It's a virtual library that lets you easily search thousands of top technology books, cut and paste code samples, download chapters, and find quick answers when you need the most accurate, current information. Try it for free at *http://safari.oreilly.com*.

Acknowledgments

Joey Lott

I'd like to thank the many people that helped directly and indirectly with this book. Thanks to Tim O'Reilly for publishing this book. Thanks to Steve Weiss for being an advocate for the book and making sure that it received all the necessary resources.

This book is only possible with the help of Elise Walter, and I'd like to thank her for all the work reviewing, editing, and coordinating every aspect of the book.

As noted on the cover of this book, there are several contributing authors. Thanks to Ezra Freedman for writing the mobile devices chapter, Kris Honeycutt for writing the 3D chapter, and Robert Reinhardt for writing the video chapter. Although this is the first publication of the book, the first drafts were written several years ago when Flash MX was the current edition of the Flash IDE. At that time, Jeffrey Bardzell was the author and Bruce Epstein was the development editor for the book. Despite several subsequent revisions, their foundational work remains.

Many technical reviewers have helped by reading chapters and testing to ensure that everything is accurate. Thanks to John Davey, Matt Sutton, Rich Shupe, Lynn Baus, Igor Costa, Jens Hauser, Stacey Mulcahy, Tim O'Hare, Jawar "JP" Puwala, and Bill Sanders.

Margot Hutchinson at Waterside Productions is the agent representing this book. Thanks to Margot for managing contract details and the like so that the authors could focus on writing.

Thanks also go to the Flash team at Adobe (formerly Macromedia), to the Flash community, and to the readers of this book.

Ezra Freedman

I would like to thank Robert Reinhardt for helping start my speaking and writing careers. I would also like to thank Joey Lott for giving me the opportunity to work with him on this book.

Kris Honeycutt

I would first and foremost like to give my heartfelt thanks to my family for their ongoing support in all my endeavors. Much respect to the people at Macromedia who made Flash what it is today, and to the team at Electric Rain for creating Swift 3D, and continuing to deliver improvements with each new release. Finally, my gratitude goes out to my coauthors and O'Reilly Media, Inc. for giving me the honor to be part of this book.

Author Bios

Joey Lott helped write this book. He writes mostly from Los Angeles.

Ezra Freedman is Senior Manager of the Multimedia Platforms Group at Schematic, a Los Angeles-based services company that develops interface and technology solutions for the Web, television, and mobile devices. He has served as lead architect and developer for many successful web and mobile applications, for such clients as

ESPN, Macromedia, and MTV. Ezra has spoken about Flash at several conferences, and recently presented a session on Mobile Content Delivery Technologies at SIG-GRAPH 2005. He lives in Venice Beach and enjoys biking to work.

Kris Honeycutt (Kagawa, Japan) is the cofounder and lead designer for Solid Thinking Interactive (*www.solid-thinking.com*), an international web and multimedia studio.

Kris began his professional career working in print and later embarked on his journey in interactive media as a freelance web designer, while continuing his formal education in graphic design and fine art photography. In his decade of experience prior to founding STi, Kris was an in-house designer for companies in both the U.S. and Japan, where he worked with clients around the globe. Over the years, his positions have included graphic designer, web designer, multimedia designer, creative director, and author. He is the lead author of *Foundation Swift 3D* (Friends of ED/Apress). While continuing to work in a variety of mediums and technologies, his favorite weapon of choice is Flash, which he has wielded to create projects for the Web, disc media, broadcast, and mobile devices. His current focus is UI design for Flash/FMS-based RIA.

Kris is a member and moderator of several online design communities, and in his spare time, he can be found both giving guidance to, as well as learning from, his peers. He enjoys spending his time outside of work with his wife Mayumi and their two sons, Kai and Riley, as well as studying traditional Japanese martial arts.

Robert Reinhardt, VP of the Multimedia Platforms Group for Schematic (*www.schematic.com*), is regarded internationally as an expert on multimedia application development, particularly in Macromedia Flash. Robert is the lead author of the Flash Bible series (Wiley), as well as coauthor of other successful web development titles. He has developed multimedia courses for educational facilities in Canada and the United States, and he is a Macromedia certified instructor for Flash courses at Portland State University. Robert has been a regularly featured speaker at the Flash-Forward, FITC, and SIGGRAPH conferences. Robert is also a partner and writer at Community MX (*www.communitymx.com*).

Technical Editor Bios

Lynn Baus is a new media designer living and working in San Francisco. Over the past seven years, she has created interactive environments and motion graphics for prominent advertising agencies, design studios, corporations, and nonprofit organizations. Her current focus is customized, permission-based, media-rich communication. In addition to her interactive and graphic design work, she is a frequent editor of books on Flash and Dreamweaver, as well as an author and instructor in the field of New Media design. She has taught courses at Columbia College and Loyola University.

Igor Costa, a resident of Brazil, is passionate about Flash—he has worked with it since Version 5, when he fell in love with it. He's a freelance Flash developer and has worked as a consultant for many Brazilian companies. He's an active member of the Flash community in Brazil, was a member of the Macromedia Flash team, and has written several articles about Flash development. His current focus is open source development for the Flash platform (*www.osflash.org*), and he is working with ActionScript 3. You can learn more about him at *www.igorcosta.com*.

John Davey is a Flash developer who has produced work for BBC, Disney, Robbie Williams, Wal-Mart, Science Museum, The Guardian, and many more. He builds everything from games to full-blown CMS sites. You can reach John at *www. developette.com*.

Stacey Mulcahy is a Flex and Flash developer who once had a torrid love affair with the Director. She currently works at Teknision Inc. in Ottawa, Ontario creating rich Internet applications that even designers like. She rants more than raves on her Flash-centric blog at *www.bitchwhocodes.com*.

Tim O'Hare is a Senior Flash Developer for Scripps Networks, the parent company of HGTV, DIY Network, Food Network, Fine Living, HGTVPro.com, Shop at Home, and Great American Country. His responsibilities are centered on the development of Flash applications for many of the Scripps Networks' online properties. Within his first year and a half with the company, Tim won two Macromedia Site of the Day awards and wrote articles for Community MX and the Macromedia Dev Center. Tim has a BFA in graphic design, and he spent five years pole-vaulting for the University of Tennessee track and field team.

Jawahar Puvvala is Core Application Developer at Nucor Corporation in Charlotte, North Carolina, where he develops server-side and client applications in Microsoft Technology. He is coauthor of *.NET for Java Developers* (Addison-Wesley) and has technical-edited several books. His educational background is in writing software for mechanical and structural engineering systems, topics on which he has published scientific journal and conference articles.

Bill Sanders is a Flash developer specializing in Flash Media Server 2 for a wide range of applications, from streaming audio/video communication to real-time data transfer. He has run Sandlight Productions (*www.sandlight.com*) for the last 20 years, has published over 40 computer books—including several on Flash—and is currently on the faculty at the University of Hartford in the Interactive Information Technology Program (*iit.hartford.edu*), where he is developing FMS2 applications on Internet 2.

Rich Shupe is the founder and president of FMA—a full-service multimedia development company and training facility in New York City. Rich teaches a variety of digital technologies in academic and commercial environments, and has lectured on these topics at Macworld, Flashforward, and other national and international events. He is currently on the faculty of New York's School of Visual Arts and teaches in both the undergraduate and master's programs. As a technical writer, Rich is a regular columnist at DevX.com and the author of multiple books, including the upcoming *Flash 8: Projects for Learning Animation and Interactivity* (O'Reilly). FMA develops CD-ROMs and web sites for clients including McGraw-Hill, Phillips, 20th Century Fox, and Nickelodeon, and trains digital media professionals in Flash, Director, Processing, HTML, XML, JavaScript, and more. Visit FMA at *www.fmaonline.com*.

Matt Sutton is an ActionScript developer based out of Chicago. He specializes in rich Internet and desktop applications that leverage the power of Flash. He's a lot like the A-Team: if you have a problem, if no one else can help, and if you can find him, he may be for hire.

CHAPTER 1

Drawing in Flash

One of the hallmarks of Flash is the use of *vector-based* graphics; vector graphics can be scaled to any size without causing the pixelation or scrunched look associated with scaled *bitmap* graphics. Vector graphics are also compact, because they are described mathematically. For example, to *render* (draw) a circle, Flash needs to store only the circle's center point and radius; from this information, it figures out which pixels to draw on the screen. In contrast, bitmap (or *raster*) graphics describe every point in an image. To draw a bitmap graphic, Flash simply does what it's told, drawing each pixel in the original image to the screen. The file size for bitmap graphics is generally much larger than that of vector graphics, and bitmaps tend to look jagged or pixelated when scaled. Vector graphics are ideal for line art and curves, offering both high quality and small storage size; bitmaps are more appropriate for photographic images that can't be described easily with vectors. Although Flash can import and manipulate bitmaps, the drawing tools create vector graphics only. This chapter focuses on how to create your own graphics with Flash's vector drawing and manipulation tools.

Although Flash's drawing tools can create straight line segments, curves, and complex shapes, they differ somewhat from those in other vector drawing programs, such as Freehand and Adobe Illustrator. Flash uses a simpler system (*quadratic paths*) for describing paths than these other programs (which use *cubic paths*). Basically, quadratic paths are adjusted with just one control handle and three data points, whereas cubic paths are adjusted with two control handles and four data points. The underlying math may be abstract, but the implications are not.

Flash's quadratic paths are not capable of quite the same level of precision as the paths you can create in most other vector programs. In practical terms, Flash does not represent paths drawn with a freehand tool as faithfully. The loss in fidelity is counterbalanced by the savings in file size and Flash's ability to simplify paths via shape recognition and line smoothing, both of which make drawing easier and help minimize file size. Whether to automatically apply smoothing, along with other options, can be specified under Edit → Preferences → Drawing. Many Flash designers find that shape recognition and smoothing enable them to create art much more quickly than in other vector drawing programs. And in spite of the intrinsic limitations of Flash's paths, it does have tools, such as the Pen and Subselection tools, which enable you to create paths with nearly the same precision as those drawn in vector drawing programs that use the more elaborate cubic paths.

Another implication of Flash's unique drawing system is that strokes and fills are treated as separate elements. In most vector drawing programs, the stroke and the fill are optional attributes of a path; you can even remove both and the path will remain. In Flash, strokes are fused to their own paths, and fills are bound by their own paths. If you delete a stroke, you also delete its underlying path. When you draw a rectangle with both a stroke and a fill, Flash effectively creates two separate paths: a stroke-path combination and a fill-path combination (their respective paths initially coincide). Throughout this book, we'll use the term *line* to describe a stroke-path combination, and *fill* to describe a fill-path combination.

A quirky (but ultimately empowering) consequence of this system is that in the default drawing mode (shape drawing versus object drawing), overlapping lines and shapes slice each other into separate, discrete lines and shapes, and/or combine to create new lines or shapes. These slicing and combining behaviors are activated when you deselect an element drawn or dragged over an existing element. Table 1-1 summarizes the behaviors of overlapping elements.

Table 1-1. Behavior of overlapping vector elements, by path type and color

Path type	Result
Lines, any color	Intersecting lines slice each other into segments; that is, two simple lines that intersect result in four line segments, each extending from the point of intersection.
Shapes (without lines), same color	Shapes merge into one insoluble shape (*union*).
Shapes (without lines), different color	The overlapping shape removes the pixels of the underlying shape (*punch*).
Combination of line(s) and shape(s)	Lines slice each other and divide shapes into pieces.

One of the benefits of describing graphics mathematically is that you can position, scale, and manipulate them with numeric precision, a process that makes more sense when you understand Flash's coordinate system. Visual elements placed on Flash's main timeline are positioned relative to the upper-left corner of the stage: the stage's upper-left corner is the *origin*—point 0,0—for Flash's coordinate system. Horizontal (x) values increase to the right, so that positive x values are to the right of the left edge of the stage. Unlike the Cartesian coordinate system you learned in school, vertical (y) values increase downward, so that positive numbers appear below the top of the stage.

Coordinates are measured in pixels. Thus, an element positioned at point 200,100 is 200 pixels from the left edge of the stage and 100 pixels from the top of the stage. Negative x values denote positions offstage to the left. Likewise, negative y values denote positions above the top of the stage. Values larger than the stage's width or height also denote offstage positions. Elements positioned offstage are not visible within the movie.

You can easily reposition, resize, and distort existing vectors; doing so is a matter of changing the location of some or all of the vectors' points on the stage. You can apply or remove fills and strokes at any time. You can even edit points within a line or change stroke attributes such as thickness and color. You can edit shapes as well, including position, reshaping, or fill attributes, such as whether to use a solid color, gradient, or even bitmap. This chapter's recipes explain how to perform common operations and how to set and manipulate these properties to create attractive and useful graphics. You should follow along in Flash to get the most out of the recipes. If you want to start over, just double-click the Eraser tool in the Tools panel, which clears the drawing canvas.

1.1   Drawing Straight Lines

Problem

You want to create a straight line segment or a shape made out of multiple straight line segments.

Solution

Use the Line tool (keyboard shortcut: N), the Pen tool (keyboard shortcut: P), or the Pencil tool (keyboard shortcut: Y) with shift-constraint (explained in detail later in this recipe).

Discussion

Often the simplest way to draw a straight line is to use the Line tool. You can do so by first selecting the Line tool from the Tools panel (Window → Tools). With the Line tool selected, drag the mouse on the stage to create a line. Pressing the mouse button creates the starting point, and releasing the mouse button creates the ending point. When using the Line tool, Flash connects the points with a straight line, and applies the active stroke attributes to the line.

You can control the appearance of the stroke, including its color, height, style, end caps, and join types. You can select the Line tool and preset these attributes in the Property inspector before drawing the line on the stage. Alternatively, you can modify an existing line's attributes by selecting the line with the Selection tool and using the Property inspector.

You can create a multisegment line by clicking the mouse close to the end of the previous line segment. Provided the mouse is close enough to an existing segment, Flash automatically joins the line segments into a single path.

Therefore, to create a path comprising a sequence of straight line segments, do the following:

1. Select the Line tool (N) from the Tools panel.
2. Press the mouse button on the stage to create a starting point.
3. Drag the mouse to another location.
4. Release the mouse button.
5. Without moving the mouse, click and drag to the next point's location, and then release the mouse button.
6. Repeat step 5 as necessary.
7. To close the path, drag the mouse back to the first point in the path before releasing the mouse button.

It is much easier to connect multiple line segments when the View → Snap To Objects option is toggled on. For maximum tolerance, under Edit → Preferences → Drawing, set the Connect Lines option to Can Be Distant. Note that the Connect Lines setting takes effect only when snapping is toggled on. When Flash snaps to an existing line, a large circle beside the cursor indicates the snap. This circle also appears when the line is drawn at an angle in a 90° increment relative to the x and y axes.

To begin a new line, unconnected to an existing line, start the new line far enough away from any existing line so that it doesn't snap to the line. You can append a new segment to an existing line by clicking close enough to one of its end points and dragging to a new location. Likewise, you can create a closed shape by dragging a new line between a line's two end points.

You may want your lines to be constrained to increments of 45° angles relative to the x and y axes. You can force Flash to draw only at these angles by holding down the Shift key as you draw. This technique is called *shift-constraint*, and it affects most of Flash's drawing tools in one way or another.

Instead of using the Line tool, you can use the Pen tool (P) to draw a straight line or a connected series of line segments. Clicking and releasing on the stage with the Pen tool creates a point. Each subsequent time you click, a new point is added, and Flash draws a line connecting the new point and the preceding point. In that way, the Pen tool is frequently more convenient for drawing a path comprised of line segments, and the Line tool is more convenient for drawing a single line segment. To use the Pen tool to draw a straight line or a series of connected line segments, follow these steps:

1. Select the Pen tool from the Tools panel.
2. Click at the starting point and release the mouse button.
3. Move the mouse (don't drag it) to a new location.
4. Click again to set the ending point.
5. Repeat steps 1 to 3 as needed.

To close the path, click again on the first point in the path. To leave a path unclosed, double-click when adding the last point. After closing a shape or double-clicking with the Pen tool, clicking the mouse on the stage again starts a new path.

When you click with the Pen tool, a point is added corresponding to the tip of the Pen tool. If you prefer, you can toggle on a precise cursor with the Pen tool, which replaces the Pen icon with a crosshair. This setting can be found in Edit → Preferences → Drawing in the Show Precise Cursors checkbox. Another useful preference in the same dialog box is Show Pen Preview, which displays the line that will be created when you click the mouse.

As with the Line tool, you can use shift-constraint to draw lines at 45° increments using the Pen tool. To do so, hold down the Shift key while selecting the points of the line. Flash will automatically snap the end point to the nearest 45° increment relative to the x and y axes.

The Pen tool differs from the Line tool in that it is capable of creating curved lines as well as straight line segments. In addition, Flash highlights points and lines drawn with the Pen tool. Drawing curves and the highlighting are discussed in more detail in Recipe 1.14.

You can also draw straight lines at 90° increments using the Pencil tool (Y) if you use shift-constraint. Using the Pencil tool to draw straight lines can be convenient if you are already using the tool to draw other lines, curves, and shapes, and you don't want to have to change between drawing tools just to draw a straight line. The obvious caveat is that the lines must be at 90° increments relative to the x and y axes.

See Also

Recipe 1.4

1.2   Drawing Curved Lines

Problem

You want to draw curved lines.

Solution

Use the Pen tool. Optionally, use the Line tool to draw a straight line. Then use the Selection tool to make the line curve. To draw curves freehand, use the Pencil tool with smoothing.

Discussion

Flash offers a number of approaches to drawing curved lines. Which you select is a matter of both context and preference.

If you plan to draw a series of connected curved segments, the Pen tool is frequently the best option. The Pen tool, as discussed briefly in Recipe 1.1, enables you to draw line segments by plotting points. However, as you draw the points, you can adjust the control points in order to draw curved segments. To adjust the control points, click the mouse at the location at which you want to add a point, and then drag while the mouse button is still pressed. You can also use the Subselection tool to adjust any of the end points and control points along a path after it has been drawn.

You can also use the Selection tool to make paths drawn with the Line tool (or any technique that results in a straight line) into curved segments. The following steps describe the procedure:

1. Draw a straight line using any of the techniques described in Recipe 1.1.
2. Choose the Selection tool.
3. Make sure that the straight line is deselected. If the line has already been selected before proceeding to the next step, you will cause the line to move, rather than curve.
4. Use the mouse (or stylus) to click on a point along the line and drag it to form a curve. You may repeat this step as many times as you want to add more curves to the line.

Although it is the least accurate of the approaches, drawing curved lines with the Pencil tool is often the most straightforward. Furthermore, using the Pencil tool you can achieve sketched looks that would be more difficult to achieve with the other approaches described in this section. Here's how to draw curved lines with the Pencil tool:

1. Select the Pencil tool (Y) from the Tools panel.
2. In the Tool panel options, set the Pencil Mode to Smooth.
3. Press and drag with the mouse to draw the curve. Flash smoothes the line automatically.

The Smooth Pencil Mode causes Flash to remove the bumps that usually appear when drawing with a freehand drawing tool. In addition to Smooth, Flash also has two other Pencil Modes: Straighten and Ink. Pencil Modes are discussed in Recipe 1.17. You can further smooth a curved line by selecting it with the Selection tool and choosing Modify → Smooth, as discussed in Recipe 1.18.

Although it is unlikely that you will have cause to use it frequently, there is at least one additional technique for drawing curves. When you want to draw a curve that is an arc of an ellipse (an oval or circle), you can achieve the effect most effectively by drawing the entire ellipse using the Oval tool, and then delete the portion of the ellipse that is unnecessary.

See Also

Recipe 1.10, Recipe 1.17, Recipe 1.18, Recipe 1.14

1.3   Modifying Curves

Problem

You want to modify the curvature of a line segment by curving a straight line segment, modifying the existing curvature, or removing the curve altogether.

Solution

Use the Selection tool (V), following up (if necessary) with the Subselection tool.

Discussion

After a path is created, the Selection tool is often the fastest and most visually intuitive way to modify the curvature of any of its segments. With the Selection tool selected from the Tools panel, hover over any line segment (it should not be selected), and the cursor changes to indicate a curve. Click and drag until the segment is curved as desired, using the path preview as a guide.

Another way to modify an existing curved line segment—and the more precise way, albeit less intuitive—is to use the Subselection tool and the control points. The Subselection tool is more precise because a segment's curvature can be defined independently at each end. If a given line segment is straight, you can add control points by selecting an end point and Alt-dragging (Windows) or Option-dragging (Macintosh). You can add new points to an existing path using the Pen tool. With the Pen tool selected, click on the path where you'd like to add the new point.

To modify a curved segment using control points, use the Subselection tool to select a point adjacent to the segment. When its control points appear, drag them and use the path preview as a guide. Dragging the control points away from the point increases the amount of curvature, and dragging them closer to the point decreases the curvature. Rotating them around the point changes the direction of the curve. When working with end points on a path, there is only one control point. However, points in the middle of a path have two control points. The control point pairs ordinarily move in mirror images to each other. To move one control point independently of the other, hold down the Alt key (Windows) or Option key (Macintosh) while dragging one of the control points.

See Also

Recipe 1.16, Recipe 1.18

1.4   Selecting a Line

Problem

You want to select a line segment or entire line.

Solution

Use the Selection tool.

Discussion

A line may be made up of one or more segments. Each of these segments may be straight or curved. In Flash, you can select individual straight line segments, contiguous curved line segments, or the entire line.

- To select a single straight line segment, click the line segment.
- To select contiguous curved line segments, click any curved line segment.
- To select an entire line, double-click any line segment on that line.

You cannot select a single curved line segment if it is connected to any other curved line segments.

When the stroke is selected, it is marked with a dotted selection. You can change the selected strokes properties, such as its color, width, and style, in the Property inspector or the Colors section of the Tools panel.

You can delete a selected line (line segment or whole line) by pressing the Delete key. If the line is part of a shape—that is, it is closed and has a fill—the shape remains; only the stroke disappears.

See Also

Recipe 1.1

1.5   Applying Line Styles

Problem

You want to apply a dashed, dotted, stippled, ragged, or hatched effect to a line.

Solution

Specify the appropriate style in the Property inspector.

Discussion

You can add a stroke effect to a shape using one of Flash's seven built-in stroke styles: Hairline, Normal, Dashed, Dotted, Ragged, Stippled, and Hatched. You can apply these styles to an existing line by selecting the line with the Selection tool and choosing the line style from the Property inspector. Alternatively, you can select any tool capable of creating strokes (Line, Pen, Oval, Rectangle, Pencil, and Ink Bottle) and choose a line style from the Property inspector before you create the stroke.

If the built-in line styles are not exactly what you want, you can customize one of the line styles to better suit your needs. For example, if you need smaller dashes in a dashed line, you can customize the dashed line style. To customize a style, click the Custom button in the Property inspector while a stroke is selected or a tool capable of creating a stroke is active. The Stroke Style dialog box opens.

You can set the attributes of each stroke style to customize its appearance. For example, for the Dashed stroke, you can specify the spacing and pixel width of the dashes. The Hatched style has six settings—Thickness, Space, Jiggle, Rotate, Curve, and Length—whose effects are evident in the Stroke Style dialog box's convenient preview window.

You can customize all the line styles, except the Hairline, which is the Solid style with a thickness of one screen pixel.

See Also

Recipe 1.1, Recipe 1.10, Recipe 1.17

1.6   Controlling How Lines Scale

Problem

You want to control how a line scales.

Solution

Set the Scale type from the Property inspector.

Discussion

Until Flash 8, there was just one option for the line scale type. The line thickness scaled with the width and height. For example, a line with thickness of 10 would appear as though it had a thickness of 20 when scaled to 200%. The only alternative for lines was to use the Hairline Line style. However, the Hairline style works only if you want a line with a thickness of one pixel.

As of Flash 8, you can specify a scale style for lines using the Scale style menu in the Property inspector. The default setting is Normal, which means that lines scale just as they have always done. However, you can also select from Horizontal, Vertical, and None. When you select Horizontal, it means that Flash does *not* scale the thickness when the line is scaled horizontally. Likewise, when you select Vertical, it means that Flash does *not* scale the thickness when the line is scaled vertically. And a setting of

None means that Flash does not scale the thickness of the line regardless of whether or not the line is scaled vertically or horizontally.

1.7   Customizing Line Caps

Problem

You want to change the style applied to the ends of line segments.

Solution

Change the line Cap style in the Property inspector.

Discussion

For most of its lifetime Flash has had exactly one line cap style: rounded. The rounded caps on lines are appropriate for many things, but not for everything. For example, when you draw a rectangle using round line caps, the corners of the rectangle are slightly rounded. Starting with Flash 8, however, Flash allows you to select the line Cap style in the Property inspector. You can select from None, Round (default), and Square.

When you select None, the line is drawn as a rectangular area with exactly the length specified. When you select Round or Square, Flash adds a cap to each end of the line segment. The end cap extends beyond the end of the line segment by half of the line thickness. For example, if the line thickness is 10, the caps extend 5 pixels past the ends of the line segment. In the case of Round, the caps are semicircles. In the case of Square, the caps are semisquares (also known as rectangles).

You can change the Cap style for any line after it's been drawn. However, note that changing the Cap style can have an effect on the Join style.

1.8   Customizing Join Styles Between Line Segments

Problem

You want to change the way in which two line segments join.

Solution

Select the adjoining line segments, and select the style from the Join style menu in the Property inspector. Both line segments must also have the same Cap style.

Discussion

As with line caps, Flash previously had only one line Join style: rounded. While a round Join style is fairly neutral, it's not appropriate for everything. Starting with

Flash 8, you can select from three line Join styles—Bevel, Round (default), and Miter. To do so, select the two adjoining line segments, and select from the Join menu in the Property inspector. Note that for Join styles to work, the adjoining line segments must also have the same Cap style.

The Bevel join style makes the joins between line segments flat and angular. The Miter join style causes the joins between line segments to be pointed. When you select the Miter join style, you can also set the sharpness by specifying a value for the Miter field in the Property inspector. The value can range from 1 to 60, and it determines at what point the miter join is beveled. The value is multiplied by the thickness of the line segments to determine how many pixels past the join the miter is beveled. For example, if the line segments have a thickness of 10 and the miter limit is set to 2, the miter can extend up to 20 pixels past the join before it is beveled. If the miter naturally converges at or before that point, the join appears pointed. Otherwise it is beveled at that point.

1.9   Creating Effects with Strokes

Problem

You want to add effects to a line, such as expanding it or softening its edges.

Solution

Use the Convert Lines to Fills command, and then manipulate the resulting fill.

Discussion

Lines and fills each have unique capabilities. Lines are best for creating complex designs, closed or open. However, fills enable special effects, such as bitmap fills. In addition, shapes can be expanded and have their edges softened.

Flash provides different tools to create these kinds of effects. For example, the Brush tool is the most direct way to paint fills. But if you don't have a graphics tablet, it is very hard to draw well with the mouse and the Brush tool.

You can get the best of both worlds—the precision of working with lines and the visual effects available with shapes—by converting lines to fills.

To convert lines to fills, follow these steps:

1. Draw the line. Any of the line drawing tools will work: Pencil, Pen, or Line tools.
2. When you are satisfied with the overall shape, convert the stroke to a fill by choosing Modify → Shape → Convert Lines to Fills. At the end of this step, the shape looks the same on stage as it did before, but it is a fill and you can start treating it as such.

3. To change the fill to a bitmap, set the active fill to the bitmap, and use the Paint Bucket tool to apply it to the shape.

To expand the width of the fill, choose Modify → Shape → Expand Fill. In the dialog box that appears, choose the number of pixels that you want it to expand. Also, select whether you want those pixels to be added to the current fill (Expand) or subtracted from the current fill (Inset).

To soften the edges of a fill, creating a blurred effect around the edges, choose Modify → Shape → Soften Fill Edges. In the resulting dialog box, you can set the width of the transition in pixels, the number of transition steps, and whether to soften outward (Expand) or inward (Inset).

To create a hollow shape, you can apply a stroke to the line and then remove the fill. Or, if you want to apply a fill (such as a gradient) to the outline, then apply Soften Fill Edges in the desired gradient, and then remove the inner fill.

See Also

Recipe 1.16

1.10 Drawing Primitive Shapes

Problem

You want to draw primitive shapes, such as ovals, circles, rectangles, and squares.

Solution

Use the Oval (O) and Rectangle (R) tools, or the Pencil (Y) tool.

Discussion

To create ovals or rectangles, select the Oval or Rectangle tool from the Tools panel, and click and drag across the stage to create the bounds of the shape. Because they are closed shapes, ovals and rectangles are automatically filled with the default fill style.

 Fills are not visible if View → Outlines mode is active. To view fills, switch to another mode, such as View → Antialias.

Set the fill style to No Color to create unfilled shapes. To create an unfilled shape regardless of the default fill style, use the Pencil tool to scribble your best approximation of a rectangle or oval. Flash will automatically convert a rough approximation to a perfect rectangle or oval, especially if the Recognize Shapes option—under Edit → Preferences → Drawing—is set to Tolerant. The Recognize Shapes option works only if you draw the shape in one continuous motion without releasing the mouse button or lifting the pen from the tablet until you've closed the shape. Also note that the only shapes that Flash can recognize with the Pencil tool are primitive shapes— ovals, rectangles, and triangles. It cannot recognize polygons with sides numbering anything greater than four. To draw regular polygons (polygons with equilateral sides) you'll need to use the PolyStar tool as discussed in Recipe 1.11.

In Flash's drawing paradigm, a shape is created with a series of points, not treated as a separate primitive object (the Oval and Rectangle tools create shapes with at least four points). Selecting any point along the curve, by using the Subselection tool (A), allows you to distort the original shape.

To create a perfect circle or square with the Oval or Rectangle tool, use shift-constraint; that is, hold down the Shift key as you drag.

When using the Rectangle tool, you have the option of drawing a rectangle with rounded corners. You can set the corner radius in the Options section of the Tools panel by clicking the Set Corner Radius icon. In the dialog box that displays, specify the radius in pixels.

See Also

Recipe 1.4

1.11 Drawing Regular Polygons

Problem

You want to draw a polygon (a closed shape made of straight lines, such as a triangle, hexagon, etc.) that has sides of equal length.

Solution

Use the PolyStar tool.

Discussion

The PolyStar tool allows you to quickly draw regular polygons with up to 32 sides. You can find the PolyStar tool nested with the Rectangle tool. There is no keyboard shortcut to the tool, so the only way to get to it is to select it from the Tools panel. Because the PolyStar tool is nested with the Rectangle tool, only one is visible at a time. Therefore, if the Rectangle tool is currently visible, click and hold the mouse on the Rectangle tool to display the pop-up menu from which you can choose the PolyStar tool. You'll know when the PolyStar tool is selected, because the icon on the Tools panel will appear as a regular hexagon instead of a rectangle.

After you've selected the PolyStar tool, you next need to select the correct options before drawing. Because the PolyStar tool allows you to draw many different types of polygons (as well as stars), you need to make the appropriate selections from the tool settings. You can access the tool settings via the Options button in the Property inspector. Clicking the Options button will open a dialog box from which you can select the number of sides. In order to draw a polygon, make sure the style is set to Polygon and not Star. The star point size applies only when drawing stars. After you've made the appropriate selections, you can click on the OK button to close the dialog box.

With the settings made, you can draw a regular polygon by clicking on the stage and dragging the mouse or stylus to the size of polygon you want. If you hold the Shift key while drawing the polygon, Flash will snap the shape to 45° increments.

1.12   Drawing Stars

Problem

You want to draw a star.

Solution

Use the PolyStar tool. Select Star from the style menu in the Options dialog box. Recipe 1.11 discusses more details of the PolyStar tool.

1.13   Drawing Other Assorted Shapes

Problem

You want to draw a shape for which there is no built-in tool within Flash.

Solution

Check to see whether there is a drawing tool available that you can add to Flash via the Extension Manager.

Discussion

Flash includes a JavaScript extension layer. What that means for you is that it is possible to find and install additional functionality for Flash—including extra drawing tools. Though you may not necessarily find a drawing tool that draws exactly what you are looking for, it is worth taking a look. A good resource for finding such extensions is the Flash Exchange at the Macromedia web site. A direct link to the Macromedia Exchange is *http://www.macromedia.com/cfusion/exchange*. Another resource with a few drawing tools is *http://www.flashextensibility.com*.

As time goes on, more Flash extensions are likely to be available, but at the time of this writing, the following are some of the most seemingly relevant:

Splat

> The Splat tool allows you to draw shapes with circular inner shapes with curved shapes extending outward from it. The default settings create what looks like a splat of paint (hence the name). But by adjusting the settings for the tool, you can readily draw flower shapes and other, more abstract shapes. Splat v2 is the same as the first version, but with a few additional options, including random colors and a noise setting that applies a random distortion to each shape drawn with the tool.

Arrow

> The Selection tool quite simply allows you to draw arrows without having to composite rectangles and triangles.

Spiral

> The Spiral tool does pretty much what it says—it draws spirals.

Dot Spiral

> According to a strict definition, a spiral is composed of a curve, and not line segments. So perhaps a more accurate term to describe what the Dot Spiral tool draws would be a spiral-like shape. The shape is composed of line segments that form what turn out to be very near to polygons, except that the angles are just a bit too wide such that the effect is something akin to a spiral. You can specify the number of points around the spiral-like shape. For example, if you specify four points, the spiral-like shape resembles a square.

The preceding drawing tool extensions can each be found at *http://www. flashextensibility.com*.

In order to install any Flash extension—be it a tool, behavior, panel, or component—you'll need the latest version of the Extension Manager. The Extension Manager is a free download from Macromedia, and you can find it at *http://www. macromedia.com/exchange/em_download/*. Each extension that you download should be packaged in a file with the *.mxp* file extension. If you have the Extension Manager installed, then your system should recognize the file type and allow you to install the extension with a few mouse clicks. You may need to restart Flash for some of the settings to take effect.

1.14 Building Complex Shapes from Simple Shapes

Problem

You want to create a complex shape for which Flash doesn't have a specific tool.

Solution

Use Flash's intersect, punch, crop, slice, and union behaviors strategically to create the shape in multiple steps.

Discussion

Flash has two drawing models—merge and object. Making complex shapes is possible using either drawing model. Which approach you take is a matter of preference, as is the type of shape you want to make. When you select a tool that supports the object drawing model (e.g., the Oval or Rectangle tools), a small Object Drawing button appears in the Options section of the Tools panel. The button (with a circular icon) enables you to toggle between the merge (default, deselected state) and object (selected state) drawing models.

When you draw on the stage using the merge drawing model, elements drawn in the same layer and frame that overlap will interact with one another by slicing, merging, and/or punching. Flash's auto-slice, auto-punch, and auto-union behaviors are unusual among vector applications. In most drawing applications, slicing, union, and punch are available, but they never happen automatically. All too often, Flash users inadvertently utilize one of the features, with Undo as the only recourse. However, you can and should use Flash's behavior strategically to create shapes that would otherwise be difficult to create.

When you place an ungrouped shape over another and deselect both shapes, Flash will automatically apply a slice, punch, or union behavior, depending on several factors. If the shapes have no outlines and are the same color, the union behavior is applied such that the two shapes merge into one shape. If the top shape has an outline or is a different color than the bottom shape, the top shape will punch out the bottom. A line that crosses another line or shape slices the line or shape it crosses.

For many shapes, the slicing, union, and punch behaviors are more efficient than using the Pen tool to plot several points, and then painstakingly modifying the Bézier curves with the Subselection tool. Figure 1-1 shows two unique shapes that were created by punching and merging shapes. The cloud formation at the top was created by laying one oval above another, all of the same color. After the overall shape was created, a linear gradient was applied to give it visual interest. The comb shape at the bottom was created by drawing a basic outline with the Pen tool, and then punching it with a simple spike shape.

When drawing, look at your subject not merely as a collection of outlines, but also as composites of simple shapes (both positive and, in the case of the comb spikes, negative).

You can prevent the slicing, punching, and cropping behaviors of overlapping elements in several ways. You can group elements (Modify → Group). You can place the elements in different layers. Or you can use the object drawing model when drawing the shapes.

When you use the object drawing model the auto-punch, auto-slice, and auto-union behaviors are disabled for those shapes. However, you can still combine elements to make more complex shapes. To do so, select the objects you want to combine, then

Figure 1-1. Create complex shapes overlapping simple shapes, using Flash's auto-union (top) and auto-punch (bottom) behaviors

modify the Union, Intersect, Punch, and Crop options from the Modify → Combine Objects menu. The Union and Punch options work like the auto-union and auto-punch features. The Intersection option combines the two objects into a new shape that is formed by the area in which the two objects intersect. The Crop option crops the bottom shape using the top shape as the mask.

If you've drawn a shape using the object drawing model and you'd like to utilize the auto-punch, auto-slice, and auto-union features, you can still do so. You need only to select the shape and ungroup it (Modify → Ungroup). After you've ungrouped an object, it behaves just like a shape drawn with the merge drawing model.

See Also

Recipe 1.31, Recipe 1.33

1.15   Drawing Complex Lines and Shapes

Problem

You want to draw a line or shape, comprising any combination of straight and curved line segments.

Solution

Use the Pen (P) tool.

Discussion

The Pen tool, also found in the Tools panel, is used to plot the points that make up a line or shape. The Pen tool can create straight or curved line segments.

To draw lines or shapes made of straight line segments, as discussed in Recipe 1.1, click with the mouse to add points, and Flash will connect them with straight line segments. To add curvature to the lines as you draw, rather than pressing and releasing immediately with the mouse, press and drag to create a new point and drag out *control points*, which control the curvature of line segments adjacent to the point. When you release, the curve is set, and continued clicking or dragging will create new points.

To close the path, click again on the first point in the path (or any point in between). To leave a path unclosed, double-click when adding the last point. After closing a shape or double-clicking with the Pen tool, clicking the mouse on the stage again starts a new path. If you forget to double-click when adding the last end point, you can click a second time on the end point or you can switch to a different tool instead; when you switch back to the Pen tool, Flash also starts a new path.

Mastering the Pen tool takes practice; however, it is the most precise and flexible drawing tool that Flash offers. Bear in mind that you can modify any part of a path, including the location of points and the curvature of the adjacent line segments, in the future.

The Pen tool is one of several ways to create complex shapes. You can also build complex shapes from primitive shapes, as shown in Recipe 1.14, and use the Pencil tool, as shown in Recipe 1.17. You can also combine these approaches. For example, you can rough out the path using the Pencil tool or the Pen tool in simple connect-the-dots fashion, and after the path is created, go back and add/modify the curves in a second pass, as shown in Recipe 1.3.

See Also

Recipe 1.16, Recipe 1.3

1.16 Repositioning Points on Paths

Problem

You want to reposition a point on a path.

Solution

Use the Subselection tool (A).

Discussion

You may want to reposition a point on an existing line or shape edge without affecting the remaining points. Use the Subselection tool in the Tools panel to select the line or shape edge, which makes the points along it visible. Click to select the point you want to modify, and drag it to a new position.

Though a line or the edge of a shape may be selected with the Subselection tool, individual points within it may not be selected. Unselected points are represented as hollow squares. Selected points are represented as solid squares if the adjacent line segment is straight and as solid circles if the adjacent line segment is curved. The control points associated with the curved segments emanating from a point appear when the point is selected. If applicable, the control points that control the curvature of the curved segment as it approaches an adjacent point also appear, as shown in Figure 1-2.

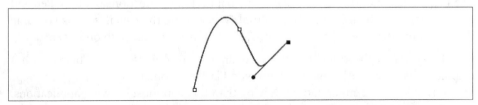

Figure 1-2. Unselected points are hollow, while selected points are solid. Control points are shown for segments attached to the currently selected point

You can reposition a selected point by dragging it with the Subselection tool. Alternatively, you can nudge it in any direction using the up, down, left, and right arrow keys. Nudging in Flash is relative to screen resolution and your view settings. At 100% zoom, it nudges one pixel relative to the stage each time you press an arrow key. Holding down the Shift key nudges it 10 times as far. At 200%, each time you press an arrow key it nudges one half pixel, relative to the stage.

You can select multiple points simultaneously, which is good for reshaping areas of a path. To do so with the Subselection tool, hold down the Shift key and click multiple points. Click a point again while still holding down the Shift key to deselect it without deselecting other points.

You can also move a point using the Selection tool (V). To do so, hover over the point with the Selection tool until the corner cursor appears, and drag the point to a new location. This approach is often unpredictable when working with curved line segments, because it adds a new line segment between the original point on the curve and the new point.

See Also

Recipe 1.3

1.17 Freehand Drawing

Problem

You want to draw directly on the stage using your input device (mouse or graphics tablet).

Solution

Use the Pencil tool (Y).

Discussion

If you don't want to deal with the intrinsic constraints of the simple drawing tools (the Line, Oval, and Rectangle tools) or the painstaking perfectionism of the Pen and Subselection tools, consider the Pencil tool. When using the Pencil tool, as you drag the mouse (or stylus on a graphics tablet), Flash draws a vector path on screen.

In most vector applications, the freehand drawing tool works much better with a graphics tablet than with a mouse. However, Flash's automatic smoothing and shape recognition system is much more forgiving than those in most drawing applications. Flash has three different Pencil drawing modes: Straighten, Smooth, and Ink. The Straighten Pencil mode excels with the straight lines. If you want to draw freehand, but you want straight line segments, use the Straighten mode because it will automatically convert the paths to the nearest straight line segment approximations. Yet if you want to draw smooth paths, you will likely find that Straighten mode will yield effects counter to what you are trying to accomplish. For smooth lines, use the Smooth Pencil mode. Use Ink mode when you want to most closely represent what you have drawn. Because precision is necessary with Ink mode, it is best left to users with graphics tablets or those adept at drawing with a mouse.

The Pencil Mode option appears at the bottom of the Tools panel when you select the Pencil tool, as discussed in Recipe 1.2. Press and hold the Pencil Mode button to select from the three options. Flash uses Straighten mode by default.

As you work, you may find that you like the smoothing or straightening of the Flash Pencil tool, but the straightening or smoothing is too heavily (or too lightly) applied for your needs. You can control the degree to which Flash applies them using the Smooth Curves, Recognize Lines, and Recognize Shapes options under Edit → Preferences → Drawing.

The four settings for the Smooth Curves option are Off, Rough, Normal, and Smooth. The four Recognize Lines and Recognize Shapes options are Off, Strict, Normal, and Tolerant. Even when the Smooth Curves and Recognize Lines options are set to Off, Flash still smoothes paths drawn with the Pencil tool somewhat.

 These Drawing Settings affect the behavior of all three Pencil modes (Smooth, Straighten, and Ink) and both Selection tool modes (Straighten and Smooth) as discussed in Recipe 1.18.

See Also

Recipe 1.18

1.18   Smoothing and Straightening Lines

Problem

You want to smooth or straighten an existing line.

Solution

Use the Straighten and Smooth modifiers of the Selection tool (V).

Discussion

Drawn shapes or lines, especially when drawn with the Pencil tool, have aberrations, such as bumps and undesired curves. You can clean up these aberrations by straightening or smoothing the line. Straighten lines that lack curved segments, and smooth lines that have curved segments.

To straighten or smooth a line or the edge of a shape, follow these steps:

1. Select the Selection tool in the Tools panel.
2. Double-click to select the whole line or shape. If a shape has both a stroke and a fill, double-click the fill to select both the fill and the stroke. Selecting strokes and shapes are discussed in detail in Recipe 1.21.
3. Click the Smooth or Straighten modifiers in the Options portion of the Tools panel (see Figure 1-3).
4. Repeat step 3 as many times as needed.

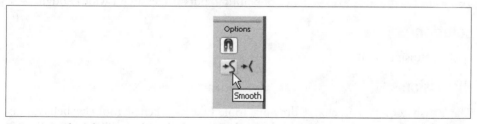

Figure 1-3. The Selection tool's Straighten and Smooth modifiers straighten and smooth an existing path

These modifiers have no effect on line segments that are already straight. Straightening shapes often results in a rectangle.

As global operations, straightening and smoothing may fix one part of a line or shape and cause trouble elsewhere. Remember that you can mix and match techniques. That is, you can straighten or smooth to approximate a shape, and switch to the Arrow or Subselection tool to rework a given area.

Smoothing and straightening is the best strategy for taking care of rough and bumpy paths, since these tools are geared toward improving the appearance of paths. In situations where the path looks good but appears to have too many points, making it hard to edit and increasing its file size, you should use the Optimize feature, as follows:

1. Select the path (including both the fill and the stroke, as appropriate) with the Selection tool.

2. Choose Modify → Shape → Optimize. The Optimize Curves dialog box appears.

3. Choose the degrees of optimization using the Smoothing slider. Higher settings optimize paths more, but they also alter the appearance of the paths more. Lower settings optimize less but maintain the appearance of the path better.

4. Choose whether to use multiple passes. This setting applies the setting specified in the preceding step over and over until no further changes occur.

5. Choose whether to show the totals message. When selected, a dialog box appears at the end of the process informing you of how many curves were removed.

6. Click OK.

See Also

Recipe 1.17

1.19 Painting Shapes

Problem

You want to emulate the experience of painting, but strokes aren't wide enough.

Solution

Use the Brush tool (B).

Discussion

The Brush tool is a freehand drawing tool. Like the Pencil tool, its behavior is affected by the smoothing settings chosen in Preferences. But unlike the Pencil tool, the Brush tool creates fills, rather than lines.

When the Brush tool is selected, the Options portion of the Tools panel displays the brush options. The Brush Size and Brush Shape options are self-explanatory, but the Brush Mode and Lock Fill options are not. Brush Mode controls how the fills painted onto the stage interact with content already on the stage in the same frame, as follows:

Paint Normal
  Paints over existing content (the default mode).

Paint Fills
  Paints over only fills, leaving existing strokes intact.

Paint Behind
> Fills the area behind existing elements, while leaving both their strokes and fills intact.

Paint Selection
> Paints over selected strokes and/or fills only, leaving all unselected content intact.

Paint Inside
> Paints only within the element in which you first click, not outside.

The differences among these modes can be seen in Figure 1-4.

Figure 1-4. Different Brush Modes make coloring easy

See Also

Recipe 1.20, Recipe 1.28, Recipe 1.22

1.20 Tapered Painting Using a Pressure-Sensitive Graphics Tablet

Problem

You want to paint tapered lines using a pressure-sensitive graphics tablet.

Solution

Use the Brush tool with the Pressure modifier toggled on.

Discussion

If you have a pressure-sensitive graphics tablet (such as a Wacom tablet) installed, the Options for the Brush tool include a button for pressure sensitivity. When pressure sensitivity is toggled off, the Brush tool paints fills just as it does with the mouse, but when toggled on, the Brush tool responds to pressure.

To create calligraphic effects, toggle pressure sensitivity on and use one of the slanted Brush shapes.

See Also

Recipe 1.19

1.21 Selecting a Shape and Changing Its Attributes

Problem

You want to select a shape and change its fill color.

Solution

Click the fill with the Selection tool.

Discussion

In Flash, fills are associated with shapes, so if you want to change a fill, you need to select its shape. To select a fill, click it with the Selection tool. You can then change its attributes using the Property inspector, the Colors area in the Tools panel, or the Color Mixer panel.

You can also delete a selected shape and fill by pressing the Delete key. If the shape has a stroke, the line surrounding the shape and its stroke remain. Otherwise, the entire shape is deleted.

Note that the fill can be selected separately from the line in which it is contained. That is, if you have a shape with both a stroke and a fill, it is possible to select the shape/fill without selecting the line/stroke surrounding it. Doing so enables you to delete the fill while retaining the closed line and stroke, or separate a shape/fill from its line/stroke.

To select an entire shape that contains both a stroke and a fill, double-click the fill. The shape/fill and line/stroke are both selected.

See Also

Recipe 1.3

1.22   Applying a Stroke to a Fill

Problem

You want to add or replace a stroke to/on an existing fill.

Solution

Use the Ink Bottle tool (S) in the Tools panel.

Discussion

The Ink Bottle adds or changes the stroke on an existing fill. It has two behaviors, depending on the nature of the fill:

- If the fill lacks a stroke, the Ink Bottle adds a line enclosing the shape and gives it the active stroke.
- If the shape already has a stroke, the Ink Bottle changes the stroke to the active stroke.

Using the tool requires two steps: setting the active stroke and then applying it to the shape. To specify the stroke formatting, select the Ink Bottle tool and choose the desired stroke color, height, and style from the Property inspector. To apply the new stroke, click anywhere on the shape itself, if it's a solid color. Otherwise, click near the edge of the fill to add the stroke.

See Also

Recipe 1.1

1.23   Applying a Fill to a Closed Path

Problem

You want to apply or modify a fill to/in a shape or closed path.

Solution

Use the Paint Bucket tool (K) in the Tools panel.

Discussion

The active fill can be applied only to a closed area, such as a closed path or an existing fill. Either way, you use the Paint Bucket to apply the active fill.

Adding a fill to an existing area requires two steps: setting the active fill and then applying it. The active fill appears in the Fill color box of the Tools panel. Clicking the Fill color box brings up the color pop up, from which you can pick the colors currently in the Color Swatches panel (see Recipe 1.25 for more on the Color Swatches panel).

In addition, you can also set the active fill to any solid color (Recipe 1.25), gradient (Recipe 1.27), or even tiled bitmap (Recipe 6.2) fill.

After you have set the active fill, apply it by activating the Paint Bucket tool and clicking anywhere within the shape or closed line. If the shape already has a fill, the fill is replaced. If a closed line lacks a fill, then a fill is added.

See Also

Recipe 1.24, Recipe 1.25

1.24   Filling in Paths with Gaps

Problem

You want to fill in a nearly closed path, but Flash won't let you, because the shape isn't quite closed.

Solution

Change the Paint Bucket's Gap Size modifier to make Flash more tolerant of gaps. Or close the gap using any drawing tool or the Subselection tool.

Discussion

Generally, fills are available to closed shapes only. However, you might draw a line that is almost, but not quite, closed. This often happens when you draw with the Pencil tool using a graphics tablet—the shape looks closed to you, but not to Flash.

You can make Flash more tolerant of shapes that don't quite close by making Flash ignore small gaps. When filling shapes with gaps, Flash creates a hypothetical straight line between the points adjacent to the gap. It does not actually close the shape, and it is not possible to apply a stroke over this straight line; Flash merely tolerates the gap, enabling a fill to be applied.

You can specify how aggressively Flash should close gaps by using the Gap Size modifier, which appears in the Options tray of the Tools panel when the Paint Bucket tool is active. Settings include Don't Close Gaps, Close Small Gaps, Close Medium Gaps, and Close Large Gaps.

Often, Flash's idea of a large gap appears quite small to our eyes, and it's common that even with the most tolerant setting (Close Large Gaps), Flash will not fill a given shape. In such cases, you will have to manually close the gap (or at least enough of it to fit in Flash's Close Large Gaps range).

To close a gap, use one of Flash's drawing tools, such as the Pencil tool, Line tool, or Pen tool. The Pen tool usually works best, because it is the most precise. Remember that you can use the Zoom tool (M, Z) to make the gap easier to see and fill.

When closing a gap manually, match the original line with the new line that you are creating to bridge the gap. To do so, click the existing line with the Selection tool, and look at its attributes in the Property inspector: color, height, and style. Then set the active stroke to the same settings.

Another way to close gaps is to manipulate the points on the line. To do so, click one of the end points with the Subselection tool, and drag it until it overlaps the other end point.

See Also

Recipe 1.16

1.25 Mixing Custom Colors

Problem

You want to mix a custom color.

Solution

Use the Color Mixer panel or the system color picker (available in the color pop up).

Discussion

When you click the Fill or Stroke color box in the Tools panel or Property inspector, Flash displays a color pop up with the colors stored in the Color Swatches panel, which by default contains the 216 colors of the web-safe palette. These colors are often insufficient to meet design needs, so you'll often need to mix your own colors.

Flash has a dedicated interface for mixing colors: the Color Mixer panel. To mix a solid color, follow these steps:

1. Open the Color Mixer panel (Window → Color Mixer).

2. In the Fill Style menu, choose Solid.

3. To mix a color, use any combination of visual and numeric controls.

   To mix a color visually, drag in the Color Space and/or drag the Brightness Control slider.

   To mix a color numerically, enter the desired values in the Red (R), Green (G), and Blue (B) fields; alternatively, enter a hexadecimal color value in the Hex Edit Text Box.

1.26   Saving and Reusing Custom Colors

Problem

You want to save or reuse a custom color.

Solution

Add the color to the Color Swatches panel.

Discussion

If you plan to reuse a color that you've mixed, you should save it as a swatch. As a swatch, it will be available in the color pop ups in the Tools panel and Property inspector, as well as the Color Swatches panel.

To add a color to the Color Swatches panel, follow these steps:

1. Mix the color and set it as the active stroke or fill color in the Colors panel.
2. Open the Color Swatches panel (Window → Color Swatches).
3. If necessary, resize the window so that a gray area is visible beneath the existing swatches.
4. Click in that gray area. The cursor becomes a paint bucket, to indicate that you are adding a new color swatch.

Another way to add a color swatch is to choose Add Swatch from the Color Mixer panel's Options menu.

To remove a color swatch, hold down the Ctrl (Windows) or Command (Macintosh) key and click the swatch. The cursor becomes a pair of scissors to indicate that you are removing a color swatch.

 Undo does not work when adding and removing colors from the Color Swatches panel.

You can restore the Color Swatches panel to the factory default—Web 216 plus a handful of premixed gradients—by choosing Load Default Colors from the Color Swatch panel's Options menu.

You can remove all colors from the Color Swatches panel, except black and white. Removing colors is useful when you are designing a custom color palette for a project. Choose Clear Colors from the Color Swatches Options menu.

The color swatches you store in the Color Swatches panel are stored along with the Flash *.fla* file. Swatches will not automatically be available to any other files. However, you can save custom color palettes—indeed, this step is highly recommended when working on projects that span multiple files. To save a color palette, choose

Save Colors from the Options menu. A standard Save dialog box appears, enabling you to save the color palette in one of two formats:

Flash Color Set (.clr)
> The default, this file type enables you to store all types of swatches, including solid colors and gradients. Only Flash can import this type of file.

Color Table (.act)
> This file type enables you to store only solid colors. Its benefit is that its colors can be imported to numerous other programs, such as Macromedia Fireworks and Dreamweaver.

You can load a Flash color palette saved in either format by choosing Add Colors or Replace Colors from the Color Swatches panel Options menu. Both bring up an Open dialog, enabling you to browse to and import a color palette file. Supported color palette file types include Flash *.clr*, *.act*, and *.gif*. The difference between Add Colors and Replace Colors is that Add Colors appends the colors in the palette to the existing collection of swatches, and Replace Colors clears the existing swatches before importing the new swatches.

See Also

Recipe 1.25

1.27 Applying Preset and Custom Gradients

Problem

You want to create a gradient.

Solution

Choose one of the gradient presets or mix a custom gradient using the Color Mixer panel.

Discussion

Gradients are a powerful and flexible graphic effect used in a variety of different ways, including pseudo-3D effects, mask effects, and more. You can apply one of Flash's preset gradients or mix your own.

Flash gradients come in two varieties: linear and radial. Every gradient contains a spectrum of colors. A linear gradient plots the spectrum across a fill in a simple left-to-right manner; the left side of the shape is mapped to the left side of the gradient spectrum, and the right side of the shape is mapped to the right side of the gradient spectrum. Colors are stretched or squeezed, as necessary, to fill the shape. A radial gradient, in contrast, plots the spectrum in a circular pattern, from the center of a shape (the left side of the gradient spectrum) to its outer edge (the right side of the gradient spectrum).

With the default color swatches active (see Recipe 1.26 to restore the default color palette), you can access Flash's preset gradients from the bottom of the color pop up, which appears whenever you click the Fill color box in the Tools panel or the Property inspector. To apply a gradient fill, select any closed line or shape or activate any shape tool that can add a fill (such as the Oval and Rectangle tools), and choose the desired gradient from the color pop up.

Gradients could previously be applied only as fills, not as lines. However, in Flash 8, it is possible to apply gradients to lines as well. To do so, select the gradient before drawing the line. Or, if you want to apply the gradient to an existing line, select the line, and select the gradient from the color pop up or in the Color Mixer panel.

If the built-in gradients don't meet your needs, you can mix your own in the Color Mixer panel. To mix a custom gradient, follow these steps:

1. Open the Color Mixer panel (Window → Color Mixer).
2. Choose the desired gradient type, Linear or Radial, from the Fill Style menu. Once a gradient style is selected, the Gradient Definition Bar appears.
3. Use the Gradient Definition Bar to specify the gradient's spectrum. Beneath the spectrum are Gradient Pointers. Each one contains a single color. Between every pair of Gradient Pointers, Flash blends the color of one into the color of the other.

   - To change a Gradient Pointer's color, click to select it, and click the Fill color box to the left of the Style menu. Select a color or mix your own using the system color picker.
   - To add an additional color to the gradient, add another Gradient Pointer: click anywhere in the Gradient Definition Bar (or just below it) between the colors where you want it to appear. As you hover your mouse over the area, a + sign appears beside the mouse cursor.
   - To make a given blend segment more or less gradual, drag the Gradient Pointers left or right. As you do, Flash automatically adjusts the blending of the two colors.

   As you mix the gradient, a preview appears in the Gradient Sample box.

You can save a custom gradient for future use by making it into a swatch. After you've mixed a gradient, open the Color Mixer Options menu, and choose Add Swatch. Flash adds the custom gradient to the Fill color pop up, and makes it available from the Tools panel, Property inspector, or Color Mixer any time a fill (or a tool that creates one) is selected.

See Also

Recipe 1.28

1.28   Applying a Fill Across Multiple Elements

Problem

You want multiple elements on the stage to share a single gradient or bitmap fill.

Solution

Toggle the Paint Bucket or Brush tool Lock Fill modifier on while filling (Paint Bucket tool) or creating (Brush tool) multiple shapes.

Discussion

By default, each shape that contains a fill has its own fill. For fill styles such as gradients and bitmaps, this means that each shape has its own gradient or its own bitmap.

You might, however, want to make a given fill, such as a gradient or bitmap fill, span from one side of the stage to the other, appearing in multiple shapes. You can cause Flash to share a fill across multiple elements in different ways. If you have already drawn a series of shapes or closed lines and you want to fill them with a shared fill, the easiest approach is to set a gradient or bitmap as the active fill, Shift-select or drag-select all of the elements, and click in any one of them with the Paint Bucket tool. This procedure fills the elements with the same locked fill, regardless of the toggle state of the Lock Fill modifier. Using this method, the fill spans from the left edge of the left-most element to the right edge of the right-most element.

Alternatively, after the elements are drawn, you can click each one individually with the Paint Bucket tool and the Options tray's Lock Fill modifier toggled on. This approach also applies a shared fill across the elements, but it sometimes has an unexpected result. It creates a fill that spans from the left side to the right side of the workspace (which is several hundred pixels wider than the stage). Consequently, the elements display only the portion of the fill that the stage represents. For example, a simple gradient fill from white to black would show only from light gray to dark gray; pure white and pure black values would be offstage.

You can lock fills when drawing with the Brush tool as well, because it creates shapes rather than lines. When using the Brush tool, if a gradient is active, and the Lock Fill modifier in the Options tray is toggled on before you paint the first brush stroke, and you start brushing on an empty stage, Flash draws only the portion of the gradient that overlaps the stage.

In both cases—the Paint Bucket or the Brush—the trick is to define the size of the fill first, then toggle the Lock Fill modifier on and continue creating shapes. Here's how:

- If you are using the Brush tool, toggle the Lock Fill modifier off, and brush a stroke that is as wide as you want the shared fill to be. (This stroke can be temporary and even drawn offstage.) Then toggle the Lock Fill modifier on, and begin brushing the desired strokes.

- If you are using the Paint Bucket tool, fill a shape (such as a rectangle) that is as wide as you want the fill to be with the desired gradient. Then toggle Lock Fill on, and use the Paint Bucket tool to fill in remaining elements. Afterward, you can remove the initial shape that you used to define the size of the fill.

It takes some practice to obtain the results that you desire when sharing fills. Just remember to define the size of the fill first, and then start applying it. You can create the appearance of several objects revealing a background by having them share a gradient or bitmap fill.

See Also

Recipe 6.2, Recipe 6.8

1.29 Stretching, Rotating, and Repositioning Fills

Problem

You want to stretch, rotate, or reposition a gradient or bitmap fill within its shape.

Solution

Use the Fill Transform tool (F).

Discussion

The Fill transform tool has simple controls for repositioning fills, stretching and shrinking fills, and rotating fills. The important concept to understand when using this tool is that it affects only the fill—not the contours of the shape.

To achieve the desired effect, drag the appropriate control handle. To apply a transformation, press the Esc key. You can apply multiple transformations to a fill, and undo the previous transformation. In addition, fill transformations are nondestructive and nonpermanent, so you can apply new transformations at any time.

See Also

Recipe 1.32, Recipe 6.2

1.30 Scaling Elements

Problem

You want to resize an existing element.

Solution

Use the Free Transform tool (Q) or choose Modify → Transform → Scale. Optionally, you can select the Modify → Transform → Scale and Rotate option to scale by a percentage.

Discussion

Flash's Free Transform tool performs a variety of transformations, including scale, stretch, distort, perspective, rotate, and reposition. Selecting the tool puts you in Free Transform mode, where you can perform most of the preceding operations. Alternatively, you can choose Scale from the Modify → Transform menu, which limits the Free Transform tool to scaling alone. You can also specify the type of transformation using the desired modifier in the Options section of the Tools panel while the Free Transform tool is active.

If you activate the Free Transform tool by selecting it directly from the Tools panel, you can scale elements as follows:

- Drag a corner handle to scale both horizontally and vertically. Before you drag, make sure that the cursor is a diagonal double-headed arrow, which indicates scale mode. To enforce proportional scaling, hold down the Shift key as you drag.
- To change the width of an element, drag a side handle, looking for the horizontal double-headed arrow cursor before dragging.
- To change the height of an element, drag a handle on the top or bottom, looking for a vertical double-headed arrow cursor before dragging.

If you initiate scaling using the main menu's Modify → Transform → Scale command, the behavior is the same as described in the preceding list, except that proportions are automatically constrained when you drag a corner handle.

If scaling visually isn't accurate enough, you can also scale numerically. To scale an element with numeric precision, choose Modify → Transform → Scale and Rotate. In the Scale and Rotate dialog box, enter the scale percent (and rotation degree) and click OK.

To scale to a given value, rather than percentage, you can set the W and H (width and height) values for a selected element using the Property inspector.

See Also

Recipe 1.31, Recipe 1.32

1.31 Distorting and Reshaping Elements

Problem

You want to skew, distort, or reshape an element.

Solution

Use the Free Transform tool (Q) in the appropriate mode.

Discussion

You can use the Free Transform tool to skew and distort elements, or to manipulate an element's envelope.

Skewing means manipulating one segment of the bounding box, but the opposite segment is unaffected. To skew an element in Free Transform mode:

1. Position the cursor over any line segment between two handles.

2. When you see a split arrow cursor, drag in a direction parallel to the current line segment to skew the element.

Manipulating a corner point independently of other points distorts a shape. If you attempt to distort a non-corner point, you effectively skew that line segment. Distortion is commonly used to create trapezoid and perspective visual effects.

You cannot distort elements in the default Free Transform mode. To enable distortion:

1. Choose either Modify → Transform → Distort or enable the Distort button in the Options section of the Tools panel with the Free Transform tool selected.

2. Hover over any corner point until you see a large white arrowhead cursor.

3. Drag the corner to the desired position. Doing so moves the one corner, stretching the element to adjust to the new dimensions.

 Holding down the Shift key when dragging a corner point in Distort mode makes the point on the opposite end of the same side move proportionately in the opposite direction.

Most transformations enable you to manipulate corner handles and side handles. What distinguishes them is how other handles react when you drag a given handle. However, manipulating a shape's envelope allows you to move points independently, resulting in highly irregular shapes. Each of the corner and side handles also has control points, akin to those used with the Pen and Subselection tools. To customize a shape's envelope:

1. Activate the Free Transform tool and enable the Envelope modifier (or choose Modify → Transform → Envelope).

2. Drag any selection handle to reposition it, without affecting any other handle. The eight handles are represented by black squares.

3. Drag any of the round tangent handles, which affect the curves of the line segments between the control handles.

See Also

Recipe 1.16, Recipe 1.3, Recipe 1.30

1.32 Rotating Elements

Problem

You want to rotate an element.

Solution

Rotate using the Free Transform tool or rotate in 90° increments using the Modify →
Transform menu commands.

Discussion

You can rotate elements to an arbitrary degree, or you can constrain rotation to regular intervals, such as 90° or 45°.

To rotate an element arbitrarily:

1. Select the Free Transform tool.
2. Hover the mouse near (but not quite over) any corner point until you see a circular rotation cursor.
3. Drag in a circular direction to rotate the element.

Holding down the Shift key constrains the rotation to increments of 45°.

You can also rotate an element by 90° clockwise or counterclockwise. To do so, select the element, and choose Modify → Transform → Rotate 90° CW (for clockwise, or CCW for counterclockwise). All rotations are performed in the X-Y plane (about the imaginary Z axis that runs perpendicular to the stage). To simulate rotation away from or toward the viewer, use a perspective skew as described in Recipe 1.31.

You can also rotate elements with numeric precision. If you need a shape to be rotated to 37°, you can draw it at 0° and then rotate it to exactly 37°.

To rotate an element with numeric precision, choose Modify → Transform → Scale and Rotate. In the Scale and Rotate dialog box, enter the rotation degree (and optionally, scale percent) and click OK.

See Also

Recipe 1.30

1.33   Creating Mirror Images

Problem

You want to flip an element along the horizontal or vertical axis to create a mirror image.

Solution

Use Modify → Transform → Flip Horizontal (or Vertical)

Discussion

Flipping an element inverts it through its center point along either the vertical or horizontal axis. Flipping an element creates a mirror image and therefore differs from rotation. To flip the selected element, choose Modify → Transform → Flip Horizontal (or Vertical). You can flip along both axes and unflip by flipping again.

You can create a bilaterally symmetrical design by duplicating a design, flipping it, and repositioning it.

See Also

Recipe 1.32

1.34   Positioning Elements Precisely

Problem

You want to position elements with numeric precision.

Solution

Set the element's X and Y coordinates in the Property inspector.

Discussion

Every element in Flash, whether it is hand-drawn artwork or a movie clip symbol, has a single registration point, which represents the location of the element. Though an element can be as large as you want, its registration point is always a single dot, a twentieth of a pixel in size.

When you position an element on stage, its X,Y coordinate is the location of its registration point. Using the X and Y fields of the Property inspector, you can specify the position for the selected element with numeric precision. (Remember that the stage's origin, [0,0], is in its upper-left corner.) Positioning with numeric precision is useful when you want to lay out elements of an animation over time, space elements out according to a mathematical pattern, or make room for elements created at runtime using ActionScript.

The location of an element's registration point can vary. For artwork that you've drawn using Flash tools, the registration point is always the upper-left corner of the element. Thus, if an element is positioned at 0,0, then its upper-left corner coincides with the upper-left corner of the stage. Other Flash elements, including symbols by default, have registration points at the center. For these elements, a positioning of 0,0 means that their centers are aligned with the upper-left corner of the stage, and that some of their contents are likely offstage.

1.35 Erasing Content

Problem

You want to erase lines and/or fills in part or entirely.

Solution

To delete an entire shape or fill, use the Eraser tool with the faucet option selected, and click on the shape or fill you want to erase. Optionally, use the Selection tool to select the shape or fill, and press the Delete key.

You can delete part of a shape or fill using the Eraser tool with the faucet option deselected.

Use the punch, slice, crop, or intersect features when you want to delete part of a shape or line to form a more complex shape.

Discussion

The Eraser tool lets you delete part or all of a shape or line. The Eraser tool works in a fairly obvious manner, for the most part. In the Options section of the Tools panel, you can select from the Eraser Shape drop-down menu. Then, as you click and drag on the Stage, it erases the portions of the shapes and lines that it crosses. However, there are a few features of the Eraser tool that are not so obvious.

In the Options section of the Tools panel, you can click on a small faucet icon to toggle faucet mode for the Eraser tool. In faucet mode, it deletes the entire shape or line on which you click.

You can also select from a variety of modes in the Options section of the Tools panel. The default mode for the Eraser tool is Erase Normal. However, you can select the Erase Fills mode to erase only fills or the Erase Lines option to erase only lines. The Erase Selected Fills option erases only fills that are selected, and the Erase Inside mode will erase only the fill enclosed within lines—assuming that you first click the mouse within that shape.

CHAPTER 2

Importing and Exporting Artwork

Importing and exporting artwork with Flash may well be one of the least-talked-about features of the application. However, as you'll read in this chapter, Flash can do a lot of quite powerful import and export functions ranging from importing simple vector artwork to exporting complex, interactive images and HTML.

Before you jump into importing any content, you may want to familiarize yourself with what formats are compatible with Flash. One useful reference, available at Macromedia's LiveDocs web site (*http://livedocs.macromedia.com/flash/flash/8/index.html*), provides you with information regarding which formats can be imported into Flash.

2.1   Importing Assets from Fireworks

Problem

You want to import assets from Fireworks into Flash.

Solution

Save the Fireworks PNG, and then use the File → Import option in Flash to import the Fireworks assets.

Discussion

Because Fireworks and Flash are both Macromedia products, they have fairly good cross-support. That means that you can directly import Fireworks *.png* files (the native Fireworks format) into your Flash documents. When you import PNG content into Flash you get several benefits:

- You don't have to worry about the hassle of saving to an intermediate step.
- You can preserve vector content as vector when possible.
- Flash can import parts of a PNG as vector and parts as rasterized bitmaps, thus providing the best possible balance between appearance, functionality, and file size.

- Another benefit is that PNG can retain an alpha channel—very useful when you want to avoid having to mask areas in your image.

The first step is to create your Fireworks PNG. Even though Flash can import PNG content, it is important to keep in mind that it cannot import all the content in vector form. Although Flash will be able to import standard lines, solid fills, linear fills, gradient fills, and standard text as vector elements, it will need to rasterize other elements. For example, contour fills and text attached to a path will need to be rasterized (Flash will do that for you if you want) to maintain the same appearance in Flash as they have in Fireworks. You will not be able to use the Flash tools to change the color or shape of rasterized elements, so it is a good idea to carefully plan your PNG content while you author it in Fireworks.

After you've created the PNG and saved it, you can import it into a Flash document:

1. Within Flash, open or create an *.fla* document.

2. Choose File → Import → Import to Stage (or press Ctrl-R) if you want to import the content both to the library and to the stage at the same time. Otherwise, if you want only to import the content to the library choose File → Import → Import to Library. If you import to the stage, you'll still be able to remove it from the stage if you want to at a later time.

3. In the Import dialog box that displays, choose the PNG that you want to import and click Open.

4. The Fireworks PNG Import Settings dialog box displays, prompting you to choose from the possible options. By default, the "Import as single flattened bitmap" option is checked. If you leave that option checked, all the content will be rasterized to a single bitmap.

   a. If you want to import the PNG as a single rasterized image, keep the "Import as single flattened bitmap" option checked.

   b. If your PNG contains any content that you want to keep vectorized, you should uncheck the "Import as single flattened bitmap" option. Doing so will enable the other options in the dialog box. The file structure has to do with how Flash should handle the imported content in terms of layers and symbols. The default setting is for Flash to import the content into a new movie clip symbol and keep the layers that are defined in the PNG. This is likely the behavior that you will want in most scenarios. Should you want to have the content imported into a single layer on the current timeline, select the "Import into new layer in current scene" option.

   c. Next, you get to select how you want Flash to handle shapes and text. The default setting is the "Rasterize if necessary to maintain appearance" option in both cases. That means that as long as Flash can import the content as vectors it will do so, but it will rasterize only that content that would not otherwise display properly. Typically, the "Rasterize if necessary to maintain appearance" option is the one you'll want. If you absolutely do not want any of the content to be rasterized, select the "Keep all paths editable" and "Keep all text editable" options. Be aware, however, that doing so can result in drastically different appearances. For example, text that has been attached to a path in the PNG will display as horizontal text in Flash unless it's been rasterized.

5. Click OK.

6. After the content is imported, it is a good idea to check the library for the new content. Often the newly imported symbols are not optimally named and organized. Any rasterized content is imported into bitmap symbols named Bitmap 1, Bitmap 2, and so on. And if you selected the option to import into a movie clip, a new movie clip is created and placed in a Fireworks Objects folder. Those movie clips will be named Symbol 1, Symbol 2, and so on. You should rename and reorganize the new symbols right away rather than waiting until later when it won't be so simple to locate them.

7. Don't forget that you can simply copy and paste directly from Fireworks into Flash—this will "wrap" your PNG in a MovieClip automatically.

2.2 Importing Content from Freehand MX

Problem

You want to import content from Freehand MX.

Solution

Import the Freehand file directly into Flash.

Discussion

As with Fireworks and Flash, Freehand and Flash have fairly good cross-support. You can import Freehand files (Version 7 up to Version 11) directly into Flash without having to export first or save in an intermediate format. One of the nice advantages that Freehand sometimes offers over Fireworks is that it provides a better way to create complex vector artwork for use in Flash. For example, if you attach text to a path in Fireworks and then import that into Flash, Flash will need to rasterize the text. With Freehand, however, you can achieve effects like text that follows a path, but Flash will be able to import it as vectorized artwork (though still not as editable text.)

To import Freehand content into Flash, complete the following steps:

1. Create your Freehand file and save it.

2. Open or create a Flash document.

3. Choose File → Import → Import to Stage if you want to import the content both to the library and to the stage at the same time. Otherwise, if you want to import the content to the library only, choose File → Import → Import to Library. If you import to the stage, you'll be able to remove it from the stage if you want to at a later time.

4. In the Import dialog box, navigate to the Freehand file you want to import, select it, and click Open.

5. In the Freehand Import dialog box, you are prompted for several options:

    a. Freehand uses a pages metaphor. If you have only one page in your Freehand document, you don't really need to care which option is selected for Mappings: Pages choices. However, if you have used several pages, you should decide whether you want the pages to be imported as different scenes or keyframes. In most cases, you should use the keyframes option.

    b. You should also specify how you want Flash to interpret the Freehand layers. By default, the layers in Freehand translate into layers in Flash. However, you also have the option of having each layer import into its own keyframe, or you can flatten all the layers so that they import to a single layer in Flash.

    c. If you have multiple pages in your Freehand document, you also need to decide which of those pages to import. You can import all the pages or specify a range.

    d. Lastly, you are asked whether to import invisible layers and background layers, and you are also asked whether to maintain text blocks as editable text in Flash. Flash will maintain only text blocks as text if possible. Otherwise, it will convert text to outlines.

6. Click OK. Flash will import the Freehand content to the current timeline following the settings you have chosen.

You will likely notice when you import Freehand MX content into Flash, however, that it also imports two new folders full of symbols in your library. The actual artwork that is imported from Freehand is imported onto the current timeline, but a bunch of unused symbols are imported to the library in a folder called Brush Tips and Freehand Objects. You can do several things with the extra symbols:

• Leave them in the Flash library. Because they are unused, they will not be exported and will not add to the file size of the *.swf* file.

• Delete the folders. Because they are not used, you can safely delete them.

• Delete the Brush Tips folder from the Freehand document's library before saving and then importing to Flash. If you do that, the symbols will not be imported.

• Another method of getting rid of the unwanted content is to choose "Select Unused Items" from the Library menu.

2.3 Importing Simulated 3D Shapes from Freehand MX

Problem

You want to import vector artwork that has a three-dimensional appearance from Freehand MX.

Solution

Use the extrude tool in Freehand MX to create a three-dimensional effect and then import the Freehand content into Flash.

Description

You can use the extrude tool in Freehand MX to add some interesting three-dimensional effects to your shapes with just a few clicks of the mouse. It can be a simple, yet effective way to add basic three-dimensional shapes to your Flash application as well. Just use the extrude tool in Freehand, save the document, and then import into Flash following the instructions from Recipe 2.2.

The extrude tool is fairly intuitive. You can find it as part of the standard toolbar in Freehand MX, grouped together with the smudge and shadow tools. See Figure 2-1 for help locating the tool.

Figure 2-1. The extrude tool in Freehand MX

With the extrude tool selected, you can move the mouse over a shape on the stage, click, and drag to cause the three-dimension effect to the shape. Figure 2-2 shows an example of that.

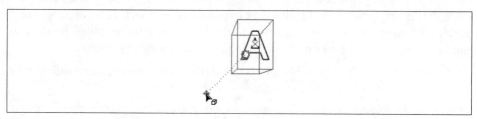

Figure 2-2. Click and drag on a shape to use the extrude tool

After you've extruded the shape, you can adjust the vanishing point and the depth by dragging the corresponding points with the selection tool. You can also double-click the extruded shape to display the rotation controls that allow you to change the angle of perspective for the extruded shape.

See Also

Recipe 2.2

2.4   Importing Acrobat PDF Content

Problem

You want to import content from a PDF to your Flash document.

Solution

Import the PDF directly into Flash.

Discussion

Since Flash MX 2004, Flash has supported importing PostScript files, including PDF. That means that you can directly import your PDF content without any additional converters. And Flash gives you several options when importing the content that allow you to control how it will treat things like text, layers, and pages.

To import PDF content, complete the following steps:

1. Create or obtain your PDF file.
2. Open or create a Flash document.
3. Choose File → Import → Import to Stage if you want to import the content both to the library and to the stage at the same time. Otherwise, if you want to import the content to the library only, choose File → Import → Import to Library. If you import to the stage, you'll still be able to remove it from the stage if you want to at a later time.
4. Navigate to the PDF, select it, and choose Open.
5. In the Import Options dialog box, you are prompted for several options:
   a. PDF documents can consist of multiple pages. When importing the content, Flash will import the pages to either different scenes or keyframes. In most cases, we recommend that you use the keyframes option.
   b. You should also choose how you want Flash to interpret the PDF layers. By default, the layers in the PDF translate into layers in Flash. However, you also have the option of having each layer import into its own keyframe, or you can flatten all the layers so that they import on a single layer in Flash.
   c. If you have multiple pages in your PDF document, you also need to decide which of those pages to import. You can import all the pages or specify a range.
   d. Lastly, you are asked whether to import invisible layers, whether to maintain text blocks as editable text in Flash, and whether to rasterize the entire import. If you choose to rasterize the entire content that you import, you can choose the resolution at which to rasterize the content, specified in dots per inch.
6. Click OK to import the PDF content. Flash will import it to the current timeline.

Importing PDF files can be resource-intensive. Larger PDFs may take a long time to import on everything but high-end machines.

2.5   Importing Illustrator AI and EPS Content

Problem

You want to import Illustrator AI files or EPS files into your Flash document.

Solution

Use Flash to import the content directly.

Discussion

The Illustrator AI and EPS formats are PostScript formats very similar to the PDF format. As such, Flash will import the contents in very much the same way as it imports PDF content. Refer to Recipe 2.4 for more details.

Flash can import Illustrator AI files that are saved as Version 6 through Version 10. Flash can import any EPS file.

 It appears that EPS content provides a more accurate representation of text that follows a curve when imported into Flash. The same Illustrator content exported as an AI file and as an EPS file imports more accurately in the EPS format when it comes to text on a path.

See Also

Recipe 2.4

2.6   Exporting Single-Frame Images

Problem

You want to use Flash to export a single frame in a popular image format, such as GIF, JPEG, or PNG.

Solution

Select the frame for which you want to export the contents and then choose to export as image.

Alternatively, change the publish settings to export the format you want and publish.

Discussion

Although you may typically think of Flash as being a tool strictly for exporting SWF content, you can also use it to export a variety of other formats, including single-frame formats such as JPEG, PNG, GIF, BMP, AI, EPS, and more. This trick can be convenient for many possible reasons. For example, you may want to export a still image of a frame or frames from your Flash movie to use for presentation or packaging purposes. And even for advanced Flash developers, the feature can be quite useful, such as to export icons that represent components that they are developing.

There are several ways you can export single-frame content from Flash. These ways can sometimes be used interchangeably, but in other cases you will want to opt for one method over another. One way is to export the content through the File menu by choosing File → Export → Export Image. We'll call this first technique the *export image technique*. The second is to change the publish settings so that Flash will know to export the image types that you want, and then to use the publish feature to tell Flash to export the file or files. We'll call this second technique the *publish settings technique*. Let's take a look at each of these two techniques in more depth, including when and why you would want to use one over the other.

The export image technique in Flash is most useful in the following scenarios:

- You want to quickly export an image file for the current frame without having to go through the extra step of changing the publish settings. If you know that you want to export the image multiple times, consider using the publish settings technique instead.

- You want to export an image file for a frame in a symbol. When this is the case, you have to use the export image technique. The publish settings technique does not allow you to export images for frames other than frames of the main timeline.

- You want to export a single-frame format other than GIF, JPEG, or PNG. For example, if you want to export an EPS or AI file, you must use the export image technique. The publish settings technique allows you to export in GIF, JPEG, and/or PNG only when exporting to a single-frame format.

- You want to publish several single-frame images from your file. The publish settings technique allows you to export only a single image corresponding to a single frame. If you want to export two or more images from the document, you'll need to export them one at a time with the export image technique.

- You want Flash to automatically crop the image to fit the artwork. For example, if your Flash document is 550×400 and your artwork is a 50×25 rectangle in the center, you may want the image that you export to be 50×25 rather than 550×400. The export image technique automatically crops the exported image to the actual artwork on the stage at that frame. Changing the dimensions of the image you export also changes the resolution (thus scaling the image), so there is no way to have Flash not crop the image with the export image technique. The publish settings technique, on the other hand, will default to the document's dimensions. Though you can change the dimensions in the publish settings technique, it will scale the content, not crop it.

To export an image with the export image technique, first move the playhead to the frame for which you want to export the artwork. Then choose File → Export → Export Image from the Flash application menu system. The Export Image dialog box appears, prompting you to choose the location, name, and format to which you want to export the current frame. Clicking Save after selecting a location, name, and format will either export the file or bring up the Export Options dialog box if the selected format requires that you choose values. The options vary depending on the format, but in each case the options with which you are presented are fairly straightforward. They involve things such as dimensions, resolution, color depth, and so on.

The publish settings technique offers advantages if you are going to export more than one format or if you are likely to export the image or images more than once. In that case, it is worth changing the Publish Settings options to export the specified format or formats, so that you can export the file or files by pressing keys on the keyboard (Shift-F12) rather than having to navigate menus, specify files and locations, and choose from options each time. You can open the publish settings by navigating to File → Publish Settings. With the Format tab selected in the Publish Settings dialog box, check each checkbox next to the formats you want to export. For each selected format, a new tab allows you to adjust the settings for that particular format. For example, if you check the JPEG and PNG format options, a JPEG and PNG tab appears within the Publish Settings dialog box. You can then choose the various tabs to adjust the settings for the corresponding formats. Those settings determine how the files will export.

By default, the files that export when you use the publish settings will be exported to the same directory as the *.fla* file and with names that correspond to the name of the FLA. For example, if the FLA is named *circle.fla*, the exported PNG would be named *circle.png*. You can modify the names and locations to which the files are exported from the Formats tab.

After you've configured the publish settings and you are ready to publish (export) the files, all you need to do is to make sure the correct frame is selected in the timeline and then press Shift-F12 and the files will be exported.

 There is a TechNote at *http://www.macromedia.com/cfusion/ knowledgebase/index.cfm?id=4ca37de4&pss=rss_flash_4ca37de4* regarding the keyboard shortcut for publish under Mac OS X.

Take note, however, that when you publish the image or images using the publish settings technique, Flash exports the first frame of the main timeline by default. Remember that you can export only images corresponding to frames of the main timeline using the publish settings technique. However, you *can* tell Flash to export a frame other than the first frame. The technique varies depending on the image format. For PNG and GIF images, you add a frame label of #Static to the frame for which you want to export the image: select the frame in the timeline, open the Property inspector, and enter the value #Static in the Frame Label field. Then, when you publish, Flash exports the image so that it corresponds to the #Static frame. If you have selected more than one single-frame image format to export, all will correspond to that same frame. For JPEG content, however, the #Static frame label will have no effect. Instead, you must select the correct frame in the main timeline before publishing.

2.7   Exporting Animated GIF Files

Problem

You want to use Flash to export an animated GIF.

Solution

Create your animation in the main timeline and then export the file as an animated GIF.

Discussion

Flash allows you to export your animations not only in SWF format, but in several other formats, including animated GIF files. As with single-frame GIF content, you can publish your animated GIFs in two ways. One way is to use the File → Export → Export Movie option. We'll call this method the *export movie technique*. The other way is using the *publish settings technique*—almost identical to the publish settings technique described in Recipe 2.6.

The single advantage that the export movie technique offers over the publish settings technique is that it allows you to export an animated GIF from a timeline other than the main timeline. Otherwise, the publish settings technique is typically more advantageous. In order to export an animated GIF using the export movie technique, choose File → Export → Export Movie. The Export Movie dialog box opens. Choose the Animated GIF option from the "Save as type" menu. After you've entered the name of the file you want to export and clicked OK, you will be presented with the Export GIF dialog box. This dialog box is almost identical to the one you get when exporting a single-frame GIF file (see Recipe 2.5), but it also allows you to specify the number of times the animation sequence should run. A value of 0 causes the GIF to animate repeatedly until unloaded from the viewer. Otherwise, you can specify a positive integer value, to loop the animation a specific number of times.

You can export an animated GIF using the publish settings technique as well. The publish settings technique offers the advantage of allowing you to export the image file repeatedly with only the press of a key on the keyboard rather than having to navigate menu systems and so forth. It also allows you to export the animated GIF from a subrange of frames (though only from the main timeline) rather than the entire timeline. In order to export an animated GIF using the publish settings technique, first configure the publish settings appropriately. Choose File → Publish Settings to open the Publish Settings dialog box. From the Format tab, select the GIF option. Select the GIF tab, and from the options for playback, choose the Animated radio button. When you select the Animated option, the additional suboptions are activated so that you can choose from them. By default, the animated GIF will loop playback continuously. You can, however, select the Repeat option and specify a number of times for the animation to repeat until it stops. After you've configured the GIF settings, you can press OK to close the Publish Settings dialog box, or select Publish to publish the GIF file. After you've set the publish settings, you can later publish the content at any point by simply pressing F12.

When you use the publish settings technique to publish your animated GIF, you can specify a subrange of frames on the main timeline for which to export the animation. By default, the entire timeline is used. However, if you add #First and #Last frame labels to the appropriate frames (on the main timeline only), Flash will export the animation between those frames, inclusive.

See Also

Recipe 2.6

2.8   Exporting Image Maps (HTML Images with Clickable Regions)

Problem

You want to export an image and an HTML page in which the HTML page contains an image map that allows the user to click on various portions of the image.

Solution

Change the publish settings so that Flash will export a single-frame image and an HTML page using the image map template. Then publish.

Discussion

Flash can export not only single-frame images and HTML pages, but also simple button functionality as an image map. An image map in HTML is a way of defining rectangular regions over an image that are clickable. A classic example is a map in which different regions can be clicked to hyperlink to another page with details about the region. Flash provides you with a simple and convenient way to create such image maps with built-in templates.

First of all, let's consider the simplest example, in which your Flash document has a single frame. On that one frame, you have artwork that you'd like to export as a single-frame image. For example, perhaps you have artwork for a world map, as shown in Figure 2-3.

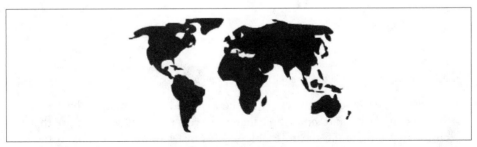

Figure 2-3. Artwork to export as a single-frame image

However, you also want to export an HTML page that will contain clickable regions over the map. The following steps outline the basic procedure:

1. Create a button symbol. In the button symbol, draw a filled rectangle on the Hit frame. This step will create an invisible button. Although you can create Flash buttons that have nonrectangular hit areas, image maps allow for only rectangular areas in the HTML. Therefore, even if you defined a nonrectangular hit area for the button, in the exported image map, the corresponding rectangular bounding box would be used to map the region. If you have any questions about creating buttons in Flash, you may want to consult Chapter 9. Also, note that the buttons that can be used for image maps must be Button instances, and they cannot be movie clips that handle button events.

2. Return to the main timeline and create a new layer above the layer or layers containing the artwork.

3. On the new layer, drag an instance or instances of the button symbol over the corresponding region or regions of the artwork. You can use the authoring tools, such as the free transform tool, to resize the button instances. The invisible buttons will show in Flash as a translucent cyan, so that you can see them on the stage. In the exported files, however, the buttons will not be visible. Figure 2-4 shows an example in which invisible buttons have been placed and resized for the world map.

4. In Flash, it is generally recommended that you use a style of ActionScript code called event handler methods to apply actions to buttons, because it has several advantages over the other option, simply called an on( ) event handler. However, when you export an image map, Flash will only recognize actions applied using on( ) event handlers. Furthermore, the only HTML event that the exported image map can detect is when the user clicks and then releases on a region. That means that regardless of which ActionScript button event you specify (press,

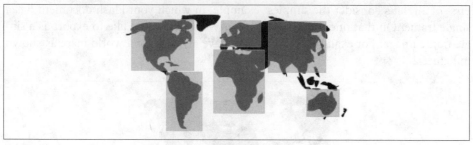

Figure 2-4. Invisible buttons will define the clickable regions

release, rollover, etc.), the effect in the exported image map is the same. For the sake of clarity and simplicity, therefore, you might as well specify that the buttons should handle the release event. In order to apply actions to the buttons, complete the following steps:

a. Select a button instance and open the Actions panel by pressing F9. In the Actions panel, you should see that the title bar says Actions—Button.

b. In the Script pane (the portion of the Actions on the right), add the ActionScript code that you want to call when the button is clicked. When exporting image maps, you have two basic options: add a hyperlink to another URL or add a JavaScript function call. In either case, the Action-Script code should be within a getURL( ) function. An example of a standard hyperlink within an on( ) event handler (as you would assign it to a button instance) is as follows:

```
on(release) {
  getURL("index.html");
}
```

An example of code that calls a JavaScript function is as follows:

```
on(release) {
  getURL("javascript: alert('You clicked on the region');");
}
```

The preceding code calls the built-in JavaScript function called alert( ). The alert( ) function opens a new message box and displays a message to the user. You can also call custom JavaScript functions if they are defined within the HTML page or in an imported *.js* file.

5. If you haven't yet saved your file, do so, then open the publish settings (File → Publish Settings) to the Format tab, and select HTML (which requires that SWF is also selected, even though you don't really need to export an *.swf* file in this case) and either JPEG, PNG, or GIF. The image format you choose is up to you, depending on what is most appropriate for your artwork. Figure 2-5 shows an example of what your Publish Settings Format tab should look like.

6. Click the HTML tab in the Publish Settings dialog box, and select the Image Map option from the Template menu as shown in Figure 2-6.

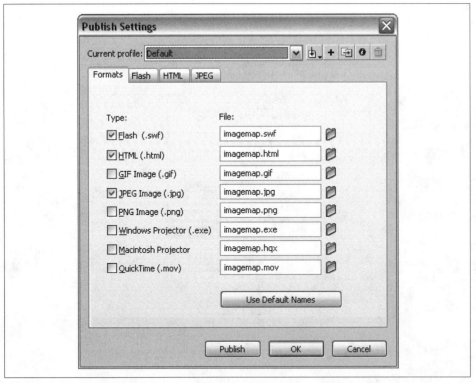

Figure 2-5. The Publish Settings Format tab

7. Click the Publish button to publish the HTML file. Because of a bug in Flash, the JPEG, PNG, or GIF will not publish simultaneously. Instead, the HTML (and SWF) file will publish. When it opens in a browser, you'll see a broken link in place of the image.

8. Still in the Publish Settings dialog box, click the Format tab again and deselect HTML, but leave JPEG, PNG, or GIF selected. Publish again. Then, when you open the HTML page in the browser, your image map should function correctly.

You can find an *.fla* file that contains everything necessary to export a sample image map included in the download of files associated with this book. The file is named *imagemap.fla*.

Should you, for some reason, want to export an image map from a Flash file that contains more than one frame, then some additional considerations may come into play. The frame in which the image appears and the frame in which the buttons appear must be considered. By default, as you learned in Recipe 2.6, Flash exports PNG and GIF files based on the artwork in the first frame, unless one of the frames on the main timeline has been assigned a frame label of #Static. With JPEG files, it

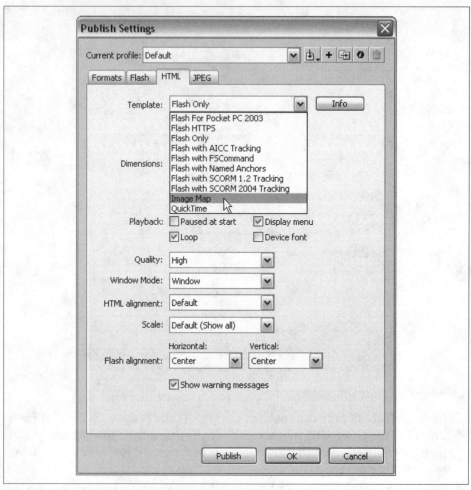

Figure 2-6. Select the Image Map template

exports the content from the currently selected frame regardless of whether a #Static label has been assigned to a frame. Images are exported according to the same rules when exporting image maps. However, Flash looks for the buttons that define the clickable regions in the *final* frame of the main timeline. You can explicitly instruct Flash to export the image map using buttons from another frame by adding a frame label of #Map to the frame.

When you have only one frame in your Flash movie, these issues of artwork and button placement are unnoticed. But when you have multiple frames in the Flash file, these minor details can greatly impact whether your image map will function. For example, Figure 2-7 shows an example of a timeline in which the buttons are defined in the first 10 frames and the artwork is defined in the last 10 frames. When such a file is exported as an image map, you will get an image file that contains none of the artwork (because the artwork is not in the first frame) and none of the interactivity (because none of the buttons are defined on the last frame).

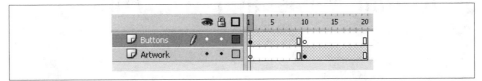

Figure 2-7. A timeline for an .fla file that will not export correctly as an image map

What you can do is (assuming you are exporting a PNG or GIF) add frame labels of #Map and #Static as shown in Figure 2-8.

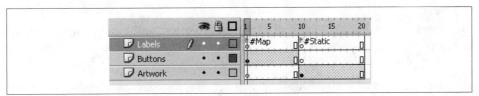

Figure 2-8. A timeline with frame labels so that it will export correctly as an image map

CHAPTER 3

Structuring Movies and Laying Out Content

After elements are in Flash, whether drawn or imported, graphics or sound, bitmap or video, you must specify where they should go, when they should appear, and when they should disappear.

Like the canvas of an image editor, or the page of a page layout program, Flash has the stage. By default, the Flash stage is 550 pixels wide by 400 pixels in height, with a white background and pixels as the default unit of measurement. But you can modify any of these settings to meet your needs.

To facilitate document layout and element positioning, Flash has rulers, a customizable grid, and guides. *Rulers* run along the horizontal and vertical edges of the page, enabling you to see exactly where a given coordinate appears relative to the stage. The *grid*, like the lines on graph paper, is a regular rectangular pattern that facilitates the creation of proportionate elements. *Guides* are horizontal or vertical lines that you can add to a document in custom locations to be used for alignment and layout purposes: they do not appear in the output file.

Another useful layout tool is Flash's Align panel, which you can use to align various elements to each other and/or the stage. In addition, the Align panel enables you to distribute multiple elements so they are spaced out evenly.

Flash also provides controls on the stacking order of elements. That is, if two or more elements overlap, you can control which appears on top of the other. In general, more recently added elements are automatically stacked on top of older elements. If you draw a circle, and then add a line of text in the same place, the text will block the original circle where the two overlap. As discussed in Chapter 1, Flash's unique drawing system is an exception—newer shapes and lines can crop and blend with older shapes when they overlap.

Flash offers a more powerful system of control over stacking order than this automatic stacking, however, called *layers*. Layers enable you to separate elements onto discrete planes; even when drawn elements on two layers overlap, they never crop or blend.

To those familiar with traditional graphics applications, such as image editors and page layout programs, all the features mentioned so far are familiar. But Flash also enables you to specify where elements are positioned in the fourth dimension: time. That is, when you are creating animations or interactivity, you must specify when elements appear or disappear, when changes occur, and how the stage should look after these changes take place.

The primary interface element used to control stage elements as they change over time is the *timeline*. The timeline contains frames, which may contain content. When a frame has content, this content is displayed (if graphic), played (if audio), and so on during playback in the Flash Player. If a frame lacks content, then it is empty, and nothing is played or displayed in the Flash Player. Every movie has at least one layer and one frame, but you can add as many frames as you need—up to 16,000. Each layer has its own frames, which means that one layer can have static content, while another layer has animated content, and a third layer may not have any content in a given moment at all.

Working with multimedia can be overwhelming at first, because you have to consider the composition on the stage, the vertical and/or logical organization in layers, the position and changes over time, and the architectural implications of symbols and the library. The key is to work with a movie's elements one at a time, rather than all at once. You should always try to isolate elements from each other, which you can accomplish by using layers, the timeline, and the library correctly. Once isolated from each other, it is easy to determine when and where elements should appear, how they should animate, and so forth.

3.1 Setting the Background Color

Problem

You want to set the background color for a Flash movie.

Solution

For static backgrounds, select a background color in the Document Properties dialog box. For background colors that can change, use a symbol instance (Graphic or movie clip) with a rectangular fill.

Discussion

There are two types of solid color backgrounds for Flash documents: static and dynamic. A static background is one in which the background color does not change, and it is the simplest to implement. A dynamic background is one in which the color may change. For example, you may want to build an application in which the user can select a background color. Because the background color *can* change, it's dynamic in such a case.

Every Flash document has a static background built into it. The default setting for Flash document backgrounds is white (although you can assign a new default color). However, you can select a new static background color from the Document Properties dialog box or from the Property inspector. To access the Document Properties dialog box, you can select Modify → Document or you can use the keyboard shortcut—Ctrl-J on Windows and Command-J on Macintosh. From the Document Properties dialog box, you can select a new background color from the Background color selector. Optionally, you can access the Background color selector from the Property inspector. The Property inspector allows you to adjust document settings when no object is selected on stage.

Whether you are accessing the Background color selector from the Document Properties dialog box or from the Property inspector, it works in the same way. When you click the current swatch, it expands the selector so you can pick from one of the 235 swatches. If none of the swatches is exactly the color you want to use, you can use the color wheel to mix a custom color. You can access the color wheel from the upper-right corner of the Background color selector.

As already noted, sometimes an application requires a dynamic background color. In such a case, Flash has no built-in background features that enable that sort of functionality. However, you can achieve the effect without too much difficulty by using a symbol instance. With Flash, you can build a library of reusable symbols. You can build a symbol that contains rectangular artwork, and you can then place an instance of that symbol on the main timeline at the lowest layer so that it appears beneath everything else on stage. As long as the rectangle has the same dimensions as the stage, it will appear to the user as a background. The advantage of using a symbol instance is that symbol instances enable you to add animation and interactivity. For example, by using a Movie Clip symbol instance, you can make the background loop through an animation in which the color slowly changes over time.

If you want to use a component that allows you to add an interactive, dynamic background with little to no programming necessary, you can use the BasicBackground component from the *Flash 8 Cookbook* components (downloadable from *http://www.rightactionscript/fcb*).

3.2   Setting Stage Dimensions

Problem

You want to set the dimensions of the stage.

Solution

Set the width and height in the Document Properties dialog box.

Discussion

Each time you open a new document, Flash uses the default document settings. Unless you've changed the default settings, new documents have dimensions set at 550×400 pixels. Although these settings provide plenty of room for doodling and experimentation, they do not work for every situation. For example, many banner ads are 468×60 pixels, yet a Flash movie optimized to fill a browser window in a monitor with 800×600 resolution should be set at (or near) 760×400. You can use Flash to author content to play on many mobile devices of varying screen dimensions. Those are just a few examples of the many standards for Flash stage dimensions.

You can change a document's basic properties in the Document Properties dialog box, which can be accessed by selecting Modify → Document. You can also access the dialog box by clicking the Size button that appears in the Property inspector when no object is selected on the stage.

Setting the document dimensions is not difficult. However, it's often important to determine the dimensions before starting a project. If you do need to change the dimensions after having started a project, you'll have to go back in to correct any layout issues that may arise as a result. When you change the document dimensions, it will not move anything on stage. The upper-left corner stays fixed, while the stage increases or decreases in dimension to the right and downward.

3.3   Setting the Frame Rate

Problem

You want to set the frame rate of a Flash document.

Solution

Set the frame rate value in the Document Properties or in the Property inspector.

Discussion

To register in the human brain, an image needs a certain amount of time—it is not instantaneous; this is referred to as persistence of vision. If an animation or video format displays images faster than the time the brain requires to process an image, the illusion of fluid motion is created. If, on the other hand, images are displayed slower than the *persistence of vision*, individual images are perceptible, and the animation or video looks uneven. In animation and video each image in the sequence is called a *frame*. Higher frame rates (more frames per second) generally result in smoother animation.

Unless you change the default settings, Flash uses 12 frames per second for new documents. However, the setting of 12 frames per second is not optimal in every situation. High-quality animation and video outlets, such as television and movies, use nearly 30 frames per second, so Flash's default setting is obviously lower in quality than those media. However, before you set the frame rate of a Flash document to 30 or greater (Flash allows a maximum frame rate of 120 frames per second) you need to consider whether the SWF will be able to run at that frame rate.

There are two basic factors that affect the actual frame rate at which an SWF plays back—the amount of processing power required by the SWF and the amount of processing power available on the computer playing back the SWF. If a computer simply cannot play back the SWF at the frame rate set for the document, Flash Player will play back the SWF at the maximum frame rate it can. And the frame rate during playback can fluctuate. For example, if an SWF has a frame rate setting of 30 frames per second, it may start at 30 frames per second as long as nothing is on stage. However, if 5 seconds into the animation there are objects flying around on stage, the frame rate might drop to 20. The effect is that the playback appears to slow down and appear choppy at times.

Although you cannot guarantee that an SWF will play back at a consistent frame rate on every computer every time, there are some steps you can take to help improve the likelihood that it will run as consistently as possible:

- Determine the minimum system requirements of your audience, and test using equivalent computers. For example, if you know that 50% of your audience uses Pentium III 1GHz computers, you ought to test using a similar system.

- Before you build the entire SWF, start with a simple test SWF that incorporates some of the most processor-intensive aspects of the project. Use that to determine what frame rates will work for the project.

- Use a utility such as the FrameRateCheckerUtility component from the *Flash 8 Cookbook* components (see the Preface). Using the FrameRateCheckerUtility you can determine the actual playback frame rate.

Flash's default of 12 frames per second is often a good option with complex animations, such as cartoons, destined for web distribution. Faster frame rates tax the processor, often forcing Flash to skip frames, which defeats the purpose of the higher frame rate. In addition, high frame rates often require more assets, hence ensuring longer downloads; usually these also require more time and effort to animate. In contrast, if you drop the frame rate lower than 12 frames per second, then the quality of the animation drops further.

More so than any other document setting, it is important to select the frame rate *before* starting a Flash project. If you change the frame rate after the project has already started, it will cause existing animations to speed up or slow down. For example, if you change the frame rate from 12 to 24, the timelines will play back twice as fast. That means that a motion tween that spans 48 frames used to take 4 seconds, but with the new setting it happens in just 2 seconds.

3.4 Applying New Default Document Settings

Problem

You use document settings other than the factory defaults for many Flash projects, and you want to apply those settings as the default rather than the 540×400, 12 frames per second (fps), white background, pixel ruler units settings that are the factory defaults.

Solution

Select the new default settings you want from the Document Properties dialog box, and click the Make Default button.

Discussion

If you frequently use document settings that are a standard for the projects you work on, but those settings differ from the Flash factory defaults, you may have to set the document properties every time you start a new Flash project. Not only can that be a slight hassle, but it can also cause difficulties if you're using a frame rate other than the default and you accidentally forget to change the settings before adding timeline animations.

If you use some set of document settings frequently, consider assigning them as the default document settings. Although Flash has factory defaults, doing so allows you to customize the default settings with the click of a button. From the Document Settings dialog box, select the settings you want to use as the defaults. Then click on the Make Default button in the lower-left corner of the dialog box. From then on, any new Flash document will use those settings as the default.

If you use several different standard document settings, consider making new document templates for each. Recipe 3.5 discusses how to do that in more detail.

3.5 Creating Document Templates

Problem

You want to create a document template that specifies basic document properties and/or includes a number of reusable assets to jump-start production.

Solution

Use Flash's template feature, either by using a built-in template or by creating and using your own custom template.

Discussion

You can optimize the production of new Flash projects by using one of the several movie templates that are built into Flash. These include standard templates for ads, broadcast, menus, mobile devices, photo slideshows, presentations, and quizzes. Each template already has appropriate movie properties settings, including size, frame rate, and so on. Furthermore, each also has a number of other assets that you can use to jump-start movie production, including graphics, ActionScript (such as custom functions or classes), sounds, layers, symbols, and even visual cues, such as custom guides.

To access the built-in templates, choose File → New, and click on the Templates tab in the dialog box. Select a template from the dialog box, and Flash creates a new document, which inherits the properties stored in the template.

You can also create your own templates. This technique is especially convenient if you create a number of movies based on the same properties, including dimensions and frame rate, that share graphic, audio, or script assets. Templates also enable programmers to create application or interface elements that designers and/or nonprogrammers can use as the basis of complex new movies.

To create a custom template, create the file to be used as a template, and choose File → Save As Template. In the Save As Template dialog box, provide a name for the template, its category, and a brief description. The entire file is saved as a template, including all graphic and sound assets, ActionScript, and visual aids such as custom guides. Creating instructions on a guide layer is optional but recommended.

3.6   Lengthening the Duration of the Movie

Problem

You want to extend the duration of a movie.

Solution

Insert frames.

Discussion

When you open a new Flash document, it contains only one frame (possible exceptions being documents based on some templates). With only one frame, the Flash document has no provision for time. To enable elements to change over time, you should add multiple frames.

An important exception to the concept of animations requiring multiple frames is ActionScript-based movies. Many Flash applications exist entirely on a single frame, with all interactivity and animation controlled at runtime with ActionScript.

Using the default frame rate of 12 fps, a single-frame movie lasts one-twelfth of a second. To lengthen a movie, to make room for changes of content, you add new frames. Figure 3-1 shows the main timeline of a movie with 12 frames. Though frame placeholders exist for frames 13 and higher, these frames do not actually exist.

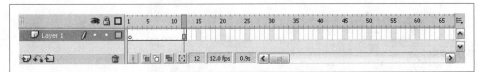

Figure 3-1. At 12 frames, this movie would last one second

In addition to frames, Flash's timeline also contains the playhead (shown in Figure 3-1). The playhead indicates the active frame. The stage displays all the contents for the frame that contains the playhead. In other words, to modify portions of a movie that occur earlier or later than the contents currently showing on the stage, drag the playhead until it is in the frame that contains the elements you want to modify.

You can add frames to a movie one at a time or in groups by using the Insert → Frame command or by pressing F5, its keyboard shortcut. The result of this action depends on a number of factors, but in all cases, new frames are always added after the selected or active frame (that is, the frame containing the playhead).

- To insert a single frame in only one layer, select a single frame in one layer, and choose Insert → Frame.
- To insert a single frame in all layers, position the playhead in the frame after which you want to add the new frame, and choose Insert → Frame.

Flash also makes it possible to add multiple frames at once. For example, if you know that your animation should be 10 seconds, and your movie's frame rate is 12 frames per second, you need to add 119 frames after the original frame. You can insert all these frames at once. You can also duplicate frame spans, one after the other.

- To insert multiple new frames, select the frame placeholder where you want the frames to end and choose Insert → Frame. Doing so inserts a new frame in the selected frame placeholder as well as in all the intervening frames between the selected frame placeholder and the original last frame in that layer.
- To duplicate a selected span of frames, select the desired frames, which can include multiple contiguous frames in multiple contiguous layers, and choose Insert → Frame.

You can add frames to the middle of a movie, and not just to the end. For example, if you have an animation that lasts 20 frames, and it goes by too quickly, you can lengthen the animation by adding several frames in the middle of the animation. To do so, position the playhead to the frame after which you want the new frames to appear, and select Insert → Frame or press F5. To add a half-second to an animation, insert 6 frames, if the frame rate is 12 frames per second.

See Also

Recipe 3.7, Recipe 3.8

3.7   Changing Contents on Stage

Problem

You want to cause an element to undergo a change; for example, appearing, disappearing, or moving.

Solution

Create a new keyframe and modify the element in the new keyframe.

Discussion

Flash has two types of frames: keyframes and frames. *Keyframes* are special frames in which you can specify a change. The first frame of every layer in a timeline is always a keyframe. *Frames* merely extend the duration of keyframes. That is, frames are dependent on and inherit from keyframes; they cannot contain any information beyond that found in the preceding keyframe.

Keyframes and frames are represented differently as well. A keyframe is depicted in the timeline with a circle. A solid circle appears if there is stage content (such as graphics or text, but not ActionScript) in the keyframe. A hollow circle appears if the keyframe lacks stage content; these kinds of keyframes are called *blank keyframes*. Frames with content—both keyframes and regular frames—are shaded gray, while blank keyframes and frames are white. Because frames are dependent on the keyframe that precedes them, the pairing of a keyframe and all successive frames can be thought of as a unit; this unit is called a *frame span*. A frame span ranges from the keyframe to the last regular frame before the next keyframe or until no more frames exist in the timeline. The last frame in a frame span has an empty rectangle in it.

Keyframes are obviously more powerful than frames, but they also add (negligibly) to file size, because users have to download whatever information they contain, such as text, graphics, sounds, animation information, element coordinate positions, and so on. Use keyframes only when you want to change the contents of a given layer. For example, to make an element in frame 1 disappear after five seconds, you would insert

58 regular frames after the keyframe in frame 1, all of which would display the same element. In frame 60, you would insert a blank keyframe. When the playhead reached frame 60, Flash would remove the element from the stage, creating the change.

Creating a keyframe is similar to adding a regular frame. The menu command is Insert → Keyframe, and the keyboard shortcut is F6. Unlike inserting new frames, when you insert a keyframe, the keyframe is added to the active frame, and not the next one. That is, if frame 60 is selected, and you add a frame, the new frame will appear in frame 61. But if you add a keyframe, frame 60 is converted to a keyframe. You should be aware of several other behaviors when inserting keyframes:

- When you insert a keyframe into a frame placeholder, all frames between the original last frame and the new keyframe are converted to regular frames.
- A newly inserted keyframe initially inherits the contents of the preceding keyframe-frame span. Because it is a keyframe, you can change or remove these contents by selecting them on the stage and moving them with the Arrow tool or by deleting them. Alternatively, if appropriate, you can insert a blank keyframe by choosing Insert → Blank Keyframe.
- You can insert multiple keyframes at once by selecting multiple frames or frame placeholders. You can insert keyframes across multiple layers and/or in a horizontal selection of frames.
- You can convert a keyframe to a regular frame by choosing Insert → Clear Keyframe.

You can use two or more keyframes in a series to create the most basic form of animation: the frame-by-frame animation. To create a simple frame-by-frame animation, follow these steps:

1. Add a graphical element to the stage. It can be text, an imported bitmap, drawn art, or any combination thereof.
2. Add a new keyframe one or more frames later. The contents of the original keyframe are copied into the new keyframe.
3. Modify the contents of the new keyframe in some way—move them; lower their opacity; enlarge, rotate, skew, or distort them.
4. Repeat steps 2 and 3 as desired.
5. To preview the animation you just created, drag the playhead to frame 1, and choose Control → Play from the main menu.

The stage can only show the contents of one frame at a time, across all layers. Again, the playhead determines which frame's contents are displayed on the stage.

Frame-by-frame animation, though providing precise control over how things move and change over time in your movie, can be a very exacting process. For most animation needs you'll likely want to rely on *tweens* (Flash's automated forms of animation)—and the role of keyframes and tweens in animation—which is covered in detail in Chapter 4.

3.8   Managing Content with Layers

Problem

You need to manage two elements independently of one another.

Solution

Place the elements in separate layers. Manage layers with layer folders.

Discussion

Layers are a common feature of graphics software that are generally used to control the stacking order of elements as well as facilitating asset management within files. Elements stored in layers higher in the stack will block elements in layers lower in the stack when there is overlap. By storing different elements in their own descriptively named layers, you can more readily manage the artwork by deleting, hiding, outlining, locking, and otherwise working with layer content independently of other layers. Although layers are used in Flash for both of these purposes, layers have additional significance:

- Use layers to prevent overlapping Flash art from automatically cropping and blending with other art. (Another way to prevent this interaction is to group elements, as described in Recipe 3.16).
- Use layers to animate elements differently.

The second point is the more significant of the two. All the contents of a layer are tied to its keyframes and frames. Certain types of content, such as Flash's automated forms of animation, *tweens*, affect entire layers. If you want to animate two elements independently of one another, such as the eyes and mouth of a cartoon character, you must put these elements on different layers. In such an example, the eyes might blink every 45 frames, while the mouth is constantly animated, requiring keyframes every few frames.

Layers are a feature of *.fla* files and authoring in Flash. When you export a Flash movie in the *.swf* file format, Flash flattens all the layers to minimize file size. Thus, layers are primarily an authoring aid.

Layer maintenance is performed in the layer stack just to the left of the timeline, as well as in the small toolbar just beneath it:

- To insert a layer, click the Insert Layer button. A new layer is inserted above the active layer.
- To rename a layer, double-click its label and type a new name. Press Enter or click elsewhere in Flash to apply the new name. Always name your layers descriptively.
- To reorder layers, drag a layer by its name, hovering in between the two layers where you want to place it, and release the mouse.

- To remove a layer and all its contents, select the layer and click the Delete Layer button.

Layers are not part of the movie's contents; remember, layers aren't even exported with the *.swf* file. A movie's contents—art, sounds, text, scripts, and more—are stored in layers and frames, much like clothes are stored in closets and drawers. Maintaining layers and maintaining movie contents are thus two different activities. These two activities come together inasmuch as content resides in a given keyframe of a given layer.

- To add content to a movie, select the keyframe in the layer into which you want to store the content.
- To modify existing content, select the appropriate keyframe and layer in which the content is stored, then select the element, and modify as needed. Likewise, to remove content from a movie, select the keyframe in the layer in which the content resides, and then select and remove the undesired element.
- In addition to copying and pasting individual elements in a movie, you can also copy and paste portions of the timeline, including entire layers and selections of contiguous frames elsewhere in the timeline, using Edit → Copy Frames. This technique is discussed in Recipe 4.13.

In addition to the standard layers with their keyframes and regular frames discussed thus far in this chapter, Flash has a handful of specialized types of layers. These specialized layers are discussed in appropriate places in this book, but they are summarized here for quick reference:

Guide layers
> Guide layers, like commented code, are for use at author time, but they are ignored when the file is output to SWF. Guide layers are discussed in Recipe 3.11.

Motion guide layers
> Motion guide layers are used for animating elements along predefined paths (rather than straight lines). The path is stored in a motion guide layer, which Flash does not render, but instead uses to control the path of an animation. Motion guide layers are discussed in Recipe 4.1.

Mask layers
> As their name suggests, mask layers are used for masks, creating an effect whereby one element controls the visibility of an underlying element. Mask layers are introduced in Recipe 6.8.

Layers are used, for one thing, to control the stacking order of overlapping elements. However, elements within a given layer also have a stacking order. In most cases, elements added more recently are stacked above elements added earlier. However, this is not universal. Vector art drawn in Flash always appears behind bitmap graphics in the same layer, regardless of the order in which they were added. There is no way to stack vector art above bitmap graphics without placing the art in a higher layer. Text, in contrast, can be stacked above bitmap graphics and art within a layer.

You can control the stacking order of elements within a layer, with the exception of vector artwork and bitmap graphics, using the commands in the Modify → Arrange menu:

Bring to Front
> Positions the selected element at the top of the stack within the current layer

Bring Forward
> Moves the element one step closer to the top of the stack within the current layer

Send Backward
> Moves the element one step closer to the bottom of the stack within the current layer

Send to Back
> Sends the selected element to the bottom of the stack within the current layer

Although these options are available, it is generally better practice to avoid stacking multiple elements within layers, and instead to put elements in their own layers, especially when the elements are of different types (for example, bitmaps and vector art).

3.9   Hiding, Locking, and Customizing the Display of Layer Content

Problem

You need to customize the look or behavior of one or more layers, including hiding or locking the contents of a layer, displaying layer graphics as low-resolution outline graphics, and/or changing the height or width of the display of frames.

Solution

Toggle the visibility, editability, outline view on or off; use the Timeline Header Options menu or the Layer Properties dialog box to modify frame display.

Discussion

When editing Flash documents crowded with art, text, and other visual assets, it becomes increasingly difficult to select and work with only the elements you want. Accidental selections and deletions, as well as inadvertent placement of content in the wrong layer, become more likely as your movie grows. Flash offers a handful of tools that can be used to prevent this confusion.

Beside the stack of layer names are three controls available to each layer: layer visibility (Eye column), editability (Lock column), and outline display (Outline column). These elements control whether contents in that layer are editable and how they are displayed:

Eye column

Controls a layer's visibility in the authoring environment. When toggled off, all the contents of the layer are hidden. In addition, you cannot edit the contents of a hidden layer or add new content. Hidden contents are exported and visible in the SWF upon export.

Lock column

Locks or unlocks all the contents of a layer. When locked, the contents are still visible, but they cannot be edited and no new stage content can be added to the layer. Interestingly, you can add frame actions, labels, and comments to a locked layer. For this reason, many developers lock a movie's actions and labels layers in order to prevent inadvertent stage content additions to those layers. If the all-or-nothing nature of layer locking is too inflexible, you can lock one or more elements within a layer by selecting Modify → Arrange → Lock.

Outline column

Toggles layer content display between full view and a low-resolution outline view. The selected setting has no impact on the exported SWF. This setting is useful with complex vector illustrations, which tax the memory and undercut performance. It is also useful when positioning an element relative to other elements: you can lock the existing elements and toggle them into outline view, and then position the new element as desired. Each layer has its own outline color, which makes it easy to distinguish contents on different layers, even when all layers are in outline view.

To toggle any of these options on or off, click the dot in the appropriate column in the desired layer. You can also toggle any of these settings for all layers by clicking the Eye, Lock, or Outline icons themselves, above the layer stack. Finally, Alt-clicking (Windows) or Option-clicking (Macintosh) one of the dots toggles the column attribute of all the other layers. For example, if you want to edit the contents of one layer and lock the contents of all other layers, Alt-click or Option-click the Lock dot in the layer you want to edit.

You can also control the appearance and functionality of layers using the Layer Properties dialog box. You can access this dialog box by selecting a layer and choosing Modify → Timeline → Layer Properties. The options in this dialog box are mostly redundant—here you can rename the layer or toggle its visibility, editability, and outline display. You can also change the layer to one of the special layer types: guide, motion guide, or mask. The Outline Color option enables you to specify the color used for elements in a layer when Outline view is toggled on. The last setting, Layer Height, is discussed in the next recipe.

Keep in mind that any visibility, editability, or outline display changes you make to a layer as described in this recipe take effect during authoring time only. After you export the movie, those specific layer settings are disregarded. They are intended for the purpose of assisting you with managing layers during authoring time. If you want to make a layer invisible when the movie is exported, convert the layer to a guide layer as described in Recipe 3.11. The majority of layer content is not editable during playback of the movie, so there is little or no need to make such a change to the exported movie. There are certain elements that have the option of being editable, however. For example, input text fields, draggable movie clips, and buttons allow for various types of editability, so to speak. If you want to toggle the editable state of such elements, do so at the level of the element, not at the level of the layer. You can read more about how to manage the editability of those types of elements in the appropriate recipes in this book. Flash does not provide a built-in tool that will automatically convert all the contents of a layer to outlines in the exported movie. You will need to add an outline to each element manually. To do so, you can use the Ink Bottle tool as described in Recipe 1.22.

See Also

Recipe 3.10

3.10   Customizing the Display of Layers and Frames

Problem

Frames and layers in the timeline are too big, require excessive scrolling, and take up too much screen space, or are too small, making it hard to see their contents.

Solution

Change the height of the layers and the width of the frames, as needed.

Discussion

The timeline is capable of displaying considerable information about a movie, its structure, and its contents. It is also used for selecting movie elements and specifying where to insert new elements. Unfortunately, you might feel that the timeline, layers, and/or frames are working against you. For example, you might have so many layers that you are either forced to scroll up and down through the layer stack constantly, or the layer stack might take up an unacceptable amount of screen space. Or your movie might have so many frames that you spend all your time scrolling left and right trying to find a given section.

Before simply adjusting the way in which Flash displays the timeline, it's a good idea to evaluate whether there might be some more basic things you can do to make the timeline easier to work with. If you're used to working with graphics programs, such as Adobe Photoshop or Illustrator, you may be trying to apply your workflow from those programs to Flash. However, it's worth noting that Flash uses a unique paradigm, and just because something works in Photoshop or Illustrator, that doesn't mean it's the best way to do something in Flash. If timelines in Flash are getting cluttered, it's possible that you're not making good use of some of the features of the program. As an example, Flash enables you to encapsulate elements in symbols. Some symbols, such as movie clips and graphics, have timelines of their own. That means you can effectively have timelines within timelines. Don't go overboard with nesting symbols, but the judicious application of symbols can make timelines much less cluttered, because the contents are distributed over more timelines.

After you've determined that you are optimizing *how* you use timelines, you can also manage the way in which the timelines are displayed within Flash. The most primitive control is the height of the timeline as a whole, which you can adjust by hovering the mouse over the black line that separates the timeline from the stage, until the mouse is a two-headed arrow. Then, drag up or down to increase or decrease the window holding the timeline.

Another way to make additional room for layers in the timeline is to lower the overall layer height. To do so, from the upper-right corner of the timeline, click the Frame View button and select Short. The Short option, toggled off by default, drops the height of every layer by 25%. The change is usually worthwhile because the legibility of the frames is barely affected.

You can also change layer height one layer at a time, using the Layer Height setting of the Layer Properties dialog box (Modify → Timeline → Layer Properties). This is particularly useful when working with sounds, because Flash displays sound waveforms in the timeline, and by heightening the layer, you achieve a better visual representation of the sound, which facilitates syncing. This technique is discussed in Recipe 17.12.

The Frame View menu also enables you to specify the width of frames. By changing frame width, you affect the amount of horizontal scrolling required to navigate the timeline. That is, lowering frame width causes more frames to be displayed and minimizes scrolling; however, it also diminished the legibility of the timeline. Frame width options include, from smallest to largest, Tiny, Small, Normal, Medium, and Large. These five settings are available in the Frame View menu.

The Frame View menu includes a pair of extreme view settings—settings that are useful only in rare circumstances. These are Preview and Preview In Context. These settings, rather than representing a frame's contents with a solid circle and/or shading, actually display the frame's contents in the frame itself. To accomplish this feat, Flash greatly increases the size of each frame, and then reduces the stage contents to fit in that frame. Preview shows only the contents of the frame, while Preview In Context shows the contents of the frame as well as nearby contents. In effect, this setting converts the timeline into a set of thumbnails, which may be useful to cartoon animators.

The trade-off between the need to scroll and the legibility of frames limits the flexibility of changing frame widths as a practical tool. That is, there is a range of acceptable frame widths, and in most contexts, you will probably use either Small or Normal. This limitation brings up the need for an alternative way of managing long timelines. Flash makes it possible to segment timelines into scenes, and many Flash developers break timelines into a series of consecutive movie clips.

3.11   Using Guide Layers

Problem

You want to add to a layer content that you do not want to be published.

Solution

Put the content on a guide layer.

Discussion

Guide layers can be used to store elements visible on the stage during authoring, which do not export with the *.swf* file. Guide layers have a number of potential uses:

Meta information
> Instructions or notes left for oneself or other developers.

Alignment
> To align several elements in different layers to a path, draw the path in a guide layer, and then drag each of the elements to it.

Asset repository
> Store assets in a guide layer for easy viewing and retrieval. In most cases, the library is a more sensible solution for this purpose, but the library can preview only one asset at a time, and you may need to choose from several actual size assets.

To create a guide layer, follow these steps:

1. Create a new layer.
2. Populate it with content, as needed, and fill it out with keyframes and frames as needed.
3. Convert it to a guide layer. To do so, right-click (Windows) or Control-click (Macintosh) the layer, and choose Guide from the context menu. Alternatively, you can specify a layer as a guide layer from the Layer Properties dialog box (Modify → Timeline → Layer Properties). You can revert a guide layer back to a regular layer the same way.

After the layer has been converted to a guide layer, the layer icon (to the left of the layer name) changes to a T-square tool.

3.12   Managing Complex Content with Layer Folders

Problem

You have too many layers to view conveniently, and you want to group them logically.

Solution

Use layer folders.

Discussion

Layer folders enable you to group related layers, collapsing them when you want to work on a different set of layers. Layer folders can be nested, as well, so it is possible to create logical hierarchies of content. Layer folders are containers only; they do not have any frames, so the only content that can be added to them are layers and other layer folders.

To insert a layer folder, click the Insert Layer Folder button beneath the layer stack in the timeline. The new layer folder is inserted above the currently active layer. It is initially empty.

Working with layer folders is reasonably intuitive:

- To put layers inside a layer folder, drag them over a layer folder so that the layer folder is highlighted, and release the mouse. Layers inside folders are indented beneath the folder to indicate the relationship.

- To move a layer out of a folder, drag it between a folder and another layer, so that a short and wide selection appears, and release.

- To nest layer folders, select a layer in an existing folder, and insert a new layer folder. The new layer folder is also nested in the original layer folder. Alternatively, you can drag-and-drop any layer folder into any other layer folder.

- To move multiple layers into a folder, Shift-select a span of layers, or Ctrl-click (Windows) or Command-click (Macintosh).

- Deleting a folder also deletes all layers nested inside it. A warning message appears in this situation.

Layer folders are a useful feature for complex Flash movies. However, designers working with a high number of assets in a single movie may want to move complex elements into movie clips, rather than storing them in nested layer folders in the main timeline. Flash movie clips have several benefits above and beyond layer folders: they are scriptable, reusable, and more self-contained. In short, though both layer folders and movie clips enable logical organization and management of complex content, movie clips are generally more architecturally sound. Movie clips are discussed in Chapter 11.

See Also

Recipe 2.5

3.13 Laying Out Page Elements Proportionately

Problem

You want to design or lay out elements proportionately, precisely, and/or harmoniously.

Solution

Use any combination of the grid, guides, and rulers.

Discussion

For certain kinds of informal art, you can get away with positioning elements by dragging and dropping them into place; a few pixels to the left or right won't make any difference. But for certain types of files, such as technical illustrations or designs based on classical architecture, layout must be precise and proportionate. Flash offers several tools to assist you in pixel-perfect layouts.

One useful tool is the grid, which covers the stage with rectangles, like graph paper. You can set the size of the rectangles using any unit of measurement—for example, every 12 pixels, or half-inch, or whole centimeter. You can toggle snap constraints on or off as well, which makes it easier to create proportionately sized and spaced elements.

To toggle the grid on or off, choose View → Grid → Show Grid. The grid appears on the stage. If you export the movie, the grid will not appear in the SWF; it is an authoring aid only.

By default, the grid comprises squares, 18 pixels (or 0.25 inches) wide. You can change the size of the width and height of the rectangles, within limits. You cannot set a side to less than 7.2 pixels (0.1 inch), or more than 288 pixels (4 inches). To change the size of the grid, enter a new width and height in the Grid dialog, accessed by selecting View → Grid → Edit Grid.

You can use the grid as a visual guide, or you can cause Flash to snap elements to the grid. For example, if you use the Pen tool to plot the points of a line, you can cause Flash to plot the points only on the intersections of the grid.

To toggle Snap to Grid on, choose View → Snapping → Snap to Grid, or check Snap to Grid in the Grid dialog box. When snapping is activated, you can control the degree to which Flash applies snapping, in the Grid dialog box's Snap To accuracy dialog box. Three options cause snapping when you click within a certain proximity to the grid. From least to most tolerant, they are Must Be Close, Normal (the default), and Can Be Distant. A fourth setting, Always Snap, snaps to the nearest grid intersection, regardless of how far away from it you clicked.

A second layout tool, a guide, is like the grid in that it crosses the stage in horizontal and/or vertical lines. The difference is that with guides, you can position them arbitrarily, rather than at set intervals, and you set them one at a time. To create guides, follow these steps:

1. Toggle rulers on, if necessary, by choosing View → Rulers.
2. To create a guide, drag from a ruler onto the stage. If you drag from the top ruler, you'll create a horizontal guide. If you drag from the side ruler, you'll create a vertical guide.
3. Repeat step 2 as often as desired.

When guides are created, you can move or remove them. To move a guide, simply drag it to the new position. To remove a guide, drag it back to the ruler from which it originated. Because guides are always movable, they can interfere with your ability to select and modify stage content. To avoid this problem, you can lock guides via View → Guides → Lock Guides. When locked, the guides remain visible on the stage, but you cannot select or move them.

Guides can be customized in the Guides dialog box. This dialog box contains some options redundant with the main menu, including checkboxes for locking guides and activating Snap To Guides. The snap feature is nearly the same as that of the grid: the Snap Accuracy setting enables you to specify the snap tolerance, with the following settings: Must Be Close, Normal (the default), and Can Be Distant. Notice that you can also change guide color in the Guide dialog box. By default, guides are bright green, but if that color is hard to distinguish from stage content, you can change it to a different color.

Flash's snap feature extends beyond the grid and guides. You can also snap to vector art on the stage. To activate this feature, turn View → Snapping → Snap to Objects on. When activated, shapes and lines drawn or moved in approximation to other shapes are snapped to them. Activating this option is useful when drawing complex shapes by combining multiple primitive shapes or lines. Snap to Objects works across multiple layers; that is, an element in one layer will snap to an element in another layer.

Another useful layout feature, which is especially helpful with spacing multiple elements, is the Align panel, discussed in Recipe 3.14.

See Also

Recipe 3.12, Recipe 3.14

3.14   Aligning, Distributing, Resizing, and Spacing Elements

Problem

You want to align or space elements relative to each other and/or the stage.

Solution

Use the Align panel for alignment, distribution, and resizing presets. Use the Snap Align feature to align elements to one another. Use the keyboard arrow keys to nudge elements for greater precision.

Discussion

Flash's Align panel includes quite a variety of unique alignment commands. As you would expect, these commands enable you to align multiple elements along a given edge or the centers. In addition, the Align panel has several options that enable you to distribute elements proportionately in space. You can even automatically resize elements.

To access the Align panel, choose Window → Align. Though the Align panel is not included in the default panel layout, you should consider adding it to the panel stack or at least memorize its keyboard shortcut: Ctrl-K (Windows) or Command-K (Macintosh).

To use the Align panel, select one or more elements with the Arrow tool. Then, decide whether you want to align the elements to each other or to the stage. If you want to align elements to the stage, toggle the To Stage button on. Doing so effectively causes Flash to treat the stage as one of the selected elements when aligning or resizing, and it automatically uses the stage edges as the outer bounds when distributing or spacing elements.

The six buttons in the Align category (the top row of buttons in the panel) function as you would expect. The first three, Align Left Edge, Align Vertical Center, and Align Right Edge, align along the specified vertical axis. That is, if you choose Align Left Edge, Flash aligns all objects along their left edges, so that wider elements will extend further to the right than narrower elements. Likewise, the top row includes three horizontal alignment buttons, which align along a horizontal axis. To align an element to the center of the stage, activate the To Stage button, and click Align Vertical Center and then Align Horizontal Center.

The six buttons in the Distribute category space the selected elements equidistantly along a vertical or horizontal axis. That is, the spaces between the selected axes for all selected elements are made the same. This is true even if the elements are of different sizes. The Align panel does not provide a preset that allows you to distribute elements such that the space between them is equal regardless of their dimensions. If you want to achieve that effect, you must use the mouse and/or keyboard to move the elements. If a close approximation is good enough, you can simply move the elements until they appear close enough. If a greater degree of precision is required, remember that the Property inspector reports the width and height as well as the coordinates of the selected element. You can use that information to align elements to a tenth of a pixel of precision. As we've already seen, using the Align panel will distribute the rectangles such that their registration points are equidistant. And because the heights are different for the rectangles, the effect would be that the space between the rectangles would vary. Instead, the rectangles are 5 pixels apart. You can achieve that effect by adding the y-coordinate and height of one element plus the number of pixels of space between elements to determine the y coordinate for the next.

The Align panel also contains a trio of buttons that enable you to resize elements so that they have the same height, width, or both. These are found in the Match Size section. When the To Stage modifier is toggled on, the selected elements are scaled to the same size as the stage, though they retain their original positioning. In all cases, the smaller element is scaled up so that it is the same size as larger elements; that is, no element is ever scaled down in a resize operation. The only exception occurs when you select an element that is larger than the stage, and you perform a match size operation with the To Stage modifier toggled on; in this situation, the element is scaled down to the size of the stage.

The Align panel is particularly useful when you want to align several elements at once. However, there are plenty of situations in which you don't want to have to open the Align panel, select elements, and choose a preset. It may be much more convenient to simply align elements with the mouse. With the Snap Align feature, you can do just that. To activate the feature, make sure that the Snap Align option is checked in the View → Snapping menu. With the feature toggled on, a dashed line appears when you are dragging an element and it has aligned to another element or to the stage.

You can adjust the settings for the Snap Align feature by choosing View → Snapping → Edit Snap Align. By default, the elements will snap their alignment to the right, left, top, and/or bottom edges. If you want them to snap their alignment relative to the center point, you can check the "Show horizontal guides" and/or "Show vertical guides" options to cause Flash to snap to the center of the selected element in the horizontal and/or vertical directions. You may have noticed that in addition to snapping elements to one another's centers and/or edges, the Snap Align feature will also display a dashed line when you have dragged an element within a certain proximity of another. By default, Flash uses a proximity of 10 pixels in both the horizontal and vertical directions. You can change those settings so that the elements will align nearer or further from one another by changing the Snap tolerance settings in the Snap Align dialog box. Additionally, the Snap Align feature will align elements relative to the stage. By default, the elements will align to an 18-pixel invisible border.

You can adjust the movie border value to change how near or far from the edge of the stage the elements will align.

See Also

Recipe 3.11

3.15   Nudging Elements with the Keyboard

Problem

You want to move an element in small increments, or you want to move elements without the imprecision of the mouse.

Solution

Nudge selected elements with the keyboard arrow keys.

Discussion

You can reposition elements with the keyboard by selecting an element and using the keyboard arrow keys (Up, Down, Left, Right). Each time you press an arrow key, Flash moves the selected element one screen pixel. That is, at 100%, Flash moves the selected element 1 pixel each time you press an arrow key, and at 200%, Flash moves the selected element 0.5 pixels.

You can nudge elements 10 screen pixels at a time, by holding down the Shift key when you nudge.

When nudging, most Snap To constraints (Snap to Objects, Snap to Grid, and Snap to Guides) are inactive. The only exception is Snap to Pixels (View → Snapping → Snap to Pixels), a somewhat quirky feature that constrains nudging to exactly one pixel, regardless of resolution. In spite of its name, Snap to Pixels does not prevent elements from being positioned in pixel fractions (for example, an x coordinate of 215.3).

See Also

Recipe 3.11

3.16   Grouping Elements

Problem

You want to bind together a collection of elements as a group; or, you want to prevent drawn lines and shapes from cropping, unioning, and punching one another.

Solution

Choose Modify → Group, or convert the collection of elements into a symbol.

Discussion

You can group a collection of entities into a single item, by choosing Modify → Group. When grouped, you can no longer edit the elements individually. For example, when grouped, you cannot directly edit text, change a fill, or reshape a line.

To modify an individual element within a group, you have to edit the group. To do so, double-click the group. The group opens, and you can modify the group, in a mode akin to symbol editing mode. When you are finished, you can return to the main stage by choosing Edit → Edit All.

Grouping is impermanent; you can ungroup a group at any time by selecting Modify → Ungroup. You can also nest groups. To do so, select an existing group and any other element, and choose Modify → Group. The original group is preserved within the new group, as a nested group.

Though grouping can be a convenient feature, especially when drawing complex art, it has no architectural benefit. In contrast, you can use graphic, button, or movie clip symbols as a way of grouping elements, and when you do, you realize all the benefits of using symbols. For example, if you group a collection of items as any type of symbol, you can apply motion tweens to it. If you group a collection of items as a movie clip, you can apply scripts to it, and so on. In short, use grouping as a temporary way to lock several items together while you work, but use symbols to make these collections more functional at runtime. Another benefit of using symbols over groups is that you can reuse them and achieve file size savings.

See Also

Recipe 3.15

3.17 Reusing Elements: Creating Symbols

Problem

You want to reuse an element in multiple places, use an element in a special capacity, such as a button, or simply optimize the use of timelines.

Solution

Convert the element to a graphic, button, or movie clip symbol.

Discussion

Architecture is one of the most important considerations in any Flash movie. *Architecture* refers to the structure and organization of a movie. You should always strive, in Flash, to keep different elements separate from one another. Yet Flash offers a number of different ways to accomplish this goal. You have seen layers and groups in this chapter. But a far more flexible and powerful solution is to use Flash symbols.

Flash *symbols* are reusable elements that have additional functionalities that vary by type of symbol. Symbols are reusable in that they are stored in a central repository in a movie, called the library. You can access the library by choosing Window → Library in any movie. When a library symbol is placed on the stage, it is called an *instance*. Instances are linked to symbols in-as-much as the symbols are the blueprints for the instances. If you change any part of a symbol, all its instances throughout the movie are updated instantly. An instance can vary from its parent symbol in the values assigned to instance properties, such as scaling, opacity, placement, and a handful of others. In addition, instances have unique identifiers, called *instance names*. One benefit of symbols' reusability is that they minimize the impact on file size: no matter how many instances of a symbol exist in a movie, the symbol is only downloaded once.

Reusability is only the beginning of the benefit of symbols. Other types of Flash elements, including imported bitmaps, sounds, and video, are stored in the library and may be reusable. But symbols extend the capabilities of Flash. Symbols make possible each of the following:

Motion tweens
> Tweens are one approach to automating animation. See Recipe 4.1.

Nested timelines
> Although all Flash symbols have their own timelines, Flash movie clip timelines are independent from the parent timeline. This feature enables complex animations and interactivity.

ActionScript events
> Events used to trigger ActionScript can be associated with symbols, including pressing and releasing the mouse, key presses, setting focus, loading data, and much more.

Availability to scripts
> Thanks to their unique identifiers and Flash's object model, you can dynamically manipulate button and movie clip symbol instances via ActionScript.

The implications of using symbols are too rich and varied to mention here. They form the substance of Chapters 9, 10, 14, and 15.

Flash contains three common types of symbols, as follows:

Graphic symbols

The simplest form of symbol, graphic symbols are like groups that are stored in the library (and hence reusable). In addition, graphic symbols can be used in motion tweens. Though graphic symbols have their own timelines, they are tied to the parent timeline. As a best practice, use graphic symbols only for single-frame, static assets.

Button symbols

These symbols respond and behave like buttons. Specifically, their timelines have four frames, in which you can insert four graphics to represent different button states (Up, Over, Down, and Hit). Buttons also respond to numerous events, including onPress, onRelease, onDragOut, onRollOver, and more, and are often used to trigger user-initiated ActionScript actions.

Movie clip symbols

The most flexible and powerful Flash symbol, movie clips are like Flash movies inside other Flash movies. Their timelines are fully independent of the main timeline, which means you can pause playback in one while the other continues to play, among other things. They have a host of events, and their numerous properties (such as opacity and position) and methods (such as playback controls, dragability, and collision detection) are all exposed to ActionScript.

New Flash developers are often unsure when to use movie clips as opposed to graphic symbols. Movie clips are much more powerful than graphic symbols, and they are generally preferred over graphic symbols. The exception is single-frame assets that you don't intend to manipulate via a script or use to trigger a script. Movie clips require (negligibly) more overhead than graphic symbols, so the latter still have a place in Flash.

To use symbols, you must first create them, and then deploy one or more instances of them on the stage. Flash offers two common ways to create symbols, from scratch and converted from an existing element:

- To create a symbol from scratch, choose Insert → New Symbol. In the Create New Symbol dialog box, name the symbol, and select its behavior (movie clip, button, or graphic). Symbol editing mode appears, which consists of a blank stage and an empty timeline. Create layers and keyframes, and add text, art, or imported assets as you would on the main stage.

- To convert an existing element to a symbol, select it, and choose Modify → Convert to Symbol. Specify a name and the behavior in the Convert to Symbol dialog. The symbol is added to the library, and the originally selected element is converted to an instance. You can convert any combination of vector art, text, groups, and bitmap graphics into a symbol.

Symbols are stored in the library. To create an instance of a symbol, so it appears in the movie, drag the symbol from the library to the stage, in the desired layer and keyframe. To create multiple instances of a symbol, you can drag-and-drop as many times as you need, or you can copy and paste the instance.

To edit a symbol, you can double-click its icon in the library or double-click an instance on the stage. Symbol editing mode opens. After you make changes and return to the movie, all instances are also updated.

 Symbols that have no instances are not exported with the SWF by default. It is possible to instruct Flash to export unused symbols using linkage settings. Linkage settings allow a symbol to be added to a movie using ActionScript.

See Also

Recipe 4.1, Recipe 9.1, Recipe 8.13

CHAPTER 4

Creating Animation

Before it was known as a platform for rich Internet applications, with its capacities for interactivity, XML, database integration, video, and real-time communications features, Flash was an animation tool. And in spite of its incredible growth in other directions, Flash remains an excellent tool for creating animations.

Animations simulate motion by playing back a series of related images, usually at a higher rate of speed than the eye and brain can process. Instead of processing each image individually, the brain connects the different images, causing the perception of motion. The effectiveness of this illusion of motion depends on numerous factors, ranging from the subjective and aesthetic to the objective, as in the case of frame rate.

Because animations usually depend on the rapid playback of many images, they are often time-consuming and painstaking to create. Drawing a single image can take hours; drawing hundreds or thousands of images to be played back at 12 frames per second or higher can be a daunting project indeed.

You can use a number of different techniques and tools in Flash to expedite and, in many cases, automate the process of creating animation, from Flash's ability to store separate discrete elements in symbols and layers to its ability to automate the animation of changes in properties, such as location and opacity. Features such as automatic acceleration and deceleration controls, rotation, and motion paths provide further control over the creation of animations. Thanks to *onion skinning*, or the ability to see multiple contiguous frames at once, Flash also simplifies positioning and modifying multiple frames simultaneously.

To build an animation, you can employ any combination of four different kinds of animation in Flash, as detailed in the following list. Each has its own strengths and limitations, so choosing the correct kind is a paramount consideration.

Frame-by-frame

Using this approach, the animator creates a succession of keyframes and manually changes the contents of each keyframe. This is the most painstaking and manual form of animation and results in the largest files. A last resort, this form of animation should be used only to create movements or effects that are impossible with the other forms of animation.

Motion tweens

The animator defines a beginning and ending state of a given element, and Flash generates a smooth transition from one to the other. Motion tweens excel with changes in position, angle/rotation, opacity, size, and other attributes of a given element.

Shape tweens

Also called *morphing*, shape tweens automate the transition of an element from one shape to another.

Tweens with custom easing

Though not strictly distinct from basic tweens, tweens with custom easing do stand out, because they enable much more sophisticated effects than standard tweens. The Custom Ease In/Ease Out panel is new to Flash 8 and is discussed in Recipe 4.4.

Scripted animation

When scripting animation, developers write ActionScript code that controls properties of a given object over time. These properties may include size, location, rotation, opacity, and so on. Moreover, the values of these properties can be changed in response to user interaction.

This chapter discusses numerous strategies for creating animation. In addition to showing the mechanics of creating certain kinds of animation, this chapter sheds light on the decision processes animators should go through to optimize the process of developing animations; there are often multiple ways to achieve the same effect, but some ways are intrinsically better than others in a given situation.

In all cases, one primary goal in developing Flash animations is to separate elements into discrete units and animate them individually. For example, rather than animating a character's face, you might animate the mouth, nose, and each eye separately. In fact, you might go even further, animating the eyelid separately from the pupil, for example. By dividing elements in this way, you simplify the movements you have to capture and, in so doing, make it more likely you can use one of the automated techniques, such as motion tweens.

4.1   Animating Changes in Location or Appearance

Problem

You want to animate a change in location, size, opacity, or color effect.

Solution

Use a motion tween.

Discussion

With its unique combination of advantages, the motion tween is the animator's friend. Motion tweens offer numerous benefits:

Power
> You can animate changes in position, overall color effect (brightness, tint, and alpha), and transformation (scale, distort, skew, etc.). Moreover, you can animate these in any combination at once.

Ease of use
> Flash does all the work for you, after you specify the beginning and ending states of the animation.

Flexibility
> You can customize the tween in several ways to create more compelling effects. With a motion tween, you can animate along motion guides, add acceleration and deceleration, adjust the duration of an animation, and add rotation. You can even orient animated elements to the motion path, on a motion-guided tween.

File size
> Because motion tweens use efficient symbols, they result in relatively compact .*swf* files.

To create a motion tween in Flash, complete the following steps:

1. Create or convert an existing element to a graphic, button, or movie clip symbol.

2. If you haven't done so already, create a layer for the animation. Also, if you are starting the tween on a frame other than frame 1, you should create a keyframe at the appropriate point on the timeline. Only one element can be placed within a keyframe if you plan to add a motion tween to it. Adding more than one element to a keyframe to which you apply a motion tween will likely cause the tween to work incorrectly.

3. Drag an instance of the symbol from the library to the stage. Ensure that you are placing the instance within the correct keyframe.

4. Define the instance's starting state: specify its location, color effect, transformation state (skewed, scaled, distorted, and/or rotated), and so on.

5. Create a new keyframe later in the same layer. The instance in its starting state is copied into the new keyframe.

6. Modify the new instance to indicate its ending state. That is, move it to a new location, transform it to a new size or degree of rotation, and/or adjust its opacity, brightness, and tint (using the Color drop-down menu in the Property inspector). When finished, you've defined the beginning and ending states of the element.

7. To insert the motion tween, click the keyframe containing the first state (or any frame in its frame span). Select Insert → Timeline → Create Motion Tween from

the main menu. You can also add the motion tween by right-clicking or Command-clicking on the starting keyframe and selecting Create Motion Tween, or by selecting the starting keyframe and then selecting Motion Tween from the Tween menu in the Property inspector.

After you have defined the tween, the frame span in the timeline turns indigo, and an arrow points from the first keyframe to the ending keyframe.

If you are motion tweening a change in location, the element animates in a straight line from the starting state to the ending state, at a constant rate. You can control both the motion path and the rate of motion in a tween. You can also cause the element to rotate in the course of the tween, or remain oriented to the path as it animates. These controls are discussed in the next several recipes.

Although motion tweens become second nature after a while, it is quite easy to make mistakes at first. These are a few common mistakes:

- Accidentally forgetting to convert the elements you want to tween to a symbol before applying the motion tween, which can cause unexpected results. If you forget to convert the elements to a symbol, one of two things might occur, depending on the context—either the elements will remain as they are, or Flash will automatically convert the elements to a graphic symbol with a name such as Tween 26. In either case, chances are good that the tween won't work. So make sure whatever you try to tween is already an instance of a symbol. You can tell when a tween will not work, because the horizontal line between the keyframes will be a dashed line instead of a solid line. The dashed line indicates that something seems to be amiss with the tween.

- If you have more than one symbol instance on the keyframe to which you are applying the motion tween, the tween will not work. This is a very common mistake. If the instance merely jumps from one state to the next state without any of the tween states, check to make sure you don't have any other instances or elements on the same keyframe. This is why it is recommended that you place each element on its own layer.

See Also

Recipe 4.2, Recipe 4.3, Recipe 4.4

4.2   Animating Along Curved Paths

Problem

You want to animate along a curved path, instead of in a straight line.

Solution

Use a motion guide. Add further realism by checking the Orient to Path modifier.

Discussion

By default, changes in location are animated in straight lines in motion tweens—going from point A to point B in the most direct route. You may want to animate an element across a curved path. Flash enables you to do so by using a *motion guide*, which is a path that you can assign to an object as it tweens.

To create a motion-guided tween, you draw a path on a special *motion guide layer*; this line is visible only in the authoring environment. Then you snap the tweened instance to the path at both the starting and stopping points of the tween, and Flash does the rest. Here are the steps in detail:

1. Create a motion tween, using a graphic, movie clip, or button symbol, as described in Recipe 4.1.

2. With the tweened layer selected in the timeline, add a motion guide layer. You may do so by selecting Insert → Timeline → Motion Guide or by clicking the Add Motion Guide button beneath the layer stack. Alternatively, right-click or Command-click the layer, and select Add Motion Guide. Flash inserts a special motion guide layer above the active layer. The active layer is indented to show that it is guided by the motion guide layer.

3. With the motion guide layer active, use any of the vector tools that allow you to draw a line, such as the Line, Pen, or Pencil tool. Tools that draw fills (such as the Brush tool) will not work for drawing motion guides.

4. When you are satisfied with the line, make sure that the line exists for the entire duration of the motion tween. For example, if the motion tween lasts from frame 1 through frame 50, make sure that the line on the guide layer is also defined from frame 1 through frame 50. If necessary, add frames to the motion guide layer.

5. Lock the motion guide layer to prevent yourself from accidentally editing the motion guide.

6. Verify that View → Snap to Objects is toggled on and that Snap To is enabled. The next steps are much easier if the motion path layer is locked and Snap to Objects is enabled.

7. In the first frame of the tween layer, drag the instance by its registration point until it snaps onto the motion path. Drag it along the path until it is in its starting location.

8. In the final frame of the tween, drag the ending instance by its registration point, until it snaps onto the motion path, and drag it along the path until it is where you want it to be when the tween stops.

9. You may want to drag the playhead back and forth to ensure that the instance does, in fact, animate along the motion path.

If your motion guide is a complex shape or crosses itself, such as a figure eight, the "guided" symbol can get confused; if this is the case, a little tweaking is required.

Add a keyframe at the "crossover point" and another at the frame after, moving the symbol to where it is next expected, and then continue the tween from there. This trick will enable you to "break" the motion guide where it crosses, and fools the eye into thinking that the motion has been continuous, when really, you have "jumped" the crossover. Using the example of a figure of 8, your motion guide shape would become a figure eight with a small break in one direction at the crossover point.

 If a motion guide path crosses itself, it can cause Flash to move the object in unexpected ways at that point. If this occurs, you can add a keyframe to the timeline at the point just before the object crosses the path and a second keyframe in the next frame. In the second keyframe, move the object just past where the path crosses itself, and the tween ought to work correctly.

For nondirectional graphics, such as a ball, motion-guided tweens are easy to implement and look good when implemented. But for graphics that have a clear direction, motion guides can pose problems. Figure 4-1 shows an airplane animated over the course of a motion guide; while the curvature is accurate, the airplane is not oriented in the right direction after the first frame.

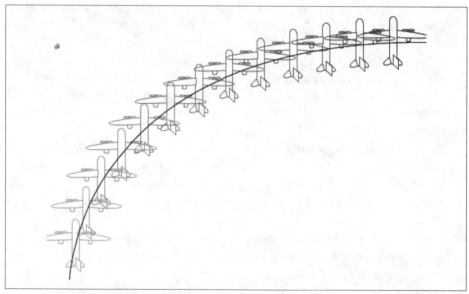

Figure 4-1. Using motion-guided tweens with directional graphics needs a little extra work

To correct this problem, you need to rotate the instances in the beginning and end states, so that they are oriented to the motion path. To rotate an instance, use Flash's Free Transform tool, as discussed in Recipe 1.32. The resulting animation is improved, but not quite ready (Figure 4-2). Notice that in the middle of the path, the plane's fuselage is at a different angle than the motion path.

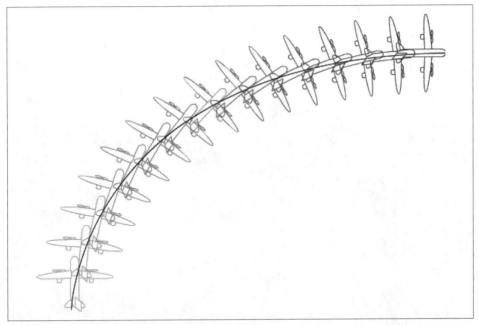

Figure 4-2. Manually rotate the instances at the beginning and end of a tween to orient each to the motion path

To force the graphic to orient itself to the path in every frame, select the first frame of the tween layer (not the motion guide layer), and in the Property inspector, check Orient to Path. As long as the instance is oriented to the path in the beginning and ending frames of the tween, this option will ensure that the instance is oriented to the path in every intervening frame as well. Notice how well the fuselage lines up with the motion path in Figure 4-3.

You can also use a single motion guide layer to control multiple layers. To do so, select the tween layer subordinate to a motion guide layer, and insert a new layer. When you do, the new layer will also be nested under the motion-guide layer and will function just like any other motion guided layer. Optionally, you can drag an existing layer underneath a motion guide layer; it will automatically nest.

To move a layer out of the influence of a motion guide layer, drag it above the motion guide layer, or right-click (Windows) or Control-click (Macintosh) and choose Properties. From the Layer Properties dialog box, change the type from Guided to Normal.

Although you will most commonly create motion guide layers as such before adding the lines for the motion path to them, it is also possible to convert an existing layer to a motion guide layer. For example, you may have drawn the line over which you want the tween to occur without remembering to first create a special motion guide layer. In such a case, you can change the layer to a guide layer. Double-click the layer

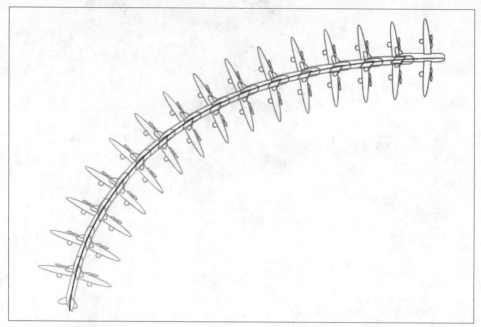

Figure 4-3. Check Orient to Path to ensure that directional graphics are oriented correctly through a tween

icon or right-click/Command-click the layer and choose Properties. Set the type to Guide. Then, drag any layers that you want to have guided by the guide layer underneath it. Set those layer types to Guided from their Properties dialog boxes.

See Also

Recipe 4.1, Recipe 4.4

4.3   Applying Acceleration and Deceleration with Easing

Problem

You want to apply acceleration or deceleration to a motion or shape tween.

Solution

Use easing.

Discussion

When you apply a motion or shape tween, Flash animates the change at a constant rate by default. However, you may want to apply acceleration or deceleration. For example, to mimic the effects of gravity on a falling ball, you'll want it to accelerate as it falls. If the ball bounces back up, you'll want to apply deceleration. You can add acceleration or deceleration by adjusting the *easing*.

Easing is applied to the same keyframe as the tween. To apply it, select the keyframe where the tween begins (or any frame before the last frame in the tween). In the Property inspector, enter a value in the Ease field, or drag the slider that appears beside it. Values range from −100 to 100. The default, 0, tweens at a constant rate. To apply acceleration, enter a negative number. To apply deceleration, enter a positive number. Negative values, or acceleration, are referred to as *easing in*, and the word *in* appears beside the easing slider when a negative number is entered. Likewise, positive numbers are referred to as *easing out*, and the word *out* appears beside the slider when a positive number is entered.

The value you specify in the Ease field is applied to the entire tween. With the value in the Ease field, you cannot ease the first half of a tween at one setting and switch a different setting for the second half. For complex and advanced easing, you can use the Custom Ease In/Ease Out utility as discussed in Recipe 4.4.

See Also

Recipe 4.1, Recipe 4.10

4.4   Applying Advanced Tweening Effects

Problem

You want to apply an advanced tween that combines several easing settings and/or has elastic or rebound effects.

Solution

Use the Custom Ease In/Ease Out utility.

Discussion

Prior to Flash 8, applying advanced tweens was a manual procedure requiring you to use several tweens back to back. For example, if you wanted to do something as simple as animate a ball that drops and bounces, it required several tweens—one as the ball dropped and accelerated, a second as the ball rebounded, a third as gravity pulled the ball downward again, and so forth until the ball finally rested. The process became even more complex if the ball's shape changed as it hit the surface, as a tennis ball might.

However, starting with Flash 8, you can accomplish such advanced and custom tweening effects with just one tween by utilizing the Custom Ease In/Ease Out utility. In order to use the utility, you must first apply a tween as discussed in Recipe

4.1. Then, with the first frame of the tween selected, click the Edit button next to the Ease field in the Property inspector. Clicking the Edit button opens the Custom Ease In/Ease Out utility.

The Custom Ease In/Ease Out utility displays the tween progress as a line moving across a graph from the lower-left corner to the upper-right corner. The lower-left corner represents the starting point of the tween, and the upper-right corner represents the stopping point of the tween. When you first apply a custom tween effect using the utility, the line is a straight line, indicating that the tween is applied in a linear fashion over the duration of the animation. However, you can adjust the line in several ways:

- Click any existing point (represented by a black square) on the line, and the corresponding control points are displayed. You can then adjust the control points to affect the curvature of the line.
- Click anywhere on the line where there is not an existing point, and a new point is added.
- Click and drag any point (except for the end points) on the line to move it.
- Hold the Alt key, and click on the points to delete them.

By default, the same custom easing setting is applied to every property. For example, if you have a motion tween for which the alpha and the location are both changed, the same custom easing graph is applied to both properties. However, just above the graph is a checkbox labeled "Use one setting for all properties." If you uncheck that option, the drop-down menu to the left of it is enabled, and you can apply different custom easing settings to each of the properties. By applying different settings to each property, you can make much more sophisticated animations than by applying the same easing settings to all the properties. Working with each property individually requires a fair amount of trial and error, but the effect can be rewarding.

4.5   Animating Rotation

Problem

You want an element to rotate during a motion tween.

Solution

Either apply rotation to the tween or use the Free Transform tool to rotate the instance(s) manually.

Discussion

Flash offers two different ways of rotating elements in a motion tween: you can use the Rotation attribute of a tween to apply rotation as a part of the tween, or you can use the Free Transform tool to rotate one or both instances at the beginning and end of the tween.

To set a motion tween's Rotation setting, select the keyframe in which the tween begins, and use the Property inspector to specify the type/direction of rotation and the number of revolutions. When adding rotation using the Rotation setting of a tween, you can enter only integers. That is, Flash forces you to specify rotation in complete 360° increments. You can specify *None* to prevent rotation; *Auto* to rotate in the direction requiring the least motion; *CW* to force Flash to rotate the instance clockwise; or *CCW* to force Flash to rotate the instance counterclockwise. This approach to rotating elements is ideal for spinning animations, such as the spinning of a basketball through the air.

When adding rotation using the Free Transform tool, which is discussed in Recipe 1.32, you can rotate only between 1° and 359°. That is, if you spin an element five times with the Free Transform tool, and leave it facing in the same direction it was originally facing, Flash won't even register that it has been rotated. Therefore, use the Rotation setting of a tween to rotate multiple revolutions, and use the Free Transform tool to rotate partial revolutions.

You can also combine the two approaches to create multiple revolutions with different starting and ending positions. When combining the two approaches, Flash adds them together. That is, if you rotate an instance 45° clockwise with the Free Transform tool, and you apply a Rotation setting of 2 clockwise, the instance will rotate 765° (720° + 45°). If you rotate an instance 315° counterclockwise and apply a Rotation setting of 2 clockwise, it will still rotate 765°, because 315° counterclockwise is the same as 45° clockwise.

When you want a rotation animation to loop, make sure that the last frame of the tween doesn't have the same rotation as the first frame. If it does, it will appear to hesitate for an instant during each rotation. The solution is to make the rotation of the last frame slightly less than the rotation of the starting frame.

See Also

Recipe 1.32, Recipe 3.2

4.6   Looping Animations

Problem

You want to create an animation, or a portion of an animation, that loops indefinitely.

Solution

Embed the animation in a movie clip symbol.

Discussion

Unless you use ActionScript to tell it otherwise, every timeline begins playback as soon as it is loaded and plays through the timeline at the document frame rate until it reaches the end. After it plays the last frame, it loops back to the beginning and plays all over again. In other words, looping animations is Flash's default behavior, and all you need to do to create one is to create any animation and export the .swf file.

But you may find that you need to loop portions of an animation, while other portions are not looped, or not looped as often. Imagine a cartoon in which a character is chased across a background; the camera follows the character, who remains in the center of the screen while the background scrolls by. Several animated elements may be in play, such as the following:

- A 5-frame loop depicting the legs while the character is running
- A 5-frame animation of the arms swinging wildly
- A single-frame graphic of the torso
- A 5-frame looping animation of the head turning back and forth
- A 10-frame loop of a distant bird's wings flapping
- A 50-frame loop of the background

Because the animation comprises elements that loop and others that don't, and because the loops are of different lengths, the animator cannot rely on the overall looping behavior of the main timeline. Each loop needs to animate independently of the others, so that the running legs loop will play nearly seven times before the background loops once.

You can loop animated elements independently by storing each looping animation in a movie clip. Movie clip timelines behave like the main timeline, in that they play back and loop by default. But they run independently of the main timeline and each other. Thus, by placing the loops into separate movie clips, and placing an instance of each on the main timeline, the animator gets the benefit of each loop's indefinite playback without having to worry that they are of different durations.

By moving animation loops into movie clips, you employ the practice, recommended in the introduction, of separating and isolating animation components from one another. This approach is architecturally more sophisticated and therefore requires more effort up front than merely storing content on different layers of the same timeline. But it is more flexible and powerful, because you can customize each one's timeline for its own needs.

Looping animations are often designed to be seamless. That is, you often don't want it to be obvious to the user when the animation reaches an end and loops back to the beginning. The 5-frame loop of the legs running in the example just cited is one such example: the animator does not want a perceptible jerk in the animation to appear every fifth frame.

To create a seamless loop, make sure that the content in the last keyframe of its timeline is near to and animating toward the first. At the same time, you don't want the last frame and the first frame to be identical—which would cause a seeming pause for a frame.

See Also

Recipe 4.13

4.7   Previewing Playback

Problem

You want to view the animations you've created.

Solution

Drag the playhead, choose Control → Play, or export the *.swf* file by choosing Control → Test Movie.

Discussion

You can play back your animations in two ways in Flash, each with its own advantages and disadvantages:

Authoring environment
> You can view an animation right in the Flash authoring environment. This is the most convenient way to preview an animation, but also the most limited, because it ignores most ActionScript and is incapable of displaying nested animations.

Creating a .swf file
> Exporting a SWF is the most reliable way to preview an animation, because it lets you see exactly what a user will see—ActionScript and nested animations included. The file opens in a new window, which you then need to close or hide before returning to the main authoring environment.

Which approach you use depends on what you need to preview. If all you need to preview is a tween or a frame-by-frame animation, the authoring environment is sufficient and more convenient. If you need to view any more than that, you'll probably need to export the *.swf* file.

To view an animation in the authoring environment, do one of the following:

*   Drag the playhead back and forth on the main timeline.
*   Choose Control → Play, or press the Enter (Windows) or Return (Macintosh) key to start and stop playback. The animation is played back at the document frame rate.

- Step backward or forward one frame at a time by choosing Control → Step Forward or Control → Step Backward. The keyboard shortcuts for these are period (.) and comma (,), respectively. Holding down the period or comma key plays the timeline very quickly—at about 25 frames per second, regardless of the document frame rate.

- Skip to the beginning (Control → Rewind) or the end (Control → Go To End).

To view the animation in the SWF, choose Control → Test Movie, or use the keyboard shortcut Ctrl-Enter (Windows) or Command-Return (Macintosh). When you are finished, close the SWF to return to your document.

See Also

Recipe 4.8, Recipe 4.12

4.8 Viewing Multiple Frames Simultaneously

Problem

You want to see multiple contiguous frames of an animation simultaneously.

Solution

Use onion skinning.

Discussion

Onion skinning shows multiple contiguous frames of an animation, which is useful for previewing animations, as well as adjusting positioning and other features of animated graphic elements. Many of the screenshots in this chapter use onion skinning to depict the different frames of an animation all at once.

To activate onion skinning, toggle on either the Onion Skin or Onion Skin Outlines button (Figure 4-4). The Onion Skin button displays the graphic itself, as it appears in multiple frames, with lowered opacity in inactive frames. The Onion Skin Outlines button displays a low-resolution outline of the graphic in multiple frames. Onion skinning applies to all visible layers in the timeline.

 If View Layer as Outlines is toggled on, onion skinning will display the outlines only, regardless of which onion skin button you toggle on.

When onion skinning is toggled on, Flash shows a span of five frames by default: two frames before the active frame through two frames after the active frame. If the active frame is (or is near) the first or last frame, it may show as few as three or four frames. Onion markers, which appear at the top of the timeline in the same area as

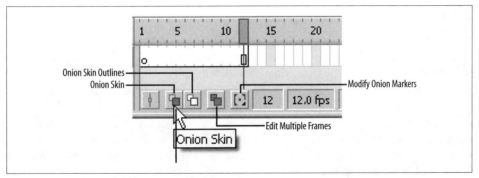

Figure 4-4. Control onion skinning in the timeline

the playhead, depict the range of frames that are displayed; the area between them is shaded.

You can control how many frames Flash includes in the onion skin span. Drag the onion markers to define a custom area, or choose one of the presets from the Modify Onion Markers menu. Presets include Onion 2, Onion 5, and Onion All. Onion 2 and Onion 5 tell Flash to use onion skinning for two or five frames before and after the active frame.

As you move the playhead, the active onion span moves along with it. For example, if the playhead is in frame 10 and the default Onion 2 is active so that frames 8–12 are onion-skinned, and you move the playhead to frame 20, frames 18–22 will be onion-skinned. You can lock the onion markers at their current positions by choosing Anchor Onion from the Modify Onion Markers menu. That way, even if you move the playhead, the onion span will not change.

Onion skinning by itself enables you to *see* the contents of several contiguous frames. Alone it does not allow you to edit multiple frames simultaneously. However, you can use the Edit Multiple Frames feature so that you can edit the contents of more than one frame at the same time. For more information on the feature, see Recipe 4.9.

See Also

Recipe 4.2, Recipe 4.10, Recipe 4.11

4.9   Editing Many Frames Simultaneously

Problem

You want to edit the contents of more than one frame at the same time.

Solution

Use the Edit Multiple Frames option.

Discussion

In the default editing mode, Flash allows you to edit the contents of only one frame at a time. However, there are cases in which you may need to edit the contents of more than one frame at the same time. For example, if you change the dimensions of your Flash document after having already created much of the animation, you may want to change the coordinates as well as the scale of the contents across the frames of the main timeline. You could certainly go through, frame by frame, making the changes one at a time. But that could be a very time-consuming and tedious process. Fortunately, Flash provides you with a means by which you can make those changes at once using the Edit Multiple Frames feature.

You can activate the Edit Multiple Frames feature by selecting the button in the timeline (see Figure 4-4). When you have toggled on the feature, you will see the range markers appear in the timeline in line with the frame numbers. You can drag the markers to modify the range. Flash will display the contents across the frames within the range on the stage at the same time, though unlike with onion skinning, here only keyframe contents are displayed (tween states are not rendered). You can select any element from any unlocked and visible layer within the range.

See Also

Recipe 4.8

4.10   Morphing Graphics with Shape Tweens

Problem

You want to morph a graphic into a different shape.

Solution

Draw the beginning and ending states of the graphic using Flash vector art, and insert a shape tween. To morph text, convert it to vector shapes (Modify → Break Apart) before inserting the shape tween.

Discussion

You can use shape tweens to morph elements from one shape to another. Like motion tweens, you apply them by defining a beginning and ending state of the element in two different keyframes of a single layer, and insert a tween, using the Tween drop-down menu of the Property inspector. Unlike motion tweens, shape tweens work only with drawn vector art. That is, symbols and text must be broken apart (Modify → Break Apart) before they can be shape tweened. When broken apart, of course, instances are no longer associated with symbols, and text is no longer editable as text. You can apply shape tweens to bitmaps only after you've traced the bitmap.

Shape tweens also have different available settings than motion tweens. Shape tweens lack a Rotation setting, although easing is still available. And shape tweens have a setting called Blend, which contains two options:

Distributive
> The default option, distributive morphs the first graphic element into the second using smooth curves.

Angular
> With this setting active, Flash attempts to preserve corners and straight lines during the tween. Use only for elements that have sharp corners and straight lines.

Shape tweens work best when morphing from one simple element into another. For example, morphing a circle into a square usually works quite well. Morphing more complex art often has undesirable results with some bizarre intermediary stages. Thanks to *shape hints*, which enable you to guide Flash as it morphs one element into another, you are not altogether without recourse; shape hints are discussed in the next recipe.

You are not limited to single lines or shapes, and you can shape-tween as many lines and/or shapes as you like. Of course, the more lines and shapes, and the more geometrically irregular they are, the less likely the results will be satisfactory.

An oft-overlooked feature of shape tweens is that they are capable of every kind of tween that a motion tween is. That is, you can position the starting and stopping states in different locations, and a shape tween will animate the motion of the artwork from one state to the next, even as it morphs the shape. Likewise, you can animate transformations, such as rotation and scaling, and you can also animate changes in color or alpha. Unless you are also morphing elements during the transition, you should use motion tweens rather than shape tweens, because they add less to the overall file size and demand less of the processor to render. However, if you are morphing an element, bear in mind that you can shape-tween more than its shape.

Although shape tweens can allow for some interesting and creative effects, they have been largely overused. If you want to use a shape-tween effect in your Flash movie, take the time to hone the result using techniques such as shape hints.

See Also

Recipe 4.11

4.11 Controlling Morphing

Problem

You want to control how Flash shape tweens a graphic, because Flash by itself does not morph it satisfactorily.

Solution

Use shape hints and/or add intermediary keyframes and manually redraw the shapes.

Discussion

When you employ a shape tween, Flash compares the starting and stopping state and does its best to correlate significant points in each state to each other to guide the tween. Unless you are working with primitive geometric shapes, such as squares and circles, Flash often struggles, and intervening frames look less like a natural transition between the two states, and more like a kaleidoscopic and quasi-random explosion of lines and shapes.

Figure 4-5 shows a shape tween of the letter A morphing into the letter B. Flash made some dubious decisions. Notice how the lower-left corner of the A morphs into the upper-left corner of the letter B rather than remaining where it is. Likewise, the upper-left corner of the A morphs around to the front of the letter B rather than staying where it is. This is a result of Flash guessing which points in the beginning of the animation should correspond to which points at the end of the animation.

Figure 4-5. Shape tweens look strange when Flash has to guess which points in the original correspond to certain points in the final graphic

Rather than forcing Flash to guess and living with the results, we can give Flash shape hints. Shape hints enable Flash developers to specify individual points that should correspond to one another before and after the tween. To use shape hints, follow these steps:

1. Select the first keyframe in the tween.

2. Add a new shape hint by choosing Modify → Shape → Add Shape Hint, or use the keyboard shortcut, Ctrl-Shift-H (Windows), or Command-Shift-H (Macintosh). A circle with the letter *a* in it appears on the stage. Though you can't yet see it, a corresponding circle with an *a* also appears on the stage in the keyframe at the end of the tween. You use this pair of hints to designate a given point in both versions of the graphic.

3. Use the Arrow tool to drag the shape hint to a point on the shape. This task is usually easier if View → Snapping → Snap To Objects is toggled on.

4. Select the last frame in the tween, and move the shape hint to a point on the shape that corresponds to the point on the first frame of the tween. When you drag the shape hint on the last frame of the tween to a point on the shape it will

turn green, and the shape hint will simultaneously turn yellow. The color change indicates that the shape hints are enabled. If the shape hints don't change color, it means that one or both of them has not correctly snapped to the outline of the shape.

5. If necessary, add several more shape hints by repeating steps 2 through 4. Each time you add a shape hint, it is given a new, unique letter; thus, the second shape hint you add is called *b*, and so on.

Using shape hints effectively often requires considerable trial and error. To determine how well the hints are working, you can scrub the playhead along the timeline between the starting and stopping frames of the tween.

You can remove a shape hint pair by right-clicking (Windows) or Control-clicking (Macintosh) on any shape hint and selecting Remove Hint from the context menu. When you remove a hint, its corresponding hint in the other keyframe is also removed, and the remaining keyframes are renamed (e.g., shape hint *b* becomes *a* when *a* is deleted), if necessary. You can remove all hints by choosing Remove All Hints from the context menu or by choosing Modify → Shape → Remove All Hints. For the Remove All Hints behavior to work properly, you must select the first frame of the tween.

Shape hints have limitations. Even after considerable trial and error, you may not obtain satisfactory results.

To improve the quality of a morphing animation beyond what is possible with shape tweens and shape hints, you'll need to draw intervening states of the animation by hand. That is, if you can't get a 12-frame segment to morph properly, try adding a new keyframe in the sixth frame and drawing or revising the graphic so that it appears as it should at the midpoint of the original shape tween. Then add shape tweens to the two new halves, applying shape hints as necessary.

See Also

Recipe 4.8, Recipe 4.10

4.12   Creating Nested Animations

Problem

You want to create an animation within an animation, such as the wheels on a car or a bird flying.

Solution

Store the child animation in a movie clip, and place an instance of that movie clip in the timeline of the parent animation.

Discussion

Certain types of animation are possible only by nesting animations within one another. For example, consider the case of a bird flying across the stage. The bird is flapping its wings, and at the same time it is moving from one side of the stage to the other. In order to achieve the correct effect, it's necessary to animate the wings flapping within a movie clip, and then you can tween an instance of that movie clip across the stage.

Flash enables nested animations with movie clip symbols. Movie clip symbols' timelines play independently of the main timeline, and you can nest practically any number of movie clips inside of each other.

To create a nested animation, follow these steps:

1. Create a new movie clip symbol by choosing Insert → New Symbol or by converting existing artwork to a symbol (Insert → Convert to Symbol). In the Create New Symbol or Convert to Symbol dialog box, name the movie clip and set its behavior to Movie Clip.

2. A new coordinate space and timeline display. Create the animation that you intend to nest inside another animation. In the example of the flying bird, you'd animate the flapping wings within the movie clip.

3. Return to the main timeline. If you started by creating a new symbol rather than converting existing artwork to a symbol, drag an instance of the new symbol to the stage. Otherwise, you ought to already have an instance of the symbol on the stage.

4. Animate the symbol instance.

One aspect of working with nested animations that can be challenging is that nested animations are not previewed in the authoring environment. When you export or test the movie, the nested animation will play. However, in the authoring environment you'll only see the first frame of the nested animation. If you want to quickly preview the nested animation within the context of the parent timeline, assuming the parent timeline has enough frames, you can temporarily change the behavior of the symbol to Graphic from the Instance behavior menu in the Property inspector. Make sure to change the behavior back to Movie Clip before exporting the movie.

See Also

Recipe 4.7

4.13   Copying Animations

Problem

You want to copy an animation, or content in contiguous layers and/or frames, to a different timeline.

Solution

Use Edit → Copy Frames.

Discussion

Like most applications, Flash enables you to copy the contents of your files and paste them into other documents or other parts of the same document. The Clipboard works for copying individual elements, but copying a timeline segment is not an individual element. For example, imagine you've created an animation on the main timeline and realize that you need to move that animation into a movie clip. The standard Copy and Paste commands won't work.

Fortunately, Flash has commands that enable you to copy and paste frames, including spans of contiguous frames across layers. To use it, drag to select the frames you want to copy in the timeline, and choose Edit → Copy Frames.

 To facilitate dragging to select frames in the timeline, be sure that Edit → Preferences → General → Span Based Selection is toggled off.

Open the destination timeline, which may be that of a symbol, or the main timeline of a different file. Select at least one frame, and choose Edit → Paste Frames. Flash pastes the frames, following these rules:

- Frames are inserted at the active frame.

  - If only one frame in the destination timeline is selected, that frame is replaced with the first frame of the copied frames. All subsequent copied frames are inserted after the selected frame of the destination timeline, and all frames that initially followed the selected frame are pushed behind the newly pasted frames. Thus, if the original destination timeline has 10 frames, and 10 frames are pasted in with the first frame selected, the resulting timeline has 19 frames.

  - If multiple frames are selected, they are replaced with the same number of copied frames. Thus, to ensure that the destination timeline has the same number of frames before and after you paste in the copied frames, select the same number of frames in the destination timeline that you copied from the source timeline.

- Layers are inserted in a manner similar to frames. That is, if you select frames in one layer of the destination timeline and paste frames from multiple layers, Flash inserts the bottom layer of the copied frames into the selected layer of the destination timeline, and it inserts new layers to hold all higher layers. Newly created layers do not retain their names, and are called Layer 2, Layer 3, and so on. To maintain the same number of layers after copying frames, select frames across the same number of layers in the destination timeline as the number of layers in the copied frames.

- Symbols' instances maintain their status. If you copy frames with instances into a movie without the parent symbol, the parent symbol for each instance is copied into the destination movie's library.

See Also

Recipe 4.12

4.14   Changing a Movie Clip's Location at Runtime with ActionScript

Problem

You want to relocate an element at runtime, through scripting.

Solution

Set a movie clip or button's _x and _y properties with ActionScript.

Discussion

By default, when you position an element on the stage, it appears in the same location on the output *.swf* movie. However, it is possible to set the positioning at runtime by using ActionScript. ActionScript can see only certain kinds of elements in a movie. In order to control an element with ActionScript, it must be an object, which means it must be a movie clip, button, or dynamic or input text field. ActionScript cannot control draw vector art, graphic symbols, or imported bitmaps, unless they are enclosed in a movie clip or button.

 In addition to the list specified in the preceding paragraph, Action-Script can control components and video objects.

In addition, for ActionScript to see one of these graphic elements, the element must have a unique identifier. You can give a movie clip, button, dynamic or input text field a unique identifier by selecting it and giving it an *instance name* in the Property inspector. After you specify a name for the object, you can address it using ActionScript.

You can control these objects through ActionScript using built-in *events*, *properties*, and *methods*:

Events
> Events refer to changes in the environment that the object is aware of. For example, a button is aware when it is pressed.

Properties

Properties describe the object. Just as a person has height, weight, and gender properties, which vary from person to person, so visual Flash objects like movie clips have properties. These include its size (`_width` and `_height`), its positioning (`_x` and `_y`), opacity (`_alpha`), and others.

Methods

Methods refer to what the object can do. Just as people can talk, run, sleep, and laugh, Flash objects have built-in behavioral capabilities as well. For example, movie clips have playback methods, such as `play( )`, `stop( )`, and `gotoAndPlay( )`.

You can access properties and methods of an instance by placing the appropriate ActionScript code on the correct keyframe of the timeline in which the instance is defined. Imagine, for example, that you have a movie clip instance named `mCircle` that exists on a layer in the main timeline on frame 1. You can then use ActionScript code on frame 1 of the main timeline to target `mCircle` and set its coordinates. Typically it is a good practice to place ActionScript code on its own layer within a timeline. That practice ensures that you'll have a better time locating it if and when you revisit it. Therefore, you should create a layer with a name such as Actions for any timeline in which you define ActionScript code.

You can access methods and properties using *dot notation*, which means that you provide the name of the object, such as `mCircle`, followed by a dot and then the name of the property or method. For example, you can set the `_x` property of a movie clip instance named `mCircle` as follows:

```
mCircle._x = 100;
```

No matter where the movie clip was positioned in the authoring environment, when the SWF plays, the movie clip is moved so that the *x*-coordinate is 100. This happens because as soon as the movie clip loads in the player, its *x* (horizontal) position is set to 100 with ActionScript. Note that the *y*-coordinate doesn't change. If you want to set the *y*-coordinate you can use the `_y` property. Movie clips, buttons, and dynamic and input text fields each have `_x` and `_y` properties that you can control with ActionScript.

See Also

Recipe 4.15, Recipe 6.5

4.15   Animating Runtime Location Changes with ActionScript

Problem

You want to animate using ActionScript.

Solution

Use the *mx.transitions.Tween* class.

Discussion

All forms of animation discussed thus far in the chapter are created at authoring time and are effectively hardcoded. After playback begins, the animations can play back only in the way that you specified at authoring time. Because they are hardcoded in this way, these kinds of animation cannot respond to the user.

You may want to create animations that respond to user activity. For example, you may want to make an object move to the location of the mouse when the user clicks it. You must use ActionScript if you want to make such an animation.

There are several ways in which you can approach animating objects with Action-Script, but each has the same basic principle—updating the values of the property or properties over time. It's possible to use event handler methods such as *onEnterFrame()* or to use an interval function with *setInterval()* to accomplish the task. However, both of those approaches are slightly more complex (and require more ActionScript) than using the *mx.transitions.Tween* class to accomplish the task.

The *mx.transitions.Tween* class enables you to animate a change in a property with just one line of code. However, to make referencing the class a little simpler, it's generally recommended that you first use an import statement. The following line of code tells Flash to look for the Tween class in a package called *mx.transitions*. That way you don't have to refer to the class by its full name each time. It's recommended that if you want to use the Tween class, you add the following import statement at the top of the code:

```
import mx.transitions.Tween;
```

After that import statement, you can simply refer to the class as *Tween* rather than *mx.transitions.Tween*.

In order to animate a property of an object using the Tween class, you must construct a new Tween object using a new statement. The basic syntax is as follows:

```
new Tween(objectToAnimate, property, easingFunction, startingValue, stoppingValue,
duration, useSeconds);
```

To start, we'll specify null for the third parameter. That means that the animation will occur linearly. (The alternative would be to use an easing function, which creates the illusion of acceleration and deceleration.) The following example tells Flash to move mCircle so that the x-coordinate starts at 0 and stops at 100. It tells Flash that the animation ought to span 10 frames.

```
new Tween(mCircle, "_x", null, 0, 100, 10, false);
```

Notice that the property name appears in quotes. If you forget the quotes, it will not work. If you want to move mCircle in both the *x* and *y* directions, you can add a second Tween object as follows:

```
new Tween(mCircle, "_y", null, 0, 200, 10, false);
```

The preceding example tells Flash to move mCircle in the y direction from 0 to 200 over the span of 10 frames. If you use both Tween objects, the movie clip will move in a diagonal line from 0,0 to 100,200 over the span of 10 frames.

> The Tween class enables you to add listener objects that get notified each time the property is incremented. Therefore, it's possible to animate more than one property at a time using just one Tween object with a listener object updating the additional property or properties. However, it is generally simpler to use additional Tween objects, as in the examples.

If you set the last parameter to `false`, the duration is in frames. You may also specify the duration in seconds simply by setting the last parameter to `true`. For example, if you set the last parameter to `true` in the preceding examples, the animation would span 10 seconds.

You can apply easing to the animation by specifying an easing function reference for the third parameter of the Tween constructor. Although you can write your own custom easing functions, it is beyond the scope of this book to discuss how to do that. However, you'll likely find that the easing functions that ship with Flash are appropriate for most projects. You can find the easing functions grouped in classes in the *mx.transitions.easing* package. The classes are called Regular, Strong, Bounce, and Elastic. Each of the classes has the following methods: *easeIn*, *easeOut*, and *easeInOut*. That may sound like a like of technical jargon. It's really simpler than it might sound. In practical terms, it means that for the third parameter you can specify something such as *mx.transitions.easing.Regular.easeIn* or *mx.transitions.easing. Elastic.easeOut*. As with the Tween class, you are likely to find it simpler to use an import statement so that you can reference the easing class in the shortened form. For example, if you want to use the *mx.transitions.easing.Elastic.easeOut* method, you can use the following import statement at the beginning of the code:

```
import mx.transitions.easing.Elastic;
```

You can simply refer to the class as Elastic from that point forward. For example, a Tween constructor might then look like the following:

```
new Tween(mCircle, "_x", Elastic.easeOut, 0, 100, 10, false);
```

CHAPTER 5

Simulating 3D in Flash

The use of 3D graphics has been a steadily growing trend in Flash design over the past years, ranging from simple accent elements, such as icons and logos, to more zealous implementations of interactive 3D environments and games. This turn toward integrating 3D and Flash has happened for a good reason. As Flash has proliferated and become a driving force in web and application design, producing solutions that stand out from the masses has become more challenging. When used appropriately, the impact of 3D graphics can add visual depth (no pun intended) and mean the difference between a good solution and an extraordinary one that commands attention.

For example, a recent project I was involved in was a real-time, multiplayer chess game created in Flash and using Flash Communication Server (now Flash Media Server). Obviously, chess is in no way a new concept, and although it's a strategy game, without an enticing interface it could be difficult to attract potential users to a chess implementation. Although a 2D interface could have been created and included all the necessary elements for play, most would probably agree that the 3D approach (see Figure 5-1) is a much more elegant design solution and entices the user to pick up and move the pieces.

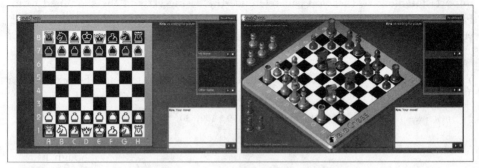

Figure 5-1. Example of game design from both a 2D and 3D approach

5.1   Solutions for Integrating 3D with Flash Projects

Problem

You want to add 3D graphics easily to your Flash projects.

Solution

Use the appropriate Swift 3D software solutions from Electric Rain.

Discussion

As Flash has progressed over time, many designers have wanted to add 3D graphics and animation to their Flash projects. It is not possible to add true real-time 3D graphics, because the Flash Player does not contain a 3D rendering engine, so it is necessary to simulate such effects. Methods for creating these simulations have varied, along with the results and practicality associated with each.

Freehand drawing methods

Illustrators have long been giving 2D drawings the illusion of depth through perspective drawing techniques. Obviously this method can require highly developed drawing skills. If the project involves animation, it can also require a lengthy time investment, reminiscent of hand-drawn frame-by-frame cell animation. Making revisions in animation or graphics with this method can result in basically the entire animation needing to be recreated. Obviously, this problem could be disastrous if working under a tight deadline or budget.

Importing prerendered images from 3D programs

Importing a sequence of bitmap images rendered in a traditional 3D design program may be a perfectly acceptable solution for some projects. However, if vector data is required, the tedious task of hand-tracing each image can be as time-consuming as perspective drawing. Manual rendition also has the downfall of making revisions difficult. Using the bitmap auto trace feature in Flash may be a possibility, but its results usually leave a lot to be desired in both quality and the resulting file size. Also, with all the traced elements residing on a single layer, animating any objects with a background can be difficult at best.

Mimicking 3D with ActionScript

Armed with ActionScript and Flash's drawing API, it is possible to create the illusion of 3D shapes and even animate them in mock 3D space, all from within Flash. Unfortunately, only basic geometric shapes can be created, and although bitmaps can be mapped to the faces of these objects, it is by no means an easy task. Achieving photorealistic results is not possible and the entire process has to be completed programmatically with no real-time visual preview. This method also requires an advanced working knowledge of ActionScript, making it difficult to accomplish for many intermediate-level designers and developers.

Using Swift 3D from Electric Rain

With the use and demand for 3D graphics and animation on the rise, a number of designers from traditionally 2D backgrounds are being drawn to 3D design for the first time. Committing to take the plunge into 3D can be a daunting task, as it is a multifaceted discipline steeped in its own software tools, lingo, and techniques. To the uninitiated, this new world can be as confusing as taking those first steps into Flash, and one of the hardest tasks of breaking into 3D is figuring out where to start. Before undertaking the actual task of even learning to work in three dimensions, you must first select the appropriate tools. The number of software solutions and the myriad of features therein can quickly make it difficult to choose your tools. The financial investment for many high-end software packages and their relatively steep learning curves can be enough to stop many would-be enthusiasts dead in their tracks before they can even create their first polygon; however, that is all changing. If your primary desire is to create 3D graphics and animation for use in Flash, the Swift 3D line of software solutions from Electric Rain (Erain) are the perfect fit. The combination of a relatively mild learning curve and low price make this midrange 3D program an ideal solution for beginner and advanced Flash users alike.

When released in April 2000, the goal of the Swift 3D standalone application was to provide the ability to render 3D graphics and animation to vector-based formats compatible with Macromedia Flash. It quickly became the premiere tool for this purpose, and the industry leader. Now in Version 4.5, Swift 3D has continually improved its integration with Flash. Along the way, there have also been additions to the Swift 3D family of products, and although the remaining portions of this chapter are focused on working with the Swift 3D 4.5 (build 471 at the time of this writing), these alternative solutions are worthy of mention.

Accompanying the release of Swift 3D 2.0 were plug-ins for 3DS Max and Lightwave (now both properties of Autodesk), as well as SoftImage; however, the Lightwave plug-in has been discontinued. The plug-ins grant users of these high-end 3D applications the opportunity to work within the environments and with powerful tools with which they are already familiar, while granting them access to the rendering and export options of Erain's vector-rendering engine, RAViX 4.

The most recent addition to the Swift 3D lineup is Swift 3D Xpress, which as the name hints is a "light" version of Swift 3D. It is not a standalone application, but rather an extension that installs into Flash MX 2004 and Flash 8 and is accessed from the Commands menu. It provides access to Swift 3D's basic tools for performing common 3D tasks without having to leave the Flash authoring environment. Because its feature list is a scaled-down version of the full application, it is discussed in more detail at the end of the chapter, so that the differences between the full and express versions are evident.

Flash and Swift 3D are like chocolate and peanut butter: each great in their own regard, but when combined, they provide rich results. However, before we get cooking, it is important that you know your way around the Swift 3D kitchen and tools contained therein. If you are new to Swift 3D, now might be a good time to open the program.

 A fully functioning trial of Swift 3D is available for download from the Erain web site (*http://www.erain.com/downloads/trials/*). The only feature that is disabled is rendering and export.

The Swift 3D authoring environment is split up between six interfaces. These include the Scene Editor, Extrusion Editor, Lathe Editor, Advanced Modeler, Preview and Export Editor, and finally the Web Assistant, which is really an information portal rather than a tool. Switching between editors is done using the tabs that run across the top of the interface (see Figure 5-2).

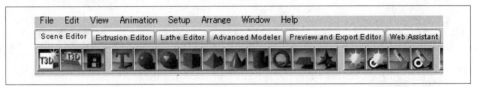

Figure 5-2. Tabs at the top of the interface for switching between editing environments

Projects will always take place in at least two of the editors (Scene Editor and Preview and Export Editor), but it is not uncommon to make use of them all to some extent. The following sections provide brief overviews of each, as well as for what they are commonly used to accomplish.

Scene Editor

The Scene Editor (see Figure 5-3) is the default view that greets you upon opening the program. As the name clearly implies, this is where you construct your scene, arranging and animating your models in 3D space, applying lighting, adjusting environmental settings, and positioning the cameras with which your 3D world is viewed. The features of the Scene Editor include:

Viewports

The most prominent elements in the Scene Editor, the viewports act as windows into your 3D world. By default, two viewports are visible, each assigned a different camera view. Whatever is showing in the left viewport is what will ultimately be rendered and exported.

Main toolbar

This toolbar contains a horizontal row of icon-adorned buttons across the top of the interface; here a simple click will let you do things like save, undo, and test render viewports. This is also where you will find shortcuts to adding simple predefined 3D objects (*primitives*), free lights, and cameras.

Properties toolbar

Here you set general scene properties, such as physical dimensions, environment, background color, and more. The categories of Layout, Camera, and Environment are always present; however, the toolbar is context-sensitive and displays other properties available for selected objects as well.

Animation timeline

In the animation timeline, objects are animated in 3D space. Structured much like its counterpart in Flash, the timeline is organized by named layers and uses keyframes. Although there are also animation timelines within the Extrusion and Lathe Editors, their usage is slightly different (as is discussed later).

Hierarchy menu

The Hierarchy menu lists all objects (models, cameras, and lights) within a scene, providing an alternative method for selection. It is also where parent-child relationships are created between objects for greater control when animating.

Rotation trackball

Allows selected objects to be rotated on all axes. Options for locking rotation to a single axis and the degree of rotation can also be set, as well as resetting an object to its default position and rotation.

Lighting trackball

The Lighting trackball lets you position scene lights. Buttons to the right of the ball provide the ability to both add and delete lights.

Gallery menu

The Gallery menu includes an assortment of different libraries, which include complete models, materials, and preset animations and lighting schemes.

Status bar

Often overlooked, the status bar provides real-time feedback regarding a number of important properties while you work, including mouse coordinates and progress.

Extrusion Editor

The Extrusion Editor's purpose is to create 3D objects by extruding a 2D path. In a nutshell, extrusion is adding depth to a one-dimensional vector path. A good analogy is comparing a single sheet of a paper to an entire ream. Although the two share the same basic shape, the ream also has depth. This is accomplished by creating a vector profile using the editor's drawing tools. You may also edit imported vectors shapes using the Extrusion Editor. See Recipe 5.2 for more details regarding importing and working with AI and EPS files. When

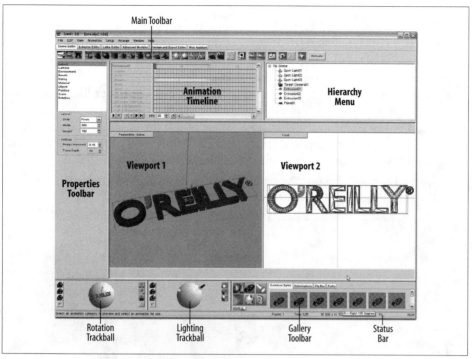

Figure 5-3. Overview of the Swift 3D interface

extruded, you also have the option to assign various bevel types to an object. Figure 5-4 shows an example of an extruded path.

The Extrusion Editor also contains an animation timeline that corresponds to the master timeline in the Scene Editor. The features and use of this timeline are discussed in Recipe 5.3.

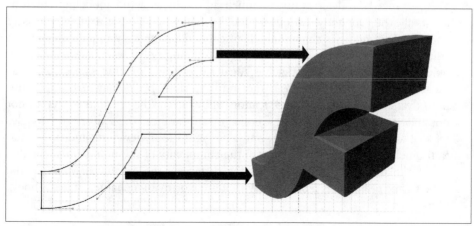

Figure 5-4. Example of 2D path extruded to 3D object

Lathe Editor

The Lathe Editor is similar to the Extrusion Editor, in that you are working with 2D vector paths; however, that is where the similarities end. The basic principle of lathing in 3D is to rotate a 2D path around a central axis, which in the case of Swift 3D is the *y* axis. You have the option to turn it a full 360°, creating a closed symmetrical shape, or to set the Sweep Angle to degree of your liking, in which case the span of degrees not covered will be subtracted from the model. When using a Sweep Angle of less than 360°, there is also the option to have the shape closed or open on the exposed ends. Figure 5-5 shows the same path as was used in the extrusion example, but lathed around the *y* axis less than 360°.

Like the Extrusion Editor, the Lathe Editor also contains an animation timeline, the features and use of which are discussed in Recipe 5.4.

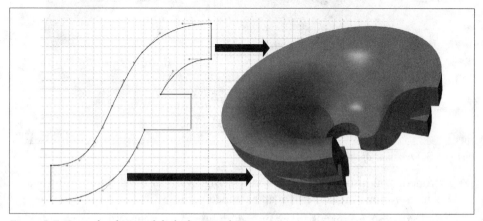

Figure 5-5. Example of 2D path lathed to 3D object

Advanced Modeler

The Advanced Modeler is not so much an editor as a full modeling environment, allowing for the creation of model mesh as well as features for precisely applying and modifying materials. It also provides the only tools that you can edit on the model mesh level, pushing and pulling polygons to create complex objects. The Advanced Modeler is ideal for creating organic shapes, such as those used in character design. Lathe and Extrusion objects may be brought into the Advanced Modeler for modification, allowing for the creation of shapes not possible using the other editors alone. In appearance, the Advanced Modeler looks a lot like the Scene Editor, but it has up to four viewports and no animation timeline (see Figure 5-6). Due to the complexity of mesh modeling, the discussion in this book only scratches the surface of the Advanced Modeler; the content and techniques associated with it are worthy of a chapter, if not a book, of its own!

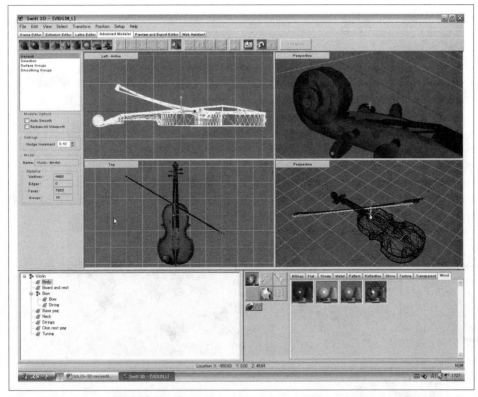

Figure 5-6. Advanced Modeler interface

When an object from one of the other editors is brought into the Advanced Modeler for editing, it ceases to be a lathe or extrusion and is no longer tied to the properties associated with both object types. Also, any animation that may have been applied in Lathe or Extrusion Editor timelines will be lost.

Preview and Export Editor

Many of the settings that determine how a final piece will ultimately appear are set in the Preview and Export Editor, which is usually the last stop for a project while working in Swift 3D. You decide not only what will be rendered and exported, but whether it will be in a raster or vector format, each of which comes with its own unique settings. A screenshot of the Preview and Export Editors can be seen in Figure 5-7.

Web Assistant

As previously stated, the Web Assistant is not an editor, and it is not actually required at all when working on projects. It acts as a resources portal for both online and offline information regarding Swift 3D, such as help files, tutorials, technical support, and product updates.

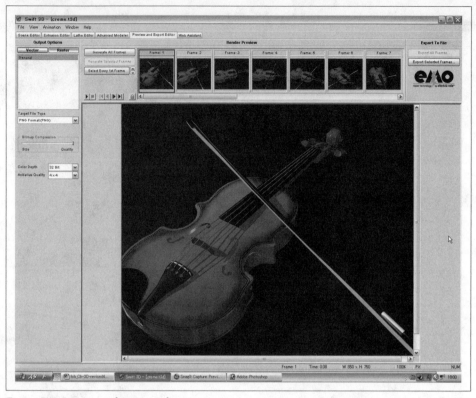

Figure 5-7. Preview and Export Editor

Basic elements of a 3D scene

A scene created in Swift 3D—and in most 3D programs—contains a number of basic elements. Although the features and options of each of these may vary from program to program, the basics remain the same. These include 3D objects (models), lighting, cameras, and environment:

3D models

Rather self-explanatory. Any object in a scene that is not a camera or a light.

Lights

Without them there isn't much to see! In Swift 3D, these include those found on the Lighting Trackball, as well as Scene Lights. Trackball lights can be thought of as "world" lighting, as they rest outside of the viewports and affect everything in your scene. Positioning these lights can be done only by using the trackball. They can be animated. Scene lights, on the other hand, appear within the viewports and can be manipulated much like any other object. A scene can contain a maximum of 16 lights, which includes the sum total of both world and scene lights.

Cameras

Any time you are using a viewport, you are looking through a camera lens. Swift contains seven standard cameras (Front, Back, Left, Right, Top, Bottom, and Perspective). These cameras are not represented within the viewports, and only the Perspective camera may be animated. The other, more flexible cameras, known as *scene cameras*, include both Free and Targeted cameras. These are displayed within viewports and can be positioned and animated like other objects. As in lighting, Free cameras are visible within viewports and can be positioned and animated like 3D models. A maximum of 250 Free and Targeted cameras may be added to a scene.

 One of the more challenging concepts for a designer coming from a 2D background grasp is the *z*-axis. While Flash contains simple *x* and *y*-axes for placing objects on the stage, 3D adds that all-important *z*-axis (the third dimension). Unlike in Flash, where you simulate depth by stacking objects on one another or change their scale, in a 3D composition you actually position the object further away in 3D space. In the Swift viewports, you can easily determine what axis you are working with by the axis indicator located in the center of the viewport.

Environment

The Environment settings in Swift 3D are comprised of three elements: Background Color, Ambient Light Color, and Environment. Background Color is used to designate the color visible in the background of a scene, just like setting the background color of the stage in Flash. Ambient Light Color is the hue of the overall lighting of a Scene and is independent of color settings made to individual lights. For example, if the Ambient Light Color is set to red, a white object in the scene will take on a red or pink hue. Finally, there is the Environment setting, which is confusing for some users when they first start working in Swift 3D, due to an understandable misconception of its use. Setting an Environment shares many similarities to applying a material to an object. In fact, it is basically just that, however instead of an object that is visible within the viewport, the material is instead being applied to an invisible sphere that encompasses the entire scene. Like materials, Environment can be designated as a solid color or various gradient types (procedural environments), as well as imported bitmap images. However, it is important to understand that unlike Background Color, Environment is not readily noticeable in the Scene Editor when applied. The Environment exists outside of the camera's field of vision and is only exposed in the faces of objects that have a reflective material applied after rendering has taken place. Refer to Figure 5-8 for a visual example of an object rendered with different Environment settings.

Figure 5-8. Example of an Environment on two spheres with reflective materials applied; sphere on the left was rendered with a solid white environment, and the one on the right with a bitmap image

5.2   Creating 3D Objects

Problem

You want to create 3D objects for use in Flash.

Solution

Use Swift 3D's multiple editors for accomplishing different modeling needs.

Discussion

Four of the five editors in Swift 3D are used for modeling of one kind or another. Each has its own specific strengths and weaknesses, and learning which editor is ideal for a specific task can greatly increase your productivity and level of success. Some planning and forethought regarding how an object is constructed will help you determine which editor is best for the job at hand. Often a combination of editors is required to achieve exactly what you want. To illustrate this point, the following example creates a chessboard and three sample pieces using the different modeling tools at your disposal in Swift 3D.

Setting up a new document

To begin, we need to first set up a new Swift 3D document. Create a new file and set the viewport dimensions, found under Layout in the properties panel, to 800×600. Select Environment in the properties panel and double click the Background Color preview to enter edit mode. Set the color to dark gray (R: 128, G: 128, U: 128), so that there will be contrast when working with the black and white elements of the chess game. Finally, assign the right viewport to the Top camera and set the secondary viewport to Front.

Building the chessboard

A chessboard is made up of 64 squares of alternating color; in this case, black and white. Though a relatively simple object, even this could be modeled in a variety of ways. Thinking over it quickly, here are a few options that you could try. They will all give you basically the same results:

- Use individual plane or rectangle primitives to create each of the black and white alternating squares. Even with numeric placement and grouping/duplicating objects, the primary disadvantage to this method is the time that it would take to precisely position each square.

- Use a checkered material and apply it to a plane or extrusion. Again, this is a possibility; however, getting the materials to line up perfectly with the edges of the shape to which it is applied might prove difficult.

- Import an AI/EPS document that contains the checkerboard vectors created in an external program. Although this approach solves the issue of placing each shape mentioned in the first example, you will still need to set all of the extruded depths to the same value, so that shapes line up. Also, relying on an external program and importing is probably overkill for this task.

These are all feasible solutions, yet there is a much simpler answer. By taking advantage of the segmentation settings of plane primitive and surface groups available in the Advanced Modeler, we can quickly create a checkerboard that is uniform in size and accurate in placement.

Enter the Advanced Modeler and click on the Plane primitive button. Under Segmentation in the plane properties, set both the width and height to 8. Working in the Perspective view, click and drag in the viewport to add the primitive plane. The Perspective view is used because primitives added to this viewport automatically maintain their proportions and are placed at the viewport's origin (X:0,Y:0,Z:0).

 When adding a primitive to one of the Orthographic viewports, holding down Ctrl (Win)/Option (Mac) constrains the objects' proportions.

What we have now looks slightly more complex than a chessboard (see Figure 5-9). The reason for this is that polygons in Swift 3D are always triangular. Each segment is thus composed of two polygons in order to make a square.

Drag-and-drop the "ER Vector—Flat Black" material, located under the Flat tab in the preset materials gallery, to the plane. This step will not only take care of the

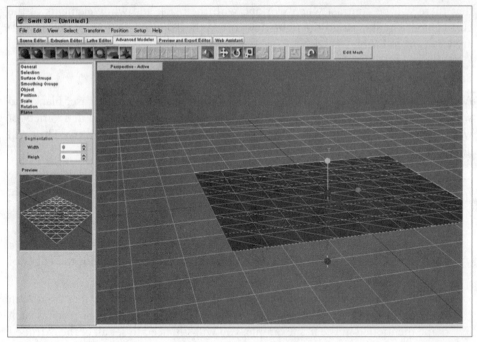

Figure 5-9. Primitive plane in the Advanced Modeler with height and width segmentation of 8 applied

material for the black squares, but will also make the wireframe more easily visible for selection purposes.

Before going any further, enter Edit Mesh mode to make the necessary tools available. If necessary, select the Plane primitive button and click the Edit Mesh button located on the right side of the top toolbar. When active, the button will be red and any object selected will turn orange.

Switch to working in the Front viewport and deselect the plane by clicking on an empty area in the viewport. Press the F key to enter Face Selection Mode. Starting at the top-left corner of the plane, select every other segment (two polygons per square). When finished, it should look like a black and orange checkerboard in the viewport (see Figure 5-10).

With the selection still active, go to Surface Groups in the properties panel (see Figure 5-11) and click the Group Selection button, which will create a new surface group comprised of what will be our white squares. To finish, drag-and-drop the "ER Vector—Flat White" material to the material preview located below the lists of available surfaces. The squares of the chessboard are now finished, and you can return to the Scene Editor.

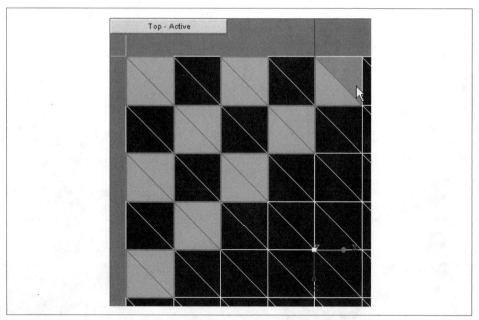

Figure 5-10. Selecting individual polygon faces in the Advanced Modeler

 You can rename surface groups by selecting them from the list and typing in a new name in the "Surface name" field.

The final step will create a slight border around the board and give it depth. In the Scene Editor, add a Box primitive to the viewport. By default, it will be placed directly in the center of the checkerboard, which is ideal for our needs.

Click the Scaling Mode icon in the top row of buttons and, while working in the Top viewport, enlarge the box until it is slightly larger than the chessboard. Manual scaling is performed by selecting an object and dragging the cursor to the left, right, up, or down while Scaling Mode is active.

Select the box and set its height, under Sizing in the Properties toolbar, to 0.005. Working in the Front viewport, position the box using the cursor and/or the keyboard arrow keys so that it rests just below the checkerboard, with little or no space between the two. When in place, apply the "ER Vector—Flat Black" material to finish the chessboard (see Figure 5-12). Select all with Ctrl-A (Win)/Command-A (Mac) and group with Alt-G (Win)/Command-G (Mac). Rename the new group "board" in the properties panel, so that it is easy to identify in the Hierarchy menu, and save the file.

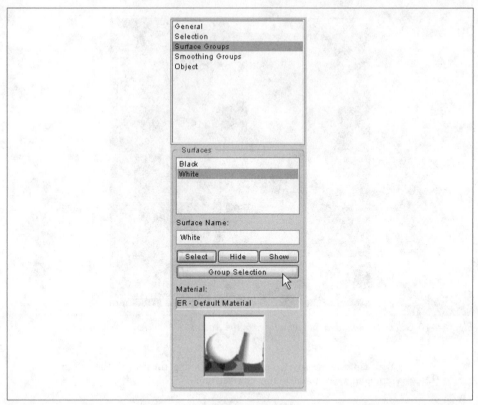

Figure 5-11. Creating surface groups in the Properties toolbar

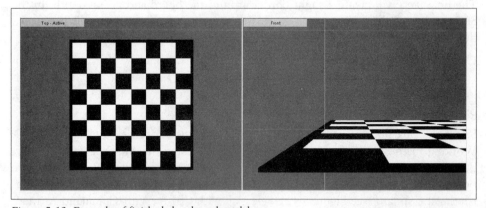

Figure 5-12. Example of finished chessboard model

 The border could have been added in the Advanced Modeler, but the point of this exercise was to teach you how to use the primitives of the Scene Editor.

Creating the chess pieces

Now that we have the playing field, we need the players. For this exercise, we will be modeling only a pawn and knight; however, after doing so you should have the experience necessary for completing the remaining pieces if you wish to do so. Modeling the pieces will make use of all four editors.

As you should recall, lathe objects are created from vector paths, so the first things we need are profile drawings of our pieces. I have chosen to draw the profiles in Adobe Illustrator and import them into Swift 3D (the original AI document may be downloaded from *http://www.rightactionscript.com/fcb/chpt5/chess.ai*). The reason I use an external program to do this is that though the Lathe and Extrusion Editors both have basic drawing tools, they simply are not of the same capability level of those found in a dedicated illustration program. Figure 5-13 shows the paths as they appear within Illustrator. Black items will ultimately be lathed objects, and the gray objects will be extrusions.

Figure 5-13. Vector path chess piece profiles drawn in Adobe Illustrator for import

Modeling the pawn

Create a new document as in the chessboard exercise. It is generally good practice in projects like this to model each major element in its own document and later combine them into a single file. This process keeps the working environment from slowing down, which can occur when a large number of model meshes are present.

Import the paths by going to File → Import... and navigating to the local copy of the AI file. After being interpreted, the paths will be brought into the Scene Editor as extruded objects.

While the group is still selected, Ungroup with Alt-U (Win)/Command-U (Mac) so that we may work with the paths individually. Select the pieces of the knight and group them (Alt-G/Command-G). In the Properties Toolbar, rename the group "Knight" and check the Hide checkbox. When finished, you should see only the pawn extrusion on the stage, with the Knight grouping visible in the Hierarchy Menu.

Select the pawn and enter the Extrusion Editor. Double-click the outline to select the entire path and copy it. Delete the path, enter the Lathe Editor, and paste the path there. This rather roundabout method is necessary because it is not possible to take an extruded path directly into the Lathe Editor or to import an external file.

If you cannot view the entire path, use the Zoom tool and zoom out until you can. Click and drag a bounding box around the entire path to select it. Using the keyboard arrow keys, move the path to the right until the left edge is aligned with the green vertical line (y-axis). In the Point Properties panel, when the x-coordinate under Properties is at 0, the path is perfectly aligned (see Figure 5-14).

Returning to the Scene Editor, you will find that the pawn model is complete (see Figure 5-15). Apply a white or black glossy material, rename the lathe object "Pawn," and hide it.

 If you wanted to create rectangular chess pieces, you could follow the same process. The only difference would be to change some of the Lathe object properties after returning to the Scene Editor. Reducing the Radial Segments to 4 and deactivating Radial Smoothing will result in a pawn with sharp corners, as displayed in Figure 5-16.

Modeling the knight

With the pawn geometry now hidden, select "Knight" in the Hierarchy menu and uncheck the Hide box. Lathe the base of the knight just as with the pawn. Once completed, position it so that the top of the base is just touching the extruded body, as shown in Figure 5-17.

The next step is to set the depth and bevel type for each of the extruded objects. Assign all objects an Outer Round bevel type, with a depth of 0.030. Bevels in Swift

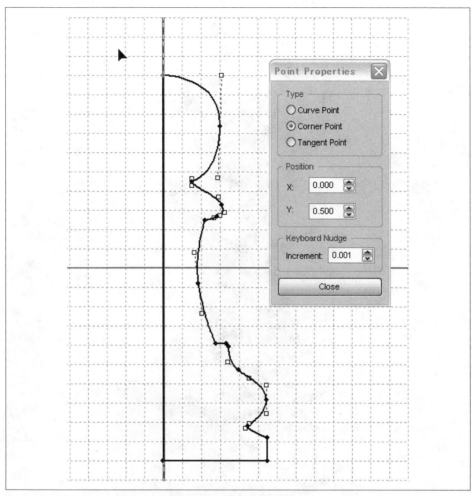

Figure 5-14. Vector path for the pawn inside of the Lathe Editor

3D are an additive process, which results in an object's geometry becoming thicker when bevels are applied. Because of this, you may need to slightly adjust the pieces of the knight so that they are symmetrical and remain aligned. Use Figure 5-18 as a reference point for setting the extrusion depth, found under Sizing.

With the sizing and bevel options set, it now seems that the base might be a little too narrow, giving the piece an unbalanced appearance. To remedy this, select the base and enter the Lathe Editor once more. Select all the points that do not rest on the center axis and move them to the right. This step will increase the diameter of the base without altering the height. The exact amount is up to you, but it should not extend past the outer edges of the knight's body.

Figure 5-15. Lathed pawn model

After applying the material of your choice, the knight model should look similar to Figure 5-19.

Figure 5-16. Pawn model without radial smoothing and reduced radial segmentation

5.3   Adding Simple 3D Animation to Flash

Problem

You want to animate 3D objects in Swift 3D for use in Flash.

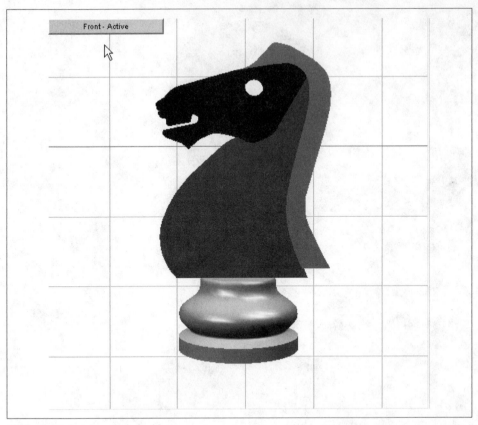

Figure 5-17. Knight with lathed base

Solution

Use drag-and-drop animations from the gallery toolbar and customize them with the timeline.

Discussion

There are two primary ways to add animation to a Swift 3D scene. If all you require are simple rotations and spins, most likely the preset Gallery Animations will fulfill your needs. The second method is manual keyframe animation, similar to that done within Flash. In either case, at the core of movement in Swift 3D is the animation timeline.

Most likely if you are reading this book, you have at least a basic working knowledge of Flash and thus have some familiarity with a timeline. Although there are specific differences between the Swift 3D timeline workflow and that of Flash, the basic concept remains the same. Motion is defined through modifying aspects of an object at specific points (keyframes) in the timeline and the software generates the neces-

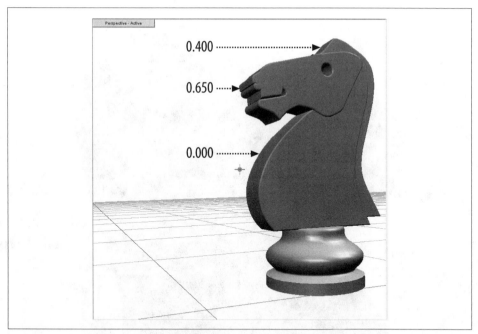

Figure 5-18. Setting depth for extruded elements of knight

sary frames in between these points. When an object is selected, the properties that are available for animation are reflected in the layers of the timeline. See Figure 5-20 to review the parts of the timeline.

> The "Animate" button in the main toolbar must be active ("red") in order to edit the timeline in any way.

Selected Objects Name
> The name of the object or group of objects that is currently selected.

Property Layers
> The list of object properties that may be animated for the current selection.

Playback Controls
> Used to control the playback of animation within the Scene Editor viewports.

Frames Per Second
> This property is just like FPS in Flash. If you want an animation to play back in Flash at the same speed as it was created in Swift 3D, this setting and the FPS of the target FLA must be the same.

Figure 5-19. Final knight with black material applied

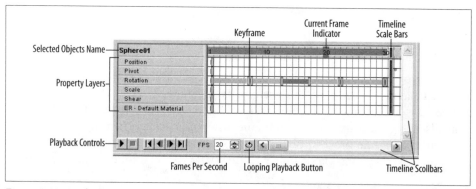

Figure 5-20. Swift 3D Animation timeline

Looping Playback Button

When this button is depressed, the animation will continuously loop until stopped. If looping playback is active when rendering a scene, the last frame of the animation will be left out in order to accommodate for a smooth loop.

Current Frame Indicator

Shows the current place in the timeline that is being viewed. By dragging this indicator to the left and right, you may also "scrub" through the animation.

Keyframe

Signifies points in the timeline where the property of an object has been modified. To set a keyframe, place the Current Frame Indicator at a desired frame and modify an object. Unlike Flash, a keyframe in Swift 3D is made up of two elements, a "Stop frame" handle and a "Start frame" handle. If these are dragged apart, the green line that represents animation in the timeline will become red, which will cause the specific animation to stop for a time equal to the number of frames it spans.

Timeline Scale Bars

By dragging these horizontally, you can increase or decrease the duration of all animation within the timeline.

Timeline Scrollbars

These act like any other scrollbar, allowing you to view items that are currently not visible due to limitations of space.

Model objects, trackball lights, scene lights, scene cameras, and the perspective camera may all be animated, but there are some common properties that cannot be animated. Some of these include:

- Environment and Background Color
- The color of lights
- Camera Lens Length
- Bevel settings

- Mesh Deformations modeled in the Advanced Modeler
- Segmentation
- The Sweep Angle of lathed objects

Here I'll provide a quick example of using the basic features of the timeline and animation gallery. The goal of the exercise is to animate the sunglasses shown in Figure 5-21. The planned animation will include the glasses spinning a full 360° horizontally along the *x*-axis while simultaneously folding the armatures to the closed position. During the process, object pivot points will be repositioned by manually animating with keyframes and applying a preset animation from the Gallery toolbar.

Figure 5-21. Sunglasses model to be animated

The first step is to organize the various part of the model for animation, forming parent/child relationships to make things easier.

I have created relationships between the objects in the Hierarchy menu (see Figure 5-22) so that all parts of the glasses are under the influence of the parent named "Glasses." This step allows me to animate the entire model at one time. Below Glasses is another grouped relationship between the frames and the lenses, and finally two more additional children, one for each armature. This structure lets me apply animation to each armature without affecting the position of the overall model.

To keep positioning simple, I will animate the armatures first, but before applying any changes, I first must reposition each arm's pivot point. Currently it is set to the center of the armature's mesh, and if I were to rotate the left arm, it would look similar to Figure 5-23. Not exactly what I had in mind.

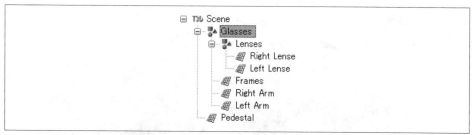

Figure 5-22. Parent/child relationships in the Hierarchy menu

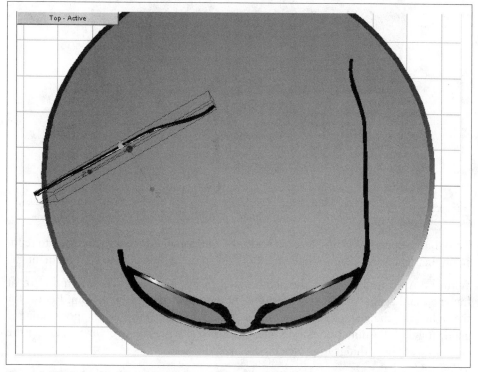

Figure 5-23. Example of rotating an object with incorrectly placed pivot point

Confirm that the Animate button is deactivated. After clicking Move Pivot Only, which is found under Position in the Properties Toolbar, use the mouse to reposition the pivot point so that it is located approximately where the hinge would be located. Doing this type of positioning requires working between the Top and Left viewports, and it often helps to switch over to wireframe view to remove visual obstacles. When in place and looking at the model through the Top viewport, check to see your progress by toggling on Lock Spin and giving the left arm a quick rotation with the trackball (see Figure 5-24).

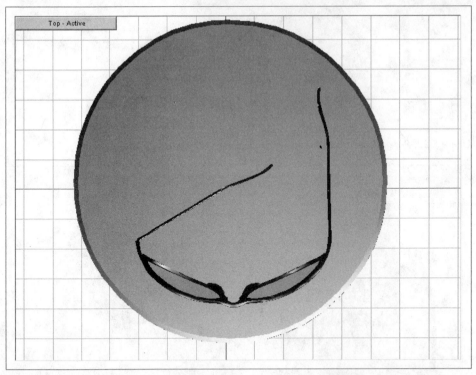

Figure 5-24. Example of rotating an object with the pivot point adjusted to the correct position

Everything appears to be in place, so undo the rotation and repeat the process to reposition the right arm's pivot point. After both are in place, it is time to start animating.

With the Animate button in the active state, place the Current Frame Indicator at frame 30 and again rotate the left arm using the trackball and Lock Spin. Repeat for the right arm; the glasses are now folded shut. To make sure that the positioning is good, toggle off Animation Mode and switch to the Perspective view, rotating the camera to see how things look (see Figure 5-25).

The positioning looks good; however, the animation preview shows that the meshes of the arms are actually coming into contact with one another and intersecting. It is always good to check an animation from multiple angles to detect problems such as this.

To solve the issue of the overlapping mesh, reenter Animation Mode and select the right armature. After dragging the Start Frame handle in the Rotation layer to the fourth frame, the right arm has a slight delay before starting to close. This keeps it from hitting the left arm and the problem is solved, as shown in Figure 5-26.

Now that the armature animations are completed, the final step is to apply the horizontal rotation to the glasses. Using the Top viewport, drag and drop the ER—Horizontal Right animation to the Glasses group. When previewing the animation, two

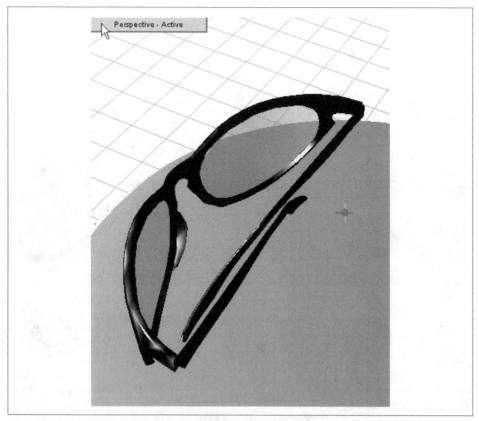

Figure 5-25. Final position of armatures in animation

problems are evident right away. First, the spin finishes 10 frames before the armature animation. Second, the glasses extend off of the pedestal as they rotate.

In order to have the armature animation end with the rotation, select all in the Glasses group and drag the Timeline Scaling Bars to the 30th frame. To fix the problem of the glasses rotating off of the pedestal, reposition them to the center of the pedestal at the 30th frame. This fix will cause the glasses to move backward along the z-axis as they rotate. Setting the Stop Frame handle of the Position layer at frame 17 caused the glasses to move to the desired position before the animation was fully completed. Figure 5-27 shows every fifth frame of the animation.

You should now have a good understanding of the animation timeline, the role that pivot points play, and structuring items in the Hierarchy menu. Armed with this basic knowledge, you will be able to apply it to create much more complex animations of your own.

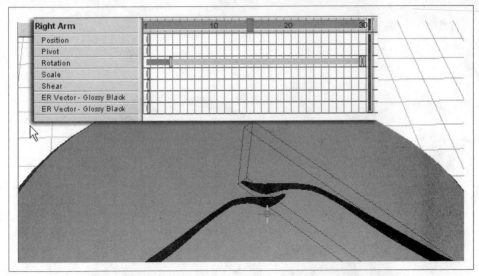

Figure 5-26. Adjusting start frame in the timeline to set a delay in the start of animation

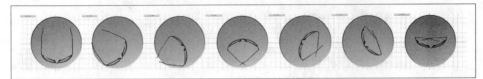

Figure 5-27. Every fifth frame in 30-frame animation of sunglasses rotating while folding

5.4 Animating a 3D Shape Morph

Problem

You want to animate a 3D model morphing into a different shape.

Solution

Use the animation timelines within the Extrusion and Lathe Editors to perform "path morphs."

Discussion

Swift 3D does not support animation within the Advanced Modeler, therefore making it impossible to animate true path deformations; however, the Extrusion and Lathe Editors both contain timelines for animating "path morphs." Animating a shape change in the object's vector path creates a path morph. This process makes it possible to have an extrusion or lathe object completely change shape through relatively easy animation techniques. You can think of standard animation in Swift 3D as the motion tweening in Flash, making path morphs equivalent to shape tweening.

To perform a path morph in either editor, add a keyframe with a change to the path. The following rules restrict the types of changes that can be made:

- Although points can be repositioned freely, they cannot be added or subtracted from a single keyframe. The same number of points must remain throughout an animation. If a point is deleted from one keyframe of an animation, it will be removed from all, therefore changing the shape of the object from start to finish.

- To assist in different kinds of drawing, the editors give the option to set point types to curve, corner, or tangent. This type must not change throughout an animation.

- New path data cannot be pasted into frames in order to morph from the original shape to the new, even if the same number of points is present in each path.

Because of these restrictions, it is often easier to animate from a more complex shape to a simpler one. Keep in mind that frames can always be reversed in Flash if the opposite is required. Figure 5-28 displays a path morph applied to the previously created pawn model, which is a lathe object.

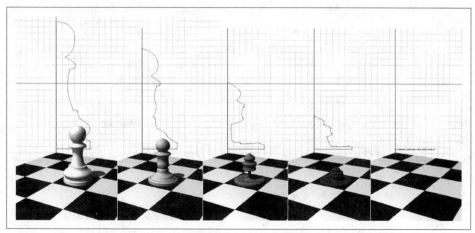

Figure 5-28. Sample frames and renders from Lathe Editor path morph

5.5   Vector-Based 3D Graphics

Problem

You want scalable 3D vector graphics and control over individual elements within the Flash authoring environment.

Solution

Render and Export vector graphics with the SWFT format and SmartLayer technology.

Discussion

As you no doubt know by now, one of Swift 3D's core features is its ability to render and export to a variety of vector formats, including SWF, AI, EPS, SVG, and SWFT. You most likely have already heard of or used the first four formats. The fifth, SWFT, is a proprietary export format of Swift 3D. Although it is similar in some ways to a standard SWF, it alone can render an object to different layers depending on specific criteria. Objects in motion, static objects, highlights, shadows, and more can all be assigned to their own layers. These layers are respected when imported to Flash via the SWFT importer that installs with the Swift 3D standalone application.

As an example of how the SWFT file format works, this example renders the first five frames of the animation used in the previous section. To render to SWFT with SmartLayer technology:

1. In the Preview and Export Editor, click Vector under the Output Options if it is not already selected.
2. Under the General category, select Swift 3D Flash Importer from the Target File Type drop-down menu, and enable Smart Layer technology by checking the Separate Stationary and Moving Objects box.
3. Select the fill type of your choice and include Highlights, Reflections, and Shadows as desired. I use Cartoon Average Color Fill, because it often provides the best quality for the smallest file sizes. I will not be rendering outlines; if you do so, they will be assigned a layer of their own as well.

Figure 5-29 shows a sample of SWFT layer structure after imported into the Flash authoring environment.

With each element residing on its own layer, greater control can be had over individual elements when working in Flash. For example, you could convert colors in motion to movie clips and set color properties dynamically.

 The SWFT importer and format are compatible only with Flash MX 2004 and up.

5.6 Realistic Raster-Based 3D Graphics

Problem

You want to make your 3D objects look more realistic than is possible with vector output.

Solution

Use raster output along with bitmap texturing in the advanced modeler in Swift 3D.

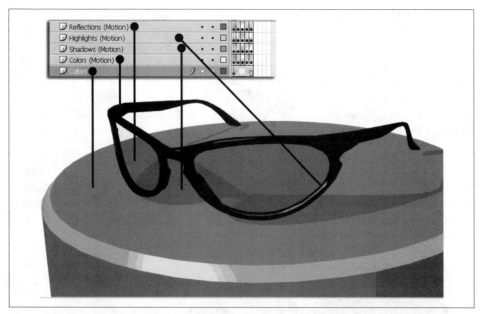

Figure 5-29. Layers corresponding to graphic elements in an SWFT file imported into Flash

Discussion

The use of bitmap texturing combined with the raster rendering and export capabilities of the Electric Motion (EMO) rendering engine results in the most photo-realistic images capable with Swift 3D. The Materials Gallery includes a number of default bitmap textures, and you may also create your own from PNG, BMP, JPG, or GIF data. Bitmap materials are an excellent way to add depth and detail without increasing the complexity of the underlying model mesh. As those familiar with low-poly (minimum number of polygons necessary) modeling for games know, this technique has the advantage of adding detail without bloating file size or increasing system demands during rendering.

 The disadvantage to using bitmaps for detail is that they will be easily distinguished as "flat" if viewed closely or from certain angles. Another visual giveaway is that shadows will not respect the shape of a bitmap texture, instead adhering to the contours of the model.

Although materials can be added to objects though the Scene Editor, advanced placement, rotation, and scaling of bitmap materials must be done within the Advanced Modeler, hence requiring extrusions, primitives, or lathe objects be converted to model meshes. Because of this requirement, it is important that you have any properties associated with these types of items finalized before moving into the Advanced Modeler. It is good practice to make a copy of such objects, setting them to hidden in the Scene Editor, so that they are available for future use if necessary.

Applying a single bitmap texture to all faces of an object is a fairly straightforward process, yet doing so to selections of polygons can take some practice. For illustrating these concepts, I have chosen to recreate the cover of a popular title from O'Reilly, *Essential ActionScript 2.0* (2004). This example can easily be adapted for creating packaging mock-ups, such as software boxes. The completed T3D and bitmap assets can be downloaded from *http://www.rightactionscript.com/fcb/chpt5/book.zip*.

Preparing the bitmap materials

The first step is to acquire the necessary artwork for all sides of the book. I did so by scanning the front and back covers, as well as the spine of my copy, and cleaning up the images in Photoshop. The right, top, and bottom image used for the edges of exposed pages was a simple texture created in Photoshop. After cleanup was finished, each image was saved as an individual PNG document, as displayed in Figure 5-30.

Figure 5-30. Bitmap materials prepared in Photoshop and saved as PNG documents; the black borders are in place to make the graphics stand out from the color of this page and do not exist in the actual files

The next step is to enter the Advanced Modeler and create the base object for the book, which in this case will be a simple Box Mesh primitive. When adding the object to the front viewport, roughly size it to the dimensions of the book. If you happen to have a copy of the book on hand, I suggest using it as reference or viewing the original bitmaps to help judge the size. It does not have to be perfect, as modifications can be made later to match up with the materials perfectly.

Before applying materials, each side of the box mesh must be assigned its own surface group. For a refresher on how to assign surface groups, see the creation of the chessboard squares in Recipe 5.2. As each group is created, it should be given a name that is easily recognizable. I have used Cover, Back, Spine, Top, Right, and Bottom. When you are working with a number of surface groups, assigning them names that correspond to the material that will be applied can be of great assistance in maintaining organization and speeding up the texturing process.

 When moving into the texturing stage of a project, it is a good idea to set all of the viewports in the Advanced Modeler to Texture Smooth Shaded and to display materials. This practice allows for real-time previews of material positioning in all viewports. These options are found under the viewport camera tabs.

With the surface groups created, it is time to start applying textures, starting with the cover. Select the cover surface group and double-click the material preview in the Properties Toolbar. This step will bring up the materials editor, as shown in Figure 5-31. In the pattern drop-down menu, select Bitmap Image and browse to *cover.png*, uncheck the X and Y tiling boxes, and click OK.

In the front viewport of the Advanced Modeler, you will now see the cover material applied. If the bitmap does not appear to be fitting correctly, enter Edit Texture mode by clicking the paint can icon in the top toolbar and use the scaling and move tools to reposition it. Right-clicking the model will also allow for scaling along along the *x*- or *y*-axis alone. If only a small adjustment is needed, this is fine; however, if a good deal of nonuniform scaling is used, distortion will soon become apparent in the material.

 A custom material that is applied to an object may be added to the materials library in the Gallery Toolbar by dragging and dropping the material preview window in the Properties Toolbar to the gallery of your choice.

If the dimensions of the box mesh are noticeably off, you'll have to adjust the various dimensions using the Vertex Selection tool and manually increasing or decreasing the size. When this is done after a bitmap material is applied, it will cause the material to scale as well; however, going back to the scaling tool in the Edit Texture mode is an easy way to resolve the problem.

When the cover graphic is in place and you feel comfortable applying and positioning materials, repeat the previous steps for both the back cover and spine of the book. If the cover is lined up, the back should be simple to apply. The spine may require additional resizing of the box's depth.

The final surface groups that require mapping are the top, right, and bottom, all of which use the *pages.png* texture. This one is applied in the same way as the others, with a few small changes. First, you must keep X and Y tiling active. The second difference, which will be obvious, is that when you go to add the material to any of the

Figure 5-31. Creating a bitmap material in the Edit Material panel

sides, the line texture will be mapped in the wrong direction. To fix this problem, enter Edit Texture Mode and right-click on one of the applicable sides of the box. When the context menu appears, select Auto Box Coordinates, as shown in Figure 5-30, and the mapping direction will be corrected. Alternatively, you could manually rotate the bitmap until it is facing the correct direction.

 An alternative approach to creating individual image files for materials is to combine them all into a single file. With this method, you can apply the same material to every side of the box and just have to reposition the bitmap to the appropriate graphic. I personally prefer to keep them separate for the purposes of editing, updating, or replacing at a later date.

Although some lighting and a ground plane have been added to the example in the figure, your final model should look similar to Figure 5-32. If you ran into trouble along the way, you may want to explore the T3D source file.

Figure 5-32. Finished bitmap-textured book

The final step is to export to a raster format for import into Flash. Swift 3D offers a variety of compatible formats, and the one you select depends very much on your needs and personal preference. Standard formats for static images include JPG, PNG, BMP, TGA, and TIF, of which all except for JPG support alpha transparency. For animation, there is direct export to SWF, which is composed of a series of raster images. There is also the option to export to video using AVI, MOV, or FLV formats.

My general preference is PNG. Even when dealing with animation, I usually export a series of PNG files instead of a raster SWF. One of the reasons for this method is that at times the anti-aliasing in SWF documents provides pixel artifacts at the edges of objects. Also, I like to have the option to edit or optimize on a per-frame level using an external image-editing application, such as Photoshop or Fireworks.

5.7   Creating 3D Buttons

Problem

You want to animate 3D buttons in Swift for use in Flash.

Solution

Import Swift-created buttons into the Flash authoring environment and control with ActionScript.

Discussion

The Swift 3D workflow involved for creating interactive elements, such as buttons for navigation, is occasionally confusing for new users, as the program itself has no scripting capabilities. Animations created in Swift 3D are strictly linear, playing from the first to the last frame; however, that all can change once imported into Flash, where content can be manipulated like any other imported asset.

This section covers two methods for creating buttons from Swift 3D graphics. The first uses a simple button symbol and bitmap data. The second uses a movie clip symbol and vector data.

Obviously the first things needed are some button graphics, which I have already created. I will be using the same source file for each example—you may download the T3D from *http://www.rightactionscript.com/fcb/chpt5/button.zip*; however, I suggest going through the following steps and previously discussed techniques to create your own, in order to experience the process from start to finish.

Taking the button concept quite literally, I modeled the nice, shiny, red, cartoony button shown in Figure 5-33. It is just waiting for someone to come along and push it! But before someone can do that, we need to get it out of Swift 3D and into Flash where a little interaction can be added.

When adding materials and lighting, I remembered that this object would be exported as both raster and vector, so I have selected fairly simple materials that will render accurately in both formats. If you have opened the T3D file, you will find that the button plunger has had applied a simple animation (10 frames) of it being depressed. This is all we need to cover each state of the button, as you will later see in Flash. Now it is time to finally export the graphics.

Creating navigation with button symbols

This is a very straightforward process, which is the same as for creating any type of button. We need only import the necessary assets and place them on the required frames of a new button symbol:

1. With your button file open in Swift 3D, enter the Preview and Export Editor and activate raster rendering mode by clicking the Raster button.

2. Set the Target File Type format to PNG, and leave the other properties at their default values.

3. Because we will be working with just two states, Up and Down, it is unnecessary to render and export the entire animation. Holding down Ctrl, select the

Figure 5-33. Example button

first and the tenth frames in the animation preview by clicking on them. To render and export only the frames needed, hold down Ctrl and click on frames 1 and 10 in the animation preview.

4. Click Generate Selected Frames. If the preview images are acceptable, finish the process by clicking Export Selected Frames. A sequentially named PNG file will be created for each frame.

With step 4, our work in Swift 3D is finished and we move into Flash:

1. Create a new Flash document and set the background color to black. You could use any color, but it is generally recommended that the background color in Swift 3D be similar to that of Flash when rendering to raster, so as to avoid any pixel halo when using transparency.

2. Select File → Import → Import to Library and navigate to the PNG files that you just exported from Swift 3D. This step is optional, but at this point it is generally a good idea to rename the imported bitmaps from their default sequential

naming to more easily recognized names, such as ON and DOWN. If you do not have preferences in Flash set to turn off bitmap smoothing, doing so will avoid any undue distortion.

3. Create a new Button Symbol and place the imported bitmaps into their appropriate frames.

4. Place the button on the stage and Enable Simple Buttons (Ctrl-Alt-B) to test.

 If you want to use multiple buttons, you may or may not have to export individual graphics for each. Depending on the camera angle and if buttons are placed near one another, you can probably get away with using multiple instances of the same button. However, if distortion occurs due to extreme lens length settings or if buttons are placed in relatively different positions, it is best to create appropriately positioned buttons within Swift 3D and export graphics for each.

Creating navigation with movie clip (MC) symbols

Although this method does require a little more work, I consider it better practice than the use of button symbols. Flash provides for increased control and manipulation of MCs, as well as providing greater potential for animation. The steps in Swift 3D are much the same; however, because we are going to render the full animation this time around, we will use vector graphics to cut down on the file size.

1. With your button file open in Swift 3D, enter the Preview and Export Editor and activate vector rendering mode.

2. Set the Target File Type format to SWFT. I have selected this format over SWF for the sole reason that it will result in a smaller file. As for the remaining settings, Separate Stationary and Moving Objects should be checked and Detail Level should be set to automatic. Combine Edges and Fills is not really applicable, because we are not rendering outlines. For this example, Fill Type (under Fill Options) is set to Area Gradient Shading. I suggest experimenting with the different types to see the results, from the standpoint of both visual quality and resulting file size. Figure 5-34 displays the sample button rendered with each of the available fill types.

We will be using the entire animation this time around, so it is necessary to click Generate All Frames and Export All Frames when rendering is complete.

After step 4 is completed, move into Flash again:

1. Create a new Flash document and, for the sake of uniformity, set the background color to black. The sample T3D file has a frame rate of 20, so Flash should also be changed to 20 fps to assure smooth playback.

2. Select File → Import → Import to Library and navigate to the button SWFT file. Importing in this manner will automatically generate a new movie clip (MC) in the library. Rename the MC "MC_redButton."

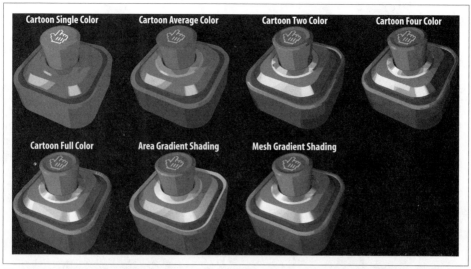

Figure 5-34. Button model rendered to each of the vector fill types

3. Open the new MC in the library for editing. The timeline of the symbol should look similar to Figure 5-35.

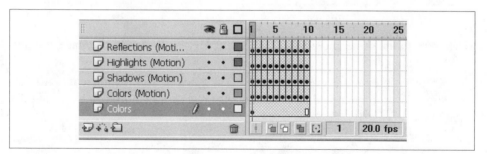

Figure 5-35. Timeline of MC_redButton with imported SWFT for button animation

4. Although the imported file is an SWFT, it is not necessary to have all the various elements on individual layers for this project. Only the objects in motion and those that are static need to be separated. Copy and paste each frame's animated content, designated by (Motion) in the layer name, and paste it into a single frame, deleting the extra layers. For the next step, convert each frame in the motion layer to a symbol. The timeline should now look like Figure 5-36.

5. The current animation includes the button depressing, but not returning to its original state. As this version will be fully animated, we require this, but did not add it within Swift 3D due to concerns of file size. Now that the graphics in motion have been converted to symbols, it is simply a matter of copying frames 2 through 9, pasting them after frame 10, and using Modify → Timeline → Reverse Frames.

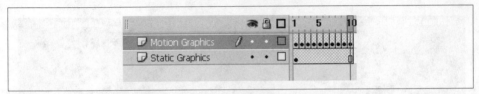

Figure 5-36. The MC_redButton timeline after grouping animated objects

6. Now that the graphics are in place, we need to add some simple ActionScript within the MC. Add two layers, naming the top one Actions and the other Labels. In the Actions layer, add a stop() to frames 1 and 10. In the Labels layer, designate frame 2 as Down and frame 11 as Up. The timeline should now resemble Figure 5-37.

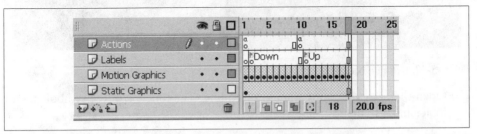

Figure 5-37. The MC_redButton timeline with Action and Label

7. Return to the scene and add an instance of MC_redButton to the stage, naming it *mybutton_mc*.

8. It is now time to add event listeners so that our button is interactive. Add an actions layer to the timeline, enter the following script, and finish by testing the movie.

```
//setup the button events
mybutton_mc.onPress = mybutton_mc.onDragOver = function(){
  this.gotoAndPlay("Down");
};

mybutton_mc.onRelease = mybutton_mc.onDragOut = function(){
  this.gotoAndPlay("Up");
}
stop();
```

5.8   Using 3D Models in Flash Not Originally Created in Swift 3D

Problem

You want to use previously created 3D models in Flash that were not created in Swift 3D.

Solution

Take advantage of Swift's capability to import common 3D file formats.

Discussion

Swift 3D can import 3DS (3D Studio) and DXF (Drawing Exchange Format) files, which are both standard file formats for exchanging data between 3D applications. Because the majority of 3D modeling and CAD programs can export to one or both of these formats, the available resource for models is exhaustive. A quick online search will return links to numerous model repositories, both free and commercial. In fact, the sheer volume of model materials available means that you could complete a project without doing any modeling on your own, if you are so inclined. A few excellent online resources for 3D models compatible with Swift 3D include:

- 3D Café—*http://www.3dcafe.com*
- Turbo Squid—*http://www.turbosquid.com*

The support for these formats can be particularly useful when working with clients whose products are intended for online, interactive display. Many manufactured goods have had a 3D model created at some point in the stages of product design and development. Thus it is often possible to obtain model data directly from the manufacturer, which not only assures accuracy in representation, but can also save valuable modeling time in the case of complex objects.

Working with each format is different from working with the others. Not only are they brought into Swift 3D by different means, but also the type of data contained in each format can vary. Although DXF, which is most often associated with AutoCAD, will only ever contain model mesh data, 3DS files may include model mesh, materials, animation, lighting, and cameras. The amount of data supported in a 3DS file is dependent upon the program in which it was created. A 3DS document from any program other than Autodesk 3ds Max (previously Discreet 3ds Max) will include only model mesh and materials, while those from 3ds Max may also include animation, camera data and lighting.

Bringing files into Swift 3D

No matter which file format you need to import, it is a simple two-step process. For DXF files, go to File → Import and select the desired document. 3DS "import" is slightly different, in that you do not actually import at all, but rather create a new Swift document based on a 3DS file. The reason that a 3DS document cannot simply be imported into an existing document is that 3DS files can contain cameras and lighting, which are scene elements and not tied directly to a model, but to the scene itself. We again return to the File menu, but this time select "New from 3DS" and select the file to be imported.

Working with imported models

Once it is imported, you can go about making changes to a model if necessary. This includes applying or modifying existing materials, adding animation, and even editing the model on the mesh level using the Advanced Modeler.

Troubleshooting files

There are times when files will not successfully import. This problem most commonly occurs with CAD DXF files, as they can vary a good deal in the type of data they contain, and not all programs write the files in the same way. If this happens, the best course of action is to see whether the model can be made available in 3DS format. If the program of origin lacks the ability to export to 3DS, a conversion program or service can also be used. At times, just opening a DXF with a different CAD program and resaving can remedy import problems.

Other problems that can happen include when objects do not import in their correct positions or have damaged polygons. In these types of situations, your only option is to reposition elements manually or repair the mesh in the Advanced Modeler.

 It is possible for a DXF file to contain only a 2D CAD drawing. If this is the case, the import process will fail, as Swift 3D supports only those files containing 3D model mesh data.

5.9   Creating a 3D Product View from Multiple Angles

Problem

You want to create an interactive 3D product view (360° with multiple camera angles).

Solution

Use Swift 3D's cameras and render files for use in Flash.

Discussion

The use of 360° product views have become a common feature of many product-centered sites, as they can provide the user with the next best thing to being able to view the product in person. However, they can be difficult to produce and develop. Although photographic solutions can provide the most realistic results, this method requires specialized photographic equipment or outsourcing to a professional photographer. There can also be added difficulties with large objects or those that are difficult to photograph. Finally, at times it is simply not possible to obtain the object to photograph, such as when it is not yet through production.

Although Swift 3D/Flash-based tours cannot provide the flexibility of real-time 3D product viewers, they are free of the high price of licensing normally associated with such solutions. Also, because the viewing is Flash-based, the user has no need to install additional plug-ins, and there is also the benefit of being able to include additional content, such as interactive hotspots, external product data, linked video, and so on.

The following product view example introduces the library of models found within the Gallery Toolbar. Here you will find "out-of-the-box" lathe and extrusion objects, as well as full 3D models. You can also save models to this gallery for future use.

Creating the animated product views in Swift 3D

1. Create a new Swift 3D document and set the layout size to 500 × 300. Set the primary viewport to front and the secondary to top.

2. In the gallery toolbar, click on the button displaying a cog to show the model libraries and scroll down to the tank at the bottom of the 3D category. Drag-and-drop an instance of the tank to the front viewport and center it.

3. Switching over to the lighting gallery, click the Stationary tab and apply the three-point lighting scheme to the scene.

4. Still working with the Gallery Toolbar, access the animation gallery and apply the Horizontal Right animation to the tank model.

5. In the animation timeline, set the FPS to 12 and activate loop animation.

Now that we have the stage, model, lighting, and animation all in place, it is time to set up the cameras. We will be using the standard front camera and a custom targeted camera:

6. To prepare the front camera, drag the frame indicator in the timeline and confirm that the model is never cropped by the edges of the viewport. If cropping does occur, advance the animation to frame 5, select the model, and use "Frame Selection" from the viewport camera tab. This step centers the camera so that the model is not being cropped at its widest point during rotation.

7. Click the Create Target Camera icon in the main toolbar and assign the primary viewport to this new camera, while changing the secondary viewport to the left camera. (See Figure 5-38.)

8. The targeted camera should be positioned at approximately a 45° angle, looking down and positioned to the right of the tank. Refer to Figure 5-39 for positioning the camera in the left and top viewports, as well as the view through the lens of the targeted camera. After the camera is positioned, confirm again that no parts are cropped during rotation, and if needed, manually adjust the camera position.

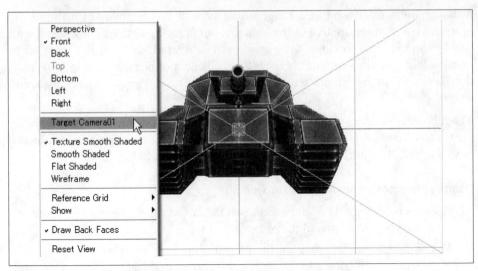

Figure 5-38. Assigning a targeted camera to a viewport

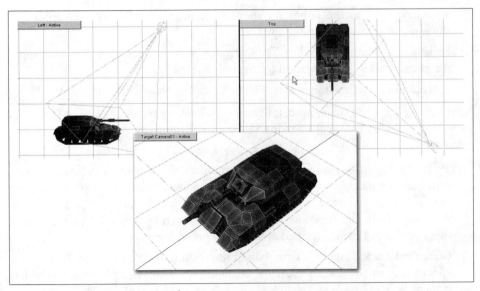

Figure 5-39. Positioning the targeted camera

Because the tank model makes use of bitmap materials, the rendering format will be raster. Render and export both camera views to SWF files. Each SWF should contain 19 frames. If there are 20 frames, the loop animation button was not activated, and there is no need to render again. Just select frames 1 through 19 and export selected frames instead of all frames.

From this point on, we will be working in Flash, importing the 3D animations and setting up the buttons for controlling the rotation and camera view.

Adding interaction in Flash

1. Create a new Flash document and set the stage size to 500×400, with a white background and FPS of 12 to match the animation done in Swift 3D.

2. Set up three layers in the timeline in the following order from top to bottom: Actions, Buttons, Views.

3. Import both the front and targeted camera SWF documents into the Flash library so that they create new MC symbols. Edit each symbol by adding an actions layer and inserting a stop( ) command on the first frame.

4. Drag instances of each MC to the stage, inserting them in the Views layer and positioning them at X: 0, Y:0. Name the front view *view1_mc* and the angled view *view2_mc*.

5. Create an MC that will be used for a button. Instances will be used for the button to change views, as well as to control the animation playing forward or backward. For this example, no over or down states are necessary—only the default up. It also requires a dynamic text box named *label_txt*, which will be used as the button label.

6. Place three instances of the button MC in the Buttons level of the timeline, two side-by-side beneath the tank and one in the upper-right corner. Name the lower-left instance *backButton_mc* and the lower-right *forwardButton_mc*. Name the button in the upper-right corner *changeViewButton_mc*. I have also created a small icon to accompany the change view button that will serve as a preview of the alternative view. It is made up of two frames and is named *icon_mc*. The stage should now look similar to Figure 5-40.

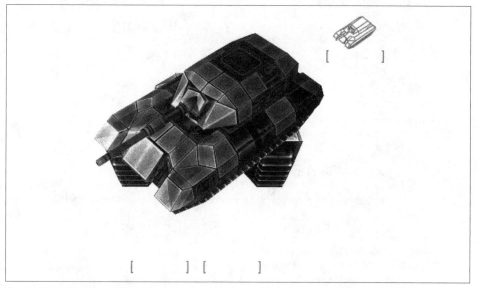

Figure 5-40. Layout of 3D product display interface

7. The final step is to add the ActionScript that will make the system interactive. In the actions frame of the main timeline, add the following code:

```
//set the default view
var currentView = 1;
//set the button labels
backButton.label_txt.text = "BACK";
forwardButton.label_txt.text = "FORWARD";
changeViewButton.label_txt.text = "Change View";
//function to set the view visibility
function setView(view:Number) {
    //comment this line out if you don't want the views to sync
    _root["view"+view+"_mc"].gotoAndStop(_root["view"+currentView+"_mc"]._
currentframe);
    _root["view"+currentView+"_mc"]._visible = false;
    _root["view"+view+"_mc"]._visible = true;
    //set the currentView
    currentView = view;
}
//function for the change view button
function changeView() {
    if (currentView == 1) {
        setView(2);
        //Line 21 and 25 are not needed if an icon is not used with the change
view button
        icon_mc.gotoAndStop(2);
    } else {
        setView(1);
        icon_mc.gotoAndStop(1);
    }
}
function moveBack() {
    //find out if we should go to the last frame
    if (_root["view"+currentView+"_mc"]._currentframe == 1) {
        var gotoFrame = _root["view"+currentView+"_mc"]._totalframes;
    } else {
        var gotoFrame = _root["view"+currentView+"_mc"]._currentframe-1;
    }
    _root["view"+currentView+"_mc"].gotoAndStop(gotoFrame);
}
function moveForward() {
    //find out if we should go to the first frame
    if (_root["view"+currentView+"_mc"]._currentframe == _
root["view"+currentView+"_mc"]._totalframes) {
        var gotoFrame = 1;
    } else {
        var gotoFrame = _root["view"+currentView+"_mc"]._currentframe+1;
    }
    _root["view"+currentView+"_mc"].gotoAndStop(gotoFrame);
}
//setup the buttons onRelease event
backButton.onPress = function() {
    this.onEnterFrame = function() {
        moveBack();
```

```
        };
    };
    backButton.onRelease = function() {
        delete this.onEnterFrame;
    };
    backButton.onDragOut = function() {
        delete this.onEnterFrame;
    };
    forwardButton.onPress = function() {
        this.onEnterFrame = function() {
            moveForward();
        };
    };
    forwardButton.onRelease = function() {
        delete this.onEnterFrame;
    };
    forwardButton.onDragOut = function() {
        delete this.onEnterFrame;
    };
    changeViewButton.onRelease = changeView;
    //set the view to view 1
    view2_mc._visible = false;
    stop();
```

Test the movie to confirm that everything works. If so, export and you are done.

5.10   Rendering Swift 3D Animations as Flash Video

Problem

You want to convert your animation from Swift 3D straight to video for Flash (FLV) and play it with Flash.

Solution

Use the export editor to render an *.flv* file and then use the new FLV player in Flash to place it on your page (or use the Flash Video Player plug-in in Dreamweaver 8).

Discussion

Swift 3D 4.5 introduced the ability to export animations, both vector and raster rendered, to the FLV (Flash Video) format. This alternative provides an excellent method for displaying movies that may be too complex to run on all computers due to processor demands. It also allows use of streaming to deliver files of large size without the issues associated with preloading an *.swf* file.

As stated, the FLV format is available when exporting from a raster or vector render. Although it is a simple process in each case, the settings available do differ. Before getting into the specific rendering options, it should be made clear that when exporting a vector-rendered FLV, the end results will *not* be vector data. It will be an FLV like any other. The difference is that this affords the possibility of maintaining the look of vector rendering, which is ideal for cartoon-like animations.

Whether rendering to vector or raster, the core FLV options stay the same. These include Encoding Focus (Quality and Bandwidth) and Keyframe Interval.

Quality

This option lets you specify whether you want the FLV compression to be focused on quality or bandwidth settings. Using the Quality setting causes the image quality to remain constant across all frames, running at a fixed bandwidth. A Quality setting at the maximum equals a bandwidth setting of 750kbs.

Bandwidth

If Bandwidth is given priority, the quality of the image will vary in order to adhere to the specified bandwidth value. This value represents kilobits per second and has a maximum setting of 750kbs.

Keyframe Interval

FLV encoding maintains its smaller file size through the use of keyframes and delta frames. Starting with the first frame of a video and at each keyframe thereafter, the entire frame of the video will be rendered. Between these keyframes, only the areas of the video that have experienced change will be rendered. These are known as delta frames. Due to this process, the overall image quality can degrade if keyframes are set too far apart; however it is a matter of give and take, as a greater number of keyframes will increase file size.

There are no special considerations to be had when working with a Swift 3D–created FLV in Flash. It can be imported or streamed just as any other. The only real shortcoming at this time is the lack of support for alpha transparency when exporting to the FLV format.

See Also

Chapter 18.

5.11   Adding 3D Graphics Without Leaving Flash

Problem

You want an easy-to-use solution for adding simple models and animations to Flash without leaving the authoring environment.

Solution

Use the Swift 3D Xpress extension for Flash MX 2004/Flash 8.

Discussion

Not everyone or every project requires the full modeling and animation capabilities that Swift 3D has to offer. If your 3D needs are rather modest and all you need to do is extrude paths and apply prepackaged animations, Swift 3D Xpress provides an extremely simple solution. Because Xpress is an extension for Flash MX 2004/Flash 8, it has an excellent workflow advantage, in that you never have to leave the Flash authoring environment.

A quick glance at the interface (Figure 5-41) and you will see many of the same elements that are in Swift 3D, albeit laid out in a different manner. Upon closer inspection, you will probably notice how much functionality has been omitted. Swift 3D Xpress includes only a Scene Editor and a version of the Preview and Export Editor, renamed "Render and Export to Flash." The Animation Timeline, Hierarchy Menu, Primitive Objects, Free Cameras, Free Lights, and Secondary Viewport are all missing from the Scene Editor, while the Extrusion Editor, Lathe Editor, and Advanced Modeler have been removed altogether. Swift 3D Xpress is basically an extrusion tool with materials and preset lighting and animation features.

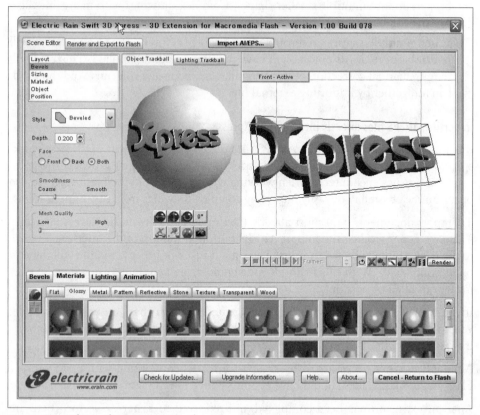

Figure 5-41. The Swift 3D Xpress interface

There are two methods by which you can extrude objects. Your choice will depend on the nature of the 2D vector artwork and what you need to accomplish.

Importing directly from Flash

To extrude text, shapes, or grouped shapes, select them and go to Commands → Swift 3D Xpress. This will open the Swift 3D Xpress dialog box from which you can modify the position and rotation of an object, as well as apply materials, animations, and bevel styles. There are a few guidelines to keep in mind when creating or selecting graphics for extrusion:

- Swift cannot extrude Flash symbols or bitmap graphics.

- Overlapping shapes that are not grouped can produce unexpected results when extruded. If you are using multiple shapes at one time, it is best if each is grouped. They must all reside on the same layer in the Flash timeline in order to be successfully used by Swift 3D Xpress.

- Use only filled objects without strokes. Although strokes can be translated into extruded objects, the results are usually unsatisfactory, as a single line can be broken up into multiple smaller shapes. Complex drawings with many lines also run the risk of memory errors.

- When multiple shapes are brought into Swift 3D Xpress, their color values will not be respected. All objects will have the same material applied. This case will require manual correction by applying new materials, or you can avoid the problem altogether by importing external files.

Importing AI/EPS files directly into Swift 3D Xpress

It is possible to import external AI/EPS files directly into the Swift 3D Xpress workspace, effectively bypassing Flash. This trick is advantageous, as it avoids the color conversion issues encountered when working with objects from the Flash stage. It also opens up the possibility of easily importing complex drawings from other applications.

To import documents, you must already have opened the Swift 3D Xpress interface. The next step is to click the Import AI/EPS button at the top of the interface, browse to the desired file, and click Import. The time it takes to process the file will depend on its complexity. With this method, you should again avoid importing lines/strokes in favor of filled objects only.

If you have a complex drawing that was created in Flash that you wish to extrude, you will have better luck exporting it from Flash as an AI or EPS and in turn importing that into Swift 3D Xpress.

Although it is not necessary to break apart fonts when working with text from the Flash stage, AI/EPS files should have all fonts converted to paths before importing.

After an extrusion has been completed and rendered to raster or vector, there are only two export options in Swift 3D Xpress. "Create Flash Movie Clip" will do just what it sounds like: exporting the 3D scene to a movie clip symbol within the current Flash document. "Export to SWF File" will create an external SWF that can be imported into an FLA or played as is. Before exporting, it is important to be aware of one of the biggest disadvantages of Swift 3D Xpress: its total lack of save features. After you have exported, there is no going back, and to make any changes, you will have to start all over again. Because of this limitation, it is critical to make sure you have what you want before hitting either of the buttons for export.

 When rendering and exporting a scene that contains animation, it is all or nothing. You cannot select to render/export a specific frame or range of frames.

CHAPTER 6

Composing Images with Bitmaps and Masks

Flash is primarily a vector editing program. Yet it can import other types of media, such as bitmap graphics, sound, and video, and it has limited tools for working with these media. To work well with import media such as bitmaps and sounds, you need to understand not only the intrinsic strengths and limitations of each form of media, but also the ways that Flash works with them.

In most cases, vector graphics are preferable to bitmap graphics for use in Flash. Vector graphics are smaller in file size as well as easier to edit and modify than bitmap graphics. In addition, bitmap graphics do not scale well, usually making them look unacceptable in Flash movies that resize to fit the size of the browser window. But sometimes bitmaps are unavoidable, especially when you need to use digital photography.

Although it is possible to convert bitmap graphics to vector graphics, using a process called *tracing*, and discussed in this chapter in Recipe 6.4, the converted graphic is often worse than the original in file size, editability, and visual quality.

Bitmap graphics may not be the Flash developer's first choice, but they are a common feature of Flash movies. Because of Flash's limited bitmap editing abilities, you should try to finalize them in a bitmap editing program, such as Macromedia Fireworks, Adobe Photoshop, or Jasc Paint Shop Pro. That is, you should set the resolution, image dimensions, tonal balance, and so on before you import the image into Flash. You can erase or paint over bitmap pixels in Flash, but that is about the limit of Flash's authoring time bitmap editing abilities.

Bitmap graphics, along with sounds and video, can increase a Flash movie's file size quite rapidly. Optimization is an important task when working with bitmap graphics. By default, Flash compresses bitmap graphics upon export. You have control over this compression and can also disable it, on a one-by-one basis, in the event that you have optimized your graphics in an external program, such as Fireworks or ImageReady.

But Flash has some advantages of its own. For one, it can animate image compositions. For example, you can create a mask, and then animate that mask or the masked content. In addition, you can script the behavior of masks, enabling dynamic masks that respond to user-initiated events during playback.

6.1   Importing Bitmaps

Problem

You want to use an existing bitmap graphic in a Flash movie.

Solution

Import it into the current document using File → Import.

Discussion

To use a bitmap graphic, such as a *.jpg* or *.gif* file, in your movie, you import it. To do so, select the frame in which you want the graphic to appear, and choose File → Import → Import to Stage. In the Import dialog box that appears, navigate to the file and click Open. The file is imported to the library and an instance of it appears on the stage. As with symbols and instances, no matter how many times you use a bitmap in a movie, the user has to download it only once. The imported image usually appears at 100% of its size. Occasionally, it may appear at a different size. To restore it to 100%, delete it, and drag out a new instance from the library.

If File → Import is grayed out, make sure that a frame in an unlocked layer is selected.

Bitmaps should be placed in their own layers. Bitmaps always stack above vector art within a layer. Even using Modify → Arrange → Send to Back cannot move a bitmap graphic behind vector artwork. Worse, if you break apart the bitmap for editing (Modify → Break Apart, discussed in Recipe 6.2), the bitmap pixels will delete any vector art that they overlap within a layer.

If you want to import the image directly to the library, but don't yet want to put it on the stage, you can take advantage of the Import to Library feature by choosing File → Import → Import to Library. The Import dialog box displays, and when you've navigated to the file and clicked Open, the bitmap is placed in the library.

Flash is able to import the following types of bitmap graphics:

- Graphic Interchange Format (*.gif*), including Animated GIF
- Joint Photographic Experts Group (*.jpg*, *.jpeg*, *.jpe*)
- Portable Network Graphic (*.png*)
- Windows Bitmap (*.bmp*, *.dib*) (Windows)

- Windows Metafile (*.wmf*) (Windows)
- Enhanced Metafile (*.emf*) (Windows)
- PICT (*.pict*) (Macintosh)

In addition, if you have the free Apple QuickTime player installed, Flash is able to install the following types of bitmap graphics:

- MacPaint (*.pntg*)
- Photoshop (*.psd*)
- PICT (*.pict, .pct, .pic*) for Windows
- QuickTime Image (*.qtif*)
- Silicon Graphics Image (*.sgi*)
- Truevision TGA (*.tga*)
- Tagged Image File Format (*.tif, .tiff*)

When you import a bitmap, Flash maintains a link to the original file. You can use this link to update the bitmap, if you change the graphic outside of Flash. To update a bitmap, follow these steps:

1. Open the library by pressing F11 or choosing Window → Library.
2. Select the bitmap from the list of assets in the library.
3. Click the Properties button at the bottom of the library. The Bitmap Properties dialog box displays.
4. Click the Update button.

After you click the button, Flash updates the graphic in the library, and all instances of the graphic throughout the movie are also updated. You can use similar steps to replace a bitmap graphic with a different graphic. Instead of choosing Update, choose Import and navigate to the new file. Again, the library and all instances are updated immediately. The graphic name in the library remains unchanged.

6.2   Editing Bitmaps

Problem

You want to edit an imported bitmap, including erasing and painting over bitmaps or using bitmaps as fills.

Solution

Use Modify → Break Apart.

Discussion

When you drag an imported bitmap instance into a Flash movie, it is locked for editing. If you select it with the Selection tool, it has a gray bounding box around it, and all you can do is reposition or scale the bitmap.

You can edit a bitmap, however. To do so, you must break it apart using Modify → Break Apart. Breaking apart a bitmap makes the pixels accessible for editing. More specifically, once it is broken apart, you can erase portions of a bitmap, or paint over them using a tool, such as the Brush tool.

Broken-apart bitmap pixels behave like the pixels of a vector shape's fill. If layered over another vector shape in the same layer, bitmap pixels remove any portion of a fill beneath them; before a bitmap is broken apart, it obscures, but does not remove, any vector shape fills beneath it in the same layer.

Breaking apart a bitmap graphic has no implications with regard to file size. That is, all the following movies using the same bitmap, *image.jpg*, would yield *.swf* files with the same file size:

- One instance of *image.jpg*, not broken apart
- Ten instances of *image.jpg*, not broken apart
- Ten instances of *image.jpg*, broken apart

An imported bitmap is stored in the library, and if it is used once on the stage, in any way, it must be downloaded in its entirety once. This rule applies even to bitmaps that are placed only partially on the stage, as well as to bitmaps that have been partially erased, masked, or resized.

In addition to enabling you to use Flash drawing and selection tools on pixels, breaking apart a bitmap also makes it easier to use a bitmap as a shape's fill. These techniques are discussed in Recipe 6.3.

See Also

Recipe 6.1, Recipe 6.3

6.3   Fitting Bitmaps Inside Shapes

Problem

You want to place a bitmap inside a shape with an irregular border.

Solution

Apply a bitmap fill to a vector shape, erase the edges of the bitmap, or use a mask.

Discussion

Flash offers three ways of filling a shape with a bitmap. No approach is better than the others in terms of file size in the exported *.swf* file, but each has its own intrinsic benefits, as discussed next. The three ways are:

- Draw a vector shape, and set its fill to any bitmap in the movie's library.
- Place an instance of a bitmap on the stage and erase its edges.
- Reveal an area of a bitmap using a mask.

You can apply a bitmap as the fill for an existing vector shape. This approach is useful if you've already drawn the vector shape, if a vector drawing tool exists that can create your shape for you (such as the Oval tool if you need to fill an ellipse), or if you are more comfortable drawing with a vector tool to create a shape than you would be trying to recreate that shape with a freehand tool, such as the Eraser tool.

Another benefit of this approach is that it is the only way to give a specific shape a tiled fill. That is, if the shape is larger than the bitmap, Flash repeats the bitmap to fill in the rest of the shape.

In addition, because the bitmap is being used as a fill, you have all the functionality of the Fill Transform tool at your disposal, which makes it easy to rotate, scale, distort, and reposition the fill relative to the shape.

To add a bitmap fill, complete the following steps:

1. Use the vector drawing tools to draw a shape on the stage. You may draw the shape with a solid fill to start, or you may add the fill afterward using the Paint Bucket tool.
2. If you've drawn the shape with a solid fill, select the fill.
3. Open the Color Mixer panel, and from the Type menu, select Bitmap.
4. When you select the Bitmap type from the menu, the selector just below becomes a scrollable region with swatches of each bitmap in the library. If you haven't yet imported the bitmap, you can click the Import button just beneath the Type menu to select the bitmap to import. When the bitmap is imported, select it from the selector's swatches.
5. If you applied a solid fill while drawing the shape, the bitmap fill is automatically applied. Otherwise, you'll need to select the Paint Bucket tool and apply the fill that way.

Note that there are advantages to applying the fill before or after drawing the shape. If you apply a solid fill while drawing a shape and then convert that fill to the bitmap, the fill is applied with the same dimensions as the imported image. If you apply the bitmap fill with the Paint Bucket tool, the image is scaled much smaller. In either case, if you want to transform the bitmap fill by rotating, skewing, translating, or scaling it, you can do so with the Gradient Transform tool as you would a normal gradient fill.

If you simply want to use a freehand drawing tool to paint away the edges of an image, the most direct way is to use the Eraser tool.

1. Drag an instance of the bitmap onto the stage.
2. Break the bitmap apart by choosing Modify → Break Apart.
3. Select the Eraser tool, and use the Options section at the bottom of the Tools panel to select the desired Erase Mode and Size.
4. Drag with the eraser over the bitmap. Be aware that Flash automatically smoothes the edges when using the Eraser tool.

A variation of this approach is to use the Lasso tool. Drag to select a region of pixels, and press the Delete key to remove the selected pixels.

Remember that even if you erase 95% of the image, the user still has to download the entire bitmap imported into Flash. Thus, if you do plan to erase most of an image, you should first crop the unneeded portions of it in an image editor, such as Fireworks or Photoshop.

Another alternative is to use a mask. Masks take more work than the preceding two methods, but you are rewarded with all the benefits of masking, including the potential to animate masks and make them dynamic and/or interactive via ActionScript. Masks are discussed in detail later in the chapter.

See Also

Recipe 6.8

6.4 Converting Bitmaps to Vector Art

Problem

You want to convert bitmap graphics to vector art.

Solution

Use Modify → Trace Bitmap.

Discussion

Flash excels with vector graphics; most of its tools are designed to edit them and Flash is optimized to work with them. Vector graphics are also scalable, in contrast to bitmap graphics, which usually lose quality when scaled (especially when scaled up). Finally, due to their editability, vector graphics are easier to animate, since you can reshape them nondestructively. Using Flash's trace feature, you can convert any bitmap graphic to vector shapes.

As promising as this conversion may sound, tracing bitmaps is often not a viable solution. For highly detailed bitmaps, such as most digital photographs, vector graphics are inferior in almost every significant way to bitmaps, including editability, file size, and image quality.

To reproduce an image using vector graphics, Flash draws vector shapes. If an image is relatively simple, with large regions of a single color, Flash can easily render the image using shapes. But if the image is detailed and intricate, as most photographs are, Flash has to draw many extremely small shapes. At some point, the overhead of creating and drawing tiny shapes becomes more file size and processor-intensive than the original pixels. And if the resulting vector shapes are larger than a pixel, the image has less detail than the bitmap, which means that it doesn't look as good.

If you are considering vectorizing a bitmap, you ought to examine your motivations. If you want to vectorize the bitmap for stylistic purposes, that's a good reason. Another good reason to vectorize a bitmap is because you want to use shape tweens on the shapes that constitute the bitmap. However, if you want to vectorize the bitmap to save file size, you're very unlikely to achieve that particular goal unless the bitmap has very few colors and consists primarily of simple shapes.

If you determine that you do want to vectorize the bitmap, complete the following steps:

1. Drag a bitmap instance onto the stage.

2. Select it with the Selection tool. Do not break it apart.

3. Choose Modify → Bitmap → Trace Bitmap from the main menu.

4. Enter appropriate settings in the Trace Bitmap dialog box, as follows:

    Color Threshold
    Determines how close colors have to be to be considered the same color and represented in the same shape. The lower the number, the more intolerant Flash is of color differences, resulting in more vectors, higher file size, and higher visual fidelity. The range is 1 to 500, with each number representing the difference in RGB colors between two pixels. The default value is 100.

    Minimum Area
    Determines how many surrounding pixels Flash considers when analyzing a pixel. This affects how large the resulting shapes are. Higher numbers merge more pixels together into single shapes, resulting in lower image fidelity and smaller file sizes. The range is 1–1000, and the default is 8.

    Curve Fit
    Controls how much smoothing Flash applies to curves. The drop-down menu has six increasingly smooth settings, ranging from Pixels to Very Smooth. Higher smooth settings result in lower fidelity to the original bitmap and smaller file sizes. The default setting is Normal.

Corner Threshold

Controls how much sharp corners are smoothened. The drop-down menu has three settings, ranging from Many Corners to Few Corners. The middle option, Normal, is the default.

5. Click OK. Depending on the settings you entered and your computer's processing capabilities, the tracing could take several seconds or minutes. When the tracing is finished, the original bitmap is replaced with the vector version of the image.

6. If desired, you can delete the bitmap from the library.

Tracing bitmap images requires you to balance the competing needs of file size and simplicity, on the one hand, and fidelity to the original image on the other. The process usually requires trial and error. Remember to use Edit → Undo to bring an image back to its original state, so you can try again.

One strategy for tracing bitmaps is to trace two instances of the same bitmap—one using low settings (yielding high quality), and one using high settings (yielding simple shapes). Then composite the two versions together using the high-quality source for important areas of the graphic and the low-quality source for less important parts of the graphic.

When you have traced a bitmap, you can sometimes further optimize the vectorized version using the Optimize feature in Flash. To use the feature, select the entire shape you want to optimize (e.g., the entire vectorized version of the bitmap) and select Modify → Shape → Optimize. The Optimize Curves dialog box will appear, prompting you for a few settings before it runs. Set the Smoothing slider based on how much you want Flash to smooth out the curves in the shape. Generally, the more smoothing you apply, the less it will resemble the original, but the greater the reduction in file size. Because you can undo after running the Optimize feature, you can use trial and error to find the setting that is most appropriate for your artwork. The Use Multiple Passes feature will automatically run the optimization repeatedly until it has determined that the shape is fully optimized. Typically, you will find it helpful to keep the Use Multiple Passes option checked unless you find that it is optimizing too much. When you've got the settings as you want, click the OK button to run the optimization. Depending on the complexity of the shape, it may take a second, or it may take many seconds. Once the optimization is done, deselect the shape on stage to see the effect. If it is acceptable, you don't need to take any further steps. If the optimization rendered the shape unrecognizable, you can undo and reapply with different settings.

If the Optimize feature didn't get enough of a file size reduction, you can still further optimize the shape using the smooth and straighten features. Using the Selection tool, select the traced bitmap shape. Then click on the Smooth or Straighten buttons at the bottom of the Tools panel. Or, optionally, choose Modify → Shape → Smooth or Modify → Shape → Straighten from the menus. You can apply smooth or straighten more than once. But check after each application to make sure that the traced bitmap shape still looks recognizable.

The following sequence of images shows the differences between different versions of a traced bitmap. The first is the original bitmap before being traced. When exported in the SWF, the bitmap in the example accounts for 56KB. The second image is a version that has been traced with a color threshold of 50, minimum area of 4 pixels, curve fit of normal, and corner threshold of normal. When exported in the SWF, the traced bitmap artwork accounts for 44KB. The third image is an optimized version of the second. The optimization was run with the smoothing set to maximum and using multiple passes. When exported in the SWF, the artwork accounts for 31KB. And the fourth image is a version of the third with further smoothing applied. When exported in the SWF, it accounts for 26KB.

Figure 6-1. You can optimize traced bitmaps using the Optimize feature as well as the Smooth and Straighten features

See Also

Recipe 6.1

6.5 Animating Bitmaps

Problem

You want to animate a bitmap graphic.

Solution

Use frame-by-frame animation; or encapsulate the bitmap in a symbol, and apply a motion tween or use ActionScript to animate the symbol.

Discussion

If you want to animate a bitmap, you can use frame-by-frame animation, motion tweens, or scripted animation. The only type of animation you cannot use with bitmaps is the shape tween (though you can shape-tween the rectangular box bounding the bitmap). Each of these types of animation works as described in Chapter 4. The only difference is that to apply a motion tween to a bitmap or animate it using ActionScript, you must first enclose it within a symbol, such as a graphic symbol (motion tweens only) or a movie clip symbol.

To improve the quality of bitmap animations, you might experiment with the following:

- Break apart the bitmap by choosing Modify → Break Apart. Use this technique even if the bitmap is enclosed within a graphic or movie clip symbol.

- Disallow smoothing. To do so, select a bitmap in the library, and click the Properties button at the bottom of the library. In the Bitmap Properties dialog box, uncheck Allow Smoothing.

- Change the bitmap's compression to Lossless (PNG/GIF). Though this option may increase the file size of the movie, it is often the JPEG compression that is to blame for banded and flickering bitmap animations, especially when the bitmap is scaled in an animation, such as zooming in or out. The Compression setting can also be found in the Bitmap Properties dialog box.

- Trace the bitmap to convert it to a vector graphic. This option is often not practical, but if the bitmap contains large regions of solid color, you'll often achieve better results if you convert it to vector graphics.

- Increase the frame rate. This may improve the appearance of bitmap animations.

See Also

Recipe 4.1, Recipe 6.2, Recipe 6.4, Recipe 6.6

6.6   Optimizing Bitmaps for Export

Problem

You want to optimize the image quality and file size of bitmap graphics included in .swf files.

Solution

Flash enables you to specify a default optimization setting for bitmap graphics as well as settings for individual graphics.

Discussion

Bitmap graphics can increase the overall file size of a Flash .*swf* file quickly, so it is important that you minimize their impact on file size as much as possible. To ensure the smallest possible file size, Flash compresses every bitmap included in an .*swf* file, using either JPEG (Joint Photographic Experts Group) compression or a lossless form of compression, such as PNG (Portable Network Graphic) or GIF (Graphic Interchange Format). The primary difference between the two is that JPEG compression is *lossy*, while PNG and GIF compression is *lossless*:

Lossy compression
> In this compression process, some information is removed. The more information that is removed, the lower the overall file quality, and the smaller the overall file size. The JPEG format that Flash uses is efficient at minimizing the file size of digital photographs without excess degradation of quality. Lossy compression is applied in degrees—a Quality setting ranging from 0 to 100 determines how aggressively Flash compresses the file. With more compression (that is, lower Quality) comes greater file size savings and greater degradation of image quality.

Lossless compression
> In this compression process, all data is preserved; it is just stored more efficiently. With lossless compression, the overall file size is reduced, yet the image suffers no loss in quality. However, it is generally not capable of the same degree of file size savings as JPEG.

By default, Flash follows two rules when exporting bitmaps, both of which you may customize:

- Imported JPEGs retain their original settings. Flash assumes that imported JPEGs have already been optimized, and it does not compress them further.
- All other bitmap types are exported with lossy JPEG compression, with a JPEG Quality setting of 80. In addition, smoothing, or anti-aliasing, is automatically applied. A Quality setting of 80 is a good default choice, because in most cases it is able to compress the image significantly while maintaining the overall image well.

You can control how Flash compresses any individual bitmap, and you can also specify the default JPEG Quality setting for all bitmaps in the document. Any setting you specify for an individual image supersedes the default export settings, which are applied only to images whose individual settings have not been specified.

To set the default bitmap settings, follow these steps:

1. Choose File → Publish Settings. The Publish Settings dialog box appears, in which you can specify how Flash exports the movie.
2. Click the Flash tab. If the Flash tab is not visible, check the Flash (*.swf*) checkbox in the Formats tab.
3. Adjust the JPEG Quality slider to a higher setting to output higher-quality bitmaps with larger file sizes, or to a lower setting to create lower file sizes and lower-quality images. The default is 80.

4. Click OK to save the settings and exit the dialog box. These settings apply to the active document only and will not affect any other Flash movie.

If you have an image with special needs—for example, one that needs to be exported with particularly high quality, or does not compress well with JPEG compression—you can specify the export settings for that image individually. These settings are specified in the Bitmap Properties dialog box, which is accessed by selecting the bitmap in the library and clicking the Properties button in the bottom of the library or selecting the Properties option from the context menu.

The Bitmap Properties dialog box has a number of settings that enable you to specify how the graphic should be exported:

Allow Smoothing

Checking this option adds anti-aliasing to the exported graphic, blurring hard edges. In most files, the effects of this setting are imperceptible and have little to no effect on file size. As a rule of thumb, check it for non-animated bitmaps, and uncheck it for bitmaps that you intend to animate.

Compression

Specify whether the graphic should be exported using lossy JPEG compression or lossless PNG/GIF compression. JPEG compression almost always yields increased file size savings, even for graphics with large regions of solid color and sharp edges, such as text. The only situation in which you should choose lossless compression is when bitmaps exported using lossy JPEG compression do not reach the level of quality you need.

Use Imported JPEG Data

This setting only appears if lossy JPEG compression is specified as the Compression type, and the imported graphic is a *.jpg* file. If both of these conditions are true, this option appears and is checked by default, which prevents the file from being compressed twice—once in the original editor and then again in Flash. Unchecking this option activates a Quality setting, which enables you to specify the compression amount for this image; the range is 0 to 100, just as it is in the Publish Settings dialog.

Use Document Default Quality

This setting only appears if lossy JPEG compression is specified as the Compression type, and the imported graphic is not a *.jpg* file (for example, if it is a *.png* or *.gif* file). When checked, the graphic is exported using lossy JPEG compression with the Quality setting specified in the Publish Settings dialog. When unchecked, a Quality setting appears, which enables you to specify the compression amount for this image.

The settings applied in this dialog box affect all instances of a bitmap symbol.

The discussion in the recipe to this point has centered on what you can do in Flash to optimize bitmaps. However, the most important decisions you'll make regarding a bitmap, which affect its quality and file size, occur before the bitmap is even imported into Flash. These decisions take place in the graphics editor from which the bitmap was exported—Fireworks, Photoshop, Paint Shop Pro, and so on.

The following techniques will help you import optimal bitmaps into Flash:

- Set the resolution to 72 dots or pixels per inch. In Fireworks and Photoshop, the resolution can be set in the Image Size dialog box. In Fireworks, Modify → Canvas → Image Size. In Photoshop, Image → Image Size.

- Set the image to the same dimensions that you intend to use in Flash. That is, avoid resizing bitmaps from within Flash. Enlarging bitmaps in Flash degrades image quality. Shrinking bitmaps in Flash does not enable you to realize any file size savings and may degrade the quality of the bitmap.

- Crop unnecessary portions of the image in your image editor before importing into Flash. Users pay for every pixel, in terms of download time, regardless of its content. Remove any borders and unnecessary white space from the top or edges, including only what you need.

- If you have Fireworks or ImageReady, optimize the graphic for the Web (that is, as a *.jpg*, *.gif*, or *.png* file) prior to export. Although Flash can import other file types, such as *.tiff*, and it can compress them as JPEG files, you should take advantage of the advanced compression interfaces and options available in Fireworks or ImageReady.

You can use the Generate size report in Flash to determine how much file size each bitmap (and every other element of the movie) is using in the *.swf* file. In order to generate the report, open the Publish Settings dialog box (File → Publish Settings). Click the Flash tab within the dialog box, and then check the Generate size report. Then, each time you export the *.swf* file, you'll get a report in the Output panel. The report tells you about how the bytes are distributed on frames and symbols. One section of the report is labeled Bitmaps, and it will tell you information about each of the bitmaps being exported in the *.swf* file. An example is as follows:

```
Bitmap                    Compressed   Compression
----------------------    ----------   -------------------
image2.jpg                    56642     1228800  Imported JPEG=102
```

The Compressed column reports on the number of bytes that the bitmap occupies in the exported file.

See Also

Recipe 6.1

6.7   Using Bitmaps with Transparency

Problem

You want to import a bitmap into Flash, but you want to retain its transparency.

Solution

Use a GIF or PNG.

Discussion

Flash can import bitmaps and retain transparency for the images. However, you have to make sure that the file you are importing actually has transparency information. The two formats capable of having transparency information that Flash can import are GIF and PNG. GIF is a lossless format best suited for content with no gradients and few colors. PNG is a lossless format, meaning that you should use this format if your bitmap contains gradient transparencies.

6.8 Masking Page Elements

Problem

You want to block or reveal one or more elements using another element.

Solution

Create a mask.

Discussion

You can use masks to hide and reveal contents of one or more layers using the contents of another layer. Every working mask has two parts: the *mask* element(s), whose outline reveals the contents of the masked element(s), and the *masked* element(s), which is hidden except where it lies directly beneath the mask. Reflecting this distinction, Flash enables you to create special mask and masked layers, which hold mask and masked elements, respectively. A mask layer is a special kind of layer, like a motion guide layer, whose stage contents are not shown in the SWF, but rather are used to reveal whatever is placed beneath them in masked layers. Where the stage is empty in a mask layer, all content in the masked layer is hidden.

To create a mask, follow these steps:

1. Create the content that you want to use as the mask. You can use any kind of visible content in any combination, including vector art, text (using embedded fonts), symbol instances, and imported bitmaps.

2. Choose Modify → Timeline → Layer Properties, and select the Mask from Type radio group.

3. On a different layer, insert the content that you want masked. Again, it can be any kind of visible content.

4. In the layer stack to the left of the timeline, drag the layer that you want masked so that it is directly beneath the layer that you want to mask it.

When you release, the masked layer will be indented beneath the mask layer, and both layers will have special blue mask icons beside them.

 Giving layers meaningful layer names, a best practice to begin with, is especially helpful when dealing with complex layer clusters, such as mask- or motion-guided tween layer clusters.

You can preview masks in the authoring environment by locking all layers that are a part of the mask group, including the mask and masked layers. You can lock layers one at a time by clicking the Lock Layer modifier for each layer. Alternatively, you can right-click (Windows) or Control-click (Macintosh) any layer in a mask group and select Show Masking, which toggles all the layers in the mask group to the locked position. To edit any part of a mask, unlock the affected layer.

In addition to the basic features just outlined, Flash masks have a few features and limitations:

- You can mask multiple layers. That is, one mask layer can have multiple masked layers associated with it. Relative to each other, multiple masked layers behave like they would if they weren't masked: content on higher layers obscures contents on lower layers.

- You cannot nest a mask layer within another mask layer. That is, you cannot mask a mask.

- Contents in mask layers fully reveal contents in masked layers. That is, a shape with 50% opacity in a mask layer still reveals the masked layer 100%.

- Mask layer clusters are not permanent. You can revert any mask or masked layer back to a normal layer or add new layers to the group at any time. A layer's status can be changed in the Layer Properties dialog box.

One popular effect is the text mask, in which text appears to be filled with a bitmap photo or some other type of advanced fill. This effect is easily achieved by placing text in its own layer, converting the layer to a mask layer, and placing a bitmap, gradient, or other image in a masked layer.

You can remove a layer from a mask group by dragging it out of the influence of the mask layer, or by selecting it and choosing Modify → Layer and choosing Normal as the layer type.

See Also

Recipe 6.3

6.9 Animating Masks

Problem

You want to create an animated mask.

Solution

Use any of Flash's animation tools to animate the content in the mask layer, except a motion-guided tween. For motion-guided tween masks, make a movie clip within which the motion-guided tween resides, and use an instance of that movie clip on the mask layer.

Discussion

Nearly all of Flash's animation features can be applied to masks, including both motion and shape tweens, frame-by-frame animation, and ActionScript-based animation.

One common animated mask effect is that of a spotlight. It is an easy effect to create and animate:

1. Create the graphic of the background as it should appear with the spotlight off it.

2. In a new layer, copy and paste the background in place (Edit → Paste in Place). This layer will contain the version of the background when shone in the spotlight.

3. Brighten the colors of the elements in this layer.

4. Create a layer above the existing two layers, and draw a circle in it.

5. Set the top layer, with the circle in it, to a mask layer, and drag the second layer so that it comes under the influence of the new mask layer.

6. If desired, lock all three layers to preview the effect. Where the circle appears, the background should be brighter. When you are finished, unlock the layers.

7. Convert the circle mask to a movie clip symbol, and assign it an instance name of mSpotlightMask.

8. Add a new layer to the timeline, select the first keyframe, and open the Actions panel.

9. Add the following code to the Actions panel.

```
mSpotlightMask.startDrag(true);
```

Flash is capable of more sophisticated animation than motion tweens, and you can take advantage of its advanced animation features when animating masks. For example, you can create a movie clip that contains a spinning shape, such as a square, and then motion-tween that movie clip instance on the main timeline as a mask. The result would be a nested animation mask, which would reveal the masked contents using complex motion.

Attempting to apply motion guides to masks can present an issue that you'll need to work around. Motion-guided tweens require a special layer, which contains the motion path. Motion guide layers and mask layers cannot be used in conjunction with one another on the same timeline. You can work around this limitation by placing the motion-guide-tween inside a movie clip, and then placing an instance of that movie clip on the mask layer. The following steps outline a basic process for combining motion-guided tweens and masks:

1. Create a layer, and place the artwork you want to mask within a keyframe on the layer. Make sure to give the layer a name that indicates what is contained on it. For example, if you place an instance of a bitmap of the Parthenon, you might label the layer Parthenon.

2. Create a new layer above the layer from step 1. Give the layer a label that indicates that it will mask another layer as well as the contents it will be masking. For example, if the layer will be masking a layer with an image of the Parthenon, consider using a label of Parthenon Mask.

3. Within the layer for the mask, draw the shape of the basic mask.

4. Select the entire mask artwork and convert it to a movie clip symbol by pressing F8. Make sure that you select Movie Clip as the behavior and give it an appropriate symbol name.

5. After you've clicked OK in the Convert to Symbol dialog box, the new symbol will be added to the library, the selected artwork on the stage will be converted to an instance of the symbol, and you will be returned to the timeline within which you had just been working. Double-click on the mask artwork symbol instance on that stage to open it in editing mode.

6. Within the symbol's timeline, add a new layer named Motion Guide, and use any of the drawing tools that create lines to draw the motion guide path.

7. Select the mask artwork and convert it to a movie clip symbol. Remember, because you're creating a motion guide, the artwork must be a symbol instance. When you've converted the artwork to a symbol you should have a movie clip nested within a movie clip.

8. Complete the motion-guided tween appropriately. See Recipe 4.2 for more details.

9. Return to the original timeline that contains the content you want to mask as well as the instance of the mask movie clip. In steps 1 and 2, you created two layers for the mask and masked content, with the layer with the mask being placed above the layer with the masked content. So you should be able to set the prop-

erties of the upper layer so that it's a mask layer, and the lower layer should automatically set its properties to be masked. For more information, see Recipe 6.8.

Flash allows you to do many things in various ways. For example, you can create a new symbol and draw the artwork within it rather than drawing the artwork and converting it to a symbol. Therefore, the preceding steps are intended as a guideline to assist you. When you're comfortable making motion-guided masks by following the steps, you can then adopt whatever workflow makes sense for you.

See Also

Recipe 3.17, Recipe 4.1, Recipe 4.12, Recipe 6.8

CHAPTER 7

Working with Text Basics

Text is one of the ways in which you can communicate with users in a Flash movie. You can use text to label buttons and movie clips, or you can use text to display detailed information to the user. You can display text that you have hardcoded into your Flash movie at authoring time or dynamic text that you generate at runtime. Equally important is that text is one of the means by which users can communicate with your Flash movie. Input text fields allow users to enter values such as their username, a quantity of a product, or information for a feedback form.

Flash text is simple, because you can accomplish a lot with text in very intuitive ways. At the same time, Flash text is complex, because Flash offers many options to manipulate and format text. Although this chapter focuses on solutions that don't require scripting, we'll see how ActionScript can offer powerful control over text. But don't panic—the ActionScript in this chapter is minimal and easy to understand.

There are a few basic things you should know about Flash text while reading the recipes in this chapter. Flash supports three kinds of text: static, dynamic, and input. Use static text to display text that does not need to update at runtime. If the text is likely to update at runtime, use dynamic text, which you can modify at runtime. And lastly, input text allows users to enter text values into your movie. Input text is a subset of dynamic text, in that you can modify them in the same way at runtime. The distinction is that users can enter values only into input text.

When you create text at authoring time, Flash defaults to static text. However, after you have selected a different text type, that text type is retained and used for subsequent text fields that you create unless you again choose a different text type. If you accidentally create a text field of the wrong text type, there is no need for alarm. You can always select the text field and modify its text type setting after the fact.

Unlike text fields created at authoring time, text fields created at runtime default to dynamic. And, in fact, you cannot even create a static text field at runtime, because static text fields are not true objects, in that they do not have instance names. Text fields created at runtime (meaning they are created using ActionScript) must be true objects.

One major benefit of using Flash as a medium for design on the Web is that you have the option of embedding the font outlines in the SWF. Thus you can be assured that the text will render the same way on every computer regardless of whether the computer has a particular font installed. Note that there are trade-offs with embedding fonts and that you also have the option of using system fonts when appropriate.

In this chapter, the topics of the recipes apply to all types of text (static, dynamic, and input) unless stated otherwise. However, the focus of this chapter is on authoring time text, and therefore the emphasis is on static text. Chapter 8 discusses more dynamic text topics.

7.1   Adding Static Text to the Stage

Problem

You want to add static text to your Flash movie.

Solution

Select the Text tool, and in the Property inspector, select Static Text as the text type. Then draw the text field on the stage, and enter a text value.

Discussion

Static text refers to text that you can create at authoring time but that cannot be modified or controlled by ActionScript. Static text is ideal for labels (meaning labels that you place on the stage, not to be confused with labels for layers within the authoring environment) and for any text values you want to hardcode into your Flash movie. Static text is the most basic kind of text you can add to a movie, because it does not require (or even allow) you to assign it an instance name or use ActionScript to assign its values.

There are four basic steps to creating static text in your movie:

1. Select the Text tool either by clicking on the Text button in the toolbar or by pressing the keyboard shortcut (T).

2. Open the Property inspector (Window → Properties) and make sure that Static Text is selected in the text type menu. The Property inspector appears in the lower portion of the Flash authoring application by default.

3. Draw a text field on the stage using the Text tool by clicking the mouse button and dragging out the text field outline. You can resize the text field later on, so you don't have to be exact. The mouse pointer shows a crosshair with an "A" next to it, and the text field that you draw is designated by a dashed line. After

you have deselected the text field, the outline disappears, and it does not show up in the exported Flash movie.

4. When you release the mouse button to stop drawing the text field, the text field automatically becomes selected, and the text input cursor appears within it. Also, notice that the outline becomes a solid line to indicate that it is selected for input. At this point, you should either use the keyboard to enter text or use the Edit → Paste command to paste text from the clipboard. If you deselect the text field without entering any text, Flash deletes the field and you will have to draw another.

After you have successfully created a static text field, you can reposition it on the stage using the Selection tool. You can also select and modify the text using the Text tool.

7.2 Changing the Appearance of Text

Problem

You want to change the appearance of text, including the font and/or the properties of the font (size, color, bold, or italic).

Solution

Select the entire text field or highlight the portion of the text you want to modify, and then set the appropriate values using the Property inspector.

Discussion

Modifying the font and font properties of text fields in Flash is the same as in most other applications. If you select the entire text field with the Selection tool, you can modify all the text contained within it. On the other hand, to modify a portion of the text, use the Text tool to highlight the part that you want to change. In either case, you can modify the font and font properties from the Property inspector.

You can also modify the appearance of dynamic text fields using HTML tags. See Recipe 8.12 for more information on how to accomplish this.

7.3 Making Text Follow a Curve

Problem

You want to add to your Flash movie text that follows a curve.

Solution

Use another application like Freehand or Illustrator to create text that follows a path, and then import that content into the Flash document.

Discussion

Flash does not currently allow you to attach text to a path or curve as other drawing applications do. However, you *can* use another program such as Freehand or Illustrator to create the text as you want it, and then import that text as paths into your Flash document.

With both Freehand and Illustrator you have two options. First of all, Flash allows you to import both Freehand and Illustrator (versions up to Illustrator 10) files directly. You can select File → Import to Stage or File → Import to Library, and then select the file that you want to import.

First, let's look at what you need to consider when you import a Freehand file. When you try to import, you will be presented with the Freehand Import dialog box, and you will be prompted to make a few choices. For single-page Freehand documents, the first two sections don't necessarily apply. But if you look at the third section, Options, you will see an option to Maintain Text Blocks. Make sure this box is unchecked. In the case of text attached to a curve, this option should not make a difference, because the text will be imported as paths (meaning that it's no longer editable text) regardless. But for other kinds of text, such as subscripted and superscripted text, if you leave the box checked, Flash will not import the text as you want it to appear.

If you use Illustrator, you can also import those files into Flash (up to Illustrator 10). Just as with Freehand files, you select the Import or Import to Library option from the File menu, and select the Illustrator file that you want to import. The Illustrator Import dialog box does not give you an option to convert text to outlines, so if you need to ensure that your text will display properly in Flash, you must convert the fonts to outlines in the Illustrator file itself.

In addition to allowing you to import Freehand and Illustrator files, Flash also allows you to import *.swf* files. And both Freehand and Illustrator allow you to export to the SWF format. When you export a Freehand or Illustrator file to an SWF, the resulting SWF contains all the text as outlines.

As an alternative, you can also create your text in an application, such as Fireworks or Photoshop, save it as an image file (PNG works well), and import the image file into Flash. Use this option only if you don't have a vector-drawing application like Freehand or Illustrator. Using vector-based applications allows you to import shapes and paths into your Flash movie. Shapes and paths scale well and require minimal file size. Images, on the other hand, do not scale well (they get pixelated) and they require more file size. If you save the text from Fireworks (or whatever application you use) as a PNG, Flash will give you some options when you import it. Make sure that you select the "Rasterize if Necessary to Maintain Appearance" option in the Text options section.

It's worth noting that you *can* manually place text along a curve using Flash. However, it can be a painstaking operation. The steps are as follows:

1. Use one of the drawing tools to draw a curve, and make the layer a guide layer.

2. Make a text field with the text value you want to attach to a curve.

3. Select the text field, and select Modify → Break Apart to break it into individual text fields for each character.

4. Use the Selection tool and/or the arrow keys to move and nudge the characters to the correct locations.

5. Use the Free Transform tool to rotate the characters to the curve.

7.4   Adding Drop Shadows to Text

Problem

You want to add drop shadows to your text.

Solution

Use the drop shadow filter.

If publishing to Flash Player 7 or lower, consider using the drop shadow timeline effect.

Optionally, create a copy of the original text, and offset it from the original to create a shadow effect.

Discussion

If you are publishing to Flash Player 8 and higher, you can use the drop shadow filter effect to apply the most convincing effect versus the other options that are readily available. The drop shadow filter allows you to set a variety of parameters. Likely the most relevant parameters are the blur, angle, distance, and color. You can apply a filter by selecting the text on stage and clicking on the Filters tab in the Property inspector.

The blur parameter determines how soft an edge the drop shadow has. The blur parameter is what visually differentiates the filter drop shadow from the other techniques described in this recipe. Prior to Flash 8 and filter effects, Flash did not have a built-in way to achieve a convincing lighting effect with drop shadows, because the edges were always too crisp. But with the blur parameter, you can soften the edges to make the drop shadow appear as though it is actually cast from an object with natural lighting—which causes a diffusion. Though not necessarily required, most frequently the blur applied to the *x* and *y* directions is equal for drop shadows. The greater the number, the softer the edges are. A value of 0 makes a drop shadow that duplicates the hard edges of the object from which it was cast.

The angle determines the direction from which the light source appears to be originating. The value is specified in degrees, which you can control via the dial that pops up from the Property inspector. The default value is 45, which casts a shadow as though the light source is located at the upper left of the object.

The distance is the number of pixels the drop shadow is cast from the object (in two-dimensional space). The default is 5. The greater the number, the further away the object appears from the surface onto which the drop shadow is cast. A value of 0 lines up with the edges of the object. That means the drop shadow isn't visible, and it appears as though the object is resting on the surface. Using a value of 0 is only useful if you are tweening to or from that value to give the appearance that the surface is nearing the object.

Drop shadows are the optimal technique, not only because they provide the most convincing effects, but also because they are so easily animated. You can apply motion tweens to changes in the parameter values for filter effects. For example, if you apply a drop shadow to text on frame 1, you can then add a new keyframe (F6) at frame 20, change the drop shadow filter parameters on frame 20 so they differ from those on frame 1, and then apply a motion tween between frames 1 and 20. Flash will automatically animate the transition between the settings.

Note that the drop shadow filter applies exactly what the name suggests—drop shadows. It does not apply perspective shadows, in which the light source appears to be at the side of the object, such that the shadow that is cast is a skewed version of the object. If you want to apply a perspective shadow, continue reading the last portion of this recipe.

If you are authoring to an earlier version of Flash Player, you cannot use filter effects. Perhaps the simplest way to add a drop shadow in that case is to use a timeline effect. In order to apply the drop shadow using the built-in timeline effect, complete the following steps:

1. Select the text instance on stage using the Selection tool.

2. Select Insert → Timeline Effects → Effects → Drop Shadow. Alternatively, you can right-click/Control-click on the instance, and choose Timeline Effects → Effects → Drop Shadow from the context menu.

3. In the dialog box, adjust the settings to create the drop shadow effect you want. You can change the color of the shadow, the transparency, and the x and y offsets relative to the text from which the shadow is being cast. If you want to see a preview of the effect after changing the settings, click the Update Preview button in the upper-right corner of the dialog box.

4. Apply the drop shadow by clicking Apply.

You should see the drop shadow applied to the text instance you had selected. If you want to edit the effect, you can select the instance on the stage and choose Modify → Timeline Effects → Edit Effect. Alternatively, you can right-click/Control-click the instance and select Timeline Effects → Edit Effect from the context menu. The dialog box opens, and you can adjust the settings and then reapply them.

The drop shadow timeline effect works. However, it has several drawbacks. One drawback is that it automatically places the text inside a graphic symbol. That result may or may not be an issue, depending on what you plan to do with the text later on. Another drawback of the built-in drop shadow effect is that it really doesn't look much like an actual shadow. It is just a simple duplication of the text with different color, alpha, and x- and y-coordinate settings. A much more realistic drop shadow effect can be achieved with the following steps:

1. Add your text to the stage. Consider naming the layer something descriptive, such as Original Text.

2. Select the text and copy it.

3. Add a new layer below the layer with the original text. Give the layer a descriptive label, such as Drop Shadow Text.

4. Paste the copy of the original text into the new layer you just created in step 3. You may find it helpful to use the paste-in-place feature so that the copy is placed on the stage with the same coordinates as the original. Use the mouse and/or keyboard to place the copy at an appropriate offset from the original text.

5. Adjust the color of the copy text. Often black is an appropriate shadow color choice. You don't need to make the color of the shadow too light yet. You can accommodate that in just a few steps when you lower the alpha.

6. Make sure that the copy text (the shadow) is selected, and break it apart twice so that it is treated as shapes instead of text. You can break apart the text by choosing Modify → Break Apart. Alternatively, you can use the keyboard shortcut of Ctrl-B or Command-B. Remember to break it apart twice. If you break it apart only once, each character will still be treated as text.

7. Make sure that the shapes are selected. If you have not clicked elsewhere after step 6, they should still be selected. If you need to select the shapes, and if you haven't yet done so, you may find it helpful to lock the layer containing the original text so that you don't accidentally select it along with the shadow shapes on the layer below it. With all the shapes selected, choose Modify → Shape → Expand Fill.

8. Choose appropriate settings for the expand fill operation. The default values of 4 and 4 will likely work well in most cases. If your text uses a very large font, consider settings higher than 4 and 4. Click OK when ready. If you find that the settings you chose were not quite correct, you can undo and then complete steps 7 and 8 again.

9. With all the shapes still selected, press F8 to convert them to a symbol. You may choose to convert them to either a movie clip or a graphic symbol. Make sure to give the symbol an appropriate name, such as Drop Shadow Text.

10. The artwork should be converted into an instance of the symbol. With the instance selected, open the Property inspector, and select Alpha from the Color Styles menu.

11. Using the control to the right of the Color Styles menu, adjust the alpha setting to an appropriate value. Values under 35% typically work well.

You can also convert your drop shadow into a perspective shadow with just a few extra steps. A drop shadow appears as though the object casting the shadow is parallel with the surface onto which the shadow is being cast. A perspective shadow, on the other hand, appears as though the object is nonparallel to the surface—typically as though it is perpendicular. In other words, a perspective shadow is the kind of shadow your text casts if it is standing up. To create such a shadow, simply complete steps 1 through 11 in the previous list, and then use the Free Transform tool to skew and shorten the height of the shadow instance.

7.5   Changing the Width of Static Text Fields (Without Stretching the Text)

Problem

You want to resize the width of an existing static text field without stretching the text.

Solution

Use the Text tool to select the text field so that the resizing square appears in the upper-right corner of it. Then, drag the resizing square so that the text field is the width that you want. Optionally, use the Selection tool, and drag any of the resizing squares.

Discussion

You can change the width of static text fields (the bounding box) using Text tool and the resizing square that appears in the upper-right corner or the Selection tool and any of the resizing squares. The height of a static text field is, however, determined solely by the font's height. In order to access the resizing square using the Text tool, you must select the text field such that the input cursor appears in the text. (It will also work if you use the Selection tool and double-click on a text field.) When the resizing square appears, you should click it and drag it to adjust the width of the text field. Optionally, you can use the Selection tool to change the dimensions of the text field from any of the four resizing squares that appear on the four corners.

Do not use the Free Transform tool or the Property inspector to change the dimensions of a static text field unless you want to stretch the text. The only exception to that rule is when the text field uses *device fonts*—fonts that are found on the client computer. However, as long as the font is embedded, Flash will scale the fonts along with the text field when using either of those techniques, as discussed in the next recipe.

7.6   Resizing Text Fields (Stretching the Text)

Problem

You want to stretch a text field horizontally and/or vertically such that its text is also stretched.

Solution

Select the text field on the stage, and modify the height and width values in the Property inspector. Or, use the Free Transform tool.

Discussion

There are two different kinds of resizing that you can perform on text—resizing the bounding box (which does not affect the width of the text within the text field) or resizing the width and height of the entire text field, including the text within it. The latter of these two types of resizing can make the text appear as though you have stretched (or squished) it.

You can accomplish this stretching effect by selecting the text on the stage and then modifying the height and width properties in the Property inspector or using the Free Transform tool.

This technique works only for embedded fonts. Because static text uses embedded fonts by default, you can stretch and squish it without any additional steps. If you want to use this technique with dynamic or input text fields, then you need to make sure that you are embedding the fonts. Also, this technique can be applied only at authoring time.

 Note that even though static text fields use embedded fonts by default, it is possible to use device fonts with static text fields if you select _sans, _serif, or _typewriter as the font face (see Recipe 7.9). If you use device fonts with any text field—even static text—you cannot scale the text field such that the fonts are stretched or squished.

7.7   Setting Margins, Indentation, and Leading

Problem

You want to adjust the margins, indentation, and the leading (the space between lines of text).

Solution

Select the text you want to modify, and adjust the values in the Format Options dialog box.

Discussion

You can modify line spacing, indentation, and right and left margin values from the Format Options dialog box, which is accessible from the Property inspector by clicking on the Format button. First, you should select the text on the stage that you want to modify. If you want to affect all the text contained within a text field, use the Selection tool to select the entire text field. If you want to modify the values for a single line within the text field, use the Text tool to place the cursor within the appropriate line of text. It does not matter whether you place the cursor at the beginning, end, or middle of the line, or even if you choose to highlight the entire line of text. Margin and leading changes affect the entire line of text.

With a text field or a line of text within it selected, open the Format Options dialog box. Then, adjust the values either by entering a new value with the keyboard or by adjusting the sliders using the mouse.

Flash uses pixels for units of measurement for text margins and indentation. The valid range for both right and left margins is between 0 and 720 pixels. The default value is 0, and that means that the text is flush with the right and/or left boundary of the text field. Indentation, however, has a valid range of −720 to 720, with a default of 0. Indentation is applied to the first line in a text field and to each line immediately after a hard return. An indentation is relative to the left margin and can never be less than the left boundary of the text field. For example, if the left margin is set to 12 and the indentation is set to 12, the indented lines will appear 12 pixels to the right of the non-indented lines, or 24 pixels to the right of the left boundary. If the left margin is set to 12 and the indentation is set to −6, the indented lines start at 6 pixels to the left of the non-indented lines, or 6 pixels to the right of the left boundary. However, if the left margin is set to 12, and the indentation is set to −24, the indented lines will appear 12 pixels to the left of the non-indented lines, or flush with the left boundary of the text field.

Flash calculates line spacing differently from margins. Instead of measuring in pixels, Flash uses points for these calculations. The difference is that whereas pixels are an absolute measurement (a pixel is always the same size), points are relative to font size. The same point value translates into more or less actual space when the font size changes. Line spacing is measured from line descender to line ascender—those are the imaginary lines that border each line of text on the top and bottom. The default line-spacing value of 0 means that the descender of the top line is touching the ascender of the subsequent line of text. However, because these imaginary lines have thickness, the actual text does not touch with a value of 0. Negative line-spacing values bring the lines of text closer, and positive line-spacing values move the lines of text further apart. Be mindful, as using too small a value will cause your lines of text to overlap.

Note that the margin, indentation, and leading settings work reliably only for text with embedded font outlines. If you use device fonts or font family groups (_sans, _serif, or _typewriter), the settings will not work reliably.

7.8   Setting Space Between Characters

Problem

You want to modify the kerning (spacing between characters) of the text in a text field.

Solution

Select the text you want to modify, and adjust the character spacing value within the Property inspector.

Discussion

Flash lets you quickly adjust text kerning by changing the character spacing value. First, select the text you want to modify (either the entire field or just a portion of the text within it). Then, use the character spacing menu to set the kerning.

Possible values for kerning range from –60 to 60, and the units of measurement are points. The physical space that a point represents is relative to the font size such that the larger the font size, the larger the space for a point. The default value for kerning is 0, and this means that there is no space between the imaginary right boundary of one character and the imaginary left boundary of another. As the point value increases, the characters move further apart, and as the value decreases, they move closer together. A value of –60 means that the left boundaries of the two characters are aligned. In practical terms, this value means that the characters overlap, and that two matching characters will occupy exactly the same space, so that they appear as one.

You can set the kerning for an entire text field, but you can also assign individual kerning to each character. The kerning value for a character indicates how much space should appear between it and the following letter. So if you want to modify the spacing between two characters, use the mouse to select (highlight) the first of the two, and adjust its kerning value.

Realistically, you can use the kerning features only with embedded fonts. When you try to use kerning with device fonts, you will not get reliable results. The spacing between letters cannot be adjusted with device fonts, but the kerning settings may result in some characters being pushed to another line.

7.9   Optimizing Static Text for Minimum File Size

Problem

You want to optimize the Flash movie's file size by using fonts on the client computer rather than embedding the fonts in the SWF.

Solution

Select the static text, and check the Use Device Fonts checkbox in the Property inspector.

Discussion

When you use static text in your movies, Flash embeds the font outline in the Flash movie by default. This result has several benefits:

- Embedded fonts are anti-aliased, resulting in smoother-looking text at larger point sizes.
- Embedded fonts can be scaled, rotated, and alpha tweened.
- The text will always appear in the correct font regardless of what client is playing the movie.

Although it may sound like embedded fonts are the optimal solution in every scenario, they have at least one major drawback: embedded fonts increase file size. If you embed the font outlines for every character in a font, it can add 10KB or more for a standard Latin character font. It can add even more when you embed nonstandard Latin characters. Double-byte fonts, such as those used for Chinese and Japanese, can require significantly more file size.

Static text fields embed fonts by default. However, they embed the outlines only for the characters they use. Therefore, a short text field with only a few characters isn't likely to add much in terms of file size to a SWF. However, if you need to embed the outlines for a font in order to display paragraphs of text, it's likely that it will add significantly more to the file size of the SWF.

If you must embed the font, or if you want to embed the font, and the added file size is not an issue for the project, there is no need to use any custom settings. However, if you find that you need to optimize the SWF in terms of file size, Flash lets you specify whether a static text field should use device fonts rather than embedded fonts delivered with the movie. To specify that a static text field should use device fonts, select the text field with the Selection tool, and then select the Use Device Fonts option from the Font rendering method menu in the Property inspector.

In the event that you want to use device fonts in order to reduce file size, plan carefully. For example, if you have two static text fields using Arial as the font, and both text fields contain significant text, it will have little effect on file size if you select Use Device Fonts for just one of the text fields.

Another important thing to keep in mind is what Flash does if it cannot find the device font on the client computer. Flash is designed so that if it cannot find the requested device font, it simply substitutes a default, available font (usually something like Times New Roman). In some situations, you may not care about this kind of substitution. But other times you may want to ensure that the font style at least remains similar by substituting serif fonts for serif fonts, sans serif fonts for sans serif fonts, and so on. Flash provides you with a solution to this problem as well. In the Font selection menu (in the Property inspector), you have three options for what are called device font types. The _sans option will always use the default available sans serif device font, such as Arial or Helvetica. The _serif option tells Flash to use the default available serif device font, such as Times New Roman. And the _typewriter option tells Flash to use the default available monospace font, such as Courier or Courier New.

7.10   Superscripting and Subscripting Characters

Problem

You want to change a character so that it is superscripted or subscripted.

Solution

Select the character or characters using the Text tool, and choose either Subscript or Superscript from the character position menu in the Property inspector.

Discussion

Flash allows you to superscript characters (as in mc^2) and subscript characters (as in x_0) in your text fields easily. First, select the text you want to superscript or subscript using the Text tool. Then, use the character position menu in the Property inspector to select either superscript or subscript.

Flash subscripts and superscripts don't have any additional settings that allow you to specify the number of points or pixels by which you want them to appear above or below the regular text. You *can* adjust the font size for subscripted and superscripted fonts, but if you do so you will notice that the placement relative to the other characters may appear "off." If you want to have more control over the placement and size of subscripted and subscripted text, you should create that text within separate text fields that you can overlay on top of the rest of your text. In order to add the correct spacing into the regular text (in order to accommodate the subscripted and superscripted text you are overlaying), you can adjust the kerning values for individual characters.

Alternatively, you can create superscripted or subscripted text using another program such as Freehand or Illustrator, and then import that content into your Flash movie.

7.11 Making Text Nonselectable

Problem

You want to prevent users from selecting text in a text field when viewing the movie.

Solution

Choose the text field on the stage, and toggle off the Selectable button in the Property inspector (so that it is not selected).

Discussion

By default, Flash text is selectable. Users can use their mouse to highlight and copy text in the movie. This is a feature you may want in many cases. But in other cases, it may not be what you want. For example, if you use text to label a button, you don't want the text to be selectable, because it will interfere with the button functionality. Also, by making text nonselectable, you can make sure that users cannot copy and paste it—which may be something you want to ensure in some cases.

Making text selectable or not is a fairly quick process. You need only to choose the text field on the stage, and then make sure that the Selectable option is toggled to the off position in the Property inspector. The Selectable option is located to the immediate right of the Line type menu in the Property inspector.

7.12 Creating Text Hyperlinks

Problem

You want to add a hyperlink to static text.

Solution

Select the text to which you want to apply the hyperlink, and add the URL to the URL link field within the Property inspector.

Discussion

You can add a hyperlink to the text of a static text field by selecting the text and entering the URL into the URL link field in the Property inspector. You can apply the link to the entire text field by selecting it with the Selection tool, or you can apply the link to just a portion of the text by highlighting it with the Text tool.

Also, notice that there is a Target menu next to the URL link field. If you do not specify a target, the hyperlink opens up in the same browser window and frame as the Flash movie (assuming that the movie is playing in a browser.) Otherwise, you can enter a target frame/window into the Target menu or choose from the four options that are already entered for you:

_blank
> Opens a new browser window.

_parent
> Opens the link in the window that is the parent to the current window.

_self
> Opens the link in the same window/frame. Choosing this option is the same as leaving the target value empty.

_top
> Opens the link in the top frame within the same window in the event that the window contains multiple frames.

 You can add hyperlinks only to horizontal, static text. You cannot add links to any vertical text, and you can add hyperlinks to dynamic text only using ActionScript.

Flash will recognize either absolute or relative URLs. For example, you can add a hyperlink such as http://www.person13.com/fcb/, which is an *absolute* URL, because it includes the domain as well as the logical path. You can also use a relative URL, such as /fcb/, in which the domain is assumed to be the same domain from which the SWF is being served. Be aware, however, that when you use an absolute URL you must provide the protocol portion. In other words, Flash can understand http://www.person13.com/fcb/, but it cannot correctly interpret www.person13.com/fcb/. If you fail to provide the protocol portion of the URL, Flash will interpret the URL as a relative hyperlink.

When the user hovers the mouse over hyperlinked text, the cursor icon changes to a hand instead of the normal arrow. This icon helps to signify that the text is clickable. However, Flash does not provide any other signs to the user that the text contains a hyperlink. Most web browsers interpret HTML hyperlinks by underlining them and changing the font to blue. This convention is understood by most web users, and so you may want to manually create this same effect. You can adjust the font color and underline the hyperlinked text so that the user can easily identify clickable text. See Recipe 8.12 for more information on how to change the text appearance of text in these ways.

Additionally, if you add a hyperlink to text and you later decide you want to remove that link, you can do so by selecting the text and deleting the value in the URL link field in the Property inspector.

7.13   Adding an Email Link to Static Text

Problem

You want to add an email link to static text such that when the user clicks on it, a new email message is opened.

Solution

Apply a hyperlink to the text (see Recipe 8.12) in which the URL is in the form of `mailto:`*`email.address@server.com`*.

Discussion

Recipe 8.12 shows you how to apply a hyperlink to static text. Using the `mailto` protocol, you can also open a new email message. For example, to enter a value into the URL link field that opens a new email message with *joey@person13.com* as the recipient, use `mailto:joey@person13.com`.

You can also specify the subject and body values by appending URL-encoded variables after the email address. For example, `mailto:joey@person13.com?subject=you rock` opens a new email message to *joey@person13.com* with a subject of "you rock," and `mailto:joey@person13.com?subject=you rock&body=a message for you` adds a message body of "a message for you."

The email hyperlink technique works only when the movie is being played in a web browser, because Flash relies on the web browser to have the capability to open the user's mail program. Therefore you cannot control what application is used to create the email message. The application choice is dependent on what default email client has been configured for the web browser. Also, be aware that while the subject and body attributes work for the majority of email clients, there are some for which these attributes are ignored.

7.14   Opening Browser Windows with Specific Parameters Using Static Text

Problem

You want to open a new browser window with specific dimensions (and/or other settings) when the user clicks the static text.

Solution

Apply a hyperlink to the text (see Recipe 8.12) in which the URL is in the form of `javascript:void(window.open('`*`url`*`', '', '`*`additional parameters`*`'));`.

Discussion

You can invoke JavaScript functions from links associated with static text fields. This technique is applicable only when you have embedded the SWF in an HTML page, and it allows you to call any function that is accessible from within the HTML page, including the *window.open( )* JavaScript method that opens a new browser window.

To create the link, select the text and add a value to the URL link field in the form of `javascript:void(window.open('`*url*`', '`*window name*`', '`*additional settings*`'));`. The `javascript` protocol lets Flash know that you want to invoke a JavaScript function. The *void( )* function should enclose the remainder of the command in order to avoid undesirable results, such as extra new windows being opened unexpectedly. Notice that the parameters for the *window.open( )* method are in single quotes rather than double quotes. You should always use single quotes when you use this technique. Double quotes will not work properly.

The first parameter that you pass to the *window.open( )* method should be the URL you want to open in the new browser window. The value can be either an absolute URL (e.g., *http://www.person13.com/fcb*) or a relative URL (e.g., */fcb*). The second parameter specifies the name of the new window. The name is a way that one browser window can communicate to another. You can specify a name that you make up, or you can even simply use an empty string (two single quotes without any other characters in between). The third parameter allows you to tell the browser application (IE, Netscape, Safari, Opera, and so on) what settings to use with the new window. For example, you can tell the browser to open the new window with specific dimensions. The following are some of the more common settings you can specify:

width
: The width of the new window in pixels

height
: The height of the new window in pixels

location
: A Boolean (true or false) value indicating whether the new window should display the location bar

toolbar
: A Boolean value indicating whether the new window should display the toolbar

screenX
: The *x*-coordinate on the screen at which to open the new window

screenY
: The *y*-coordinate on the screen at which to open the new window

Specify the settings as a comma-delimited list for the third parameter. The following is an example of the entire value you can enter for the URL field in the Property inspector. The example would cause Flash to call a JavaScript method that opens a new browser window with width and height of 100×100:

```
javascript:void(window.open('http://www.person13.com/fcb', '',
'width=100,height=100'));
```

7.15   Calling ActionScript Functions from Static Text

Problem

You want to invoke an ActionScript function in the current movie when the user clicks on static text.

Solution

Apply a hyperlink to the text (see Recipe 8.12) in which the URL is in the form of asfunction:*actionscriptFunctionName*[, param1, parame2...paramN].

Discussion

In addition to all the other kinds of linking you can do with static text fields, you can also link to an ActionScript function using the same basic technique. Select the text to which you wish to apply the link, and then add a value to the URL link field in the form of asfunction:*actionscriptFunctionName*[, param1, parame2...paramN]. The asfunction protocol tells Flash to invoke an ActionScript function. You should then provide the name of the function to invoke. And if the function should be invoked with parameters, you can optionally provide a list of those values as well. Consider the example in which the ActionScript function is defined as follows:

```
function greet(sName:String):Void {
    // Assume that tMessage is a dynamic text field on the stage.
    // Read Chapter 8 for more details about dynamic text fields.
    tMessage.text = "Hello, " + sName;
}
```

You can invoke the *greet()* function from a static text field by applying the following value to the URL link field:

```
asfunction:greet,friend.
```

In this example, when the user clicks on the static text field, the following message appears in the text field:

```
Hello, friend
```

The ActionScript function must be defined on the same timeline in which the static text field exists. For example, if you create a static text field in the main timeline and apply a URL link to it of asfunction:greet,friend, the *greet( )* function must be defined within the main timeline. If the *greet( )* function is defined within another timeline's scope, Flash will not know where to find the function, and nothing will happen when the user clicks on the text.

You can find more information on how to define functions, as well as function scope, in the *ActionScript Cookbook* (O'Reilly, 2003).

7.16 Making Small Fonts Readable

Problem

You want to use a small point size for your text, but anti-aliasing makes the font unreadable.

Solution

Use device fonts or adjust the anti-aliasing settings for the text.

Discussion

Most fonts use *anti-aliasing* to ensure that the font doesn't appear to have jagged or sharp edges. To achieve this effect, the font's edges are actually blurred very slightly. Although that makes fonts look nicer at larger font sizes, it can cause text to appear rather unreadable once you decrease the point size below 10 points. However, if you want to use small point sizes, you still have some options:

- Use device fonts. Using device fonts can have several benefits. As discussed in Recipe 7.9, using device fonts can reduce the file size of the SWF. Additionally, device fonts aren't anti-aliased, which makes them appear more legible at smaller point sizes. However, device fonts may not be the optimal solution in every case. Remember that when you tell Flash to use device fonts, it will use a font on the user's computer. If the user doesn't have the font, it will substitute the default system font. Thus device fonts are not appropriate when you require a specific font face. Furthermore, device fonts won't respond in a predictable manner to some advanced formatting settings.

- Apply the anti-alias for readability setting. In Flash 8, you can select the Anti-alias for readability option from the Font rendering method menu in the Property inspector. The setting causes Flash to still apply anti-aliasing to the text, but it will apply the anti-aliasing with settings that will cause smaller fonts to still appear legibly. The Anti-alias for readability option will work well for some fonts at some point sizes. If you want the text to still appear with anti-aliasing but you want to use smaller font sizes of 9 or 10, try the setting. If it doesn't work, you can try the remaining options detailed in this list.

- Apply custom anti-aliasing. If you want the text to use anti-aliasing, but the Anti-alias for readability setting doesn't make the text legible enough, you can still try the custom anti-aliasing option. Select the Custom anti-alias option from the Font rendering method menu. Then adjust the Thickness and Sharpness settings in the Custom Anti-Aliasing dialog box. The text on stage will preview the changes so you can see what effects the adjustments are having.

- Use no anti-aliasing. Although anti-aliasing can make text look less jagged, when the font point size is small enough any amount of anti-aliasing makes the text illegible. Although you can use device fonts, as noted previously, that option means that you cannot guarantee that a specific font will be used to render the text. If you want to use a specific font, you must embed the font as is done by default. However, you can opt to remove anti-aliasing from the text even if it continues to use the embedded font outline. You can do so by selecting the Bitmap text (no anti-alias) option from the Font rendering method menu.

Even though the Font rendering method options let you specify rendering options, there are some fonts that simply will not anti-alias particularly well. However, you can find a large selection of pixel fonts online that are specifically designed so that they do not anti-alias. One great resource of pixel fonts is *www.fontsforflash.com*. Pixel fonts are made so that each part of the font occupies an actual pixel on the screen, rather than appearing between pixels, as can occur with standard, anti-aliased fonts. That means that the text will appear clear, even at lower font sizes. However, you need to use the fonts only at the size at which they were designed. For example, if a font is designed at 8 pixels, you should use it only at 8 pixels. Any other font size can cause parts of the font to appear offset from whole pixels—with the effect being blurry or jagged text.

7.17 Checking Spelling

Problem

You want to check the spelling of text within your Flash document.

Solution

Use the spellchecking feature in Flash.

Description

Flash includes a spellchecker that can check spelling throughout your Flash document, including frame and layer labels, ActionScript, and text. However, in order to use the spellchecker, you must first configure it. To do so, choose Text → Spelling Setup. Within the dialog box, you have many options via which you can configure the spellchecker to best suit your needs. You can instruct it to check the spelling in a variety of locations, though perhaps the most practical is to have it check the contents of text fields. Second to that, you may also choose to have it check your Action-Script for spelling. If you do have it check your ActionScript for spelling, however, depending on your coding style, you will probably return many reported misspellings on variable names and such.

Within the Checking options section of the Spelling Setup dialog box, you may want to check the "Suggest phonetic matches" and "Suggest typographical matches" options. That way, when you run the spellchecker, Flash will make suggestions to you for words it reports as misspelled.

After you've configured the spellchecker, click OK to close the dialog box. Then you can check the spelling at any point by choosing Text → Check Spelling. If Flash reports any misspellings, you will have the option to change them or ignore them. You can also add words to your custom dictionary so that Flash will recognize them next time you check the spelling.

CHAPTER 8

Working with Dynamic Text

In Chapter 7, you had a chance to read extensively about static text—the sort of text that you can create and change only at authoring time. Static text can be useful in many situations, but it also has its limitations. Frequently applications require that you be able to display text dynamically to the user. For example, if you are creating an application that displays catalog contents, you need to be able to display the information dynamically, based on what the user selects. Sometimes using dynamic text is not so much a necessity as a matter of convenience. If you manage the content for a small Flash web site, you may want to update the information on the web site frequently. If you use static text, you have to open the *.fla*, change the text, re-export the *.swf* file, and upload it to the server. And perhaps someone else at the company is responsible for actually creating the updated content, but they don't know how to use Flash. So you are then responsible for assisting someone each time the content needs to be updated. Your job is simplified greatly if you can set up your *.swf* file to load the text from an external text file. Then, anyone who can edit a text file can make changes to the content without having to have specialized Flash knowledge.

There are several other limitations of static text. Static text cannot scroll. If you use static text, make sure you have allotted enough space within your Flash movie to display all the text that you want the viewer to see. If you have a large amount of text, that can be somewhat difficult. Additionally, static text cannot accept user input. With static text alone, you cannot prompt the user for a username and password, comments, email address, or any other text-based information.

In this chapter, you will read about how to use dynamic text to both display text and accept user input. You'll also see how to scroll text, use HTML within Flash, apply formatting, and much more.

8.1 Creating Text that You Can Modify at Runtime

Problem

You want to create a text field that can be controlled by ActionScript (in order to update the text content at runtime or animate using ActionScript).

Solution

Create a dynamic text field in the same way you would create a static text field (see Recipe 7.1), except that instead of selecting Static Text from the text type menu, choose Dynamic Text. Also, give the text field an instance name.

Alternatively, you can create dynamic text fields at runtime using the *createTextField( )* ActionScript method:

```
// Create a new dynamic text field in current timeline.
var tField:TextField = this.createTextField("tField", 1, 0, 0, 100, 20);
```

Discussion

If you want to be able to control text at runtime, you must use dynamic or input text fields. Although you can place static text in your movie at authoring time, Action-Script knows little about those text fields. However, ActionScript can access dynamic and input text fields while the movie is playing.

Technically, ActionScript is capable of reading the contents of static text fields. However, static text fields are not objects, and ActionScript does not have control over them as it does with dynamic and input text fields. Fortunately, while dynamic text fields are drastically different from static text in terms of what you can do with them, the process for creating a dynamic text field is almost identical to creating a static text field. Here are the steps you should follow:

1. Select the Text tool either by clicking the Text button in the toolbar or by pressing the keyboard shortcut (T).

2. Open the Property inspector and make sure that Dynamic Text is selected from the text type menu.

3. Draw a text field on the stage using the Text tool by clicking the mouse button and dragging out the text field outline. Unlike with static text fields, you can set a dynamic text field height in addition to its width.

4. When you release the mouse button to stop drawing the text field, the text field is automatically selected, and the text input cursor appears within it so that you can enter text if you want. However, unlike static text fields, you do not have to enter text into a dynamic text field at authoring time, and so you can choose to deselect the field without entering any values.

5. Give the dynamic text field object an instance name. Make sure that the text field is selected, and then specify an instance name in the Property inspector. The instance name must adhere to the ActionScript rules for naming identifiers. In simple terms, the name cannot include spaces and cannot begin with a number, and the name should contain only letters, numbers, and the underscore character.

You must always assign an instance name to dynamic text fields. Otherwise, Flash won't know how to refer to the text field via ActionScript.

Technically, it *is* possible to assign text to text fields even if they don't have instance names. It is possible to assign a variable name to a text field instead. However, assignment of variable names to text fields continues to exist for legacy purposes for compatibility with Flash 5 and earlier. But it is no longer recommended that you assign a variable name to a text field. You should always use an instance name, as discussed in this recipe.

Flash also allows you to create dynamic text fields at runtime using ActionScript instead of drawing it on the stage at authoring time. The method for doing this is *createTextField( )*, and you can invoke it from any movie clip (including the main timeline) in order to create a new dynamic text field within the clip. In order to use *createTextField( )*, you must know several pieces of information:

Instance name
   You must provide the method with an instance name for the new text field.

Depth
   All text fields (as well as movie clips and buttons) must have a unique, numeric depth value. Generally speaking, the depth value should be a positive number starting at 1. Make sure to always use a unique depth value, because if you use a value that has already been assigned to another object, the original object will be deleted.

x- and y-coordinates
   You must provide Flash with the coordinates at which to place the new text field within the coordinate system of the movie clip.

Width and height
   You must provide Flash with the width and height (in pixels) of the new text field to create.

The *createTextField( )* method returns a reference to the newly created text field (as of Flash Player 8).

Here is an example of how you can create a dynamic text field in the current movie clip. This example creates a text field named tField that has a depth of 1, is positioned at 120,50, and has dimensions of 100 × 20 pixels.

```
var tField:TextField = this.createTextField("tField", 1, 120, 50, 100, 20);
```

If you don't know the exact dimensions of the text field that you want to create (because the dimensions are to be determined by the text you assign it via Action-Script), you can assign the value 0 to both the height and width when creating the text field, and then set the entire text field to autosize based on the contents. Likewise, you can always modify the *x* and *y* coordinates of the text field later on using the _x and _y properties.

8.2 Changing Text at Runtime

Problem

You want to customize text field at runtime in order to display text retrieved from a text file, a database, user input, and so on.

Solution

Set the value of the text field's text property.

Discussion

Every dynamic and input text field has a text property that controls what is displayed to the user at runtime. You can use ActionScript to set the text property for a text field, and the value you assign to the property is displayed:

```
// Display the assigned string value in the text field.
tMessage.text = "Don't think about pink crocodiles.";
```

You can also use variables and more complex expressions on the right side of the equals sign (known as an *assignment statement*):

```
// Assign a value to a variable, sUsername.
var sUsername:String = "Fred";

// Use the sUsername variable, and concatenate its value with a quoted string
// to create a dynamic value to assign to the text field. In this case, the
// text field displays: "Fred, don't think about pink crocodiles."
tMessage.text = sUsername + ", don't think about pink crocodiles.";
```

If using a multiline text field, you can add line breaks using a newline character. You can use either the special characters \n or \r within the quoted string, or you can use the ActionScript constant, newline. Both are equivalent, but you must use the \n or \r character within quotes, and you must use the newline constant outside of quotes.

```
// The following two lines are equivalent, but the first is more convenient.
tMessage.text = "Don't think about pink crocodiles\n...or yellow walruses.";
tMessage.text = "Don't think about pink crocodiles" + newline + "...or yellow
walruses.";
```

The whole purpose of dynamic text is that you can assign values to it at runtime instead of being limited to authoring time only. This feature is extremely useful in many situations. For example, as in the preceding examples, you might want to customize the output so that the user's name is included in a message. In more practical situations, you need to use dynamic text any time you want text values on the stage to update based on user interaction. For instance, in a shopping cart, you want the shopper's total purchase price to reflect the items they have selected. Additionally, you can populate dynamic text fields with data drawn from external sources, such as text files, databases, and web services. (These last few examples involve some slightly more complex ActionScript that is not within the scope of this book. For more information, see the *ActionScript Cookbook*, O'Reilly.)

8.3   Accepting User Input

Problem

You want to accept user input at runtime.

Solution

Use a text input or text area component.

Alternatively, create an input text field in the same way as you create a dynamic text field (see Recipe 8.1), except that instead of selecting Dynamic Text from the text type menu, select Input Text. Additionally, in most cases you should make sure that input text fields have a border, so that the user can see where to insert text. Optionally, you can create an input text field using ActionScript by first creating a dynamic text field with *createTextField( )* and then setting the object's type property to input.

Discussion

Flash provides two ways of accepting text input from the user: components and dynamic text fields. Each has its own advantages and disadvantages, so you should learn about each to best determine which to use.

In the UI components that ship with Flash, you can find two components for accepting user input: TextInput and TextArea. The text input component provides you with a rather simple way to create an input control that looks like a standard HTML text input control. All you need to do is drag-and-drop an instance from the Components panel to the stage, and give it an instance name in the Property inspector. Although the text input component makes it very simple for you to create a way to accept text that the user enters, that is not a distinct advantage over the dynamic text field, because the latter is quite simple as well. However, the text input component does offer at least two advantages. One is that the component is part of the standard UI components, and as such it provides the same common functionality, such as built-in style management (see Chapter 15). That means that you can apply the same styles (such as font color, font face, etc.) to the text input component instances as all other component instances within the movie using just a few lines of simple Action-Script code. You don't have to actually apply the changes to each instance individually. Another advantage is that the text input component has the slightly recessed appearance of a standard HTML text input control. Though you could create that same effect in just a few minutes with the drawing tools, it is convenient to be able to simply drag-and-drop an instance. The flip side is that if you don't want your input control to appear like a standard HTML text input, it is rather difficult to make changes to the appearance of the component in that respect. Furthermore, perhaps the most distinct disadvantage is that a text input component adds 27KB to your *.swf* file size.

The text area component is much like a standard HTML text area. It is a multiline field with a built-in scrollbar. Like the text input component, the text area component has the advantage of ease of use and built-in style management. It also has the same disadvantages as the text input component.

The other option for accepting user input is an input text field. Input text fields are practically the same as dynamic text fields. In fact, the only difference is that a user can type or paste text into an input text field, something that is not possible with a dynamic text field. Therefore, it should come as no surprise that creating an input text field is almost the same as creating a dynamic text field. You should follow the same instructions as in Recipe 8.1, but in step 2, specify Input Text rather than Dynamic Text. Additionally, in most cases you should add a border, to ensure that the user can see where they can input text. You can add a border to an input text field by selecting it on the stage and pressing the "Show border" button in the Property inspector (see Figure 8-1).

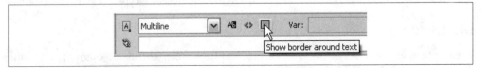

Figure 8-1. Select the "Show border" button in order to display a border around a text field

When you add a border to a text field at authoring time, the border color defaults to black. There is no way to modify this value at authoring time. What's more, when you specify a border for your text field at authoring time, Flash also adds a white background to it. As with the border, you cannot change the color of the background (nor can you turn it off) at authoring time. You can, however, modify these settings at runtime using ActionScript. All dynamic (including input) text fields have four properties related to border and background:

border
> This property is either true or false, and determines whether the border shows up. When you choose to turn on the border at authoring time, Flash sets the border property to true.

background

> This property is also either true or false, and it determines whether the background shows up. When you turn on the border at authoring time, Flash sets not only the border property to true, but also the background property.

borderColor

> This property determines the color value of the border. The default value is 0x000000, but you can assign any number value that represents a valid color.

backgroundColor

> This property determines the color value of the background. The default value is 0xFFFFFF, but you can assign any number value that represents a valid color.

Here is an example of some ActionScript that modifies the border and background colors for a text field:

```
tField.borderColor = 0x0000FF;
tField.backgroundColor = 0xCDCDCD;
```

Or, if you want to keep the border on but hide the background you can do so like this:

```
tField.background = false;
```

Optionally, if you don't want to use the standard border and/or background for a text field, you can add artwork on a layer beneath the text field. If the text field's border and background are off, then the artwork on the lower layer will give the appearance of being the border and background for the text field. This technique enables you to add more complex borders and backgrounds.

You can also create an input text field at runtime using ActionScript. See Recipe 8.1 for more information on creating text fields at runtime, and follow the same process. Then, in addition, set the new text field's type property to input:

```
var tInputField:TextField = this.createTextField("tInputField", 1, 120, 50, 100, 20);
tInputField.type = "input";
```

If you're adding a text field programmatically and you want to add a border programmatically, you can accomplish that by setting the border property of the text field to true:

```
tInputField.border = true;
```

Although this approach is not used frequently, it is entirely possible to assign a value to an input text field or text input component instance at authoring time or at runtime. You can assign a text value to an input text field at authoring time in the same way as you can add a value to a dynamic text field. If you want to add a value to a text input component instance at authoring time, enter the value for the text parameter in the Component Inspector panel. If you want to assign a value to an input text field or a text input component at runtime, the code is the same: assign the value to the text property of the instance. For example:

```
tInputField.text = "Some value";
```

For an example of why you might use this functionality, consider the following code snippet, which assigns an initial value to an input text field that tells the user what to enter.

```
tUserName.text = "<type your name here>";
```

If you want to use an input text field instead of a text area component, follow the preceding instructions. Then, in addition, set the text field to display more than one line of text.

8.4   Accepting Password Input

Problem

You want to accept text input from the user, but you want it to display on the screen as asterisks rather than the actual characters to ensure that other users won't be able to read it.

Solution

If you are using a text input component, set the password parameter to true.

If you are using an input text field, choose Password from the Line type menu in the Property inspector. Or, alternatively, assign a value of true to the instance's password property using ActionScript.

Discussion

Regular input text fields and text input components display all the entered text in plain view of anyone who can view the computer monitor. This is not always a good idea for fields into which the user is supposed to enter information relating to security—information such as passwords or credit card numbers. Password fields can be used for any kind of information you don't want to make visible to all people in the same room as the user. Instead of displaying the actual character that the user inputs, a password field displays asterisks to correspond to each character. This way the user can see how many characters they have entered, but not the actual value. This affects only the display of the value, not the actual value itself as it is processed within your Flash movie.

How you create a password field depends on what type of input control you are using. If you are using an input text field, you can make it a password field by selecting the password option from the Line type menu in the Property inspector. Password fields can be only single-line fields.

If you created the input text field at runtime with ActionScript code (or even if you didn't), you can use code to make it a password field. All you need to do is set the password property to true:

```
tInputField.password = true;
```

You can also make text input component instances into password fields. To do so, select the instance, open the Component Inspector panel, and set the password parameter to true.

8.5   Limiting the Length of User Input

Problem

You want to restrict the number of characters that a user can enter into an input text field or text input component instance.

Solution

With the text field selected, enter a nonzero numeric value in the Maximum Characters field of the Property inspector. Optionally, set the instance's maxChars property to a nonzero numeric value using ActionScript.

Or, if you are using a text input component, set the maxChars parameter to a nonzero numeric value.

Discussion

In some scenarios, you want to restrict the number of characters that a user can type into an input field. For example, you may want to limit a user to five characters when entering a U.S. zip code. Flash lets you limit the length of the input for both input text fields and text input components.

For an input text field, you can use the Maximum Characters option in the Property inspector (see Figure 8-2). Enter a nonzero numeric value while you have selected the input text field instance on the stage. A value of 0 allows the user to enter an unlimited number of characters.

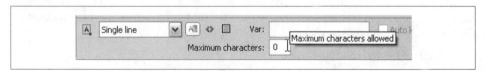

Figure 8-2. Use the Maximum Characters field to limit the number of characters that a user can enter into an input text field

Optionally, you can use ActionScript to set the maximum number of characters by assigning a value to the instance's maxChars property. For example:

```
tInputField.maxChars = 10;
```

If you're using a text input component instance, you can set the instance's max-Chars parameter in the Component Inspector panel. A value of null or 0 allows the user to enter an unlimited number of characters. A nonzero numeric value allows the user to enter the corresponding number of characters.

You can also restrict the allowed characters that a user can enter into an input text field.

8.6 Setting Allowable Characters for Input

Problem

You want to restrict allowable characters for an input text field or text input component instance.

Solution

Use the Character Options to embed only those characters you want to allow the user to input.

Use the text field's restrict property to assign a list or range of characters to include or not include.

Discussion

If you are using an input text field, there are two ways you can restrict the allowable characters. One way is to embed the font and to use the Character Options to specify which characters to embed. Because only that subset of characters gets embedded, the user can enter only those characters. For example, if you want to make sure that a user can only enter a number into an input field, you can embed only the number characters.

The downside of relying on embedding a font to restrict allowable characters is that embedded fonts increase the file size of the Flash movie. You can use ActionScript to restrict the allowable characters even with device fonts. The restrict property for a text field determines what characters can be entered by the user. You can assign a string value to the restrict property that contains all the characters you want to allow. The following example restricts the allowable characters for tInputField to the lowercase letters from a to g and the uppercase letters X, Y, and Z:

```
tInputField.restrict = "abcdefgXYZ";
```

The restrict property affects what characters an input text field can display. If the user presses a key, there are several possible results. If the user presses a key that is in the restrict property value, the character appears in the text field. If the user presses a key that isn't directly in the restrict property value but can be shifted to a character in the restrict property value (adding or removing a Shift key), the shifted value appears in the text field. For example, if the user presses the z key yet only the Z character is allowed, the Z character will appear in the text field. If the user presses a key for which there is no shifted or unshifted value in the restrict property, no character is added to the text field.

You can also specify ranges of characters by using the dash between the starting and ending (inclusive) letters or numbers. The following example restricts the allowable characters to the ranges of the upper- and lowercase letters, as well as the numbers. Therefore, the disallowed characters include all punctuation and other non-alphanumeric characters.

```
tInputField.restrict = "a-zA-Z0-9";
```

In addition to specifying allowable characters, you can also disallow characters with a restrict string by using the caret character (^). All characters and ranges in a restrict string following the caret will be disallowed. For example:

```
tInputField.restrict = "^abcdefg"; // Allows all except lowercase a through g
tInputField.restrict = "^a-z";     // Disallows all lowercase letters (but
                                   // allows all other characters including
                                   // uppercase)
tInputField.restrict = "0-9^5";    // Allows numbers only, with the exception of 5
```

You can also specify allowable characters using Unicode escape sequences. For example, if you want to disallow users from entering the → character into a field, you can specify its Unicode code point in the restrict property as follows:

```
tInputField.restrict = "^\u001A";
```

To allow a literal character that has a special meaning when used in a restrict string (such as a dash or caret), you must *escape* the character in the restrict string by preceding it with two backslashes (not just one):

```
tInputField.restrict = "0-9\\-"; // Allow numbers and dashes
tInputField.restrict = "0-9\\^"; // Allow numbers and caret marks
```

If you want to escape the backslash character, you must precede it with three backslashes for a total of four backslashes:

```
tInputField.restrict = "0-9\\\\"; // Allow numbers and backslashes
```

The text input component has a restrict parameter that corresponds to the restrict property of text fields. You can assign a value to the parameter using the Component Inspector panel. The only difference between values assigned to the restrict property of a text field using ActionScript and the restrict parameter of a text input component using the Component Inspector panel is that when you want to specify a backslash character in the string for the parameter, you need to use only two consecutive backslashes rather than four.

8.7   Retrieving User Input

Problem

You want to retrieve the text that a user has entered into a text field, text input, or text area instance for further processing.

Solution

Use ActionScript to access the value by way of the instance's text property.

Discussion

You must use ActionScript in order to retrieve the value from an input text field, text input, or text area. However, the code that is required is short and simple. You can access the text value using the instance name and its text property.

This following code writes the value of an input text field to the Output window when you are testing your movie. The text field in this example has an instance name of tInputField. In order for this code to work, it must be placed on a frame in the same timeline in which the text field exists:

```
trace(tInputField.text);
```

Text that you retrieve from an input text field, text input, or text area is always a string value. The string data type can perform differently in some operations than a number data type. For example, when you use the plus sign with two numbers, they are added together. But when you use the plus sign with two strings, the values are appended to one another. Therefore, if you want to perform mathematical operations on a value that you retrieve from an input text field, you should convert that value to a number data type. You can do this very quickly using either the *parseInt( )* or *parseFloat( )* functions.

The *parseInt( )* function takes a string value, and returns an integer (a whole number) if possible. The *parseFloat( )* function takes a string value, and returns a floating-point number (a number with a decimal place) if possible. Here is an example of how you can use these functions to convert text field values to numbers:

```
var nFloat:Number = parseFloat(tInputText.text);
var nInteger:Number = parseInt(tInputField.text);
```

Typically you'll retrieve the value from a text field, text input, or text area only after the user clicks a button or otherwise signifies that she has entered the information and wants Flash to do something with it. If you retrieve the information before that, you're likely to retrieve empty values. That means that the code that you use to handle the text should be placed within a method or function that gets called once the user has clicked the button, pressed a key, and so on. Refer to Chapter 9 for more information on handling button events. However, the following is a simple example of some code that displays the user's input in the Output panel after she clicks the button with an instance name of btSubmit. The Output panel is only available within the test player, and therefore the example is only relevant for demonstration purposes. A more practical example requires slightly more sophisticated code. You can find several relevant, related examples in Chapter 13.

```
btSubmit.onRelease = function( ):Void {
   trace(tUsername.text);
};
```

8.8   Resizing Dynamic or Input Text Fields

Problem

You want to resize a dynamic or input text field.

Solution

Use the Text tool to select the text field, and then drag the resize square found in the lower-right corner of the text field. Alternatively, use the Selection tool.

Optionally, you can use ActionScript to resize the text at runtime. Set the autoSize property of the text field to left, right, or center in order that it will automatically resize itself to accommodate the text value:

```
tField.autoSize = "left";
```

Or, you can set the _height and _width properties of the text field to specify the dimensions in pixels:

```
tField._height = 200;
tField._width = 300;
```

Discussion

Dynamic and input text fields differ from static text fields in several ways when it comes to resizing. When resizing a dynamic or input text field at authoring time, it differs from resizing static text in two ways:

- The Text tool resize square displays in the lower-right corner of the dynamic or input text field.
- You can resize dynamic or input text fields in both the horizontal and vertical directions.

In order to resize the text field at authoring time, select the text field using the Text tool. Then, click and drag the resize square to adjust the dimensions. Optionally, click and drag from any of the resize squares using the Selection tool.

Be careful about adjusting the width and height of a text field using the Property inspector. The actual effect depends on whether you are using device fonts or an embedded font with the text field. If you are using device fonts, the text will appear to scale in the authoring time preview, but it will appear in the normal font size during runtime with the bounding box resized. On the other hand, if you are embedding the font in the text field and you use the Property inspector to resize the field, the authoring time preview accurately indicates how the text will appear at runtime. The text will scale without necessarily maintaining the aspect ratio. The effect is that the text can appear squished or stretched.

If you use the Free Transform tool to change the dimensions of dynamic or input text, the authoring time preview will not accurately reflect the runtime effect if the text uses device fonts. The authoring time preview will display the text as being scaled without maintaining the aspect ratio. However, at runtime the text does maintain the aspect ratio such that the characters are scaled proportionately. The Free Transform tool has the same effect on dynamic and input text fields regardless of whether they used device fonts or embedded fonts.

Another way that dynamic and input text fields differ greatly from static text fields is that you can also use ActionScript to resize them at runtime. There are two different techniques for resizing a text field with ActionScript. To begin with, if you want a text field to automatically resize to accommodate whatever value is assigned or entered into it, you can set its autoSize property to left, right, or center:

```
tField.autoSize = "left";
```

The text field's name (tField in the example code) is the name that you entered for the instance name in the Property inspector. The autoSize property values of left, right, and center each cause the text field to resize to fit the contents. The difference is in which direction the text field resizes. If you set the value to left, the upper-left corner of the text field remains fixed while the field resizes in to the right and downward. A value of right causes the text field's upper-right corner to stay fixed. And a value of center causes the text field's upper-center point to stay fixed.

If you set the text field to autosize, both the width and height may change to accommodate the text. If you assign a nonzero width to the text field when you create it, the autosize width will not surpass that width. However, if there is not enough text to warrant the width of the text field when it was created, it is possible that the text field will have a width that is less than the original. When you want to afford more control over how the field resizes, set the _height and _width properties to specific values:

```
tField._height = 60;
tField._width = 150;
```

Setting the width and height values adjusts the bounding box of the text field and does not stretch the text itself.

8.9   Creating Multiline Text

Problem

You want to display multiple lines of text and/or allow the user to input multiple lines of text.

Solution

Use a text area component.

Alternatively, use a dynamic or input text field and select Multiline or Multiline No Wrap from the Line type menu in the Property inspector. Optionally, you can set the text field's multiline property to true via ActionScript.

Discussion

There are two ways you can work with multiple lines of text within Flash: a text area component and a text field instance that has been configured to accept multiple lines. Each option has its own advantages and disadvantages.

The text area component provides functionality much like the text area form control in HTML. The text input component allows a single line of input; the text area component allows multiple lines of input. However, the text area component is not only for input, but also for displaying text. It provides automatic scrolling functionality, so that if the text extends beyond the boundaries of the text area, a scrollbar will appear, allowing the user to scroll to see the entire contents. That makes text area components useful both for allowing a user to input multiple lines of content and for displaying text content.

To use the text area, complete the following steps:

1. Drag an instance from the Components panel onto the stage.

2. Give the instance a name in the Property inspector.

3. If you want to assign a text value to the component instance, you can do so either at authoring time or runtime:

   - You can assign a text value at authoring time by way of the Component Inspector panel. Assign the value to the text parameter.

   - You can assign a text value at runtime using the text property of the instance. For example, the following code assigns a value to a text area with an instance name of ctaOutput:

     ```
     ctaOutput.text = "Flash Cookbook";
     ```

     Assigning values to text area components at runtime instead of authoring time has plenty of potential advantages. One of the most significant is that you can load data from an external file and use it to populate the text area. For more information on loading text from external files, see Chapter 19.

The text area component has several advantages. One is that it is very simple to set up scrollable text with a text area—something that is a little more complicated with a standard text field. Additionally, because the text area component is built on the same framework as the other Macromedia UI components, you can use built-in features such as style management to quickly change the styles of all components in your Flash application. However, the text area is not without disadvantages. As with many of the Macromedia UI components, the text area can add a hefty increase to your .swf file's size. A .swf file with nothing other than a text area is already 40KB. Furthermore, if you want to customize the scrollbars beyond simple style changes (changing the color, and so on), you're likely to find it more of a hassle than it's worth.

The other option for accepting and displaying multiple lines of text is to use a dynamic or input text field. By default, dynamic and input text fields display only a single line. A single-line text field won't display more than one line of text, even if you include line breaks in the text value or if the user presses the Enter key while entering text. In order for a text field to accommodate multiple lines of text, you must tell Flash that it is a multiline text field. You can do this either at authoring time or at runtime.

At authoring time, you can make a text field multiline by selecting it with the Selection tool and then selecting the Multiline or Multiline No Wrap option from the Line type menu in the Property inspector. The Multiline option creates a multiline text field that automatically performs word wrapping. The Multiline No Wrap option creates a multiline text field that does not perform automatic word wrapping.

You can also tell Flash to make a text field multiline at runtime using ActionScript. The multiline property can be either true or false. It defaults to false, but setting it to true allows the text field to accommodate multiple lines:

```
tField.multiline = true;
```

See Recipe 8.11 for more information about controlling word wrapping of multiline text fields at runtime.

8.10 Creating Scrolling Text

Problem

You want to create scrolling text.

Solution

Use a text area component.

Alternatively, create a multiline text field and button or movie clips for scrolling up and down. Then add some ActionScript to update the text field's scroll property when the button or movie clips are pressed.

Discussion

In the event that you want to use a standard scrollbar to scroll text horizontally and/or vertically, you can use the text area component with its built-in scrollbars. You can add a text area to the stage simply by dragging an instance from the Components panel to the stage. If you are planning to use the text area with ActionScript at all, make sure to give it an instance name using the Property inspector. If you want to add text to the text area you can follow the instructions provided in Recipe 8.9.

With a text area, the scrollbars (vertical and horizontal) appear only when necessary. However, with some simple ActionScript you can specify whether and when the scrollbars should appear. Each text area component instance has a property named vScrollPolicy and a property named hScrollPolicy. The vScrollPolicy property determines the behavior of the vertical scrollbar, and the hScrollPolicy property determines the behavior of the horizontal scrollbar. The properties can accept values of on, off, or auto. The default value is auto, which means that the scrollbar appears only when necessary. A value of on means that the scrollbar is visible even when unnecessary; a value of off means that the scrollbar does not appear, even when necessary. The following code example sets the vertical scrollbar to be on and the horizontal scrollbar to be off for a text area instance named ctaOutput:

```
ctaOutput.vScrollPolicy = "on";
ctaOutput.hScrollPolicy = "off";
```

There are times when you don't want to use a text area component. For example, due to file size issues, you may not have the option of including the 40KB text area component in your project. Another reason you may opt not to use the component is that you might want to create a custom scrolling mechanism. Whatever your reasoning, you can add a small amount of ActionScript code in order to scroll a text field.

Dynamic and input text fields have an ActionScript property named scroll. Each text field line is assigned an index by Flash, and the scroll property contains the index of the top visible line in a given text field. For example, if the text field is scrolled all the way to the top, the scroll property has a value of 1, because the first line is the top visible line. Not only does the scroll property report the index of the top visible line, but it also allows you to set that value. For example, regardless of how a text field has been scrolled, you can scroll it to the top by assigning a value of 1 to the scroll property of that instance.

```
tField.scroll = 1;   // Scroll a text field named tField to the top.
```

If you want to scroll a text field down one line, use the increment operator (++) with the instance's scroll property. You can scroll a text field up one line by using the decrement operator (--) with the instance's scroll property. Typically, you'll want to scroll a text field up and/or down using a movie clip or button instance in conjunction with an *onPress( )* or *onRelease( )* event handler method (see Chapter 9 for more details on handling button events with event handler methods). The following example scrolls a text field named tField to the next line when the user clicks on a movie clip with an instance name of mScrollDown, and scrolls the text up one line when the user clicks on a movie clip with an instance name of mScrollUp:

```
mScrollDown.onPress = function( ):Void {
  tField.scroll++;
};

mScrollUp.onPress = function( ):Void {
  tField.scroll--;
};
```

The preceding code allows the user to scroll the text up and down one line at a time. Each time the user wants to scroll one more line, he has to click the appropriate movie clip or button again. That can require a lot of clicks to scroll any substantial amount. If you want to add continuous scrolling functionality, you can do so by using the setInterval( ) command to tell Flash to repeatedly call a function that scrolls the text field. Call *setInterval( )* within an *onPress( )* event handler method, and then clear the interval within an *onRelease( )* event handler method. The following code is an example:

```
// Define a custom function that Flash can call on an interval. The function accepts two
// parameters - the text field to scroll and the amount by which to scroll the text field.
// A positive number for the nScrollAmount parameter will cause the text field to scroll
// downward, while a negative number will cause the text field to scroll upward.
function scrollField(tField:TextField, nScrollAmount:Number):Void {

    // Add the scroll amount to the text field's scroll property.
    tField.scroll += nScrollAmount;

    // Refresh the stage so that the animation is as smooth as possible.
    updateAfterEvent( );
}

// Declare a variable into which you'll store the interval ID. That way you can clear the
// interval later on, so as to stop the scrolling.
var nInterval:Number;

// Assign an onPress( ) event handler method to the button or movie clip that the user can click
// to scroll the text upward. In this example the movie clip instance name is mScrollUp.
mScrollUp.onPress = function( ):Void {

    // Clear the interval just to make sure that you don't accidentally get multiple intervals
    // calling the same function running simultaneously.
    clearInterval(nInterval);

    // Set an interval so that Flash will call the scrollField( ) function every 50 milliseconds.
    // If you want the scrolling to occur faster, decrease the second parameter. If you want a
    // slower scroll, increase the value. Also, pass along the reference to the text field you
    // want to scroll. In this example the text field is named tField. And you should also
    // specify a value of -1 for the fourth parameter so that the text field scrolls upward.
    nInterval = setInterval(scrollField, 50, tField, -1);
};
```

```
// Assign an onRelease( ) event handler method to the same button or movie clip. In
this example
// that movie clip is mScrollUp. When the user releases the click on the button
simply clear the
// interval. That causes Flash to stop calling the scrollField( ) function.
mScrollUp.onRelease = function( ):Void {
  clearInterval(nInterval);
};

// Make sure that the interval is stopped if the user releases the mouse while no
longer over
// the movie clip.
mScrollUp.onReleaseOutside = mScrollUp.onRelease;

// Then assign onPress( ) and onRelease( ) event handler methods to the movie clip or
button that
// should cause the text to scroll downward. In this example the movie clip instance
is named
// mScrollDown. The code for the onPress( ) and onRelease( ) event handler methods on
the
// downward scroll movie clip or button is almost the same as the code for the upward
scroll movie
// clip or button. The only difference is that the fourth parameter passed to
setInterval( )
// should be 1 instead of -1 since you want the text to scroll downward.
mScrollDown.onPress = function( ):Void {
  clearInterval(nInterval);
  nInterval = setInterval(scrollField, 50, tField, 1);
};

mScrollDown.onRelease = function( ):Void {
  clearInterval(nInterval);
};

mScrollDown.onReleaseOutside = mScrollDown.onRelease;

// The following code populate the text field with text so that you can test the
scrolling
// functionality.
for(var i:Number = 0; i < 100; i++) {
  tField.text += i + newline;
}
```

The scroll property handles scrolling in the vertical direction. You can also scroll in the horizontal direction using the hscroll property if the text field has word wrapping turned off. The scroll property value is given in line numbers; the hscroll property is given in pixels. The minimum value for hscroll is 0, and that value indicates that the text is scrolled all the way to the right. If the text extends beyond the right boundary of the text field, you can increment the hscroll property to move the text within the field to the left.

8.11   Specifying Wrapping of Multiline Fields

Problem

You want to set the word wrapping setting for a multiline text field or text area.

Solution

If you are using a text area component, set the `wordWrap` parameter to `true`.

For a text field, choose the appropriate selection in the Line type menu (see Recipe 8.9 for more information) in order to accomplish this at authoring time. Set the value of the `wordWrap` property using ActionScript to modify word wrapping at runtime.

Discussion

If you are working with a text area component, the default behavior is that it wraps words. You can toggle the `wordWrap` parameter on and off, which can be found in the Component Inspector panel. Select the instance on stage, open the Component Inspector panel, and change the value of the `wordWrap` parameter. A value of `true` (the default setting) makes the text wrap to the next line if and when it is too long to fit within the horizontal boundaries of the text area. A value of `false` means that new lines appear only when they have been placed there by way of a newline, carriage return, or form feed character. (In addition, if the text area is configured to render HTML, <p> and <br> tags will cause new lines of text.) Otherwise, the text continues to extend horizontally, even though it may not fit within the boundaries of the viewable area.

There are two ways to specify the word wrapping settings for multiline text field: one for authoring time control, and another for runtime control. Both ways result in the same effect at runtime, but the former is done using the Property inspector, and the latter is done with ActionScript.

When a multiline text field is not set to wrap words, new lines are created only when a newline character is encountered (in the case of dynamic text being set at runtime) or when the user enters a carriage return (for input text fields). Therefore, in non-word-wrapping text fields, some text might appear outside of the text field's horizontal viewable area. By setting the text field to wrap words, Flash will intelligently wrap the text to a new line so that all the text fits within the text field horizontally (though it still may not fit within the text field vertically—see Recipe 8.10 for information about scrolling text). If possible, Flash will avoid splitting words when it performs a line wrap. However, if a line contains non-breaking text that is too long to fit on a single line, Flash will fill the first line and then wrap to the next line even in the middle of a word.

When you create a multiline text field at authoring time, you can select from either Multiline or Multiline No Wrap in the Line type menu. Each option creates a multi-line text field, but the former automatically wraps words and the latter does not.

You can also use ActionScript to control the word wrap by setting the wordWrap property of the text field. By default, wordWrap is set to false, which means that the lines continue, even beyond the visible area of the text field, until a line break or carriage return is encountered. If you set wordWrap to true, however, Flash will wrap lines of text to make sure that the contents fit (horizontally) within the viewable area of the text field:

```
tField.wordWrap = true;
```

8.12 Using HTML Tags in Text

Problem

You want to use HTML tags in text fields or text areas.

Solution

For text area components, set the html parameter to true using the Component Inspector panel. Then assign the HTML text to the component's text parameter.

For text fields, activate the Render Text as HTML option within the Property inspector. Or set its html property to true using ActionScript. In either case, after you've set the text field to render HTML, you can then assign the HTML text to the field's htmlText ActionScript property. (You cannot assign HTML text to a text field at authoring time.)

Discussion

You can instruct Flash to render text field and text area content as HTML rather than plain text, which is an effective and relatively simple way to apply some formatting to your text without having to use extensive ActionScript. For example, you can add hyperlinks, color, and style changes all with basic HTML tags.

There are two main steps in using HTML in your text fields and text areas. The steps in either case amount to basically the same thing—telling Flash to render the text within the instance as HTML rather than plain text, and assigning the HTML to the instance. However, the steps are slightly different depending on whether you are using a text field or a text area.

If you are using a text area, complete the following two steps:

1. With the text area selected, set the html parameter to true using the Component Inspector panel.
2. Assign the HTML text to the text area by way of the text property within the Component Inspector panel.

If you are using a text field, complete the following two steps:

1. Tell Flash that it should render the text for that field as HTML. You can accomplish this one of two ways:

   - Select the text field with the Selection tool, and select the Render as HTML option to the right of the Selectable option and the Line type menu in the Property inspector.

   - Use ActionScript to set the text field's html property to true:

     ```
     tField.html = true;
     ```

2. Assign the HTML value to the text field's htmlText property. When you have instructed Flash to render the text field as HTML, you should *not* assign the HTML code to the text property as you would do for plain text. Instead, use the htmlText property as shown here:

   ```
   tField.htmlText = "<font color='#0000FF'>blue text is fun<font>";
   ```

The following HTML tags are supported by dynamic text in Flash:

<a>

Use this tag for creating hyperlinks. Flash's support of the tag includes the following attributes:

href

The URL to which you want to hyperlink. You may use standard http or https protocols. You can also specify the mailto, javascript, or asfunction directives.

target

The name of the window into which the hyperlink should be opened. If no target is specified, then the link is opened in the same window as the Flash movie.

<b>

Use this tag to embolden text.

<font>

Flash's support of the <font> tag includes three attributes:

color

Use the color attribute to set the color of text. The value must be a hexadecimal value that begins with a # (e.g., #0000FF for blue and #00FF00 for green).

face

The face attribute sets the name of the font. You can specify any font name, comma-delimited list of font names, or one of the three Flash font groups (_serif, _sans, or _typewriter.)

size

The size attribute sets the size of the text.

<i>

Use this tag to italicize text.

<img>

Use this tag to display an external *.jpeg* file or *.swf* file, or to display a movie clip within a text field or text area. Flash supports the following attributes for the `<img>` tag:

align

You can optionally specify how to align the content within the text field or text area. Choose from `left` (default) or `right`.

height

The height to which you want to resize the content.

hspace

The number of pixels of space to the left and right of the content. The default is 8.

id

The instance name by which the image or movie clip can be addressed using ActionScript. This attribute is necessary only if you plan to target the content with code.

src

The URL of the *.jpeg* or *.swf* file to load and display. Optionally, you may specify the linkage identifier of a movie clip symbol in the library.

width

The width to which you want to resize the content.

vspace

The number of pixels of space above and below the content. The default is 8.

<li>

Use the `<li>` tag to create a bulleted list. Flash does not support the `<ul>` and `<ol>` tags to differentiate between an ordered and unordered list.

<p>

Use the `<p>` tag to create a new paragraph. Flash supports the following attributes for the tag:

align

Specify `left`, `center`, or `right` to indicate how you want the text to align within the text field or text area. The default is `left`.

class

The `class` attribute allows you to apply CSS formatting to the text. In order to use the `class` attribute you should first apply a StyleSheet object to the text field. CSS works only with text fields, and not with text areas. You can read more about using CSS with text fields in Recipe 8.15.

<span>

Use this tag to apply CSS formatting to your HTML text. In order to apply CSS, you must first have applied a StyleSheet object to the text field. The tag only works with text fields, and not with text areas. Flash supports the following attribute for the span tag:

class

The CSS class you want to apply to the text.

<u>

Use this tag to underline text.

8.13 Entering International and Nonstandard Characters

Problem

You want to enter international and/or nonstandard characters into text fields, text inputs, or text areas.

Solution

For text fields you can use the Alt-sequences to enter the characters at authoring time. Or, you can copy and paste from another application.

For text fields, text areas, and text inputs, use the Unicode escape sequences to add these characters at runtime.

Discussion

Flash uses Unicode for character encoding, so that it can support a wide range of languages and special characters. And because of this support, Flash movies can display any character as long as the user's computer has the appropriate font.

If you are using characters available on a standard keyboard, you can enter those characters without any special considerations. However, if you want to enter other characters, there are two different ways to do this: you can enter the values at authoring time (for text fields) or you can use ActionScript to add the values at runtime.

When you enter Unicode values to a text field at authoring time, you can either copy and paste the characters from another application or you can enter them using the Alt-sequences. For example, you can enter Alt-0169 (Windows) or Option-G (Macintosh) to add the copyright symbol (©) to a text field at authoring time.

If you want to use ActionScript to display any of these nonstandard characters in a dynamic (or input) text field at runtime, you can use the Unicode escape sequences within the string you assign to the text field's text property. For example, the escape sequence \u00a9 is the Unicode escape sequence for the copyright symbol:

```
// This code, when placed on the same timeline as the dynamic text field,
// tField, displays: this is a copyright symbol: ©
tField.text = "this is a copyright symbol: \u00a9";
```

If you are loading the text from an external source using ActionScript, and then applying it to the text field, text input, or text area at runtime, you can load and display any Unicode text and it should render properly within Flash. If, for example, you are loading text from a text file, make sure the text file is saved as UTF-8 or UTF-16. If you save the document as UTF-16, you need to make sure that contains a byte order mark. Otherwise Flash will interpret the content as UTF-8. Most editors that save to UTF-16 automatically add the byte order mark.

8.14 Ensuring that Text Displays in the Original Font

Problem

You want to make sure that your movie's text will display in the correct font even if the user does not have that font installed on her system.

Solution

Embed the font. Or, if you want to continue to use device fonts, choose one of the font groups from the font menu (text fields) or set the fontFamily style (text area and text input) to one of the font groups. This latter option does not guarantee that Flash will use the exact font you use during authoring time, but it does guarantee that Flash will substitute at least a similar font.

Discussion

By default, Flash uses device fonts for dynamic and input text fields as well as for text input and text area components. If you don't use a font that the user has installed on her computer, Flash will substitute the default font. In many cases, this is not something that you want to have happen. So you have two options:

- Embed the font. This approach guarantees that the exact font will be used every time the movie is played, regardless of the fonts available on the user's computer. The downside is an increase in file size. However, each font is embedded only once, even if it is used in multiple text fields, text inputs, and/or text areas.

- Continue using device fonts, but select one of the three font groups (_sans, _serif, or _typewriter) instead of a specific font. These font groups allow you to tell Flash what style of font to use. The benefit is that there is no increase in file size since you are not embedding fonts. The downside is that you don't get as much control over the fonts as you do when you embed the font.

How you can go about embedding a font or selecting a font group depends on whether you are using a component (text input or text area) or a text field. In order to embed a font for a text field, select the instance on the stage using the Selection tool, and then click on the Embed button in the Property inspector. From the Character Options dialog box, you should choose Specify Ranges. Choose to embed only the ranges of characters you plan to use so as to keep the file size increase to a minimum. If you know that you will display only uppercase and punctuation characters, for example, then choose those ranges. If you plan to use all the standard characters in the Latin character system, then choose Basic Latin, which includes uppercase, lowercase, numeric, and punctuation. If you plan to use the text field for user input, including the Basic Latin characters is usually a good idea. You can also add specific characters by entering them in the "Include these characters" field. Embedding specific characters is useful if you plan to use only a few characters and/or if you plan to use nonstandard characters such as symbols. You can select multiple ranges by holding the Ctrl key (Windows) or Command key (Macintosh) while clicking on the ranges with the mouse. That is all that is required to embed fonts for a text field.

When you are using large character sets, such as Japanese and Chinese fonts, you should avoid embedding the entire font. Doing so will significantly increase the file size of the movie. Instead, use device fonts. Or, if you need to embed fonts, embed just the necessary subset.

If you want to use a font group with a text field, select the text field on stage and then choose the font family from the Font menu in the Property inspector. Choose from _sans, _serif, or _typewriter.

There is no authoring time way to embed fonts or specify a font group for a text input or text area. However, the ActionScript code to accomplish the task is relatively simple. Assuming that you want to use an embedded font with a text input or text area, you first need to embed the font in the Flash movie. One way to do that is to create a font symbol. A font symbol resides in a shared library. That ability is beneficial if you plan to include the same font in multiple Flash movies that are loaded into a parent movie at the same time. However, that is a rather unlikely event. And font symbols have the distinct disadvantage that they require you to embed the entire font. Therefore, a much more practical approach is to embed the font using a text field. Create a dynamic text field off the visible portion of the stage. There is no need to place any text within the text field. Nor do you even need to give it an instance name. But you do need to embed the font using the text field in the same manner as described three paragraphs previously by means of the Character Options dialog box. Once you've embedded the font in the Flash movie in that manner, you can apply that font to a text input or text area by means of the *setStyle( )* method. There are two steps: tell the instance that it should use an embedded font, and then tell the instance which font to use. The basic syntax is as follows:

```
componentInstance.setStyle("embedFonts", true);
componentInstance.setStyle("fontFamily", "name of font");
```

For example, assuming that you have embedded the Times New Roman font, and you want to apply that font to a text area instance named ctaOutput, your code should look like the following:

```
ctaOutput.setStyle("embedFonts", true);
ctaOutput.setStyle("fontFamily", "Times New Roman");
```

If you want to apply the same font to every component instance in your Flash application (including Buttons, Lists, and so on), you can apply the *setStyle( )* method calls to the global style object as follows:

```
_global.style.setStyle("embedFonts", true);
_global.style.setStyle("fontFamily", "Times New Roman");
```

8.15   Applying CSS

Problem

You want to apply CSS (cascading style sheets) to a dynamic text field.

Solution

Use a StyleSheet object to load the CSS from an external file, and then apply it to the text field.

Optionally, use the TextLoader component.

Discussion

The StyleSheet class allows you to apply CSS to text fields in your Flash application. While there are several ways in which you can create and populate a StyleSheet object within Flash, the most useful is to load an external CSS document. You can define a CSS document using a standard text editor or a CSS editor such as Dreamweaver or Top Style.

After you've defined the CSS document, save it to the same directory to which you are saving the *.swf* file. Then, within Flash, use the following code:

```
// Set the text field so that it can render HTML.
tField.html = true;

// Create a StyleSheet object.
var cssStyles:TextField.StyleSheet = new TextField.StyleSheet( );

// Define an onLoad( ) event handler method for the style sheet so that it knows what
to
// do with the CSS once it has loaded.
cssStyles.onLoad = function(bLoaded:Boolean):Void {
  if(bLoaded) {

    // Apply the style sheet to the text field.
    tField.styleSheet = this;
```

```
        // Assign the HTML text to the text field.
        tField.htmlText = "HTML text";
    }
};

    // Load the CSS.
    cssStyles.load("CSS document");
```

As you can see from the code, you can apply a style sheet to a text field using the styleSheet property of the text field. You must apply the style sheet to the text field *before* you assign the HTML to it.

You can define both tag styles and style classes in your CSS document. Flash supports the following styles:

color
> A hexadecimal representation of the color value to apply to the text. Use a # prefix. For example, red is #FF0000.

display
> How you want the text to display. You can choose from block, inline, or none. A value of block means that the text appears in its own block. A value of inline means that it appears in line with surrounding text. A value of none means that the text does not display.

font-family
> The name of a font or font group.

font-size
> The point size to use for the font.

font-style
> Either normal or italic.

font-weight
> Either normal or bold.

margin-left
> The number of pixels in the left margin.

margin-right
> The number of pixels in the right margin.

text-align
> You can choose from left, center, or right.

text-indent
> How many pixels to indent the text from the left margin.

text-decoration
> Either bold or underline.

The following is an example of a simple CSS document. The first block defines a style for a tag named <body>. The second block defines a style class named code.

```
body {
  font-family: "_sans";
  color: #0000FF;
}
.code {
  font-family: "_typewriter";
  color: #FF0000;
}
```

The following ActionScript example loads the preceding CSS from a document named *styles.css* and then applies it to a text field named tOutput:

```
tOutput.html = true;

var cssStyles:TextField.StyleSheet = new TextField.StyleSheet();
cssStyles.onLoad = function(bLoaded:Boolean):Void {
  if(bLoaded) {
    tOutput.styleSheet = this;
    tOutput.htmlText = "<body>If you want to use CSS with Flash, use a <span
class='code'>StyleSheet</span> object.</body>";
  }
};
cssStyles.load("styles.css");
```

If you feel uncomfortable with the ActionScript necessary to apply CSS to a text field, you can use the TextLoader component discussed in Chapter 13 to both load text and CSS without any ActionScript code.

CHAPTER 9

Adding Interactivity

Although Flash is a great platform for delivering linear animations, linear animations represent just a small fraction of the many possibilities for the types of content you can deliver using Flash. Linear animations might not require any user interaction. But most types of Flash content do.

Buttons are one of the primary ways in which users can interact with your Flash movies. Using buttons, you can allow users to cause actions to occur by rolling over buttons, clicking on buttons, and other similar types of events. You can use both button symbols and movie clip symbols as buttons in your Flash applications. This chapter explains the advantages and disadvantages of both.

Buttons are the basic building blocks of user interaction mechanisms in Flash. In addition, you can build specialized buttons to use as menus, and you can use specialized controls such as dials and sliders. Each of those topics is discussed in this chapter as well.

Users can also interact with Flash using the mouse and keyboard. This chapter shows you how to apply custom mouse cursors—even interactive cursors. And you'll also read about how to detect keyboard activity.

There are additional ways in which users can interact with Flash applications. Some of those topics are not discussed in this chapter because they have chapters dedicated to them already. You can read more about using text for interactivity (links, user input, and so on) in Chapters 7 and 8. Additionally, Flash has standard UI components that you can use for building user input forms and navigation controls. Those components are discussed in more detail in Chapters 13 and 14.

9.1 Creating Buttons from Scratch

Problem

You want to create a button.

Solution

Create a new button symbol in the library, and then drag an instance of it onto the stage.

Optionally, use a movie clip symbol.

Discussion

Flash buttons are a convenient way to add user interaction to your movies. In order to use buttons in your movie, you must first create a button symbol in the library. Flash allows you to define up, over, and down states for your button symbols, and it automatically displays them when the user has used the mouse pointer to activate the button states. Then, after you have created the symbol, you can place instances of that symbol on the stage within your movie.

Here are the steps to create a button from scratch:

1. Create a new symbol. You can accomplish this by choosing Insert → New Symbol from the menu, or by pressing Ctrl-F8 or Command-F8. This step will open up the Create New Symbol dialog box.

2. In the Create New Symbol dialog box, enter a value in the Name field. This name is what appears in the library next to the symbol to help you to locate it. So use a descriptive name—a name that indicates what the button is used for or how the button looks. A good example would be something such as SendEmail-Button or BeveledOvalButton.

3. In the Behavior section of the Create New Symbol dialog box, select Button, so that Flash will know to treat the symbol (and its instances) as a button. Button symbols have specialized timelines, so it is important that you select Button as the behavior before you add any content to the timeline.

4. Click the OK button to close the dialog box and finalize the creation of the new symbol.

5. After you have clicked OK, Flash will automatically open the new symbol for editing. You will see a timeline with four specially named frames in it—Up, Over, Down, Hit. All buttons have this special timeline.

6. Create artwork in the default layer on the keyframe at the Up frame. You can add artwork using the drawing tools by placing an instance of a movie clip symbol or graphic symbol (but not another button symbol) or by importing an image. This artwork is how the button will look by default—when the user is neither hovering over it with the mouse nor clicking on it.

7. Insert a keyframe and contents at the Over frame. Flash will automatically display this frame when the user moves the mouse over the button. If you want to copy the same contents from the Up frame to the Over frame, select the Over frame in the default layer and choose Insert → Keyframe or press F6. This is a

convenient way to create an exact copy of the previous frame if you want to modify only some aspect of the up contents (such as changing a fill color). Otherwise, if you want to add completely different content to the Over frame, add a new blank keyframe by selecting the frame and choosing Insert → Blank Keyframe or pressing F7.

8. Insert a keyframe and contents at the Down frame. Flash displays this frame when the user clicks on the button. Follow the same instructions from step 7, but apply them to the Down frame instead of the Over frame.

9. At this point, you are done editing the button symbol. (You can read more about using the Hit frame in Recipe 9.3.) You should return to the timeline to which you wish to add an instance of the button. You can return to the main timeline several different ways:

   • Choose Edit → Edit Document

   • Choose the scene (by default, Scene 1) from the Edit Scene menu in the Scene toolbar

   • Choose the scene (by default, Scene 1) from the Navigation menu in the Scene toolbar

10. Open the library either by choosing Window → Library or by pressing F11 or Ctrl-L or Command-L.

11. From the library, select the button symbol, and drag an instance of it onto the stage where you want it.

That is all there is to creating the button. If you test your movie (Control → Test Movie) and experiment by moving the mouse over the button and clicking on it, you should see the button change states.

When you create a button, it is not absolutely necessary that you define over and down states. If there are no keyframes defined for either of those states, Flash will simply continue to display the up state when the user mouses over or clicks on the button.

Button symbols have the advantage of built-in state detection (up, over, and down). However, there are certain inherent limitations with buttons. The limitations start to get more apparent as you start to use more ActionScript code. Most notable is that buttons cannot reference themselves via ActionScript code, nor can they be added to the stage with code. Although these issues may seem irrelevant to the beginning Flash developer, they can have rather significant implications with regard to building highly dynamic Flash applications. For that reason, many Flash developers who use a lot of ActionScript code tend to give preference to movie clips over buttons. Movie clips can reference themselves, and it's possible to add movie clip instances to the stage using code. Furthermore, movie clips can respond to the same events as buttons (such as mouse-overs, clicks, and so on). The only disadvantage of movie clips is that they don't have built-in state detection, as do buttons. However, with a little finessing, you can actually create a movie clip that does handle button states. To do so, complete the following steps:

1. Create a new symbol by pressing Ctrl-F8 or Command-F8.
2. Enter a name, and select Movie Clip as the behavior.
3. When you click OK, the symbol will open in editing mode.
4. Rename the default layer to Artwork, and create two more layers named Labels and Actions.
5. Create keyframes for the first three frames of each of the layers.
6. Select the first keyframe of the Actions layer, open the Actions panel (F9), and add the following line of code:

   ```
   stop( );
   ```

7. Add frame labels to the keyframes on the Labels layer. Use the labels of _up, _over, and _down.
8. Add artwork to the keyframes of the Artwork layer. The artwork on the frames should correspond to the up, over, and down states.

After you've created the symbol by completing the preceding steps, you can return to the main timeline and create an instance of the symbol as described in the steps for a button symbol instance. The only difference between how the movie clip instance and button instance will behave is that the movie clip instance requires you to add the appropriate ActionScript code for event handling before it will respond to the up, over, and down states. The button instance will respond with those states even if no event handling code has been applied to it.

At this point, you have successfully created a button or movie clip that responds to mouse events such as rolling over and clicking. It responds by displaying the corresponding button state as you have defined it in the symbol's timeline.

9.2 Creating Buttons that Animate

Problem

You want to create a button that will animate in one, two, or all three of its states.

Solution

Add a movie clip instance to the button's keyframes in which the movie clip contains animation.

Optionally, use a movie clip and some ActionScript to control the timeline.

Discussion

Buttons (and movie clips with button states) allow you to define only one frame for each of their states, and that limitation may at first appear to be a challenge when you want to add animations to your button states. However, you can achieve this goal by adding movie clip instances containing animation to the keyframes of the symbol's timeline. This trick works because a movie clip's timeline can play independently of the timeline that contains it.

There are many different combinations to choose from when talking about adding animations to buttons. Some of the more common are as follows:

- Animate the up state, and have non-animated over and down states. For example, you might have a button that spins until a user moves the mouse over it, at which point it would stop spinning.

- Animate the over state, but not the up or down states. This is the reverse of the previous scenario. For example, a button could remain static until the user moves the mouse over it, at which point it could begin to spin or animate in some other way.

When a button state is activated, either by the user clicking on the button or moving the mouse over or away from the button, Flash automatically moves the playhead in the button's timeline to the corresponding frame. This playhead is moved to that frame only, however, and does not continue to play subsequent frames. But by utilizing a movie clip, you can achieve your goal. For example, you can animate the over state of a button by following these steps:

1. Create a new button with up and down states as outlined in Recipe 9.1. Use a blank keyframe for the over state.

2. Create a new movie clip symbol with animation taking place over multiple frames. (See movie clip and timeline recipes in Chapters 8 and 9 for more information on how to do this.)

3. Return to the button symbol's timeline.

4. Move the playhead to the over frame.

5. Select all the contents on the stage on the over frame, and delete them.

6. Open the library, and drag an instance of the movie clip symbol from the library onto the stage at the over frame in the button symbol.

After you have completed these six steps, you have successfully created a button that animates when the user moves the mouse over it. In order to see the button work, you must create an instance of the button symbol within your movie, and test it.

If you want to create a button that animates on a different state, you can accomplish this by placing an instance of an animating movie clip within the button at the corresponding frame. For example, you can create a button that animates on the up state by placing an animating movie clip instance within the button's up frame.

Although the preceding steps are helpful for adding continuously animating button states, they don't directly address the scenario in which each button state animates to the next. For example, you may want to make a button in which the transition between the up and over states is a gradual animation rather than relying on the default functionality in which Flash simply jumps from the Up frame to the Over frame. While you can accomplish this feat using a variation of the technique described earlier in this recipe, it's much more practical to accomplish it using a movie clip instance rather than a button instance. You can then use some relatively simple ActionScript to control the playback of the timeline appropriately:

1. Create a new movie clip symbol.

2. Within the symbol add two new layers, for a total of three. Name the three layers Labels, Actions, and Animation.

3. Define six keyframes on the Labels layer. Give the keyframes the following frame labels: up, over, out, press, release, and outside. The up frame should be on frame 1. The exact frame numbers of the subsequent keyframes depend on the animation between button states. Although the up state doesn't have any animation, it's generally a good idea to leave a few frames between it and the next keyframe so that the frame label is visible in the timeline. Therefore, if each animation requires nine frames, the keyframes can appear on frames 1, 10, 20, 30, 40, and 50.

4. On the Actions layer, there ought to be a keyframe on frame 1 as well as the frames just prior to the out, press, release, and outside frames. And there ought to be a keyframe on the frame at which the outside animation stops. If the animations each require nine frames and the frame labels appear on frames 1, 10, 20, 30, 40, and 50, then the keyframes on the Actions layer appear at frames 1, 19, 29, 39, 49, and 59.

5. On each of the keyframes on the Actions layer, add the following ActionScript code:

   ```
   this.stop();
   ```

6. On the Animation layer add the artwork and any tweens. The up frame ought to have the default up state of the button. The over frame ought to be the starting point for the transition from the up to over state (meaning the first frame of that animation is likely identical to the up state). The out frame ought to be the starting point for the transition from the over to the up state. The press frame ought to be the starting point for the transition from the over to the down state. The release frame ought to be the starting point for the transition from the down to the over state. The outside frame ought to be the starting point for the down to the up state. Figure 9-1 shows an example of what the timeline might look like.

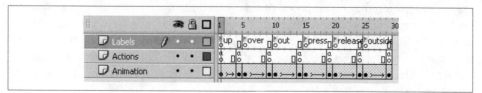

Figure 9-1. An example of a timeline for an animated button movie clip

7. Exit out of editing the symbol, and return to the main timeline or the point at which you want to add an instance of the animated button movie clip.

8. Add an instance of the movie clip symbol, and give it an instance name. This example uses the instance name mButton.

9. On the timeline to which the instance was added, add the following Action-Script code:

```
mButton.onRollOver = function( ):Void {
  this.gotoAndPlay("over");
};
mButton.onRollOut = function( ):Void {
  this.gotoAndPlay("out");
};
mButton.onPress = function( ):Void {
  this.gotoAndPlay("press");
};
mButton.onRelease = function( ):Void {
  this.gotoAndPlay("release");
};
mButton.onReleaseOutside = function( ):Void {
  this.gotoAndPlay("outside");
};
```

That ActionScript code tells the movie clip to play the correct transition animation for each mouse event.

9.3 Defining the Area that Activates the Button

Problem

You want to define the area that causes the button's over state to be triggered.

Solution

Define a shape in the button's Hit frame.

Discussion

By default, any shape that is defined within a button can trigger the button's over state when the mouse is moved over it. In many cases, this behavior is sufficient, because buttons are often composed of solid shapes. However, in other situations you may run into problems when you rely on the default behavior. Consider, for example, a button that is composed of text. When the user moves the mouse directly over the shapes of the characters that compose that text, the button's over state is activated. However, if the user moves the mouse such that it is generally over the text, but not directly over the character shapes, then the button's over state is never activated. This result can be very frustrating for the user who is trying to move the mouse over the button.

In these types of situations, it is best to define a hit area. You can accomplish this by drawing a shape that defines the area you want to use to activate the button's over state at the button's Hit frame. The contents of the Hit frame are never displayed in the resulting movie, but that shape is used by Flash to determine what area should activate the button.

If you are using a movie clip to handle button events rather than an actual button instance, then you don't have the option of simply adding an extra keyframe with the label _hitarea, as you might have assumed. You can actually use ActionScript to apply a hit area to a movie clip, but that course is a bit convoluted. Instead, the simplest approach is to add invisible artwork within the movie clip symbol. The steps are as follows:

1. Open the movie clip symbol for editing.
2. Add a new layer, and give it a label of hit area.
3. Open the Color Mixer panel (Window → Design Panels → Color Mixer).
4. Select the Stroke color and turn the Alpha setting to 0.
5. Select the Fill color and turn the Alpha setting to 0.
6. From the Tools panel, choose one of the drawing tools most appropriate for creating the hit area shape. For example, if you want to define a rectangular hit area, choose the Rectangle tool.
7. Draw the hit area shape on the stage within the Hit Area layer. The artwork should be invisible. However, if you select it with the Arrow tool, you should be able to see that it is there.

9.4   Creating Hotspots with Invisible Buttons

Problem

You want to define hotspots in your movie in which there is no visible button.

Solution

Create a button with no content except a hit area.

Or, if you are using a movie clip as a button, create a movie clip with the shape you want, and set the alpha value of the movie clip to zero.

Discussion

More often than not, you will want the user to be able to see a button within the movie so that she can locate it and click it. However, there are reasons you might want to use invisible buttons to create hotspots in your movie. Here are a couple examples of the uses of hotspots:

- Define clickable regions of a map or other image
- Add hidden or surprise functionality

In any of these scenarios, you will want to create an invisible button. You can quickly create an invisible button by defining the hit area and nothing else. Remember that a hit area is never displayed in your Flash movie. It remains as an invisible shape that causes the button over state to be activated when the user moves the mouse over it. Therefore, when you define a button that has no contents other than on the Hit frame, the button will be active in the movie, but will be invisible to the user (except that the hand cursor will appear when the user moves the mouse over it.) When you create an instance of an invisible button in your Flash movie, the instance will show up as a transparent, light blue shape on the stage while you are authoring. This is for your benefit so that you can see where the instance exists. However, the light blue shape will not show up in the resulting movie.

Alternatively, if you are using a movie clip as a button instead of a button symbol, you need to use a slightly different approach to creating an invisible button:

1. You should define the movie clip symbol with a single frame, and on that frame, draw the hit area shape.
2. Create an instance of the movie clip in the movie to act as a button.
3. Select the movie clip instance, and locate the Color menu in the Property inspector.
4. Select the Alpha option from the Color menu.
5. Adjust the alpha value to 0%.

With either the button symbol or movie clip symbol techniques, you should name the instances and assign actions to them as you would to any other button or movie clip instance.

9.5   Making Buttons Respond to Clicks

Problem

You want your button to respond when the user clicks on it.

Solution

Define an *onPress( )* and/or *onRelease( )* event handler method for the button instance.

Discussion

Buttons can handle a variety of different events, or user actions, including detecting when the user clicks on them. Furthermore, Flash treats each click as two separate events—the press and the release. And you can handle each of these events separately by defining an *onPress( )* and/or an *onRelease( )* event handler method for the button instance. The *onPress( )* event handler method is invoked when the user presses the button, and the *onRelease( )* event handler method is invoked when the user releases the button.

If the terminology and concepts mentioned in the preceding paragraph are unfamiliar to you, or if you don't yet feel very comfortable with ActionScript, don't give up! Even though it may appear daunting at first, the procedure for adding actions to buttons is really not difficult, and it is something you can easily get the hang of with a little practice. No matter what actions you add to a button, the procedure is always the same (and this applies to both button symbol instances and movie clip instances):

1. Make sure you have named the instance on the stage.

2. In the Flash authoring environment, open the timeline in which the button instance exists.

3. If you have not yet created a special layer for actions, do so now. Create a new layer at the top of all existing layers, and label it Actions.

4. Within the Actions layer, create a keyframe at the same frame in which the button instance is first defined. If the button is first defined on the first frame of the timeline, you don't need to do anything for this step.

5. Click on the keyframe in the Actions layer so that it is selected. It should highlight to let you know that you have selected the frame.

6. Open the Actions panel either by pressing F9 or by choosing Window → Actions.

7. Enter ActionScript code into the script pane using the syntax shown in the following code block. In this example code, the *onPress( )* method is defined. If you want to define another of the event handler methods, you need only to substitute the onPress portion of the code with the correct event handler method name (such as onRelease). Also, in this example btInstance is the name for the button instance. You should replace that name with the name of your button instance.

```
btInstance.onPress = function( ):Void {
   // Actions to occur when the button is pressed go here.
}
```

8. Add the actions that you want to occur when the event is handled in the *method body*—the part of the code between the opening curly brace and the closing curly brace. For example, if you want to call a *trace( )* action when the button is pressed, your code would look like this:

```
btInstance.onPress = function( ):Void {
   trace("You pressed the button.");
};
```

9.6 Making Buttons Respond to Mouse Rollovers

Problem

You want your button to respond to mouse rollovers.

Solution

Define an *onRollOver( )* and/or *onRollOut( )* event handler method for the button instance.

Discussion

You can configure your buttons to respond to mouse rollovers and rollouts using the *onRollOver( )* and *onRollOut( )* methods, respectively. If you define an *onRollOver( )* method, it will get invoked any time the user moves the pointer over the button instance. Likewise, the *onRollOut( )* method, if defined, gets invoked whenever the user moves the point off of the button instance.

The following are examples of the correct syntax for defining these event handler methods for a button instance:

```
btInstance.onRollOver = function( ) {
    // Actions to occur when the user moves the mouse over the button go here.
};

btInstance.onRollOut = function( ) {
    // Actions to occur when the user moves the mouse off the button go here.
};
```

If you are not yet familiar with the process for adding actions to buttons by way of event handler methods, see Recipe 9.5 for detailed instructions.

9.7 Making Buttons Respond to Dragging and Releasing Off the Instance

Problem

You want your button to respond when a user clicks on the button and drags off of it and/or when the user releases the button after having dragged off of the button.

Solution

Use the *onDragOff( )* and/or *onReleaseOutside( )* event handler methods.

Discussion

Although the most common button events are click- and rollover-related events, you can also handle several other kinds of user actions. Among these events are the user actions of clicking on a button and dragging off of it, and clicking on a button, dragging off of it, and then releasing.

In order to understand how and when to use these additional events, consider first that the typical behavior of a button the responds to click releases is as follows: the user clicks on the button, and when they release, the actions are triggered. As long as the user has not yet released the button, they can change their mind by dragging the mouse pointer off the button before releasing it. At that point, when they release, the button actions are not triggered. Normally this is the behavior that you would want from a button. However, in some situations you want to make sure that the actions are also triggered when the user releases the button outside the button instance. For example, if the button is moving on the stage while the user clicks it, it may move out from under the mouse pointer before the user has the opportunity to release. Another good example is when creating sliders. Sliders are generally constrained to a certain region over which they can be dragged. If the user tries to drag the slider outside that region, the slider will stop at the boundary, but the mouse pointer will continue. If the user releases the button after having dragged off the button, you still want to handle the event. In these cases, you should also detect when the user releases outside using an *onReleaseOutside( )* event handler method. The correct syntax is:

```
btInstance.onReleaseOutside = function( ) {
  // Actions to occur when the user releases the button outside the button instance.
}
```

In some situations, you might want to define different actions for a basic release and a release outside the button instance. However, in most cases you will want to define the same actions. Rather than define the same actions twice (once in the *onRelease( )* method and once in the *onReleaseOutside( )* method), you can simply assign the value of one method to the other. Here is an example:

```
// First, define the onRelease( ) event handler method.
btInstance.onRelease = function( ) {
  // Actions to occur when the user releases the button outside the button
  instance.
}

// Next, assign the value of the onRelease( ) method to the onReleaseOutside( )
// method. So in either event, the same actions are invoked.
btInstance.onReleaseOutside = btInstance.onRelease;
```

9.8   Building Menus with Buttons

Problem

You want to create menus such that you can press one button and then roll over and release on others.

Solution

Set all the button instances to track as menu items.

Discussion

The normal behavior for buttons is such that if you press one button (but don't yet release) and then drag the mouse pointer over another button, the other button will not respond to the rollover event. And if you release on top of a button other than the one on which you first pressed, the release event will not be activated either. In many cases, this is the behavior that you want from your buttons. However, when working with buttons that compose menus, you may want to alter that behavior such that buttons in the menu respond to rollover and release events even if the user first pressed another button in the menu. This behavior is particularly important for pop-up menus in which the user has to press one button to expand the menu.

You can quickly modify the behavior of a button in this way by setting it to track as a menu item. With button symbol instances, you can choose this option from the Property inspector. If you select the button instance on the stage, you can choose Track as Menu Item from the tracking menu.

The preceding technique works for button symbol instances at authoring time. If you want to track movie clip symbols as menu items or if you want to perform the same task at runtime, you can use the trackAsMenu property. The trackAsMenu property is a property for both button and movie clip instances, and can have a value of either true or false. By default the value is false, meaning that the instance is not tracked as a menu item. By setting the property to true, Flash immediately begins tracking the instance as a menu item. One of the advantages of using this technique is that you can switch back and forth between tracking an instance as a menu item or not.

```
btInstance.trackAsMenu = true;
```

9.9   Using Slider Controls

Problem

You want to use a slider control.

Solution

Use an instance of the RightActionScript HorizontalSlider or VerticalSlider.

Discussion

Slider controls are useful and even necessary in a whole host of possible applications. The ways in which you might use a slider include, but are not limited to:

- Adjusting the volume of a sound
- Adjusting the pan of a sound
- Changing color values for a movie clip
- Changing transparency for a movie clip
- Allowing users to select values for a form

However, Flash does not have any (practical) built-in slider controls that you can use in your applications. While there are a few sliders in the Buttons Common Library, they are difficult to use and to customize. If you want to use a slider component, it is recommended that you either write your own (which is outside the scope of this book) or use a third-party component. In this recipe, you'll find instructions for using and customizing the RightActionScript HorizontalSlider and VerticalSlider components.

Using a horizontal or vertical slider doesn't require many steps. In order to add an instance to a project, drag an instance from the Components panel to the stage. If you then test the movie, you'll see a functioning slider at the default dimensions and with the default artwork.

 The horizontal and vertical sliders have identical parameters and they work identically. The primary difference between them is that one is horizontal and one is vertical.

By default, the sliders have minimum values of 0 and maximum values of 100. However, you can set the range by using the Component Inspector panel. Update the values for the minimum and maximum parameters. For example, if you want to use slider controls to control the red, green, and blue elements of a color value, then you probably want to work with a range of 0 to 255. Or perhaps you want to use a slider to allow a user to select a year in a range from 1900 to 2100. You can also use negative numbers. For example, you might want to use a range from –10 to 10.

If you want to retrieve the value of a slider instance, you can retrieve by percent or by value. The percent is always in the range 0 to 100 regardless of the range set by the minimum and maximum parameters. The value is the value from the range that corresponds to the percent. If the range is set to the default of 0 to 100, the percent and value are equal. Regardless of which you want to retrieve, you have to use some simple ActionScript. The percent is returned by the percent property, and the value is returned by the value property. The following code uses a trace( ) statement to display the percent and value of a slider instance called sldrVolume:

```
trace(sldrVolume.percent);
trace(sldrVolume.value);
```

Most frequently, you'll want to retrieve the value only when the user moves the slider. The slider components can send out notifications when that occurs. You simply have to write some ActionScript code to listen for those notifications.

In order for the slider to send a notification, you have to tell it where to send that notification, by way of a method called *addEventListener()*. The *addEventListener()* method for the sliders is defined such that it requires three parameters: the name of the event, a reference to an object for which the function is defined, and the name of the function. The name of the event dispatched by sliders is called *change*. The following code tells sldrVolume to call the *onVolumeChange()* function when the user moves the slider:

```
sldrVolume.addEventListener("change", this, "onVolumeChange");
```

The next step is to define the function. The function always gets passed one parameter. That parameter is an object with two properties: type and target. The type property specifies the type of event (change), and the target property is a reference to the component that dispatched the event (sldrVolume). The following function uses oEvent.target to reference the slider instance that just dispatched the event. It then references the value property from that slider instance. It uses a *trace()* statement to display the value in the Output panel.

```
function onVolumeChange(oEvent:Object):Void {
    trace(oEvent.target.value);
}
```

The horizontal and vertical sliders are each composed of two basic elements: the thumb bar and the track. Although the default artwork may be suitable in many cases, it is likely that you'll want to customize the appearance in some projects. Therefore, you can customize the thumb bar and/or the track element. To do so, complete the following steps:

1. Make a new movie clip symbol for each element you want to customize.

2. Select the Linkage option from the library menu for the symbols, and click the Export for ActionScript option. Assign a linkage identifier to each.

3. The linkage identifiers must be unique within the Flash document. Consider something descriptive such as VolumeSliderThumbBar and VolumeSliderTrack. When you click the Export for ActionScript option, Flash will automatically populate the linkage identifier field with the symbol name. As long as you've used a unique and descriptive symbol name, it's okay to use that for the linkage identifier as well.

4. Click OK in the Linkage Settings dialog box.

5. Use the Arrow tool to select the slider instance for which you want to customize the appearance.

6. In the Component Inspector panel, enter the linkage identifier(s) for the custom artwork symbol(s) that you want to use. For example, if you assigned a linkage

identifier of VolumeSliderThumbBar to the symbol you want to use for the thumb bar element, enter VolumeSliderThumbBar for the thumbBarLinkage parameter.

The changes won't be reflected in the live preview during authoring time. However, when you export (or test) the movie, you'll see the custom artwork.

When you build the movie clip for the track, align the track artwork so the upper-left corner is at position 0,0 within the symbol. When you build a movie clip for the thumb bar, align the artwork so it is centered at 0,0. If you notice that the artwork doesn't align correctly in the SWF, it's likely that you have to realign the artwork within the symbols.

For the thumb bar states (up, over, and down) you need only to specify the artwork for the states on frames 1 (up), 2 (over), and 3 (down) on the timeline of the movie clip symbol that you specify as the custom thumb bar.

9.10   Using a Dial Control

Problem

You want to use a dial control.

Solution

Use an instance of the RightActionScript `Dial` component.

Discussion

Like slider controls, dial controls are a moderately common element in Flash applications. You can use dials to control audio settings (volume, pan, and so on), mimic analog devices (such as radios), and much more. However, as with slider controls, Flash has no (practical) built-in dial controls. That means that you either have to make your own dial control or use a third-party component. In this recipe, I'll discuss how to use the RightActionScript `Dial` component.

Adding a dial is as simple as dragging an instance from the Components panel to the stage of a Flash document. When you test the movie, you'll notice that the dial automatically responds to mouse events. As you mouse over it, the dial highlights. As you click on the dial, it visually changes to the down state, and you can drag the mouse to move the dial.

As with the slider control, you can retrieve the value from a dial as a percent or in a range. The default range is from 0 to 100, so unless you change the range, the percent and value are equal. However, you can set the range in the Component Inspector panel with the minimum and maximum parameters. For example, if you want to use the dial to control the red element of a color, you might want to change the range from 0 to 255. You can retrieve the percent (always from 0 to 100) using the percent property. You can retrieve the value using the value property. Both require Action-Script. The following code uses trace( ) statements to display the values in the Output panel:

```
trace(dlVolume.percent);
trace(dlVolume.value);
```

Most commonly you'll want the dial to send a notification when the user changes the setting. Just like the slider components, the dial component dispatches events to any listening object. You can add a listener using some ActionScript code with a method called *addEventListener()*. You need to pass that method three parameters: the name of the event, the object for which the function is defined, and the name of the function you want it to call when the value updates. The name of the event dispatched by a dial is called *change*. The following code tells a dial called dlVolume to notify a function called *onVolumeChange()* when the value changes:

```
dlVolume.addEventListener("change", this, "onVolumeChange");
```

You can then define a function with the same name specified in the third parameter, and when the value of the dial changes, the dial will automatically call that function. It will pass that function one parameter—an object with a type property and a target property. The type property specifies the name of the event. In the case of a dial component, the type is always change. The target property is a reference to the dial that dispatched the event. The following defines a function that uses a *trace()* statement to display the value of a dial:

```
function onVolumeChange(oEvent:Object):Void {
  trace(oEvent.target.value);
}
```

By default, the dial rotates on a range from 45° to 315° where 0° is at the bottom of the dial. That is to say that the stops on the dial are at angles on the lower-left and lower-right sides. If you want, you can adjust the range over which the dial can rotate by way of the minimumAngle and maximumAngle parameters. To do so, simply change the values via the Component Inspector panel.

Although the default artwork may be suitable for many projects, it is likely that you'll want to occasionally use custom artwork. The component has just one element, and that element is entirely customizable. You can customize the dial by completing the following steps:

1. Make a new movie clip symbol.
2. Add the artwork to the movie clip. Make sure that the point of rotation is at 0,0 within the symbol.
3. Select Linkage from the library menu for the movie clip symbol.
4. Check the Export for ActionScript option.
5. Give the movie clip a unique and descriptive linkage identifier.

6. Click the OK button.

7. Select the dial instance for which you want to use the customized artwork.

8. In the Component Inspector panel, enter the linkage identifier from the new movie clip for the dialLinkage parameter.

The custom artwork won't display in live preview during authoring time. However, when you export the movie, it will display properly in the SWF.

9.11 Creating Custom Cursors

Problem

You want to create a custom mouse cursor in place of the standard arrow/hand.

Solution

Use the *Mouse.hide( )* method to hide the standard cursor, and then use ActionScript to tell a movie clip instance to follow the mouse.

Discussion

Although you cannot really replace the cursor icon in your Flash movies, you can create the illusion of a custom mouse cursor:

1. Create a movie clip symbol in which you add the artwork for your custom icon.

2. Create an instance of the movie clip symbol on the stage in the main timeline, and make sure to give it an instance name. You should make sure the instance is on a layer that appears above all the other layers in the main timeline.

3. Hide the standard mouse cursor with the *Mouse.hide( )* method. Assuming that you want to hide the standard arrow/hand cursor from the moment the Flash movie starts to play, place the following code on the first keyframe of the main timeline:

4. Mouse.hide( );

5. Define a function that updates the movie clip to the mouse location by assigning the values of _xmouse and _ymouse to the _x and _y properties of the movie clip:

6. function updateCursorLocation( ):Void {

7. mCustomMouseCursor._x = _xmouse;

8. mCustomMouseCursor._y = _ymouse;

9. updateAfterEvent( );

10. }

11. Instruct Flash to continuously call the function using *setInterval( )*. You can call *setInterval( )* with two parameters—a reference to the function and a number of

milliseconds to use as the interval. To make the cursor move smoothly use an interval of something near 50 milliseconds:

12. setInterval(updateCursorLocation, 50);

13. In the event that you use any ActionScript code within your Flash movie in order to attach movie clips, add a line of code that tells Flash to move the cursor movie clip to a high stacking order. That step will ensure that the cursor movie clip does not accidentally get hidden beneath other instances. Use the *swapDepths()* method, and pass it a value of *this.getNextHighestDepth()*:

```
mCustomMouseCursor.swapDepths(this.getNextHighestDepth( ));
```

After you have completed the preceding steps, you can test the movie, and you should see your custom cursor instead of the standard arrow.

9.12   Creating Animated Cursors

Problem

You want to create an animated mouse cursor.

Solution

Create a custom cursor as in Recipe 9.11, and create animation within the custom cursor's movie clip symbol.

Discussion

You can create animated cursors by extending upon the technique in Recipe 9.11. An animated cursor is simply a custom cursor in which the cursor movie clip symbol contains animation—either frame-based animation or ActionScript-based animation. For example, you can create a cursor of a spinning box by following the steps in Recipe 9.11, but within the cursor movie clip symbol, create a spinning box animation either by using a motion tween or by using ActionScript to continually update the rotation.

9.13   Creating Interactive Custom Cursors

Problem

You want to create a cursor that can change state depending on what the user is doing.

Solution

Create a cursor movie clip symbol with three keyframes labeled up, over, and press. Then, create ActionScript code for the cursor instance such as described in the discussion.

Discussion

After you have created a basic custom cursor, you may discover that you want the cursor to respond to various events by changing state. When you use the default cursor, for example, it changes from an arrow to a hand icon when the user moves the mouse over an object with button event handlers. When you use a custom cursor, you do not get this behavior inherently. You can, however, create a cursor that responds in the same way. And, in addition, if you want, you can create a special press state for the cursor as well—a state that is activated whenever the user clicks the mouse button. The first step in creating an interactive custom cursor is to create the three states within the movie clip symbol. You can do this by doing the following:

- Rename the default layer in the symbol's timeline to Labels.
- Define three keyframes on the Labels layer. Label these keyframes (in this order) up, over, and press.
- Create a new layer named Artwork.
- On the Artwork layer define three keyframes that match up with the keyframes in the Labels layer.
- On each of the keyframes of the Artwork layer, place the artwork that corresponds to the state for that label. For example, on the frame that matches up with the up label, place the artwork for the cursor's default up state. If any of the states are animated, then the animation should be contained within another movie clip symbol, and you should place an instance of that symbol at the appropriate keyframe in the cursor symbol.
- Follow steps 2 and 3 from Recipe 9.11 for creating the custom cursor.
- Add the following additional code to the keyframe on the main timeline:

```
// Populate the aOverItems array with references to all the objects to which you
want the
// mCustomMouseCursor to respond with an over state. In this example, the array
is populated with
// mItem1 and mItem2. You should change those values to suit your own movie. The
rest of the code
// does not need to change.
var aOverItems = new Array(mItem1, mItem2);

// Declare a variable to keep track of the current cursor state.
var sMouseState:String = "up";

// Stop the playback of the mCustomMouseCursor instance's timeline.
mCustomMouseCursor.stop();

// Set an interval at which the checkState( ) function is called.
setInterval(checkState, 50);

function checkState( ):Void {
```

```
    // Loop through all the aIverItems references and perform hit tests. If the
  mCustomMouseCursor
  // overlaps any of those items, then change the mCustomMouseCursor state to the
  over state. Or,
  // if the mouse state is press, go to the press state.
    for(var i = 0; i < aOverItems.length; i++) {
      if(mCustomMouseCursor.hitTest(aOverItems[i])) {
        if(sMouseState == "press") {
          mCustomMouseCursor.gotoAndStop("press");
        }
        else {
          mCustomMouseCursor.gotoAndStop("over");
          sMouseState = "over";
        }
        return;
      }
    }

    // Otherwise, if nothing else, change the state to the up state.
    mCustomMouseCursor.gotoAndStop("up");
    sMouseState = "up";
}

// Add onMouseDown( ) and onMouseUp( ) event handler methods to assign the state
based on whether
// the user has clicked the mouse. Note that you shouldn't use onPress( ) and
onRelease( ) because
// that would interfere with other buttons and movie clips in your application.
mCustomMouseCursor.onMouseDown = function( ):Void {
  sMouseState = "press";
};

mCustomMouseCursor.onMouseUp = function( ):Void {
  sMouseState = "up";
};
```

The only part of the preceding code that you need to adapt for your specific project is the first line of code in which the aOverItems array is defined. The aOverItems array contains references to the objects in the movie to which you want the cursor to respond. In the example, the cursor is told to respond to objects (movie clips, buttons, or text fields) named mItem1 and mItem2.

9.14   Hiding the Hand Cursor

Problem

You want Flash to continue to display the arrow mouse icon instead of the hand icon even when the mouse is moved over a button (or movie clip acting as a button).

Solution

Set the useHandCursor property to false for all the movie clips and buttons for which you wish Flash to continue to use the arrow icon.

Discussion

The default behavior for Flash is that when the user moves the mouse over any button instance or any movie clip instance with button event handlers, the cursor changes from the arrow icon to a hand icon. However, it is possible for you to tell Flash to retain the arrow icon throughout by setting the useHandCursor property for the button and movie clip instances. For example, if you want Flash to retain the arrow icon even when the user moves the mouse over a button instance named btSubmit, you can use the following code on a keyframe within the timeline in which the button instance exists:

```
btSubmit.useHandCursor = false;
```

If at a later point you want Flash to use the hand cursor again when the user moves the mouse over objects, you can set the useHandCursor property to true again.

9.15   Detecting Keystrokes

Problem

You want to detect when the user presses a key on the keyboard.

Solution

Add a listener object to the Key class.

Discussion

If you want to detect key presses with Flash, you've got to write a small amount of ActionScript code. In order to handle keyboard interactivity, Flash uses a specific ActionScript class called Key. The Key class detects when keys are pressed and released, and it reports which keys have been pressed. When the Key class detects that some keyboard event has occurred, it sends out a notification to any object that has been registered with it as a *listener*. A listener object is an ActionScript construct that you can register with the Key class once, and each time the Key class dispatches notifications, the listener object can respond appropriately. All you need to do is tell the listener object what ActionScript code it should run when it gets a notification.

Key class listener objects can receive notifications for two types of keyboard events: keys being pressed and released. In order to handle those events, define event handler methods on the listener object with the names *onKeyDown( )* and *onKeyUp( )*.

The *onKeyDown( )* method, as the name would suggest, gets called when a key is pressed. And similarly, the *onKeyUp( )* method is called when a key is released.

If defining listener objects and custom event handler methods is new to you, don't worry. It requires only a few lines of code. The following code defines a listener object as well as an *onKeyDown( )* and *onKeyUp( )* method for the object:

```
var oKeyListener:Object = new Object();
oKeyListener.onKeyDown = function():Void {
  // Code you want to run when the key is pressed. For example:
  trace("Key pressed");
};
oKeyListener.onKeyUp = function():Void {
  // Code you want to run when the key is released. For example:
  trace("Key released");
};
```

When you've defined the listener object and its event handler methods, the next thing you need to do is register it with the Key class. That step is important, because otherwise the Key class won't know to send the notifications to that listener. To register a listener object with the Key class requires only a single line of code. The *addListener( )* method requires a single parameter referencing the listener object you want to register. The following example registers a listener object named oKeyListener with the Key class:

```
Key.addListener(oKeyListener);
```

Frequently, you'll want to know more than simply that some key has been pressed. Rather, you'll want to know *which* key has been pressed. The Key class has built-in functionality that can report that information using the *getCode( )* method. The *getCode( )* method returns the numeric code that corresponds to the key that was pressed, and the *getAscii( )* method returns the ASCII code that corresponds to the key that was pressed. For uppercase alphabetic character and numeric keys, the *getCode( )* and *getAscii( )* methods return the same values. The character codes for upper- and lowercase alphabetic characters are the same, so if you want to differentiate between upper- and lowercase, you should use *getAscii( )*. However, for non-alphanumeric keys such as Shift, Enter, arrow keys, and so on, you should use the *getCode( )* method, because the Key class also has some built-in constants that you can use to compare with character codes.

You can use the String class's *charCodeAt( )* method to get the ASCII code for a particular character in order to compare it with the character code of a pressed key. Even though the name of the method would suggest that it returns a character code, it returns the ASCII code, so you can compare the value with the value returned by *Key.getAscii( )*. The following code creates a listener object that tests to see if the user has pressed a lowercase r key:

```
var oKeyListener:Object = new Object();
oKeyListener.onKeyDown = function():Void {
```

```
  // Create a string with the value of the character you want to use in the
comparison.
  var sCharacter:String = "r";

  // Retreive the character code for the character.
  var nCode:Number = sCharacter.charCodeAt(0);

  // Check to see if the code of the key that was pressed matches the character code
of
  // the character for which you are wanting to check.
  if(Key.getAscii() == nCode) {
    trace("You have pressed the r key.");
  }
};

  Key.addListener(oKeyListener);
```

The *getCode( )* method returns codes for lots of non-alphanumeric keys, making it a good choice for determining whether and when keys like the arrow keys have been pressed. To make your job even simpler, the Key class has some built-in constants that return the character codes for some common keys such as the up, down, right, left, shift, backspace, and enter keys. You can find a complete list in the Help panel by searching for Key class. The following code creates a listener object that detects when the right arrow is pressed:

```
var oKeyListener:Object = new Object();
oKeyListener.onKeyDown = function():Void {

  if(Key.getCode() == Key.RIGHT) {
    trace("You have pressed the right arrow key.");
  }
};

  Key.addListener(oKeyListener);
```

CHAPTER 10
Managing Playback

By default, a Flash movie begins playback as soon as it loads, playing through the end of the movie, and looping back to the beginning and playing again. Unless you are making a simple animation, you'll probably want to control playback or enable user control. For example, most interactive movies, such as games and business or learning applications, need to stop on the first frame (or the first frame following a preloader). Even for animations and video, you'll often need to provide playback control buttons for the user. Flash has several ActionScript methods for controlling playback, including pausing and starting playback, skipping to different portions of the movie, and advancing the playhead one frame at a time. These include *stop( )*, *gotoAndPlay( )*, *gotoAndStop( )*, *nextFrame( )*, *prevFrame( )*, *nextScene( )*, and *prevScene( )*. Fortunately, these methods are easy to implement.

To script in Flash, you must understand the relationship between events that occur in the movie and ActionScript statements associated with them. Every script executed in Flash occurs in the same sequence:

1. An event occurs in the movie (examples include button presses, the playback of frames, movie clips being dragged, keypresses, and loaded data).
2. An event handler associated with that event is triggered.
3. The actions or statements enclosed in that event handler are executed.

If a series of actions is enclosed in an event handler, and the corresponding event never occurs, the script is never executed. If an event occurs several times, actions enclosed in the corresponding event handler are executed several times.

Chapter 9 discusses several button-related events and event handlers, including *onRelease*, *onRollOver*, and *onDragOver*. Different Flash objects have different event handlers associated with them. These events are covered along with their objects throughout this book. Movie playback actions, like all other actions in Flash, are triggered by events. To give control to the user, tie playback actions to buttons. To trigger playback actions automatically, you can add scripts to keyframes. Scripts attached to keyframes, called *frame actions*, are activated as soon as their keyframe loads.

When you place an action in a keyframe, you don't need to specify an event handler, because the event is implied. Frame actions may look bare, because they lack explicit event handlers, but remember that an event handler actually is present and active—it is just implicit. Frame actions are the only actions that have implicit event handlers.

For basic playback control, the actions discussed in this chapter are most commonly applied to buttons and frame actions, though this relationship is not exclusive. Although these recipes and code examples focus on these objects and their associated events, you can use the same techniques with other objects, events, and event handlers.

10.1 Pausing a Movie After It Loads

Problem

You want to prevent the movie from playing when it loads.

Solution

Insert a *stop( )* action on the first frame (or the first frame following the preloader), or, if applicable, set the play parameter/attribute in the HTML document to false.

Discussion

Because you want to pause playback automatically and immediately, rather than relying on a user-initiated event, such as a button press, you can add the *stop( )* action to frame 1:

1. Create a layer in the timeline called Actions.
2. Select frame 1 of the Actions layer of the main timeline.
3. Open the Actions panel (Window → Actions, or F9, or Option-F9 on the Mac).
4. Add the *stop( )* action by typing it into the Script pane (the main portion of the Actions panel).

 The *stop( )* action doesn't require that you specify any additional information when you call it; it stops the current timeline (the timeline from which it is executed) as soon as it is called. Frame scripts are indicated by a small "a" character in the timeline in the keyframe in which you added the action. If you test the movie (using Control → Test Movie), you'll see that when the movie loads, it is paused in the first frame. When testing movies with ActionScript, you should test the actual *.swf* file (Control → Test Movie) rather than using playback in the authoring environment (Control → Play). Though you can activate simple actions during playback in the authoring environment (Control → Enable Simple Frame Actions), it is best to get in the habit of testing the actual *.swf* file. When a timeline's playhead stops, the Flash movie is still running. That is, the movie is still rendering graphics, responding to events, and playing sounds. In addition, other timelines, such as movie clip timelines, may continue to play back.

After you've used a *stop( )* action, be aware that unless you create another script restarting playback—on a button, for example—there is not necessarily a way for the user to get the movie to play again.

 Users have some control over playback from the context menu, accessed by right-clicking (Windows) or Control-clicking (Macintosh) in the Flash player. Commands include Play, Rewind, Forward, and Loop. Making users rely on the context menu for playback is not good design for at least two reasons. One reason is that it is not an obvious user interface, and that makes the application less usable. Secondly, it is possible to customize the context menu such that the playback options are not displayed. As such, the context menu is not even a standard or consistent mechanism for playback control.

Although adding a *stop( )* action is probably the easiest and most common way to stop a movie in the first frame, it is not the only way. You can also use HTML to prevent initial playback. To do so, set the `play` parameter of the `<object>` tag to `false` (for example, `<param name=play value=false>`) and likewise set the `play` attribute of the `<embed>` tag to `false`. The following code snippet shows the HTML code needed to embed a Flash *.swf* file in a web page, so that it is visible in all major browsers. The attributes needed to prevent playback are highlighted. This code is discussed in detail in Chapter 21.

```
<object classid="clsid:d27cdb6e-ae6d-11cf-96b8-444553540000" codebase="http://
fpdownload.macromedia.com/pub/shockwave/cabs/flash/swflash.cab#version=7,0,0,0"
width="550" height="400" id="someMovie" align="middle">
<param name="allowScriptAccess" value="sameDomain" />
<param name="movie" value="someMovie.swf" />
<param name="play" value="false" />
<param name="quality" value="high" />
<param name="bgcolor" value="#ffffff" />
<embed src=" someMovi.swf" play="false" quality="high" bgcolor="#ffffff" width="550"
height="400" name="someMovie" align="middle" allowScriptAccess="sameDomain"
type="application/x-shockwave-flash" pluginspage="http://www.macromedia.com/go/
getflashplayer" />
</object>
```

Alternatively, you can use Flash to generate the HTML that sets the `play` parameter to `false` for both the `<object>` and `<embed>` tags. To do so, use the File → Publish Settings → HTML → Paused At Start checkbox.

Generally, using *stop( )* is better that relying on HTML parameters/attributes, because it works in all environments. The HTML option works only if you publish the SWF in an HTML document. If you publish the movie in a projector, or test it during authoring, HTML parameters and attributes aren't available.

See Also

Recipe 10.4, Recipe 21.1

10.2 Preventing the Movie from Looping

Problem

You want to prevent a movie from looping back to the beginning when it reaches the last frame.

Solution

Add a *stop( )* action to a keyframe in the final frame, or set the HTML loop parameter/attribute to false.

Discussion

You can prevent a movie from looping by using a *stop( )* action or by using HTML attributes to control the movie.

To use a *stop( )* action, complete the following steps:

1. If you haven't already done so, add a layer for your ActionScript code to the timeline. Give the layer a label of Actions.

2. Insert a keyframe in the Actions layer at the final frame within the timeline. To add a keyframe, choose Insert → Keyframe, or press F6.

3. Select the keyframe that you just added, and open the Actions panel by pressing F9.

4. Add the *stop( )* action by typing it into the Script pane.

To use HTML to prevent looping, create/change the loop parameter in the <object> tag, so that its value is false (e.g., <param name="loop" value="false">). Likewise, set the <embed> tag's loop attribute to false. As noted in Recipe 10.1, generally, using a *stop( )* action is preferred over relying on HTML attributes.

See Also

Recipe 10.1, Recipe 21.1

10.3 Dividing the Timeline into Segments

Problem

You have a lengthy timeline and want to divide it into logical sections.

Solution

Divide the timeline into scenes, frame segments, or movie clips.

Discussion

Movies with significant animation and video can have hundreds or even thousands of frames. To facilitate authoring, you may want to divide your timeline into segments. Flash offers several ways of dividing movies in time. Which you select depends on various factors, including which makes sense intuitively, whether and how you intend to implement ActionScript in the movie, and even more broadly, how you intend to architect the overall project.

Flash documents can have a maximum of 16,000 frames per timeline.

If you are an animator, and you are developing cartoons meant to be played from beginning to end in order, without user interaction, the traditional division of the timeline into scenes is probably a good option. Using Flash scenes, you can break the timeline into arbitrary sections, working on one at a time. At runtime, Flash plays the scenes back, without interruption, in order (though you can reorder scenes, as needed). From the point of view of ActionScript and Flash movie architecture, scenes are primitive and generally more trouble than they are worth. But for long, linear animations and videos that lack interactivity, scenes are a good selection.

Every Flash movie has at least one scene—the main timeline that appears when you create a movie. You can subdivide this timeline into multiple scenes; that is, the main timeline comprises all of the scenes that you create in a movie. The benefit of scenes is that they enable you to work on one portion of a movie at a time, without having to scroll through or worry about portions of the timeline outside your area of focus. A 2-minute movie, at 12 frames per second, has 1,440 frames. Divided into scenes, you can cause the main timeline to display a much more manageable number of frames at a time. Not only the number of frames is a factor; so is the number of layers. Typically, the longer a timeline, the more layers there are likely to be. And the content on any given layer may only be placed on the stage for a small portion of the entire timeline. The result is that you can end up with large numbers of layers, and at any given point along the timeline, the majority of the layers do not contain any visible elements. If you divide the timeline into scenes, the number of layers per scene can end up much more manageable as well.

The only timeline you can break into scenes is the main timeline. You may not break the timelines within symbols into scenes.

To create a new scene, choose Insert → Scene from the main menu. Immediately, the Flash environment looks like you've opened a new file. The timeline has only one, empty layer, and the stage is empty. In addition, you'll see a new scene name listed above the stage. The first new scene is called Scene 2 by default.

You can rename and reorder scenes using the Scene panel, Window → Other Panels → Scene. To rename a scene, double-click its name in the Scene panel and type the new name. To reorder scenes, drag-and-drop them into position in the Scene panel. Flash plays through scenes in the order listed in this panel, from top to bottom. You can also duplicate and delete scenes using the Scene panel.

Although scenes make it easy to isolate segments of a movie to author one section at a time, they are overkill when all you want to do is mark logical segments of your movie. You might mark logical segments in your movie to make the timeline easier to read during authoring, or you might want to mark frames so that you can point to them using ActionScript. In these cases, you can use *frame comments* and *frame labels*. Frame comments and labels appear as text strings in keyframes of the timeline.

Frame labels are exported with the SWF, which means that they are available to ActionScript and contribute (minimally) to file size. Frame comments, in contrast, are stripped out of the exported SWF, which means that they are useful only during authoring time and do not contribute to the SWF's file size. Frame labels are particularly useful when skipping the playhead to different sections of the timeline, as discussed in Recipe 10.4.

To add a frame label:

1. Select a keyframe in the timeline.
2. In the Property inspector's Frame Label field, type a name for the frame. Frame labels must contain only letters, underscores, and numbers, and should begin with a letter or underscore.
3. To make sure the label applies, press Tab or Enter, or click anywhere else to deselect the field and apply the label.

To insert a frame comment, rather than label, follow the preceding steps, then select Comment from the Label type menu in the Property inspector.

Another way to segment portions of a movie is to encapsulate them in movie clip symbols. This approach offers considerable flexibility, especially with regard to ActionScript. Movie clips enable any combination of linear and nonlinear/interactive playback.

Finally, yet another approach to segmenting movies is to store them as separate *.swf* files, and load them into a parent or shell *.swf* file when the user needs them. This approach (discussed in Chapter 21) has many benefits, including optimizing download management, improved authoring workflow and maintenance, and high potential for interactivity.

See Also

Recipe 10.4, Recipe 10.7, Recipe 3.17

10.4 Skipping the Playhead to a Different Frame of the Timeline

Problem

You want to skip the playhead ahead or back within a timeline.

Solution

Use the *MovieClip.gotoAndPlay( )* or *MovieClip.gotoAndStop( )* method. Optionally, if you want to specify a scene to which you want to have the playhead move, you may use the *gotoAndPlay( )* or *gotoAndStop( )* global function.

If you want to simply move the playhead to the next frame or the previous frame, use the *MovieClip.nextFrame( )* or *MovieClip.prevFrame( )* method.

Discussion

Flash has several ways by which you can instruct the playhead to move to a specific frame in a timeline. Some of the ways tell the playhead to go to a frame and then keep playing from there. Others tell the playhead to go to a frame and then stop. That is logical enough. But what may not be obvious is the reasoning for two sets of each. You can use either the methods of the *MovieClip* class or the global functions of the same name. Typically, the methods of the *MovieClip* class are preferable, because they allow more flexibility in most ways than the global function counterparts. The global functions remain in Flash, because the *MovieClip* class methods were not introduced until Flash 5. That means that for Flash to continue to support Flash 4 content, it must support the global functions.

Both the *gotoAndPlay( )* and *gotoAndStop( )* methods of the *MovieClip* class skip the playhead to a specific frame of the timeline. As their names suggest, *gotoAndPlay( )* skips the playhead to the specified frame and begins playback from that point, and *gotoAndStop( )* skips the playhead to the specified frame and pauses playback. Both functions require that you pass a parameter indicating the frame to which you want the playhead to move. You can indicate the frame either as a number or as a quoted string value indicating the frame label.

Which timeline is affected is determined by which movie clip you use to call the method. To call the method, first reference the movie clip. Follow the movie clip reference with a dot (.), and then the name of the method. There should be no spaces between the movie clip reference, the dot, or the name of the method. The following example instructs the timeline of a movie clip instance named mAnimation to go to the tenth frame and stop:

```
mAnimation.gotoAndStop(10);
```

If mAnimation happens to have a frame label of AnimationStart at the tenth frame, you could accomplish the same thing as the preceding example with the following code:

```
mAnimation.gotoAndStop("AnimationStart");
```

The benefit of using frame labels is that even if the frame number changes, your code will still work. For example, if you later added a few frames to the beginning of the mAnimation instance's timeline, what was previously at frame 10 would move to a later frame. If you referenced the frame by number in your code, you'd also need to change the code for your Flash movie to work correctly. On the other hand, if you use a frame label, as long as the frame label moves to the appropriate frame within the timeline, your code will still work.

If you want to add some code to the main timeline that sends instructions to the main timeline itself, you need to know how a timeline can refer back to itself. As you saw in the previous examples, you need to use a movie clip reference in order to call the *gotoAndStop( )* or *gotoAndPlay( )* method. But unlike other movie clip instances that you place on stage, you cannot add an instance name to the main timeline. Instead, you can use a special ActionScript keyword called this. The this keyword allows an object (such as the main timeline) to refer to itself without having to know its own name. The following code is an example of how you can instruct the main timeline to go to frame 40:

```
this.gotoAndPlay(40);
```

Often, Flash developers want to use the timeline playback methods such as *gotoAndStop( )* or *gotoAndPlay( )* to allow the user to control the playback of a time-line. For example, you may want to allow a user to jump to different sections of an animation. Or you may want to allow the user to rewind and play an animation again. In the majority of scenarios, you want to target one timeline from another timeline or object. For example, you may want to add buttons that allow the user to jump to different sections of the timeline. Therefore, you will want to place the *gotoAndStop( )* and/or *gotoAndPlay( )* method calls within button event handler methods such as *onPress( )* or *onRelease( )*. When you do that, you have to be aware of an issue called *targeting* or *addressing*. You need to make sure that you provide Flash with the correct way to locate the timeline you want to control, or it won't be able to do as you have asked. This is similar to sending a postal letter: if you send it to the wrong address, it doesn't matter what's in the letter. So you need to make sure you provide the correct address so that Flash can find the correct timeline. Address-ing issues are discussed in more detail in Recipe 11.11.

If you want to move the playhead to the next frame or previous frame of a timeline, you can use the *nextFrame( )* and *prevFrame( )* methods, respectively. Both of the methods move the playhead to a frame and then stop the playback at that point. They are particularly useful methods when you are creating something like a slide-show presentation in which the user gets to move the playhead back and forth through the timeline one frame at a time. The methods don't require any parameters, and you should call them using the same type of dot-syntax as is used with the *gotoAndStop( )* and *gotoAndPlay( )* methods. For example:

```
mAnimation.nextFrame( );
```

If you want to jump back and forth by more than one frame at a time, you can use the _currentframe property as part of an expression. The _currentframe property returns the number of the frame through which the playhead is currently moving. You can add or subtract from that value to get the number of a frame that is a specific distance before or after the current frame. For example, if you want to tell Flash to move the playhead within mAnimation 10 frames forward, use the following code:

```
mAnimation.gotoAndStop(mAnimation._currentframe + 10);
```

Notice that the _currentframe property is referenced using dot-syntax—just as when calling one of the methods of a movie clip. The property returns the current frame for the movie clip from which it is called.

Using _currentframe as part of an expression to skip ahead or backward by more than a single frame can create the need for something called bounds checking. *Bounds checking* refers to a script that tests whether the specified frame target is within the bounds of the timeline; for example, if the playhead is on frame 12 and a *gotoAndStop( )* method sends it back 20 frames, the action would attempt to send the playhead out of the bounds of the movie.

Bounds checking is not absolutely necessary in the sense that leaving out bounds checking will not cause an error: Flash ignores any script that attempts to send the playhead to a frame before frame 1 or after the last frame in the timeline. That is, if the script is on frame 12 and a script attempts to send it back 20 frames, the playhead will remain on frame 12. In the opposite case, where a script attempts to send the playhead beyond the last frame, Flash advances the playhead to the last frame. Thus, if the playhead is on frame 92 of a 100 frame movie, and a script attempts to advance the playhead 20 frames, Flash will move it to frame 100. Therefore, bounds checking is needed to achieve certain behaviors. You would need it, for example, if you wanted the button that skips backward to behave the same way as a button that skips forward. That is, if you wanted a button either to rewind by 20 frames, or to rewind to the first frame when the playhead is on a frame lower than 20, you would incorporate bounds checking into the script:

```
btSkipBackward.onPress = function( ):Void {
  var nFrame:Number = mAnimation._currentframe - 20;
  if(nFrame < 1) {
    mAnimation.gotoAndStop(1);
  }
  else {
    mAnimation.gotoAndStop(nFrame);
  }
};
```

As mentioned previously, Flash continues to support the *gotoAndPlay()* and *gotoAndStop()* global functions. The global functions are very similar to the MovieClip methods already described. However, they affect only the timeline from which they are called. That makes them less useful as you start to create more complex animations and applications with Flash.

One reason that many people still use the global functions instead of the recommended methods is that both the *gotoAndPlay( )* and *gotoAndStop( )* global functions allow you to specify a scene to which you want to have the timeline jump. With either of the functions, you can specify up to two parameters. If you only specify one parameter, it should be the number or label of the frame to which you want the timeline to move. For example:

```
gotoAndPlay(1);
```

If you specify two parameters, the first should be the name of the scene to which you want the playhead to move. The second parameter should be either the number or label of the frame. For example:

```
gotoAndPlay("Scene Two", 1);
```

 You may use the scene label parameter only with the *gotoAndStop()* and *gotoAndPlay()* methods when targeting the main timeline.

Although the global functions may, at first, appear to have a distinct advantage when you are using scenes, the recommended approach is to continue to use the *MovieClip* class methods with frame labels. Simply add a frame label to the first frame of each of your scenes. For example, you can add a frame label of Scene_Two to a scene in your document. Then, from the main timeline, the following code will cause the playhead to jump to the first frame of the scene.

```
this.gotoAndStop("Scene_Two");
```

See Also

Recipe 9.2, Recipe 9.8

10.5 Creating a Basic Interface to Control Timeline Playback

Problem

You want to create a button bar to give users control over movie playback.

Solution

Create the buttons or use premade buttons from the common library. Then use button event handler methods to call the *stop( )*, *play( )*, and *gotoAndStop( )* methods as appropriate.

Discussion

You can create a set of buttons to give control over playback to the user. Whether your movie contains animation, video, or even a series of slide-like pages with a voice-over soundtrack, playback controls make it possible for users to stop and start the movie, fast-forward over parts they've seen before, or rewind to parts they want to see again.

Creating a set of playback controls involves two major steps: creating the buttons that will serve as the interface, and writing the code that will make the buttons functional.

For a basic set of controls, you will need at least three buttons (or movie clips that handle button events)—one for stopping the playback, one for pausing the playback, and one for resuming the playback. Refer to Chapter 9 for more information about creating buttons or movie clips that act like buttons. Optionally, one fast way to put together an interface is to use one of several button sets available in the Common Libraries (Window → Common Libraries → Buttons).

After you've created the buttons, next create instances on the stage. Make sure to give them each instance names. The example code in this recipe uses the instance names btStop, btPause, and btPlay. If you use different instance names, make sure to adjust your code appropriately.

With the buttons (or movie clips) on the stage with instance names, the next step is to add the ActionScript code. There are a variety of ways you could write the code depending on the exact setup of your Flash file. However, the following code should work in the majority of scenarios. Just add the code to the appropriate keyframe of the timeline. For example, if you have placed the button instances on the first frame of the main timeline, you should create a new layer with a label of Actions, and then add the code to the first frame of that layer.

```
// Declare a variable, and assign it a reference to the timeline you want
// to affect. In this example the value of this is used. Assuming the code
// is on the main timeline, this refers back to the main timeline. If you
// want to affect a movie clip named mAnimation that is on the main
// timeline, then change the this reference to mAnimation. The purpose of
// the variable, mTimeline, is that it provides you with one central
// location to define which timeline you want to affect.
var mTimeline:MovieClip = this;

// Define an onPress( ) event handler method for the stop button. When the
// user clicks on the button tell the playhead to go to and stop on frame
// 1.
btStop.onPress = function( ):Void {
```

```
    mTimeline.gotoAndStop(1);
};

// Define an onPress( ) event handler method for the pause button. When
// the user clicks the button tell the playhead to stop at the current
// frame.
btPause.onPress = function( ):Void {
  mTimeline.stop( );
};

// Define an onPress( ) event handler method for the play button. When the
// user clicks the button tell the playhead to start playing from the
// current frame.
btPlay.onPress = function( ):Void {
  mTimeline.play( );
};
```

See Also

Recipe 9.2, Recipe 10.1, Recipe 10.4

10.6   Playing the Timeline Backward

Problem

You want to play the timeline backward.

Solution

Use the *prevFrame()* action within an *onEnterFrame( )* event handler method in combination with bounds checking.

Discussion

By default, each movie clip timeline (including the main timeline) plays back in a forward direction. And Flash does not have a built-in function or method that can automatically instruct a timeline to play in reverse. However, with just a bit of ActionScript code, you can cause a timeline to play backward.

The basic idea is as follows: at the frame rate of the movie, tell Flash to move the playhead back one frame. Instructing the playhead to move back one frame is fairly simple. The only challenge is to then tell Flash to call the *prevFrame( )* method at the frame rate of the movie. That too is fairly simple, because there is a built-in event handler method named *onEnterFrame( )* that gets called at the frame rate of the movie. Therefore, in order to instruct a timeline to play in reverse, you should define the *onEnterFrame( )* event handler for the movie clip such that it calls *prevFrame( )*. The following example instructs a movie clip named mAnimation to play backward:

```
    mAnimation.onEnterFrame = function( ):Void {
      this.prevFrame( );
    };
```

As you can see, you can define an *onEnterFrame( )* event handler method, just as with the other already-familiar event handler methods such as *onPress( )* and *onRelease( )*. Also notice that within the event handler method, you can refer to the movie clip object by its self-referencing this.

 The *onEnterFrame( )* event handler method is an event handler method for movie clips only. It will not work for buttons.

There's one catch with the code in the preceding example. The *prevFrame( )* method can move to the previous frame only if there is one. And because movie clip time-lines start on frame 1, the playhead cannot move before that. Therefore, what you can do is add an if/else statement within the *onEnterFrame( )* event handler method that checks to see whether the current frame is the first frame. You can check the first frame using the _currentframe property. If the current frame is the first frame, you can use a *gotoAndStop( )* method to go to the last frame of the timeline. That way, the playback will loop in reverse. You can determine the final frame of a time-line using the _totalframes property. The following is a modification of the preceding code, causing the playback of mAnimation to loop in reverse:

```
mAnimation.onEnterFrame = function( ):Void {
  if(this._currentframe == 1) {
    this.gotoAndStop(this._totalframes);
  }
  else {
    this.prevFrame( );
  }
};
```

Assuming that the movie clip mAnimation exists on the first frame of the main time-line, you can cause it to play in reverse simply by adding the preceding code to the first frame of the main timeline.

If you want to allow a user to have a timeline play forward *or* backward, place the *onEnterFrame( )* definition within an *onPress( )* or *onRelease( )* event handler method of a button. Then, to play the timeline forward, use another button. Within the second button, add ActionScript code that removes the *onEnterFrame( )* definition and then calls the *play( )* method. The following code makes references to btBackward, btPause, and btForward as the button instance names. If you use different instance names, change the code accordingly.

```
// This example uses a variable to create
// a reference to the timeline you want to affect. Assuming you place this
// code on the main timeline then the value of this will refer to the main
// timeline. If you want to affect another timeline, change the value from
// this to the instance name.
var mTimeline:MovieClip = this;

// Define an onPress( ) event handler method for the backward button. When
// the users clicks the button define the onEnterFrame( ) event handler
```

```
// method for the movie clip.
btBackward.onPress = function( ):Void {
  mTimeline.onEnterFrame = function( ):Void {
    if(this._currentframe == 1) {
      this.gotoAndStop(this._totalframes);
    }
    else {
      this.prevFrame( );
    }
  };
};

// Define an onPress( ) event handler method for the pause button. When
// the user  clicks the button use the delete operator to remove the
// onEnterFrame( )  event handler method definition. Notice that there are
// no parentheses  in that line of code. Then, call the stop( ) method.
btPause.onPress = function( ):Void {
  delete mTimeline.onEnterFrame;
  mTimeline.stop( );
};

// Define an onPress( ) event handler method for the forward button. When
// the user clicks the button use the delete operator to remove the
// onEnterFrame( ) event handler method definition. Then call the play( )
// method.
btForward.onPress = function( ):Void {
  delete mTimeline.onEnterFrame;
  mTimeline.play( );
};
```

See Also

Recipe 10.5, Recipe 10.7

10.7   Creating Seek Buttons

Problem

You want the timeline to fast-forward or rewind visually as long as the user holds down a button.

Solution

Use the *gotoAndStop( )* method in conjunction with the _currentframe property to skip back or forward in the timeline. Add the *gotoAndStop( )* method within an *onEnterFrame( )* event handler method, so that it gets called repeatedly at the frame rate of the movie. Use button event handler methods to define and remove the *onEnterFrame( )* method based on the state of the button.

Discussion

In Recipe 10.6, you learned how to play a movie clip's timeline in reverse. Using very similar principals, you can add functionality to your Flash movie that causes a timeline to visually rewind or fast forward. There are several elements involved. First, you need to create buttons to trigger the rewind and fast-forward functionality. Then, you need to apply *onPress( )* and *onRelease( )* event handler methods to the buttons. Within the *onPress( )* event handler methods, define an *onEnterFrame( )* event handler method for the movie clip you want to affect. The *onRelease( )* event handler method should remove the *onEnterFrame( )* definition. That may sound like a lot of information, so here's an example.

Imagine that you have a button on the main timeline with an instance name btRewind. Also on the main timeline is a movie clip with an instance name of mAnimation. When the user clicks on the btRewind button, you want the timeline of mAnimation to play in reverse rapidly. Then, when the user releases the button, you want the mAnimation timeline to stop. You can accomplish this task with code that is actually quite similar to some of the code from Recipe 10.6.

```
// As with the code in Recipe #"Playing the Timeline Backwards," this
// example uses a variable to create a reference to the timeline you want to
// affect. Assuming that you place this code on the main timeline, then the
// value of this will refer to the main timeline. If you want to affect
// another timeline, change the value from this to the instance name.
var mTimeline:MovieClip = this;

// Define an onPress( ) event handler method that gets called when the
// user clicks on the button.
btRewind.onPress = function( ):Void {

  // Define an onEnterFrame( ) event handler method to repeatedly call the
  // code that moves the playhead within the timeline.
  mTimeline.onEnterFrame = function( ):Void {

    // Declare a variable to determine how many frames you want the
    // playhead to move back with each iteration. The greater the value,
    // the faster the rewind will appear.
    var nFrames:Number = 5;

    // Check to see if the frame to which you are sending the playhead is
    // a valid frame, and then move it.
    if(this._currentframe - nFrames < 1) {
      this.gotoAndStop(1);
    }
    else {
      this.gotoAndStop(this._currentframe - nFrames);
    }
  };
};

// Define an onRelease event handler method that gets called when the user
```

```
// releases the click on the button.
btRewind.onRelease = function( ):Void {

  // Use the delete operator to remove the definition for the
  // onEnterFrame( ) event handler method. That causes Flash to stop
  // calling the onEnterFrame( ) code.
  delete mTimeline.onEnterFrame;
};

  // Assign the same definition from the onRelease( ) event handler method
  // to the onReleaseOutside( ) event handler method. That way, if the user
  // clicks on the button, drags the mouse off the button, and releases the
  // button, the rewind will stop. Otherwise, the rewinding would keep
  // going.
  btRewind.onReleaseOutside = btRewind.onRelease;
```

Likewise, you can create a button to cause a movie clip's timeline to fast-forward. The code is practically identical to the preceding example, but instead of subtracting from the _currentframe value to determine the frame to which you want the playhead to move, you should add to it.

It's typically preferable to use an interval function rather than an *onEnterFrame( )* event handler method in order to perform actions repeatedly. However, in this recipe and the previous one, the *onEnterFrame( )* event handler method is actually a good choice. That is because the *onEnterFrame( )* event handler method gets called at the frame rate. So by placing the *prevFrame( )* method within an *onEnterFrame( )* method, the playhead moves backward at the same rate that it would normally play forward. However, the faster you want the timeline to rewind, the choppier the animation can appear if you use the *onEnterFrame( )* technique. If that problem occurs, you can consider using an interval function.

Define a function that accepts a single parameter that determines how many frames the playhead should move. And within the function, call the *gotoAndStop( )* method to move the playhead accordingly. Then make sure to call the *updateAfterEvent( )* function so the stage refreshes. For example, the following function will move the playhead of the timeline within a movie clip named mAnimation:

```
function movePlayhead(nFrames:Number):Void {
  mAnimation.gotoAndStop(mAnimation._currentframe + nFrames);
  updateAfterEvent( );
}
```

Then you need to use *setInterval( )* to have Flash call the function at a particular frequency. Because you'll likely want the interval to start only when the user presses a button, you should place the *setInterval( )* function call instead of an *onPress( )* event handler method. When you call *setInterval( )*, remember to assign the return value to a variable. That way you'll be able to clear the interval later. Also, pass three parameters to *setInterval( )*—the reference to the function, the interval in milliseconds, and either a 1 (for fast-forwarding) or a –1 (for rewinding). The interval should probably be 50 or less. The exact value depends on the frame rate of the movie (as rewinding and fast-forwarding should be relatively faster than normal playback) as well as your own preferences. The smaller the interval in milliseconds, the faster the animation.

```
// Declare a variable outside the onPress( ) event handler method.
```

That way, even though you assign a value to it from within the event handler method, you can still reference it elsewhere.

```
var nInterval:Number;

// Define an onPress( ) event handler method for the button.
btRewind.onPress = function( ):Void {

  // Call setInterval( ), passing it the reference to the function you
  // want it to call, the interval in milliseconds, and either a 1 or -1
  // depending on the direction in which you want the timeline to play.
  nInterval = setInterval(movePlayhead, 50, -1);
};

// Define an onRelease( ) event handler method for the button such that
// the interval is cleared when the user releases the button.
btRewind.onRelease = function( ):Void {
  clearInterval(nInterval);
};

// Assign the same definition from onRelease( ) to the onReleaseOutside( )
// event handler method. That way the rewinding will stop even if the user
// drags the mouse off the button before releasing it.
btRewind.onReleaseOutside = btRewind.onRelease;
```

The following example will generally work for most scenarios. You can place the code on a keyframe in which the buttons and the movie clip timeline you want to control exist. The code assumes that you have buttons with instance names of btRewind, btFastForward, btPlay, btStop, and btPause. If you use different button instance names, change the code accordingly.

```
// Declare a variable to hold the reference to the movie clip whose
// timeline you want to affect. Storing the movie clip reference in a
// variable in this way makes it very simple for you to modify this code
// to work with any timeline, as you need to change only a single
// reference. The example uses the this keyword to reference the timeline
// in which this code is placed. But you can change that value to target
// any valid movie clip.
var mTimeline:MovieClip = this;

// Declare a variable to store the interval identifier. That way you can
// clear the interval to stop the rewinding or fast-forwarding.
var nInterval:Number;

// Declare and define a variable to store the rate at which the
// function should be called. The smaller the value, the faster the rewind
// and fast-forward will appear.
var nRate:Number = 50;
```

```
// Define the onPress( ) event handler method to cause the timeline to
// stop playback.
btStop.onPress = function( ):Void {
  mTimeline.gotoAndStop(1);
};

// Define the onPress( ) event handler method to cause the timeline to
// pause playback.
btPause.onPress = function( ):Void {
  mTimeline.stop( );
};

// Define the onPress( ) event handler method to cause the timeline to
// resume playback.
btPlay.onPress = function( ):Void {
  mTimeline.play( );
};

// Define the onPress( ) event handler method to cause the timeline to
// rewind. Use setInterval( ) to tell Flash to call the movePlayhead( )
// function (defined later in the code) at the rate defined earlier,
// moving the playhead of the timeline back one frame at a time.
btRewind.onPress = function( ):Void {
  nInterval = setInterval(movePlayhead, nRate, -1);
};

// Define the onRelease( ) event handler method so that the interval is
// cleared (and hence the rewinding stops) when the user releases the
// button.
btRewind.onRelease = function( ):Void {
  clearInterval(nInterval);
};

// Make sure that the onReleaseOutside( ) has the same definition as
// onRelease( ).
btRewind.onReleaseOutside = btRewind.onRelease;

// Define the onPress( ) event handler method to cause the timeline to
// fast-forward. Use setInterval( ) to tell Flash to call the
// movePlayhead( ) function at the rate defined earlier, moving the
// playhead of the timeline forward one frame at a time.
btFastForward.onPress = function( ):Void {
  nInterval = setInterval(movePlayhead, nRate, 1);
};

// Define the onRelease( ) event handler method so that the interval is
// cleared (and hence the fast-forwarding stops) when the user releases the
// button.
btFastForward.onRelease = function( ):Void {
  clearInterval(nInterval);
};

// Make sure the onReleaseOutside( ) has the same definition as
// onRelease( ).
```

```
btFastForward.onReleaseOutside = btFastForward.onRelease;

// Define the function that gets called on the interval.
function movePlayhead(nFrames:Number):Void {
  mTimeline.gotoAndStop(mTimeline._currentframe + nFrames);
  updateAfterEvent();
}
```

See Also

Recipe 10.4, Recipe 10.6

CHAPTER 11

Managing Movie Clips

Movie clips are among the most important types of symbols in your Flash movies from several standpoints. First of all, movie clip timelines are able to play back independently. This means that you can create movies within movies. Using movie clips correctly can help organize your Flash document and make your main timeline much more manageable.

Secondly, movie clips can be programmatically controlled—much more so than any other types of symbol instances. Graphic symbol instances cannot be controlled by ActionScript at all, and button symbol instances can be controlled only in a limited sense. But when you begin to work with ActionScript, you begin to use more and more movie clips in your movies.

As you can read in the recipes in this chapter, by using ActionScript you can perform many types of actions in your Flash movies. For example, you can adjust the transparency, color, and rotation of a movie clip instance using ActionScript. You can also use ActionScript to create duplicates of existing instances or even to create new instances of movie clips that exist only in the library. You can use ActionScript to create all kinds of animation effects, such as fades.

Although the recipes in this chapter are intended to demonstrate how you can introduce some basic ActionScript to begin creating more advanced Flash movies, non-code-based solutions are also included.

Many of the recipes in this chapter rely on functions for some of the more advanced portions of the discussions. The topic of functions is simultaneously simple and complex. A function is a convenient way to group together functionality. If we have a group of actions that we want to call upon again and again, we can place those actions into a function, and then call the function each time. And the actions don't always have to be exactly the same each time you call the function. You can pass the function some pieces of information called *parameters*, and then you can tell the function how to respond based on the parameter values. Let's take a look at some of the details on how to define and use a function.

There are two basic types of functions—named and anonymous. First, we'll look at the named function. We call these types of functions *named* because we give them a name right in the definition. All named function definitions follow this basic syntax:

```
function functionName (parameters):ReturnType {
    // Actions to perform when the function is called.
}
```

The function keyword tells Flash that what you are defining here is a function. That keyword is always followed by the name of the function. The name of the function is up to you, but it should indicate what the function does. Also, you cannot use any reserved words, such as function, Math, MovieClip, and so on, and you cannot use any names that are also the names of movie clips, buttons, text fields, or variables within the same timeline. Next in the definition comes the opening and closing parentheses. Regardless of whether you are going to define the function to accept parameters, the opening and closing parentheses must be there. If the function *is* going to expect parameters, you can indicate those parameters in the parameters list between the parentheses. If there is more than one parameter, you should use a comma to delimit the list. The names you give to the parameters are the names by which you can references those values—in other words, they are variables. Following the closing parenthesis are the opening and closing curly braces. Within the opening and closing curly braces should be what we call the *function body*—all the actions that you want to occur when the function is called.

After you have defined a function, you can invoke it by name. You should provide the function name, the function call operator (the opening and closing parentheses), any parameters, if applicable, and a final semicolon. This syntax is nothing new to you if you have used any ActionScript whatsoever. For example, the *trace( )* action is really just a built-in function:

```
trace("Yay!");
```

Now that you've had a chance to read over the definition of a function, let's take a look at a few examples. First, here's a very basic function that moves a movie clip named mSquare to position 10,10:

```
function moveMovieClip( ):Void {
    mSquare._x = 10;
    mSquare._y = 10;
}
```

Our function would be much more useful if we could tell it to movie the movie clip to various locations each time instead of always to the same location of 10,10. So we can rewrite the function using parameters:

```
function moveMovieClip(nX:Number, nY:Number):Void {
    mSquare._x = nX;
    mSquare._y = nY;
}
```

Now we can call the function to move the movie clip to lots of different locations:

```
moveMovieClip(90, 30);
moveMovieClip(180, 300);
```

And if we want, we can make the function even more extensible by making the movie clip a parameter as well. Then we can use the same function to move not only the square_m movie clip, but also many others:

```
function moveMovieClip(mClip:MovieClip, nX:Number, nY:Number):Void {
  mClip._x = nX;
  mClip._y = nY;
}
```

Here are a few examples of how we might invoke the function now:

```
moveMovieClip(mSquare, 90, 30);
moveMovieClip(mCircle, 180, 300);
```

The other type of function—an anonymous function—is not much different from its named counterpart. The difference is, of course, that it does not have a name. Instead, anonymous functions must be assigned to a variable. This is very handy when we want to assign the function to a method of an object, as we'll see in Recipe 11.1.

The syntax for an anonymous function definition is as follows:

```
function (parameters):ReturnType {
  // Function body
};
```

As you can see, it is almost identical to the named function definition. The two differences are that the name portion is omitted and the function definition is followed by a semicolon. As previously mentioned, an anonymous function is not very useful in isolation and is typically used to assign a definition to a method of an object. Here's an example that defines an *onEnterFrame( )* method for a movie clip:

```
mSquare.onEnterFrame = function( ):Void {
  trace("This is a method defined by an anonymous function.");
}
```

11.1 Performing Actions Repeatedly Over Time

Problem

You want to do some action or actions repeatedly over time.

Solution

Use a *setInterval( )* action to tell Flash to invoke a function at an interval in milliseconds. Or, alternatively, you can use the *onEnterFrame( )* method for a movie clip to have an action or group of actions execute at the frame rate of the movie.

Discussion

Admittedly the concept of performing actions repeatedly over time is not exclusive to movie clips, but it is something that you will use very often in conjunction with movie clips.

There are basically two ways to have Flash automatically perform an action or group of actions repeatedly. The first way we'll take a look at uses interval functions. An *interval function* is a function that Flash invokes at a frequency (in milliseconds) that you define. For example, you might want to set up a function that moves a movie clip to the right by six pixels, and then you can tell Flash to call that function every hundred milliseconds. The result would be that the movie clip would appear to animate to the right across the stage. Of course, the application of interval functions is not limited to moving a movie clip. But that should give you an idea of at least one way in which you can use this technique.

In order to set an interval for a function you should use the aptly named *setInterval( )* global function. The *setInterval( )* function takes at least two parameters: a reference to the function and the number of milliseconds between each function call. The *setInterval( )* function also returns an interval ID that can later be used to stop the interval if you want. And obviously, in order to use *setInterval( )*, you will need to have first created the interval function itself. An interval function is nothing other than a regular function (named or anonymous) that gets called at the specified frequency. You don't have to do anything special or different with the function itself to get it to work as an interval function.

 Even though you don't have to do anything beyond that of a regular function, if your interval function might run faster than the frame rate of the movie, and if the interval function updates some visual aspect (such as the location of a movie clip), you should place a call to the global function *updateAfterEvent( )* as the last line in the function body. This function tells Flash to update the display even if it is between frames or enter frame events, which will ensure a smooth animation.

```
// Define an interval function. Notice that this is just a regular, named function.
function exampleIntervalFunction( ):Void {
  trace("This is an interval function");
}

// Call setInterval( ). Pass it a reference to the interval function and a number
// of milliseconds between each call. In this case, we're telling Flash to call
// the interval function once every thousand milliseconds, or, in other terms, once
// every second.
var nIntervalID:Number = setInterval(exampleIntervalFunction, 1000);
```

You also have the option of passing parameters to an interval function by appending those values to the parameters list of the *setInterval( )* function.

```
// Here we define an interval function that expects two parameters.
function exampleIntervalFunction(sCharacter1:String, sCharacter2:String):Void {
  trace("parameters: " + sCharacter1 + " ," + sCharacter2);
}


// Now, we define the interval, and tell Flash to pass the values "a" and "b" to
// the interval function each time it is called.
var nIntervalID:Number = setInterval(exampleIntervalFunction, 1000, "a", "b");
```

You'll notice, however, that the same values are always passed to the interval function. Even if you use variables in the *setInterval( )* function, those variables are evaluated only once. Therefore, often the most useful situations in which to pass parameters to interval functions are those in which you use a single interval function for slightly different tasks. For example, you might want to write a single interval function that can move any movie clip in any direction. Then you can create multiple intervals that call the same function, but that tell Flash to move different movie clips in different directions.

```
// First, we define the interval function. The function accepts a reference to a
// movie clip and the change in the x and y directions. It then moves the movie clip
// appropriately.
function moveMovieClip(mClip:MovieClip, nX:Number, nY:Number):Void {
  mClip._x += nX;
  mClip._y += nY;

  // Add an updateAfterEvent( ) call here, as this function updates the position
  // of a movie clip.
  updateAfterEvent();
}


// Create an interval that calls moveMovieClip( ) every three hundred milliseconds
// in order to move a movie clip named mSquare one pixel at a time in the y
// direction.
var nMoveSquareIntervalID:Number = setInterval(moveMovieClip, 300, mSquare, 0, 1);


// Set another interval at which the moveMovieClip( ) is called every five
// hundred milliseconds. But this time, instead of moving mSquare, we're moving
// mCircle one pixel at a time in the x direction.
var nMoveCircleIntervalID:Number = setInterval(moveMovieClip, 500, mCircle, 1, 0);
```

You can also tell Flash to stop calling the interval function using the *clearInterval( )* global function. This function needs to know which interval to stop, so this is where the interval ID comes in handy. Because you've saved the ID to a variable at the time when you initially set the interval, you can pass that variable to the *clearInterval( )* function:

```
clearInterval(nIntervalID);
```

It is also possible to use object methods as interval functions. This procedure is not discussed in this book, but you can find more information on this subject in the *ActionScript Cookbook* (O'Reilly, 2003).

As an alternative to using interval functions, you can also use the built-in event handler method *onEnterFrame( )*. The former technique is preferred because it allows you more control over how often the actions are being called. The *onEnterFrame( )* technique is dependent on the movie's frame rate. However, there are some cases in which you want some action or actions to occur at the frame rate of the movie. For example, Recipe 10.6 explained how to use an *onEnterFrame( )* event handler method to play a movie clip's timeline in reverse. In that case, you want the playhead to move backward at the same rate at which it would normally move forward. You can, of course, use some simple mathematics to determine the correct frequency at which to call an interval function. But because the *onEnterFrame( )* method is already called at that frequency, it is a good fit.

The *onEnterFrame( )* method is what is called an *event handler method*. This means that when the enter frame event occurs in Flash, this method is automatically invoked. The enter frame event occurs at the frame rate of the movie. So if the frame rate is 12 frames per second, the enter frame event occurs 12 times per second, and, in turn, the *onEnterFrame( )* method for any and all movie clips is invoked. The enter frame event is somewhat of a misnomer, because this event occurs regardless of whether the playhead is entering a frame. The event occurs at the frame rate if the movie is playing or stopped. Therefore, as long as the frame rate is high enough (the default of 12 frames per second is generally sufficient for most actions), you can use an *onEnterFrame( )* method to have Flash perform actions repeatedly.

Even though Flash tries to call the *onEnterFrame( )* method for all movie clips, the method is undefined until you define it. So normally, no actions necessarily take place when the enter frame event occurs. It is up to you to define this method for a movie clip. In order to do so, you need only to assign a function reference to the *onEnterFrame( )* method for that movie clip. The function reference can be either to a named or anonymous function. The most common practice is to define the function inline as an anonymous function, as shown here:

```
mClip.onEnterFrame = function ():Void {
  trace("This gets called at the movie's frame rate.");
};
```

You should notice that when you assign the function reference to the *onEnterFrame( )* method, you do not include the function call operator (*( )*) after *onEnterFrame*. This is very important. If you add the function call operator, it will not work.

```
// This will not work. It is incorrect to add the function call operator after
// the name of the method to which you are assigning the function.
mClip.onEnterFrame()  = function ():Void {
  // ...
};
```

11.2   Applying Transparency to Movie Clips

Problem

You want to adjust the transparency of a movie clip.

Solution

Select the movie clip instance during authoring time and adjust the Alpha Color value in the Property inspector.

Alternatively, you can modify the transparency at runtime using ActionScript to set the movie clip's _alpha property.

Discussion

By adjusting the alpha (transparency) value of a movie clip instance, you affect the appearance of the transparency of all the contents of that instance. The valid alpha range is from 0% (completely transparent) to 100% (completely opaque), and the default value for all new movie clip instances is 100%. Notice, however, that the alpha value applied to a movie clip instance is multiplied by the alpha values of each of the nested contents to yield the resulting transparencies. For example, if you apply a 50% alpha value to a movie clip instance, and that instance contains two nested movie clips—one with 100% alpha and the other with 50% alpha—the result is that the first nested movie clip displays at 50% alpha (which is 50% of 100%) and the second nested movie clip displays at 25% alpha (which is 50% of 50%).

One way to modify a movie clip instance's transparency is at authoring time. The advantage of adjusting a movie clip instance's alpha value at authoring time is that you can accomplish this task without having to use any ActionScript. The process is as follows:

1. Select the movie clip instance on the stage.
2. Locate the Color Styles menu in the Property inspector, and select the Alpha option.
3. Modify the percentage in the form field that appears to the right of the Color Styles menu.

Another option is to modify a movie clip's transparency at runtime using Action-Script. The ActionScript for modifying an instance's alpha is really quite simple. All that is required is one line of code—an assignment statement that sets the value of the instance's _alpha property. The _alpha property should contain a numeric value from 0 to 100. If you assign _alpha a value of less than 0, the movie clip will display at 0% alpha, and if you assign _alpha a value of greater than 100, the movie clip will display at 100% alpha.

The following is an example of the proper syntax for assigning a value to a movie clip's _alpha property. In this example, the movie clip instance is named mClip, and the value 70 is assigned to the _alpha property for that movie clip. Use your own movie clip instance name and the value you want to assign to the _alpha value.

```
mClip._alpha = 70;
```

The advantage of setting a movie clip's transparency using ActionScript is that you can allow for greater user interaction. For example, setting a movie clip's alpha value at authoring time does not allow for much interactivity. However, you can create all kinds of interesting effects by adjusting the alpha with ActionScript. One such example is that you can create buttons that increment and decrement an instance's transparency:

```
// Apply actions when the user clicks and releases btIncrement, a button instance.
btIncrement.onRelease = function( ):Void {

  // Add five to the _alpha property of mClip.
  mClip._alpha += 5;
}

// Apply actions when the user clicks and releases btDecrement, a button instance.
btDecrement.onRelease = function( ):Void {

  // Subtract five from the _alpha property of mClip.
  mClip._alpha -= 5;
}
```

By adjusting the alpha for a movie clip, you can create transparency effects, and you can also create effects where instances seem to fade in and out of the movie. In order to accomplish this task, you need to either use a motion tween or an ActionScript technique—both of which are covered in Recipe 11.3.

11.3 Fading Movie Clip Instances In and Out

Problem

You want to create an effect in which a movie clip appears to fade in or out of your movie.

Solution

Use a motion tween between an instance of the movie clip at 100% alpha to an instance of the movie clip at 0% alpha, to create a fade-out effect—or the reverse to fade-in.

Alternatively, you can use an interval function (or an *onEnterFrame( )*) event handler method to increment or decrement a movie clip's _alpha property over time.

Additionally, you have the option of using the *mx.transitions.Tween* class.

Discussion

You can create the effect of a movie clip fading in or out of your movie by adjusting the instance's alpha setting over time. By starting out with 100% alpha and gradually adjusting the value to 0%, the movie clip will appear to fade out, and by starting at 0% and gradually adjusting the alpha to 100%, the movie clip will appear to fade in. Or, you can also have the movie clip only fade in or out partially to create your own custom fading effects. For example, you might choose to lower the transparency of one or more movie clips when another is selected. Instead of completely fading those movie clips down to 0%, you can create a dimming effect by lowering the alpha to 50%.

You can create a fading effect at authoring time by using a motion tween between two instances of the same movie clip with different alpha settings. The following steps outline the basic process:

1. Create the first instance of the movie clip on a keyframe that contains no other content. Make sure to position the movie clip where you want it.

2. Create a new keyframe after the first on the same layer. This new keyframe should be a duplicate of the original, which you can accomplish by selecting the frame at which you wish to create the new keyframe and choosing Insert → Keyframe or pressing F6. You should create the new keyframe after the first by the number of frames over which you want the fade to take place. For example, if your first keyframe is at frame 15, and you want the fade to take 30 frames, create the new keyframe at frame 45.

3. Adjust the alpha settings of the two instances appropriately. For example, if you want to create the effect of the movie clip fading in, adjust the alpha value of the first instance so that it is at 0%, and leave the second instance at 100%.

4. Create a motion tween between the two keyframes. You can also create fading effects at runtime using ActionScript to modify the _alpha property value over time. The preferred technique for accomplishing this is to use an interval function. Alternatively, you can also use the *onEnterFrame( )* method. Both of these techniques are described in Recipe 11.1.

First, let's look at how to do this using an interval function. A simple fade function would take a single parameter—the reference to the movie clip to fade. We'll assume at first that we want to fade the movie clip down from complete opacity at a constant rate of one percentage point at a time. Here, then, is the function:

```
function fadeMovieClip(mClip:MovieClip):Void {
  var nAlpha:Number = mClip._alpha;
  mClip._alpha = nAlpha - 1;
  updateAfterEvent();
}
```

Note that I didn't use the decrement operator in the preceding example. That is because Flash Player internally keeps track of alpha values on a scale from 0 to 255, and the _alpha properties effective range is from 0 to 100. Due to the way in which Flash Player converts between the scales, the effects are unexpected when using the decrement operator. Using the preceding technique (assigning the current _alpha value to a variable, and then subtracting 1 from that variable) corrects the issue.

Then you can set up an interval over which to call this function for a particular movie clip. The number of milliseconds for the interval that you should choose depends on how quickly you want the movie clip to fade. The smaller the interval, the faster the movie clip will fade. The following example creates an interval in which *fadeMovieClip( )* is called every 100 milliseconds and is passed a reference to a movie clip:

```
var nFadeSquareIntervalID:Number = setInterval(fadeMovieClip, 50, mSquare);
```

Now, one difficulty with this solution to this point is that it continues to decrement the _alpha property even after having reached 0. So the movie clip can end up with negative _alpha values. Although this is not inherently a problem, it can create other problems, and it is best to stop decrementing the _alpha property once it reaches 0. We can do this by adding an *if* statement to the function definition. Here's the new *fadeMovieClip( )* definition:

```
function fadeMovieClip (mClip:MovieClip):Void {
  if(mClip._alpha > 0) {
    var nAlpha:Number = mClip._alpha;
    mClip._alpha = nAlpha - 1;
    updateAfterEvent();
  }
}
```

And yet, there are still a few minor things we can do to improve upon this solution. Now we can also adjust the function definition a little, so that we can pass it a parameter indicating what value to use when changing the _alpha property. Instead of always decrementing by one, we can now specify positive and negative values to fade the movie clip both up and down. In this case, we'll also want to modify the *if* statement slightly, so that it also makes sure the _alpha property is no greater than 100:

```
function fadeMovieClip (mClip:MovieClip, nRate:Number):Void {
  if(mClip._alpha > 0 && mClip._alpha < 100) {
    var nAlpha:Number = mClip._alpha;
    mClip._alpha = nAlpha + nRate;
    updateAfterEvent();
  }
}
```

With the latest *fadeMovieClip( )* function, we can fade movie clips up and down using positive and negative rate values. Here are two examples in which we assume that mSquare has an initial _alpha value of less than 100 and mCircle has an initial _alpha value of greater than 0:

```
var nFadeSquareUpIntervalID:Number = setInterval(fadeMovieClip, 50, mSquare, 1);
var nFadeCircleDownIntervalID:Number = setInterval(fadeMovieClip, 50, mCircle, -1);
```

Although this code works perfectly well, it has a slight defect: the interval doesn't stop. That won't normally cause any difficulties or errors, but it does mean that the Flash movie continues to use processor resources to keep calling the interval function, even though the task has completed. If enough intervals get set and none of them is cleared, after a while, Flash can start to slow down the entire computer. So it is generally a good practice to clear any interval after it's no longer necessary. You already learned how to do that in Recipe 11.1, by using the *clearInterval( )* function. The only catch is that in this case, you've created a function (*fadeMovieClip( )*) that is abstract enough that it can accommodate many different movie clips and intervals. Therefore, you cannot call *clearInterval( )* within the function using a hardcoded interval ID reference. Instead, you need to store the interval IDs in an associative array as you create them. The following code may seem a little confusing, because it is rather advanced. However, rest assured that using this same code, you'll be able to apply fades to any movie clip with just very minor modifications. The first thing you should do is define an associative array to contain the interval IDs. You can do that using the Object class constructor as follows:

```
var oIntervalIDs:Object = new Object( );
```

Then, instead of assigning each interval ID to a variable as in the previous examples, you can assign the IDs to elements of the associative array. Use the name of the movie clip as the index, or key, of the associative array. That way you'll be able to reference the ID later on simply by knowing the name of the movie clip. You can retrieve a movie clip's instance name using its _name property. The following code shows how you can create two intervals as in the previous example, but this time assigning the IDs to elements of the associative array:

```
oIntervalIDs[mSqaure._name] = setInterval(fadeMovieClip, 50, mSquare, 1);
oIntervalIDs[mCircle._name] = setInterval(fadeMovieClip, 50, mCircle, -1);
```

You then need to modify the *fadeMovieClip( )* method just slightly. Add an *else* clause to the *if* statement so that if the _alpha value is beyond the valid range, Flash will clear the appropriate interval. The new function should appear as follows:

```
function fadeMovieClip (mClip:MovieClip, nRate:Number):Void {
  if(mClip._alpha > 0 && mClip._alpha < 100) {
    var nAlpha:Number = mClip._alpha;
    mClip._alpha = nAlpha + nRate;
    updateAfterEvent( );
  }
  else {
    clearInterval(oIntervalIDs[mClip._name]);
```

```
    }
  }
```

Although that may appear to be a lot of advanced code, you can copy and adapt it to fade any movie clip.

You can use buttons to initiate the programmatic fading by placing the call to *setInterval( )* inside the *onPress( )* or *onRelease( )* event handler method:

```
// In this example, I assume that the interval function, the btFadeUp button, and the mSquare
// movie clip are defined on the main timeline.
btFadeUp.onRelease = function ():Void {
  oIntervalIDs[mSquare._name] = setInterval(fadeMovieClip, 50, mSquare, 1);
}
```

You can accomplish basically the same tasks with the *onEnterFrame( )* event handler method. However, it does not allow you quite as much flexibility as an interval function. You're likely to notice choppier animations unless you have a high frame rate and/or you are fading the movie clip slowly. However, if you prefer using an *onEnterFrame( )* technique, you can use the following code as an example. Many of the same principles apply as with the interval function technique.

```
mClip.onEnterFrame = function():Void {

  // Decrement the _alpha value by one.
  var nAlpha:Number = this._alpha;
  this._alpha = nAlpha - 1;

  // Check whether the value is out of range. If so, delete the onEnterFrame( ) event handler
  // method. Notice that you should not include the function call operator after onEnterFrame.
  if(this._alpha > 100 || this._alpha < 0) {
    delete this.onEnterFrame;
  }
};
```

If you want to fade a movie clip's alpha up, increment the _alpha property's value instead. If you want the movie clip to fade more rapidly, increment or decrement the value by more than 1.

Flash ships with an ActionScript class called *mx.transitions.Tween*. You can use the class to add an alpha tween programmatically with the following syntax:

```
var twShape:mx.transitions.Tween = new mx.transitions.Tween(movieClip, "_alpha",
null, startingAlpha, endingAlpha, durationInFrames);
```

For example, you can add an alpha tween that fades a movie clip named mShape from 0 to 100 over 10 frames using the following code:

```
var twShape:mx.transitions.Tween = new mx.transitions.Tween(mShape, "_alpha", null,
0, 100, 10);
```

Optionally, you can replace the null reference with a reference to one of the built-in easing functions. Those functions are as follows:

mx.transitions.easing.Back.easeIn
mx.transitions.easing.Back.easeOut
mx.transitions.easing.Back.easeInOut
mx.transitions.easing.Bounce.easeIn
mx.transitions.easing.Bounce.easeOut
mx.transitions.easing.Bounce.easeInOut
mx.transitions.easing.Elastic.easeIn
mx.transitions.easing.Elastic.easeOut
mx.transitions.easing.Elastic.easeInOut
mx.transitions.easing.Regular.easeIn
mx.transitions.easing.Regular.easeOut
mx.transitions.easing.Regular.easeInOut
mx.transitions.easing.Strong.easeIn
mx.transitions.easing.Strong.easeOut
mx.transitions.easing.Strong.easeInOut

You can try the different function references to see the effects. Some of the easing effects may not be noticeable with alpha tweens, but they are with other types of tweens (rotation, x and y, etc.).

The following example alpha-tweens a movie clip named mShape from 0 to 100 over 10 frames using a regular ease in:

```
var twShape:mx.transitions.Tween = new mx.transitions.Tween(mShape, "_alpha", mx.
transitions.easing.Regular.easeIn, 0, 100, 10);
```

Make sure that you do *not* include the function call operator (( )) when you reference the easing functions.

Additionally, you can specify the duration of the tween in seconds rather than frames. If you want to do that, change the durationInFrames parameter to a duration given in seconds. Then, add one more parameter—a value of true. The extra parameter tells Flash to interpret the duration as seconds rather than frames. For example, the following code creates an alpha tween over five seconds:

```
var twShape:mx.transitions.Tween = new mx.transitions.Tween(mShape, "_alpha", null,
0, 100, 5, true);
```

11.4 Adjusting Movie Clip Instance Color

Problem

You want to adjust the color of a movie clip instance.

Solution

Select the Tint option from the Color Styles menu in the Property inspector, and modify the red, green, and blue values as well as the tint amount.

Alternatively, use an ActionScript `ColorTransform` object to modify the color at runtime.

Discussion

You can adjust the tint on each movie clip instance individually, creating unique colors for each, even though they are all derived from a common library symbol. This can be a powerful technique for creating variations on a single movie clip instance.

At authoring time, you can modify an instance's color settings from the Property inspector:

1. Select the instance on the stage.
2. Open the Property inspector, locate the Color Styles menu, and select the Tint option.
3. Adjust the available settings:
   - Set the red, green, and blue color values individually, or choose a color from the color selector. These settings affect the tint of the color to apply to the instance.
   - Choose a value for the Tint Amount. The valid range is from 0% to 100%.

When you apply a tint to a movie clip instance, Flash modifies each of the instance's color values relative to their original value. The result is a tint, rather than a fill effect. In other words, if the movie clip instance originally had blue, orange, and yellow colors within it, and you apply a red tint to it, the blue, orange, and yellow values become redder. *How much* redder the colors become depends on the value you choose for Tint Amount. If you choose 0%, no tint is applied. If you choose 100%, the red color ends up replacing all the other color values. The values in between result in a tint of increasing intensity.

The Tint option in the Color Styles menu gives you moderate control over the tint you apply to the movie clip. For more advanced authoring time control, use the Advanced option instead. If you choose Advanced from the Color Styles menu in the Property inspector, you then have the option to open the Advanced Color Settings dialog box.

In the Advanced Effect dialog box, there are eight values for you to modify. These values are the red percentage, red offset, green percentage, green offset, blue percentage, blue offset, alpha percentage, and alpha offset. For more information on how these values work together to produce a tint, read the further discussion later in this recipe on modifying these values using ActionScript.

You can also apply a tint to a movie clip instance at runtime using ActionScript. The ActionScript *ColorTransform* class lets you make runtime adjustments to a movie clip's color. Here are the steps to follow:

1. Import the *ColorTransform* class with an import statement. The class is in a package called *flash.geom*, so the import statement looks like this:

   ```
   import flash.geom.ColorTransform;
   ```

2. Create a new ColorTransform object using a new statement with the ColorTransform constructor. You can pass the constructor eight parameters, specifying the red multiplier, green multiplier, blue multiplier, alpha multiplier, red offset, green offset, blue offset, and alpha offset. We'll discuss the details of those parameters in just a minute. For now, just know that the multiplier values have a range of –1 to 1 and the offsets have a range of –255 to 255. The following example makes a ColorTransform object that applies a red tint by effectively subtracting the green and blue parts from the colors:

   ```
   var ctClipColor:ColorTransform = new ColorTransform(1, 0, 0, 1, 0, 0, 0, 0);
   ```

3. Apply the object to the movie clip instance by way of the transform. colorTransform object. Every movie clip has a transform property that, in turn, has a colorTransform property. You can assign the ColorTransform object to that property as follows:

   ```
   mClip.transform.colorTransform = ctClipColor;
   ```

When you apply a tint at authoring time, you can see the results on the stage. Therefore, when using that technique, there is not always a need to be able to understand *how* the tint gets applied in order to predict what the result will be. However, when you make changes to an instance's color at runtime, you need to be able to predict what your number values will produce visually. In order to make these predictions, you need to understand how Flash calculates the tint based on the values of your transform object (or from the Advanced Effects dialog box if you are making authoring time changes). All calculations are based on the original color values of each pixel, which I refer to as R0, B0, G0, and A0. The original color values are multiplied by the multiplier values, and then the offset is added to that product. Here are the equations that are used in the calculations to give you a better idea:

$$newRed = (R0 \times redMultiplier)/100 + redOffset$$
$$newGreen = (G0 \times greenMultiplier)/100 + greenOffset$$
$$newBlue = (B0 \times blueMultiplier)/100 + blueOffset$$
$$newAlpha = (A0 \times alphaMultiplier)/100 + alphaOffset$$

You might notice that it is possible to produce values outside of the valid range (0 to 255.) For example, if you have an R0 value of 150, and you use a red multiplier value of 1 and a red offset value of 180, the resulting red value is 330. In such cases, Flash will convert the value to something within the valid range by way of some calculations that are a bit too complex to discuss in this book. Suffice it to say that if you use values outside the valid range, the resultant color will be difficult to predict.

When you use the advanced authoring time settings or the ActionScript runtime technique to modify tints, you can reset the movie clip instance to its original color by using the following `ColorTransform` object.

```
var ctColorReset:ColorTransform = new ColorTransform(1, 1, 1, 1, 0, 0, 0, 0);
```

You can retrieve the current `ColorTransform` object for a movie clip by simply reading the value of the `transform.colorTransform` property.

```
var ctCurrent:ColorTransform = mClip.transform.colorTransform;
```

You can then use the `redMultiplier`, `greenMultiplier`, `blueMultiplier`, `alphaMultiplier`, `redOffset`, `greenOffset`, `blueOffset`, and `alphaOffset` properties to update the value. For example, the following code subtracts 10 from the current blue offset.

```
ctCurrent.blueOffset -= 10;
```

If you want the changes to affect the movie clip, you have to reassign the object to the `transform.colorTransform` property:

```
mClip.transform.colorTransform = ctCurrent;
```

The advantage of updating the properties of the current object instead of constructing a new `ColorTransform` object is that you can make incremental changes to the color relative to the current values. In the preceding example the blue offset was decremented by 10. That enables animated effects whereby colors change gradually over time.

11.5   Animating Color Changes

Problem

You want to animate changes in a movie clip instance's tint over time.

Solution

Create two instances of the movie clip on two keyframes on the same layer. Modify the color settings in the first one to reflect how you want the movie clip to appear when the color animation begins. Modify the color settings in the second one to reflect how you want the movie clip to appear when the color animation ends. Create a motion tween between the two keyframes.

Discussion

As with just about any other properties of a movie clip, you can animate changes in color/tint over time. You can achieve a smooth gradation over time from one color/tint to another by using a motion tween:

1. Create a new layer for the movie clip instance, and create a new keyframe beginning on the first frame in which you want the animation to begin. If you want the movie clip to appear and begin animating its color starting at frame 1, you don't need to create an additional keyframe in this step.

2. Create an instance of the movie clip on the stage and place it into the keyframe you created in step 1.

3. Determine the number of frames over which you want the animation to take place, and create a new keyframe on the same layer at the appropriate frame. For example, if your first keyframe is at frame 15, and you want the animation to last for 30 frames, create a new keyframe on the same layer at frame 45. The new keyframe should be a duplicate of the first. You can do this by selecting the frame in the timeline and then choosing Insert → Keyframe or by pressing F6.

4. Adjust the Tint or Advanced color settings for the two instances. Set the first instance's color to what you want it to be when the animation begins. And set the second instance's color to what you want it to be when the animation ends.

5. Create a motion tween between the two keyframes.

The result of this process is that the movie clip instance will gradually shift from the initial tint to the final tint. And, of course, you can combine this kind of tween animation with any other tweenable properties. For example, you can also change the position of the movie clip instance at the same time as the color is changing.

Although it is possible to programmatically tween color changes, it is a complex process that is not discussed in this book.

11.6 Brightening Movie Clip Instances

Problem

You want to brighten a movie clip instance.

Solution

Apply a brightness percentage to the instance.

Discussion

You can create the effect of brightening or lightening a movie clip instance by applying a brightness percentage to it. The default value for brightness is 0%, which represents the original colors. As the percentage increases, the colors get lighter and lighter until, at 100%, all the colors are completely white. You can access an instance's brightness settings by selecting the instance and then choosing the Brightness option from the Color Styles menu in the Property inspector. After you have selected the Brightness option, the control for selecting/entering the percentage appears to the right of the Color Styles menu.

11.7 Transforming Movie Clips (Rotation, Scaling, and Skewing)

Problem

You want to rotate, scale, or skew a movie clip instance.

Solution

Use the drawing tools to modify the instance on the stage at authoring time.

For some properties, such as rotation and scaling, you can modify the values at run-time using ActionScript with the _rotation and _xscale and _yscale properties. Skewing is possible using a Matrix object.

Discussion

Not only can you modify movie clip instance locations and colors, you can also transform them in other ways, such as by rotating, scaling, or skewing them. This feature is extremely useful, because it allows you to perform these transformations on all the contents grouped within the movie clip. And even more beneficial is how you can then animate these transformations as well.

You can transform a movie clip instance at authoring time just as you can modify any symbol instance, as discussed in various recipes in Chapter 3. Use the authoring tools to perform rotation, scaling, and skewing tasks.

You can then animate these transformations over time by using a motion tween, just as you would use a motion tween to animate color or position changes over time. In addition to transforming a movie clip at authoring time, you can also perform these modifications at runtime using ActionScript. One of the advantages of using Action-Script to perform these changes is that you can add a greater degree of user interactivity. For example, you can create sliders and buttons that allow a user to scale a movie clip to virtually any size using ActionScript.

The _rotation property allows you to specify the number of degrees to rotate a movie clip in the clockwise direction. The default value for _rotation is 0, which means that the movie clip appears in the same orientation as the parent movie clip. Because there are 360 degrees in a complete turn, a value of 360 causes the movie clip to appear in the same orientation as a value of 0. By specifying increasingly positive values for the property, you cause the movie clip to rotate clockwise, and by specifying increasingly negative numbers, you cause the movie clip to rotate counter-clockwise. You are not limited to any range of values for _rotation.

```
// Rotate mClip one hundred eighty degrees (a half turn).
mClip._rotation = 180;
```

To animate the rotation of a movie clip, adjust the value of the _rotation property repeatedly within an interval function. The following example continually rotates a movie clip named mShape in a clockwise direction:

```
// Set an interval at which Flash calls rotateMovieClip( ) every 50 milliseconds,
each time
// passing the function two parameters - a reference to mShape and the amount by
which to rotate
// the movie clip.
var nInterval:Number = setInterval(rotateMovieClip, 50, mShape, 1);

// Define rotateMovieClip( ). It accepts two parameters, corresponding to the
parameters passed to
// it from the call to setInterval( ). It then adds the rotation increment to the
current
// _rotation value of the specified movie clip.
function rotateMovieClip(mClip:MovieClip, nRate:Number):Void {
  mClip._rotation += nRate;
}
```

You can scale a movie clip in both the *x* and *y* directions using the _xscale and _yscale properties. These values are given in percentages, and therefore the default value for each is 100. You can scale a movie clip in one or both directions, but if you want to maintain the aspect ratio, make sure to set both _xscale and _yscale to the same value. For example, if you want to scale a movie clip to three times its original size, you should use code similar to the following:

```
mClip._xscale = 300;
mClip._yscale = 300;
```

You can use buttons, sliders, or any other user interaction mechanism to set the rotation and scaling for a movie clip. Here is an example of several buttons that cause a movie clip to scale using an interval function. The code assumes that there are buttons named btScaleUp and btScaleDown and that the movie clip is named mShape. If you use different instance names, change the code accordingly.

```
// Declare a variable to store the interval ID so you can stop it later.
var nIntervalID:Number;

// Define the onPress( ) event handler method for the btScaleUp button. When the user
presses the
// button, set an interval so that the scaleMovieClip( ) function (defined later)
gets called at a
// particular frequency. Pass the scaleMovieClip( ) function the reference to the
movie clip you
// want to tween and the increment. A positive increment causes the movie clip to
scale up. You
// can cause the movie clip to scale faster by decreasing the interval (50 in the
example) and/or
// increasing the increment (1 in the example).
btScaleUp.onPress = function():Void {
  nIntervalID = setInterval(scaleMovieClip, 50, mShape, 1);
};
```

```
// Define the onRelease( ) event handler method for btScaleUp. When the user releases
the button
// clear the interval so the movie clip stops scaling.
btScaleUp.onRelease = function( ):Void {
  clearInterval(nIntervalID);
};

// Assign the same definition from onRelease( ) to onReleaseOutside( ) so the button
stops scaling
// even if the user moves the mouse off of the button before releasing.
btScaleUp.onReleaseOutside = btScaleUp.onRelease;

// Define the onPress( ), onRelease( ), and onReleaseOutside( ) event handler methods
for the
// btScaleDown button. See the previous comments for more details. The only
difference is that a
// negative value is used as the increment so that the movie clip scales down.
btScaleDown.onPress = function( ):Void {
  nIntervalID = setInterval(scaleMovieClip, 50, mShape, -1);
};
btScaleDown.onRelease = function( ):Void {
  clearInterval(nIntervalID);
};
btScaleDown.onReleaseOutside = btScaleDown.onRelease;

// Define the scaleMovieClip( ) function. It should accept two parameters – the movie
clip to
// scale and the amount by which to scale it.
function scaleMovieClip(mClip:MovieClip, nRate:Number):Void {

  // Increment both the _xscale and _yscale properties and then call
updateAfterEvent( ) to ensure
  // a smooth animation.
  mClip._xscale += nRate;
  mClip._yscale += nRate;
  updateAfterEvent( );
}
```

As with an alpha animation, you can animate the changes to a movie clip's rotation
and scaling using an *onEnterFrame( )* method. The same inherent advantages and
disadvantages arise. Here is an example that increases the movie clip's scaling and
rotation continually:

```
mClip.onEnterFrame = function( ):Void {
  this._rotation++;
  this._xscale++;
  this._yscale++;
};
```

11.8 Moving a Movie Clip in Front of or Behind Another Movie Clip (or a Button or Text Field)

Problem

You want to move a movie clip in front of or behind another movie clip, button, or text field.

Solution

Use layers or the arrangement commands to adjust the order of instances at authoring time.

Use the *swapDepths( )* method to change the stacking order of any two instances at runtime.

Discussion

When you are working with multiple movie clip, button, and/or text field instances on the stage at the same time, you need to be aware of their stacking order. For example, if you have a movie clip that is supposed to animate behind a text field, you need to make sure that the text field appears in front of the movie clip. You can make these kinds of adjustments at authoring time either by placing the instances on different layers and arranging the layer order or by changing the order using the arrangement commands. You can move an instance forward or back by selecting the instance and then choosing Modify → Arrange → Bring Forward/Send Back/Bring to Front/Send to Back.

The authoring time techniques work just fine when you want to maintain a constant stacking order of all the instances in the movie. But when you want the order to change, you need to use ActionScript to effect that change at runtime using the *swapDepths( )* method. In some cases, it is important that you be able to programmatically change the depths of instances in this way. For example, if you create a puzzle in which the user can drag the pieces around on stage, you want to make sure that the piece that is currently being dragged appears on top of all the other pieces.

In order to understand how to use *swapDepths( )*—a relatively easy method—you first need to understand how Flash determines stacking order. For the convenience of the developer, Flash uses layers within the authoring environment. However, the exported SWF does not contain any information about layers. Instead, it knows only about *depths*: whole number values determining the stacking order. Every instance in the movie is assigned its own depth whether you assign it explicitly using the *attachMovie( )*, *duplicateMovieClip( )*, *createEmptyMovieClip( )*, or *createTextField( )* methods, or whether it is done automatically for all authoring time instances. But regardless of how the instances are created, they all must have a unique depth. The depth determines the stacking order in which they appear on the stage. An instance of greater depth appears on top of an instance of lesser depth.

 Instances created at authoring time have depths beginning at –16383 and continuing upward in increments of one.

You can use the *swapDepths( )* method to switch the depths of any two instances. You should invoke the method from one of the instances, and pass a reference to the other instance to the method as a parameter. For instance, if you want to switch the depths of two movie clips on the same timeline named mSquare and mCircle, your code could look like this:

```
mSquare.swapDepths(mCircle);
```

The preceding example could also be written:

```
mCircle.swapDepths(mSquare);
```

Both the examples result in the same thing—the two movie clip instances change positions in the stacking order.

There are many scenarios in which you may want to change the stacking order of instances in your movie. One common example was mentioned earlier—ensuring that the movie clip that is selected or being dragged appears on top of all the other instances. And another example is that of creating animations that appear to move in three dimensions. For example, if you have two movie clips that appear to spin in a loop along the z-axis (meaning they seem to move back into the screen), you need to make sure that the movie clip that is currently appearing to be nearer to the viewer has a higher depth.

Here is a simple example with two movie clip instances named circle and square on the main timeline. The two movie clips are slightly overlapping. The circle movie clip has the following actions:

```
mCircle.onPress = function( ):Void {
  this.swapDepths(mSquare);
};
```

In this example, each time the user clicks the circle, the circle and square appear to change order. You can also create a slightly more intelligent system by which the circle is always brought to the front of the square when it is clicked by adding a conditional statement that uses the *getDepth( )* method to compare the current depths of the two movie clips. In this slightly modified code, the depths are changed only if the depth of mCircle is not already greater than the depth of mSquare:

```
mCircle.onPress = function( ):Void {
  if(this.getDepth( ) < mSquare.getDepth( )) {
    this.swapDepths(mSquare);
  }
};
```

You can add a similar action to the square movie clip so that when the square movie clip is clicked, it comes to the front of the circle.

```
mSquare.onPress = function( ):Void {
  if(this.getDepth( ) < mCircle.getDepth( )) {
    this.swapDepths(mCircle);
  }
};
```

11.9   Creating New Movie Clips Based on Existing Movie Clips

Problem

You want to create a duplicate movie clip instance based on an existing instance.

Solution

Use the *duplicateMovieClip( )* method.

Discussion

With the *duplicateMovieClip( )* method, you can quickly create duplicates of movie clip instances already on the stage. This method creates a copy of the movie clip instance from which it is invoked with a new instance name and depth:

```
// Create a new movie clip named mNewInstance based on the movie clip named
// originalInstance that already existed on the stage. The new movie clip is
// created at depth 1.
mOriginalInstance.duplicateMovieClip("mNewInstance", 1);
```

 Make sure that you use a unique depth for the new movie clip. If you use a depth that corresponds to an existing instance, that existing instance will be overwritten.

Additionally, you can specify a third, optional parameter for the *duplicateMovieClip( )* method. This parameter is known as the *initialization object*, and the properties and values of the initialization object are assigned to the new instance. The parameter value should be in the form of an ActionScript *Object* object, which you can create one of two ways:

- Using the constructor and assigning properties and values via dot notation:

```
var oInitialization:Object = new Object( );
oInitialization.property1 = "value1";
oInitialization. property2 = "value2;
```

- Using the object literal notation:

```
var oInitialization:Object = { property1: "value1", property2: "value2"};
```

Both of these techniques are absolutely valid, and neither is better than the other. Sometimes you may find that you want to use the object literal notation, because it allows you to create the object in line with the *duplicateMovieClip( )* method:

```
mOriginalInstance.duplicateMovieClip("mNewInstance", 1, { property1: "valeu1",
property2: "value2"});
```

However, in other cases, the object literal notation is either inconvenient or impossible. Generally, the more properties you want to assign to an object, the more it makes sense to use the constructor technique, because it offers a much more readable format.

```
var oInitialization:Object = new Object( );
oInitialization. property1 = "value1";
oInitialization. property2 = "value2";
mOriginalInstance.duplicateMovieClip("mNewInstance", 1, oInitialization);
```

The initialization object, or init object, can be extremely useful in at least two ways:

- You can use the initialization object to initialize the new instance with its own values for built-in movie clip properties, such as _x, _y, _rotation, and so on. By default, the duplicate retains the values for these properties from the original movie clip.

    ```
    // Create a duplicate movie clip positioned at 300,300.
    mOriginalInstance.duplicateMovieClip("mNewInstance", 1, {_x: 300, _y: 300});
    ```

- You can use the init object to initialize a new instance with copies of the custom method definitions (such as event handler methods) of the original movie clip. By default, custom method definitions are not copied from the original to the duplicate movie clip. However, you can use a for ... in loop to populate an initialization object with all the custom properties and methods of the original movie clip, and then pass that initialization object to the *duplicateMovieClip( )* method:

    ```
    // Create the init object.
    var oInitialization:Object = new Object( );

    // Use a for...in loop to loop through all the custom properties and methods of
    // the original movie clip instance, and add them to the init object.
    for(var sItem:String in mOriginalInstance) {
      oInitialization [sItem] = mOriginalInstance[sItem];
    }

    mOriginalInstance.duplicateMovieClip("mNewInstance", 1, oInitialization);
    ```

You can use a for statement to create multiple duplicates at the same time. The basic syntax is as follows:

```
for(var i:Number = 0; i < numberOfDuplicates; i++) {
  originalInstance.duplicateMovieClip(newInstanceName, depth);
}
```

When you create the new movie clips, make sure each has a unique instance name and a unique depth. Typically, you can generate unique instance names by concatenating the for statement's index variable value with a base name. For example, you might use a base name of mSquare and concatenate that with the value of the for statement's index variable to get instance names of mSquare0, mSquare1, mSquare2, and so on. Then, for the depth, you can either use the value of the for statement's index variable or you can use the *getNextHighestDepth( )* method that is discussed in Recipe 11.10. The following example creates five duplicates with instance names mSquare0 through mSquare4:

```
for(var i:Number = 0; i < 5; i++) {
  mSquare.duplicateMovieClip("mSquare" + i, i);
}
```

When you generate duplicate movie clips in batches as shown in the preceding code, you may notice that you don't have a very convenient way to refer to the new instances. When you create a single duplicate with a specific name, you can refer to the new movie clip quite simply. For example, the following code creates a duplicate of mCircle with an instance name of mNewCircle. Then it applies an *onPress( )* event handler method to the new movie clip.

```
mCircle.duplicateMovieClip("mNewCircle", 1, {_x: 100, _y: 100});
mNewCircle.onPress = function( ):Void {
  trace("You clicked on mNewCircle.");
};
```

However, when you use a for statement to create the duplicates with dynamic instance names, you need a different way to refer to the new movie clips. For example, if you are creating duplicate movie clips with instance names mSquare0, mSquare1, mSquare2, and so on, you *cannot* use the following code to assign an *onPress( )* event handler method to them after you've created them:

```
for(var i:Number = 0; i < 5; i++) {
  mSquare.duplicateMovieClip("mSquare" + i, i);

  // This code will not work.
  "mSquare" + i.onPress = function( ):Void {
    trace("You clicked on a duplicated square.");
  };
}
```

Fortunately, the *duplicateMovieClip( )* method returns a value—a reference to the movie clip it just created. You can assign that value to a variable and then reference the movie clip by way of the variable. The following example code will work:

```
// Declare a variable to use in order to reference the duplicate movie clips.
var mDuplicate:MovieClip;

for(var i:Number = 0; i < 5; i++) {
```

```
// When you duplicate the movie clip, assign the return value from the method to
the mDuplicate
// variable.
mDuplicate = mSquare.duplicateMovieClip("mSquare" + i, i);

// Reference the new movie clip by way of the mDuplicate variable.
mDuplicate.onPress = function():Void {
  trace("You clicked on a duplicated square.");
};
}
```

11.10 Generating Unique Depths

Problem

You want to generate unique depth values so that you don't accidentally overwrite existing content when you use methods such as *duplicateMovieClip( )*, *attachMovie( )*, *createEmptyMovieClip( )*, or *createTextField( )*.

Solution

Use the *getNextHighestDepth( )* method.

Discussion

The *getNextHighestDepth( )* method is a particularly useful method when you are creating movie clips (or text fields) programmatically. If you add a lot of content programmatically, it can start to get somewhat difficult to keep track of which depths have been used and which have not. And if you accidentally use a depth that was already used, you will overwrite the content that had previously been placed within that depth. The *getNextHighestDepth( )* method, as the name suggests, returns the next unused depth within a movie clip. That means you don't need to worry about keeping track of which depths have been used.

To use the *getNextHighestDepth( )* method, call it from a movie clip using standard dot-syntax. The method doesn't require any parameters, and it returns the next unused depth within the movie clip. The following example uses a *trace( )* statement to output the next unused depth within a movie clip named mClip:

```
trace(mClip.getNextHighestDepth( ));
```

You can get the next available depth within the main timeline by using the self-referencing this. For example, on the main timeline you can use the following code to write the next available depth to the Output panel:

```
trace(this.getNextHighestDepth( ));
```

Typically you'll want to use the *getNextHighestDepth( )* method in conjunction with one of the methods that creates movie clips (or text fields) such as *duplicateMovieClip( )* or *attachMovie( )*. The following example duplicates mSquare and creates a new instance named mNewSquare:

```
mSquare.duplicateMovieClip("mNewSquare", this.getNextHighestDepth( ));
```

11.11 Controlling Movie Clip Playback from Different Timelines

Problem

You want to use ActionScript within one movie clip's timeline in order to control another movie clip.

Solution

Use a relative target path.

Discussion

You can control one movie clip from another movie clip's timeline by using the correct target path. A target path is the address by which Flash can locate a movie clip instance (or button or text field instance), and target paths come in two varieties: relative and absolute.

An absolute target path is a way for Flash to locate an instance from the top down. All absolute target paths begin with _root or _level0 (or _level1, _level2, and so on), which is the topmost structure in a Flash movie. For example, if a movie clip instance named mClip exists on the main timeline, you could reference it with the absolute target path of _root.mClip. Flash then begins looking first at _root, and then locates a movie clip instance named mClip within _root. If there is a movie clip instance named mNested nested within mClip, then an absolute target path would be _root.mClip.mNested.

Absolute addresses may seem like a good way to target instances. However, there are some drawbacks. One of the major drawbacks is that in many, if not most, cases, your code will stop working if and when you load the *.swf* file into another *.swf* file. Flash Player 7 and higher versions support a _lockroot property that enables you to correct that. However, if you are publishing to previous versions of Flash, you cannot work around it without changing your code. Another drawback of absolute addresses is that they tend to lend themselves to poor programming practices. If you have a lot of absolute addresses in your code, it can be a bit more difficult to read. What's more, if you later want to nest a movie clip inside another movie clip for one reason or another, you may need to change your code to accommodate the change.

A relative target path is a way for Flash to locate an instance relative to the timeline from which the command is issued. When you reference a movie clip in the fashion that has been used throughout most of this book, Flash assumes that you want it to look for a movie clip with that instance name within the current timeline. For example:

```
mShape._rotation = 20;
```

In the preceding example, Flash looks for a movie clip named mShape within the timeline from which the command was issued. Additionally, if you add such a reference within a function, Flash will look for a movie clip with that instance name within the timeline for which the function is defined. For example:

```
function rotateMovieClip( ):Void {
  mShape._rotation = 20;
}
```

In the preceding example, Flash looks for a movie clip named mShape that exists on the same timeline in which the *rotateMovieClip( )* function is defined.

Likewise, the same applies to movie clip references within event handler methods. For example, the following code looks for a movie clip named mShape that exists within the same timeline in which the code is defined:

```
btRotate.onRelease = function( ):Void {
  mShape._rotation += 20;
};
```

In addition, there are a few special keywords you should know when working with relative paths. One of those is the this keyword. The this keyword allows an object or timeline to refer to itself. Therefore, the following two statements are equivalent:

```
mShape._rotation = 20;
this.mShape._rotation = 20;
```

Additionally, if you use the this keyword within a regular function, it will refer to the timeline within which the function is defined. For example, the following function definition is the equivalent of the previous *rotateMovieClip( )* function example:

```
function rotateMovieClip( ):Void {
  this.mShape._rotation = 20;
}
```

 There is an exception with functions and the keyword this: when the function is an interval function. In that case, the this keyword returns undefined.

However, within event handler methods, the this keyword refers to the object for which the event handler method is being defined—not the timeline within which the code exists. For example, for the following to work, mShape would need to be nested within btRotate. Otherwise, the reference is undefined.

```
btRotate.onRelease = function( ):Void {
  this.mShape._rotation += 20;
};
```

In addition to being able to refer to themselves, movie clips (and buttons) can refer to the movie clip object (if any) that contains them using the _parent property. For example, if mClip is on the main timeline, then mClip can target the main timeline to do things such as control the timeline playback. The following code applies an *onPress( )* event handler method to mClip such that when it is clicked, the main timeline would stop playback:

```
mClip.onPress = function( ):Void {
  this._parent.stop( );
};
```

11.12 Creating Simple Drag-and-Drop Functionality

Problem

You want to be able to create a draggable movie clip.

Solution

Use the *startDrag( )* and *stopDrag( )* methods.

Discussion

You can cause a movie clip to follow the mouse pointer using the *startDrag( )* method, and you can tell the movie clip to stop following the mouse pointer using the *stopDrag( )* method. Depending on the effect you want to create, you can use these methods in several different ways.

First of all, you can place the *startDrag( )* method call on a frame to cause the movie clip to begin following the mouse pointer as soon as the playhead enters that frame. For example, if you place the action on the first frame of the movie, the specified movie clip will follow the pointer from the very beginning of playback:

```
mClip.startDrag( );
```

When you use the *startDrag( )* method in this way, you'll usually specify a value for the first, optional parameter of the method. The first parameter is a Boolean value indicating whether the movie clip should snap to the pointer. The default value is false, which means that the movie clip will follow the mouse pointer at the same distance that existed between them at the time the method was invoked. For example, if the movie clip instance was on stage at 0,0 and the mouse pointer was at 300,300 when the method was invoked, wherever the user moves the pointer, the movie clip will be offset by 300 pixels up and to the left. However, if you specify the value true when you invoke the *startDrag( )* method, the initial offset is disregarded, and Flash automatically snaps the center of the movie clip instance to the mouse pointer. The result is that the movie clip follows the mouse pointer with no offset. The effect can be used to create custom mouse cursors.

```
mClip.startDrag(true);
```

In other cases, you don't want to start dragging the movie clip based on the play-head entering a frame, but rather based on the user's interaction. For example, if you create a puzzle using Flash, you want the pieces to be draggable only when the user clicks and drags them. In these cases, you want to enable dragging when the use clicks the mouse (a press event), and you want to stop dragging when the user releases the mouse. Therefore, you should place the *startDrag( )* method call in an *onPress( )* event handler method that you define for the movie clip instance, and you should place the *stopDrag( )* method in the *onRelease( )* event handler method you define for the movie clip instance:

```
mClip.onPress = function( ):Void {
  this.startDrag( );
};

mClip.onRelease = function( ):Void {
  this.stopDrag( );
};
```

In the preceding code example, there are a couple of things to notice. First of all, within the event handler methods, you reference the movie clip instance with the this keyword. The other thing to notice is that in the example, the *startDrag( )* method does not have any parameters. In most simple drag-and-drop cases, you don't want the movie clip to snap to the mouse pointer. Instead, you want the movie clip to get dragged from whatever point the user clicks on it. On the other hand, if you do want the movie clip to snap to the mouse pointer, you can do so by specifying true as the first, optional parameter for the *startDrag( )* method. The *stopDrag( )* method never needs any parameters.

```
mClip.onPress = function( ) {
  this.startDrag(true);
};

mClip.onRelease = function( ) {
  this.stopDrag( );
};
```

11.13 Constraining Drag-and-Drop Areas

Problem

You want to allow a movie clip to be draggable only within a certain region.

Solution

Use the optional parameters for the *startDrag( )* method to specify a region over which the movie clip can be dragged.

Discussion

By default, draggable movie clips can be moved anywhere on the stage. However, there are many situations in which you may want to define an area in which a movie clip can be dragged. Two examples of this include:

- If your movie contains various sections, and you don't want the user to be able to drag movie clips over other sections. For example, if you have a puzzle movie with instructions or other text on the right side, and the puzzle pieces on the left, then you could define a draggable area for the movie clips that includes only the left side of the movie.

- When you create sliders, you want to make sure that the slider can be dragged only along a line.

Fortunately, ActionScript makes it relatively simple to define a draggable area for your movie clips. In Recipe 11.12 you can read about how to use the *startDrag( )* method in a basic way to create draggable movie clips. However, in addition to the optional Boolean parameter that determines whether the movie clip snaps to the pointer, the *startDrag( )* method also accepts four more optional parameters. These four additional parameters determine the rectangular area over which the movie clip can be dragged by defining the left, top, right, and bottom coordinate values. The coordinates should be given as values within the movie clip instance's parent. For example, if you have a movie clip instance in the main timeline named mClip, and you want that movie clip to be draggable only within a rectangle in which the left edge is where x is 10, the top edge is where y is 30, the right edge is where x is 150, and the bottom edge is where y is 300, your code might look like this:

```
mClip.startDrag(true, 10, 30, 150, 300);
```

In the preceding example, the snap to parameter is true, which means that the movie clip will snap to the mouse pointer. Also, if the preceding code is placed on a keyframe of the main timeline, the movie clip would automatically begin following the mouse pointer as soon as the playhead entered that frame. But instead of following the mouse pointer anywhere on stage, it will follow the pointer within the rectangular area you have defined. If, instead, you want the movie clip to be draggable within that region only when the user clicks and drags it, the code should be placed within an *onPress( )* event handler method, and the accompanying *stopDrag( )* method should be placed within an *onRelease( )* event handler method. Notice that the *stopDrag( )* method still does not require any parameters, even when you use it to stop a drag action within a region.

```
mClip.onPress = function( ):Void {
  this.startDrag(true, 10, 30, 150, 300);
};
mClip.onRelease = function( ):Void {
  this.stopDrag( );
};
```

11.14 Changing Movie Clip Visibility

Problem

You want to make a movie clip invisible or visible.

Solution

Set the _visible property.

Problem

Movie clip instances default to being visible. However, you can also programmatically toggle the visibility of a movie clip using the _visible property. You may be wondering why you would want to set the _visible property to false rather than simply setting the _alpha property to 0. There is a very important distinction to make between these two properties. When you set the _alpha property to 0, the movie clip may appear invisible, but it will still respond to mouse events, and can otherwise receive focus in the movie. In the event that you want to use a movie clip as an invisible button, this is exactly what you want. However, if you want to temporarily hide a movie clip from the user such that it does not even respond to mouse events, you should set the _visible property to false.

```
mClip._visible = false;
```

You can also reinstate visibility by setting the _visible property to true:

```
mClip._visible = true;
```

A perfect example of how you might use the _visible property is to hide a button until some other user activity (or perhaps a server response) has occurred. One such scenario might be that you might want to hide the Continue button from the user until they have completed all the requested tasks for the given "page." On the frame on which the page is created in your Flash movie, you can initialize the button to be invisible:

```
btContinue._visible = false;
```

Then, after all the tasks have been completed, you can make the button visible:

```
btContinue._visible = true;
```

The _visible property is a very important property as you begin to move from basic Flash movie architecture to more advanced architectures. You can actually create multiple "pages" all within a single keyframe, and by using the _visible property you can switch between them. This has many advantages, including:

- It is easier to maintain user state. For example, if you have a form as one of your pages, you can allow the user to switch back and forth between the form and other sections without losing the information the user has filled out already.

- You can generate your entire movie using ActionScript. Although when you use Flash as a standard animation tool, it does not always make sense to try to generate your entire movie using code, in many other cases it can be quite advantageous, because you can have more programmatic control over things.

You can see many more examples of how to use _visible to perform these kinds of advanced ActionScript tasks in the *ActionScript Cookbook* (O'Reilly).

11.15 Relocating or Moving Movie Clips

Problem

You want to move a movie clip instance on the stage using ActionScript.

Solution

Set the movie clip's _x and/or _y properties.

Discussion

Both the one-time relocation of movie clips and the continual relocation of movie clips to produce animation are discussed in recipes in Chapter 3.

11.16 Detecting Collisions (or Overlaps) Between Two Movie Clips

Problem

You want to be able to detect when two movie clips have collided or are overlapping.

Solution

Use the *hitTest( )* method.

Discussion

There are plenty of reasons why you might want to detect whether two movie clips are overlapping. Here is a brief list of just a few examples:

- Create collision effects whereby two movie clips bounce off of one another.
- Create movie clips that cannot pass through other movie clips. An example of this would be the walls of a maze.
- Detect overlaps between movies to switch the stacking orders.

You can detect when two movie clips are overlapping by using the *hitTest( )* method. This method has two variations on its use. We'll look at the first one in this recipe.

The other variation is used primarily for more advanced collision detections, and you can read about it in the *ActionScript Cookbook* (O'Reilly, 2003).

The basic use of the *hitTest( )* method involves passing the method a reference to the other movie clip instance with which you want to perform the test. Flash then performs a test between the movie clip instance from which the method is invoked and the movie clip instance you pass the method as a parameter.

```
mOne.hitTest(mTwo);
```

If the bounding boxes of the two movie clips overlap, the method returns true. Otherwise, the method returns false. It is important here to note that because the bounding boxes are used to perform the test, only rectangular movie clips can return completely accurate results. If the movie clip shapes are not perfectly rectangular, the results may sometimes be a little different from what you want. In most cases, the differences are not so drastic that it makes a big difference. If you need to perform more accurate collision tests, you should refer to the more advanced collision detection recipes in the *ActionScript Cookbook* (O'Reilly, 2003).

Because the *hitTest( )* method returns a Boolean value, you usually use it in a conditional statement.

```
if(mCircle.hitTest(mSquare)) {
  trace("The circle and square are overlapping.");
}
```

11.17 Adding Movie Clips at Runtime

Problem

You want to be able to add movie clips to your movie at runtime.

Solution

Set the movie clip symbol to export, and use *attachMovie( )* to add the instance to the movie.

Discussion

You can add movie clips to your Flash movie at runtime using ActionScript. Previously, you read about how to use *duplicateMovieClip( )* to create duplicates of an existing movie clip. However, you can actually add new instances to the stage using ActionScript without even having any prior instances that you created during authoring time. This is a really powerful technique, because it allows you to construct your Flash movies almost entirely with ActionScript.

In order to add movie clip instances to the stage at runtime without any previous instances, you need to do two things:

1. Export the movie clip symbol. Flash does not include all symbols from your library in the exported SWF. In order to ensure the smallest file size, Flash exports only those symbols that are used in the movie. Therefore, if you don't create any authoring time instances of a movie clip symbol, Flash will not export it in the final SWF unless you tell it to do so. You can tell it to do this by using the Linkage settings from the library:

   a. Open the library by choosing Window → Library or by pressing Ctrl-L.

   b. Select the movie clip symbol in the library, and either right-click/Control-click the item in the symbol list, or open the Library menu and select the Linkage option.

   c. In the Linkage Properties dialog box that displays, check Export for Action-Script and Export in First Frame.

   d. When you check Export for ActionScript, the Identifier field will become enabled. Flash automatically fills the field with the same name as the library symbol.

   e. Click OK.

2. Within your ActionScript code, at the point at which you want the new movie clip instance to be created, add a call to *attachMovie( )*. The *attachMovie( )* method creates a new movie clip instance nested within the movie clip from which it is called. The method requires at least three parameters: the name of the symbol's linkage identifier, the name of the new movie clip instance to create, and a depth at which to create the new movie clip. The first two parameters should be strings, and the third parameter should be numeric.

The following creates a new movie clip instance named mCircle. The instance is based on the symbol in the library with a linkage identifier of Circle. With the assumption that you place the code on a keyframe on the main timeline, mCircle will be created within the main timeline.

```
this.attachMovie("Circle", "mCircle", 1);
```

The preceding code creates mCircle with a depth of 1. You can use the *getNextHighestDepth( )* method to get a valid depth without having to hardcode a value.

```
this.attachMovie("Circle", "mCircle", this.getNextHighestDepth());
```

You can read more about depths in Recipe 11.9. You can read more about the *getNextHighestDepth( )* method in Recipe 11.10.

Most of the concepts that apply to duplicating movie clips also apply to attaching movie clips. Refer to Recipe 11.9 for more details.

CHAPTER 12

Creating Presentations and Slideshows

Presentations and slideshows are two common types of applications that people want to be able to create. Presentations are used at business meetings, demonstrations, and conferences; they allow the user to organize information and present it in a visual manner. Slideshows can be used in much the same manner, but typically a slideshow automatically advances from one slide to the next, whereas a presentation is controlled by the presenter. You can use a slideshow to allow clients to see images of products or to show off your vacation photos.

There are plenty of programs on the market that allow you create presentations and slideshows. For example, Microsoft PowerPoint is a popular product that is specifically for the purpose of creating presentations. And Adobe Acrobat allows you to create slideshows. So why would you want to use Flash to create presentations and/or slideshows? There are many good reasons why Flash can be a good choice for creating these types of applications, including these:

- Flash provides many more options for a richer-looking product. You can incorporate images, text, animations, and nice transitions without having to using extra programs or rely on a built-in, predefined set of clip art.

- Presumably, if you are reading this book, you already own a copy of Flash. You may or may not own a copy of another program for creating presentations and slideshows.

- The Flash player has a very large distribution. That means that if you want to publish your presentation for others to view, Flash is a good choice.

- If you are already familiar with Flash, but not yet familiar with another application, Flash enables you to avoid the learning curve associated with learning a new program.

Although Flash can be a great way to create presentations and slideshows, it was previously less accessible to many people than something like PowerPoint. Flash didn't really provide a very convenient way to author such things without knowing quite a bit of ActionScript. However, with this book, your job just got a whole lot easier. In this chapter, you'll see three primary ways you can create presentations and slide-shows:

- Templates built into Flash
- A Flash slide presentation
- *Flash 8 Cookbook* components

Each of these techniques has particular advantages and disadvantages. The following table should help you to determine which options make the most sense for you.

	Template	Slide presentation	Component
Available in both Flash Basic and Flash Professional?	Yes	No, Professional only	Yes
Allows for transition effects?	No	Yes	Yes
Allows you to conveniently add a timer to auto-advance slides without adding ActionScript?	Yes	No	Yes
Allows you to automatically load external JPEG files without having to add any extra ActionScript?	No	No	Yes
Allows you to customize the look of the controllers?	Depends on the template. For presentation templates, yes. For slideshow templates, no.	Yes	Yes

All *Flash 8 Cookbook* components can be found at *http://www.rightactionscript/fcb*.

12.1   Building a Presentation Using the Built-in Template

Problem

You want to create a presentation in Flash using a built-in template.

Solution

Open a new Flash document based on one of the presentation templates, modify the assets and timeline, and export.

Discussion

Flash ships with four presentation templates with which you can create your own presentations. The templates provide the same functionality with the predefined ActionScript code. Essentially, the presentation that you export will pause on the first frame. The user can then navigate between the presentation's frames using the back and forward buttons on the stage or by using the right and left arrow keys on the keyboard. The benefit of the template is that you don't have to know any ActionScript to be able to create a simple presentation in relatively little time. But be aware that using the template does not allow for many bells and whistles.

You can open a new Flash document based on a template by choosing File → New or by pressing Ctrl-N or Command-N to bring up the New Document/New From Template dialog box. The dialog box has two tabs—General and Templates. Choosing the Templates tab reveals categories of built-in templates. You should choose the Presentation category, and you will see that there are four built-in presentation templates. Each only differs from the others by the design elements. Because you'll likely be choosing to use your own design, which template you choose is mostly irrelevant. Selecting the template and clicking OK opens a new Flash document already containing the template's content.

After you've opened a new document from a presentation template, you can see that it contains five frames. The movie will pause on the first frame when first run, and it will pause on each of the subsequent frames as you navigate through them using the buttons or the keyboard right and left arrows. Although there are several layers within the document, you need only keep the topmost layer labeled Actions. That layer contains all the ActionScript code that makes the application work when you export the movie. The other layers contain the artwork that you are likely to want to replace anyway. So you can feel free to delete all the layers but the Actions layer.

 There's a possibility that the timeline may be hidden when you open a presentation template. If that is the case, you can display the timeline by clicking the Timeline button in the upper-left corner just above the stage.

If you want to have a background that appears consistently behind the contents of each frame in your presentation, create a layer and then place the background artwork on the first and only keyframe in that layer. You may then want to lock the background layer so that you don't accidentally make changes to it later. Then create a layer for the contents that should change from frame to frame. Make sure that the new contents layer appears above the layer for the background. Create a new keyframe in the contents layer for each frame of your presentation, and place the corresponding artwork on the stage. Figure 12-1 shows an example of what your timeline might look like.

You may notice from the figure that you do not need to add any extra keyframes or actions to the Actions layer, even if you add frames to the timeline beyond the default six frames.

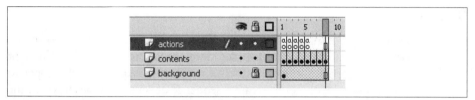

Figure 12-1. An example of a modified timeline from a Flash document based on a presentation template

The preceding describes how to create a presentation that you can navigate using the keyboard's right and left arrow keys. However, with just a slight addition, you can add button-based navigation as well. All you need to do is add another layer to your timeline and place two button instances on the stage at the first (and only) keyframe in that layer. You don't need to assign any ActionScript to the buttons, but you do need to give them specific instance names. Place an instance of your back button symbol on the stage and, using the Property inspector, give it an instance name of backBtn. Do the same for your forward button symbol, and use the Property inspector to give it an instance name of forwardBtn. The specific instance names are important, because the ActionScript code in the template uses those instance names and assigns the necessary code to the corresponding buttons.

Should you want to make the frames of your presentation a little livelier, you can, of course, add movie clip content to the keyframes on your content layer. Remember that movie clips can play back their timelines independently of the timeline in which the instances are placed. That means that even if you place an instance of a movie clip on a keyframe for which your presentation will be paused, the movie clip's timeline will play. This technique allows you to create animations within each frame of your presentation if you want. Also keep in mind that movie clips will loop their playback. You can use very simple ActionScript to stop the playback when the end of the movie clip's timeline has been reached. See Recipe 10.2 for more details on how to do that.

See Also

Recipe 10.2

12.2 Building a Presentation Using a Slide Presentation

Problem

You want to use a Flash Slide presentation to display and navigate your content.

Solution

Create a new Slide presentation, add contents to the slides, and export the movie.

Discussion

Slide presentations are part of a Flash Professional–only feature of screens-based development. The idea behind screens-based development is to provide a different interface for creating applications that doesn't necessarily require the developer to use the timeline. Instead, you get to create a sequence of screens between which the user can navigate. There are two types of screens: Forms and Slides. Forms require you to add ActionScript to make things work; Slides do not. Therefore, for this recipe, Slides are much more applicable. Although you can do much more complex sorts of things with screens, in their simplest sense, they provide a very simple interface for creating presentations.

To get started with a Slide presentation, open a new Flash document by choosing File → New. When the New Document/New From Template dialog box opens, make sure the General tab is selected and then choose Flash Slide Presentation from the list of document types. Click OK, and a new Slide presentation document will open in Flash.

You'll notice that the interface for a Slide presentation document is different from a standard Flash document. Though the timeline does exist for each screen, it is hidden by default. In addition, a Screen Outline pane appears to the left of the standard Document pane (the pane displaying the stage). The Screen Outline pane contains thumbnails of all the screens in your presentation. By default, the new Screen presentation has one top-level slide named Presentation and one nested child slide named slide1. You can think of the top-level slide as being the equivalent of the main timeline in a standard Flash document. You cannot delete it, and all other slides must be nested within it. Any contents added to the top-level slide automatically get displayed in all nested slides. Therefore, the top-level slide is a good place to place your background artwork and/or navigational buttons.

Slide presentations pause on each slide by default, and they have built-in actions that allow the user to navigate back and forth between slides using the right and left arrows on the keyboard. Therefore, to add additional screens of content to your presentation, you should add additional slides nested within the top-level slide. You can add new slides to the presentation in several ways. Clicking on the plus symbol button in the Screen Outline pane will add a new slide to the presentation immediately following the currently selected slide or appending a new slide to the children of the top-level slide if it is selected. Alternatively, you can also right-click or Command-click on a slide and choose the Insert Screen option from the menu that appears.

Figure 12-2 shows an example of the Screen Outline pane for a Slide presentation with two nested slides. The top-level slide contains the background artwork that appears throughout the rest of the slides when the application is run. The two nested slides are the content between which the user can navigate using the arrow keys.

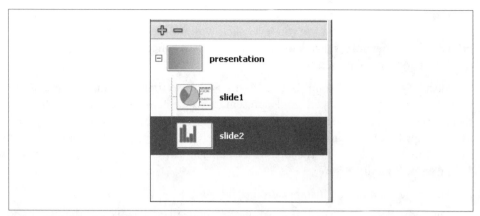

Figure 12-2. The Screen Outline pane for a sample Slide presentation

You may find screens-based projects unresponsive during authoring time and slow to export. Though the screens idea is a nice concept, it is still fairly early in development and can sometimes be a hassle to work with.

12.3   Adding Back and Forward Buttons to a Slide Presentation

Problem

You want to add back and forward buttons to a Slide presentation.

Solution

Add two button instances on the top-level slide and add ActionScript to instruct Flash how to respond when the user clicks the buttons.

Discussion

Though the Slide presentation adds keyboard navigation by default, it does not add any button-based navigation. You have to add that functionality yourself if you want it, requiring a fairly simple, two-step process:

1. Add button instances to the top-level slide.

2. Add ActionScript to tell Flash how to respond when the user clicks on the buttons.

Adding button instances is something with which you should already be familiar. If it is a new concept to you, review Chapter 9. Essentially, you want to create a back button symbol and a forward button symbol, and then drag instances of each symbol onto the top-level slide. Because you're placing the instances on the top-level slide, they will appear throughout the nested slides. An important thing to keep in mind is that all artwork on the top-level slide will appear below the artwork in the nested slides. Therefore, make sure that the button instances are not going to be hidden by artwork in the nested slides.

The next step is to add the appropriate ActionScript, so that Flash knows what to do when the buttons are clicked. Slide presentations in general do not tend to lend themselves to good coding practices, and to further complicate things, the required ActionScript is somewhat convoluted. Fortunately, however, you can apply some of the built-in behaviors from the Behaviors panel in order to have Flash apply the ActionScript for you:

1. Select the back button instance on the slide.

2. Open the Behaviors panel. If it is not already displayed as part of the panel set, you can open it by choosing Window → Development Panels → Behaviors or by pressing Shift-F3.

3. Click the Add Behavior button (the plus sign in the Behaviors panel) to open the menu of behavior options, and choose Screen → Go to Previous Slide. This command adds the necessary code for the button instance.

4. Select the forward button instance on the slide.

5. In the Behaviors panel, open the Add Behavior menu and choose Screen → Go to Next Slide.

After you've completed these steps, you can test your application—you should be able to navigate between the slides using either the keyboard or the buttons you just added.

 Although much of the code provided as behaviors can help you to get your simple applications working without knowing much Action-Script, the code they add does not necessarily represent good coding standards or best practices.

See Also

Recipe 12.2

12.4 Adding Transitions to Slide Presentations

Problem

You want to add transitions (fades, wipes, and so on) to your Slide presentation.

Solution

Use the built-in transitions and apply them to the slides.

Discussion

Flash Professional includes a set of standard transition effects you can use to determine how slides will animate when appearing and disappearing. You can add these transition effects to your slides using the Behaviors panel. To do so, just complete the following steps:

1. Select the slide in the Screen Outline pane for which you want to add the transition effect.

2. Open the Behaviors panel (Window → Development Panels → Behaviors or Shift-F3).

3. Click on the plus button to open the Add Behavior menu, and choose Screen → Transition.

4. In the Transitions dialog box, choose the options, including the type of transition, the direction (in or out), the duration of the transition in sections, the type of easing, and any other options specific to the transition type. Then click OK.

5. If you want to add a second transition, repeat steps 3 and 4. For example, you may want to add a transition for the slide as it appears and another for when it disappears. A transition applied to the in direction corresponds to the appearance of the slide, and a transition applied to the out direction corresponds to the disappearance of the slide.

See Also

Recipe 12.2

12.5   Building a Presentation Using the Flash 8 Cookbook Components

Problem

You want to build a presentation application using the *Flash 8 Cookbook* components instead of using a template or a Slide presentation.

Solution

Use the Presentation component.

Discussion

The Presentation component that is included with the *Flash 8 Cookbook* components is specifically designed to allow you to create presentation applications that unite some of the best qualities of the template and the Slide presentation options mentioned in previous recipes. Using the Presentation component, you can quickly and simply put together a basic presentation, but without having to know any ActionScript or advanced Flash techniques. What's more, the Presentation component allows you to add transition effects without having to rely on a Slide presentation—a Flash Professional–only feature.

The Presentation component is designed to work in one of two ways: either with sequential keyframes on a timeline or with specially named movie clip symbols in the library. The former is, arguably, the simpler of the two techniques, while the latter provides a slightly more robust feature set.

The first way that you can use the Presentation component allows you to set up a presentation in a manner that is almost identical to the template technique discussed in Recipe 12.1. You can set a target for the component, and the component will automatically pause the playback of the target timeline and allow the user to navigate through the frames using the right and left arrow keys. By default, the target timeline for a Presentation component is the timeline in which the instance has been placed. For example, if you place an instance of the Presentation component on the main timeline, the main timeline will be paused and navigable with the arrow keys. You can also choose to specify another movie clip instance for the component to target. You can do so by setting the component's container parameter using the Component Inspector panel. In order to specify another movie clip instance to target, you must have a working understanding of target paths in Flash (see Chapter 10 for more information). The container parameter should be relative to the timeline in which the component instance has been placed. For example, if the component is placed in the main timeline and you want to have it target a movie clip instance in the main timeline with the name mContents, you should use the value of mContents for the container parameter. If you specify another movie clip instance as the target, only that movie clip instance will be controlled with the arrow keys. For example, if you set the container parameter to mContents, the timeline of mContents will be paused and navigable, but the main timeline will no longer be controlled by the component.

You can use many of the same techniques that you used with the presentation templates when working with the Presentation component. For example, if you want to have a continuous background throughout each screen of your presentation, add a layer to the bottom of the content timeline that contains that artwork on a single keyframe that extends the length of the timeline. That way, even though the contents layer will change with each keyframe, the background artwork will remain constant. You may want to refer to Figure 12-1 for a visual representation of what that would look like (though you will not need an actions layer in such an example). You should also make sure that the Presentation component instance itself remains constant throughout the timeline, if applicable. Therefore, you may want to place the Presentation component instance on its own layer similar to how you create the background layer.

The second manner in which you can use the Presentation component is by working with specially named movie clip symbols. The sequential frame technique is fine for; most presentations, but it does not allow you to add transitions between the screens, the second technique does. In order to use the Presentation component in this manner, follow these steps:

1. Create an instance of the Presentation component.

2. Create a movie clip symbol for each screen of the presentation. The movie clip symbols will be programmatically added to the application by the component and, as such, they are consistently aligned so that the 0,0 coordinate point within the movie clip symbol's coordinate space lines up with the 0,0 coordinate point of the container movie clip's coordinate space. In practical terms, that means that if the Presentation component instance itself is being used as the container (the default behavior) then each screen will be aligned so that its 0,0 point will be aligned to the upper-left corner of the component instance. If the main timeline is used as the container, the screens will be aligned to the upper-left corner of the stage.

3. Set each movie clip symbol to export and give them specific linkage identifiers. Setting a symbol to export is necessary to allow Flash to programmatically add the content, and because the component looks for symbols with particular identifiers, it is important that the linkage identifiers match the correct pattern. The linkage identifiers should be Slide1, Slide2, Slide3, and so on. You can set the symbols to export and give them linkage identifiers by selecting the symbol in the library, right-clicking or Command-clicking on the symbol name, and choosing Linkage from the menu that appears. In the Linkage Properties dialog box select the Export for ActionScript option. Doing so will also select the Export in First Frame option automatically. Leave both checkboxes selected. Then specify the linkage identifier and click OK.

Following the preceding steps sets up a basic presentation using the Presentation component and specially named movie clip symbols.

You can also add a constant background to a presentation that uses the named movie clip technique. All you need to do is create a movie clip symbol that contains the background artwork, set it to export, and give it a linkage identifier of PresentationBackground.

12.6 Adding Buttons to a Presentation Using Flash 8 Cookbook Components

Problem

You want to add next and previous buttons to a presentation made with the Presentation component.

Solution

If using the frames technique, add button instances named btNext and btPrevious.

If using the named movie clip technique, add another movie clip symbol with nested button instances named btNext and btPrevious.

Discussion

The Presentation component does not add next and previous buttons by default. Instead, it allows you to specify whether you want them, what they should look like, and how they should be placed relative to the contents of the presentation. However, should you opt for adding next and previous buttons, you can do so without having to add any ActionScript code. How you can add the buttons varies slightly depending on which technique you have used to construct the presentation— sequential frames or named movie clips (see Recipe 12.5 for more details).

If you have constructed your presentation using sequential frames, you can add next and previous buttons by adding a layer to the timeline in which the sequential frames have been placed, and adding the button instances to the layer. The key is that the button instances must have specific instance names. Using the Property inspector, you can give them instance names of btNext and btPrevious. The component will take care of the rest.

If you have used the named movie clip technique to construct your presentation, adding next and previous buttons is just slightly different. What you should do is create a new movie clip symbol and place the two button instances inside the movie clip symbol. Just as with the presentation content movie clips, the buttons' movie clip will be added programmatically and aligned similarly. So make sure that you place the buttons within the movie clip's coordinate space appropriately. Then, so that the component will be able to apply the correct actions, give the two nested button instances the instance names of btNext and btPrevious. The only remaining step is then to set the symbol to export and to give it a linkage identifier of Presentation-Buttons.

12.7 Adding Transition Effects to a Presentation Using the Flash 8 Cookbook Components

Problem

You want to add transition effects between the screens of a presentation you have created using the Presentation component.

Solution

Set the transitionType parameter of the Presentation component instance.

Discussion

The Presentation component makes it quite simple for you to add transition effects between the contents of your presentation. By default, the transition is a basic cut from one screen to the next. However, you can also add other types of transition effects simply by changing the value of the transitionType parameter for the Presentation component instance.

See Also

Recipe 12.5

12.8 Building an Image Slideshow Using a Flash Template

Problem

You want to create a slideshow that uses a Flash template.

Solution

Open a new Flash document using the Modern Photo Slideshow template, add your own images, and export.

Discussion

Flash ships with a slideshow template that enables you to create an image slideshow without having to know any ActionScript. The slideshow template works very similarly to the presentation templates, in that it pauses on the first frame of the main timeline and then enables the user to navigate back and forth through contents placed in sequential frames. A quick look at the contents of an *.fla* file shows that the main timeline contains several layers. Most of the layers contain artwork that remains constant throughout the entire slideshow. The layers labeled Captions and Picture Layer each contain multiple keyframes, however. Presumably you will want to modify the contents of those two layers, at the very least. Replace the contents of each keyframe with your own images and caption text. If your slideshow contains fewer images than the template, you can delete the extra frames from each layer. If your slideshow contains more images than the template, you can add extra keyframes to the Captions and Picture Layer layers, and add extra regular frames to the other layers.

You may also want to customize the look of the rest of the template as well. You can do so without much difficulty by replacing the artwork within the symbols used or by removing and/or replacing contents altogether. However, be aware that there is no simple way to change the appearance of the controller, and the controller must be included in the application for it to work.

12.9   Building an Image Slideshow Using the Flash 8 Cookbook Components

Problem

You want to build a slideshow that uses a *Flash 8 Cookbook* component.

Solution

Use a Presentation component to create a slideshow based on images you import into Flash during authoring time.

Use a SlideShow component to create a slideshow based on external image files that are loaded at runtime.

Discussion

You can use the Presentation component that is discussed in previous recipes in this chapter to create a photo slideshow. To do so, follow the same directions as when creating a standard presentation, using imported images as the contents for each screen. If you want the slideshow to play back automatically without the user having to press buttons, you can set the Presentation component instance's timer parameter to a positive numeric value indicating the number of seconds between each image.

The SlideShow component provides slightly different way to create a slideshow. Instead of having to import your images, arrange then in Flash, and so on, you can actually tell Flash to load the images as the movie runs. In order to understand the information, the component needs you to provide the information about the images in an XML document. Even if you've not used XML before, it is still very simple to learn and apply to this task. The following is an example of an XML document that will work with the SlideShow component to create a slideshow with four images:

```
<images>
  <image url="one.jpg />
  <image url="two.jpg" />
  <image url="three.jpg" />
  <image url="four.jpg" />
</images>
```

The outermost XML tag (`<images>` in the example) is called the *root element*. XML documents that will work with the SlideShow component should have a single root element that contains nested elements for each of the images in the slideshow. The nested elements (`<image>` in the example) should each have an attribute named `url` that has a value indicating the name and location of the JPEG to load. The value can be a relative URL (as in the example) or an absolute URL (such as *http://www. person13.com/image.jpg*).

You can create an XML document using any editor that will save a text file without any special formatting. For example, WordPad on Windows will work just fine. You can also use more sophisticated editors such as BBEdit, PrimalScript, or Dreamweaver to create your XML documents if you prefer. Because the XML document you are creating is really quite simple, no particular editor is likely to offer significant advantages over the others.

When you've defined your XML document and saved it, tell Flash to use that information with a SlideShow component instance. After creating a SlideShow instance on the stage, set the xmlURL parameter to point to the XML document that you have just created. The simplest thing to do is to save the Flash files, XML document, and images all to the same directory. Then set the xmlURL parameter to the name of the XML document. For example, if you have created an XML document named *images.xml* within the same directory as your Flash files, you can set the xmlURL parameter for the SlideShow component to *images.xml*. It is also possible to use an absolute URL, such as *http://www.person13.com/images.xml*.

Set the timer parameter for the SlideShow component to a positive numeric value indicating the number of seconds between each image in the slideshow. You can also select from a list of available transitions.

The images for the slideshow load into the SlideShow component instance. That means that if you scale and/or move the SlideShow instance, the images will all be affected in a like manner. If you want to add a background to your slideshow, add artwork to a layer below the layer in which you have placed the SlideShow instance. If you want to add a frame or any other artwork that should appear over the images, place that artwork in a layer above the layer in which you have placed the SlideShow instance.

After you've created the XML document and set the parameters of the SlideShow component instance, you can test the movie. You should see the slideshow run automatically. When you transfer your application, make sure that you include all the necessary files. If you've used relative URLs when specifying where Flash can find the XML document or the images, make sure you include those files along with the *.swf* file.

12.10 Adding Titles and Captions to a Slideshow Using the Flash 8 Cookbook Components

Problem

You want to add titles and/or captions to the images in your slideshow that you have created using the SlideShow component.

Solution

Add title and/or caption attributes to the tags within the XML document, and add dynamic text fields named tTitle and tCaption to your Flash document.

Discussion

The SlideShow component allows you to specify title and caption text for each image by adding attributes to the XML tags. Each nested tag can have a title attribute and a caption attribute, as shown in the following example:

```
<images>
    <image url="one.jpg title="Image One" caption="The first image" />
    <image url="two.jpg title="Image Two" caption="The second image" />
    <image url="three.jpg title="Image Three" caption="The third image" />
    <image url="four.jpg title="Image Four" caption="The fourth image" />
</images>
```

Flash will then look for dynamic text fields named `tTitle` and `tCaption` located within the same timeline in which you have placed the SlideShow instance. The component will automatically assign the corresponding title and caption values to the text fields as each image appears.

See Also

Recipe 12.9

CHAPTER 13

Building Flash Forms

Forms are the primary way of gathering user input in any type of computer application, and Flash applications are no exception. If you want to prompt the user for information such as email address, preferences, registration information, and so forth, you'll likely be using a form of one sort or another. Flash forms are typically made up of Flash components from the User Interface component set. The UI component instances are sometimes referred to as *form controls* and consist of the following basic types:

Button

> A Button component allows the form to respond to mouse clicks. The Button component is very similar to a Button symbol in a general sense, but it is specifically designed to interact with Flash in a standardized manner.

CheckBox

> The CheckBox component allows the user place a checkmark in a box next to a question, which is useful for yes/no and true/false questions, for example.

ComboBox

> A ComboBox component is more informally referred to as a drop-down menu. Using a combo box, you can present a variety of options from which the user can select just one.

List

> A List component is similar to a ComboBox except that the options are displayed slightly differently and you can allow the user to select more than one option.

NumericStepper

> A NumericStepper component allows the user to choose from a specified range of numeric values.

RadioButton

> A RadioButton operates somewhat similarly to a checkbox in that it can be selected or not. However, radio buttons are not really used by themselves. Typically radio buttons are grouped together to present the user with a set of possible

responses from which he or she can select just one. If any one radio button in a group is selected, the others in the group are automatically deselected.

TextArea

The TextArea component allows the user to input multiple lines of text. Should it be necessary, the component will automatically scroll to accommodate the text.

TextInput

A TextInput component allows the user to input a single line of text. TextInput components also allow you to create password input controls.

In addition to the preceding list of components, you can also use input text fields as a way of gathering user input in a Flash form. In fact, the TextArea and TextInput components are really just fancy text fields with some extra functionality built in.

In the recipes in this chapter, you'll get a chance to familiarize yourself with the Flash form controls. You can find out how to add form controls, how to add values to them, how to retrieve values from them, and how to submit that information to a server-side script for further processing—by sending an email or inserting information into a database.

13.1 Adding a Form Control for Gathering Text Information

Problem

You want to add a form control to your Flash application for the purposes of gathering text-based information from the user (e.g., email address).

Solution

Use a TextInput or TextArea component, or use an input text field.

Discussion

You have several options available when you want to add a form control that allows the user to input text. There are two standard UI components that you can use: TextInput and TextArea. Additionally, if you prefer, you can opt for a standard dynamic text field. Which of these three options you prefer depends mainly on the context in which it will be used.

If you want to prompt the user for a single line of text (such as a zip code, an email address, or a one- or two-word response to a question), your choice is between the text input component and a single-line input text field. The text input component provides the following potential benefits:

- The component is designed to look much more like an HTML text input control, appearing to be slightly sunken into the screen.
- The component styles can be adjusted globally along with all the other components. Therefore, you can change the appearances of all the components in one location rather than having to change each instance's settings. (See Chapter 15 for more details on component styles.)

On the other hand, an input text field has the following potential benefits:

- A standard dynamic text field is much smaller in file size than the component equivalent.
- A text field doesn't have the standard artwork of the component, thus allowing you to quickly and easily add customized artwork behind the text field.

When you want to allow the user to input multiple lines of text, you have the choice between the text area component and a multiline input text field. The text area component provides the same potential benefits that the text input component does. In addition, consider that a text area component can automatically scroll when the user adds more text than can be displayed at one time.

After you've decided which type of text input form control you are going to use, the next step is to add that form control to your Flash application, give it an instance name, and set the parameters for that form control.

You can add a text input or text area component by dragging an instance from the Components panel onto the stage just as if you were adding an instance of a movie clip symbol. If you don't already see the Components panel, you can open it by choosing Window → Components or by pressing Ctrl-F7 or Command-F7. You can add an input text field instance by choosing the Text tool, making sure the text type is set to Input Text, and drawing the text field on the stage. (For more information regarding dynamic text fields, see Chapter 11.)

Regardless of which type of text form control you add, you should give it an instance name. And you can accomplish that in the same way for each type. With the instance selected on the stage, enter a name in the instance name field within the Property inspector. The instance name is important for being able to retrieve the information from the form control later on. Without it, you won't have a way to reference the control.

Typically, the default settings for a TextInput or TextArea component should be fine as they are for standard text form control purposes. With a text field, you may want to change some of the settings depending on how you are using it. If you are using the text field to allow the user to input multiple lines of text, make sure to choose multiline as the line type. And if you want the text field to display a border, select the option for showing the border around the text. (You can read more about setting text field properties in Chapter 11.)

You can change the dimensions of a TextInput or TextArea component instance either by assigning new values for the width and height via the Property inspector or by using the tools to scale and transform the instances. Be aware, however, that TextInput components are designed to allow for only a single line of text to be input. So even if you change the height of the control, the user will still be able to input only a single line of text.

If you want to change the dimensions of an input text field, you should be sure to do so by choosing the Text tool, selecting the text field instance, and dragging the resize square in the lower-right corner of the instance. If you try to resize the instance using the Property inspector or the scale or transform tools, you will scale the text rather than changing the dimensions of the bounding box.

13.2   Adding a Password Form Control

Problem

You want to add a form control that allows the user to input a password value (or something like a credit card number) that cannot be read by others who can see the computer screen.

Solution

Use a TextInput component with the password parameter set to true, or use an input text field with the line type set to password.

Discussion

Typically, you want to design a form so that potentially sensitive information cannot be easily read by others in the same room as the user. Password and credit card numbers are two of the most common examples of this type of information. The conventional solution is to use what is known as a password form control. The password form control allows the user to input their information, but rather than displaying the information in plain text, it is represented by asterisks. This device lets the user to know that the computer is responding to their input, but it does not permit passersby to read the information. Even though the information does not display in clear text on the screen, it is stored within Flash in the correct format so that it can be utilized by the program.

You can create a password form control in two ways. These two ways are really just slight variations on the standard, single-line text form control discussed in Recipe 13.1. Both the input text field and the TextInput component allow you to change a single parameter to convert them into a password form control.

With a TextInput component, all you need to do is select the component on the stage and change the password parameter to true.

For an input text field, select the instance on the stage and change the line type to password.

See Also

Recipe 13.1

13.3   Adding a Menu Form Control

Problem

You want to add a form control that allows the user to select a value or values from a menu.

Solution

Use a ComboBox or List component.

Discussion

The ComboBox and List components provide you with a simple way to add menu form controls to your Flash application. Flash Professional includes a Menu component that requires some slightly more advanced ActionScript than this book discusses, but for the purposes of this discussion, the term "menu" is meant in a general sense. Combo boxes are often referred to in laymen's terms as drop-down or pop-up menus. A combo box will display only one menu item at a time, though you can open and close the menu to display more items at once. A user can select only one item at a time from a combo box. A list, on the other hand, cannot be opened and closed, but instead displays multiple selections at the same time. If the list contains too many items to fit within the vertical space, the list will be made scrollable. Though lists allow a user to select only one item at a time by default, it is possible to enable them to accept multiple selections.

You can add either a combo box or a list component by dragging an instance from the Components panel onto the stage. After you've created the instance, you should be sure to give it an instance name using the Property inspector. The instance name provides the way in which you can later retrieve the selected value or values from the menu form control.

The next thing you should do is add values to the component instance. Without values within the menu control, it would be of little use to someone trying to make a selection. There are a variety of ways in which you can add values to menu form controls, including adding values using a graphical user interface and by way of Action-Script code.

Adding values through the graphical user interface (via the Component Inspector panel or the Property inspector) has the advantage that you don't need to know

ActionScript to add values. And for short lists of values, this technique will work just fine. When you select your combo box or list instance and open the Property inspector or Component Inspector panel, you will see that among the available parameters are two called "labels" and "data." The labels parameter determines the values that get displayed in the form control. The data parameter allows you to specify additional values that are associated with the labels, but hidden from the user. Setting the data parameter is optional, but you should be sure to set the labels parameter for each form control, or else the user will not be able to see what he is selecting. In many cases, you may not need to specify any data values. It depends on the type of application you are building. The data values are usually used when your application needs to interface with a server-side script that requires specially formatted identifiers that differ from the labels that you want to display. For example, you may want to use a combo box to display to the user a list of products, such as Flash, Dreamweaver, ColdFusion, and the like. However, when you submit that information to the server, the server-side script may require specific numeric identifiers that it uses to correspond to the correct information in a database. If you are the one developing the server-side script, then you will know what the server-side requirements are. Alternatively, if you are working with someone else who is developing the server-side script, you may want to consult the developer to ask if there are any such special requirements.

You can add values for the labels and the data parameters in the same way. Within the Component Inspector panel or the Property inspector, double-click in the value column on the right where you see the square brackets displayed ([ ]). Doing so will open the Values dialog box from which you can add, remove, and reorder the values for the selected parameter.

You can also add values to a menu form control via ActionScript. Adding values with ActionScript obviously means that you need to be somewhat familiar with how to write code, but it also offers several advantages. If the values are actually being retrieved at runtime (e.g., if they are drawn from a database), you must use ActionScript. Additionally, when you want to populate a form control with a long list of values, using the graphical interface can be rather unwieldy, and ActionScript provides a slightly more user-friendly interface at that point. For example, if you want to populate a combo box with the names of the 50 United States, you would likely find it easier to do so using ActionScript rather than the Component Property inspector.

Within ActionScript, there are a few different ways you can add values, depending on whether you want to add one value at a time or add a whole list of values at once. You can add a single value at a time using the *addItem( )* method. The *addItem( )* method must be called using dot syntax and the instance name of the combo box or list. The method requires at least one parameter—the label that you want to display. That parameter should be a string value, so place the value in quotation marks. The following is an example that adds the label of Flash to a combo box with an instance name of ccbProducts:

```
ccbProducts.addItem("Flash");
```

You can optionally add both a label and data value with the *addItem( )* method by passing two parameters. The first parameter is the value used as the label, and the second parameter is used as the data value. For example:

```
ccbProducts.addItem("Flash", 1);
```

Flash also allows for yet another variation on the *addItem( )* method, in which you can pass the method an object that contains a label property and optionally a data property. The effect is the same as with the other variations already discussed, and it involves some slightly more advanced ActionScript knowledge, so that discussion is left for the *ActionScript Cookbook* (O'Reilly).

If you want to add more than one item at a time to the form control, the data provider technique is the option you'll want to use. You can assign an array of values to the component instance's dataProvider property using ActionScript, and Flash will take care of the rest. If you're familiar with ActionScript arrays, you may know that there are several ways to make new arrays. Any which way you make an array will be fine with the dataProvider property, but for simplicity, I'll show only one way in this discussion. To assign four items to a combo box with an instance name of ccbProducts using the dataProvider property and an array created using array literal notation:

```
ccbProducts.dataProvider = ["Flash", "Dreamweaver", "ColdFusion", "Fireworks"];
```

Note that to create an array with array literal notation, you should enclose a comma-delimited list of quoted string values in square brackets. If you omit the square brackets, the quotes, or the commas, you will get an error.

The preceding example demonstrates how to add items in which each item has a label, but no corresponding data value. It is possible to use an array of objects to assign both label and data values for each item, but that example requires slightly advanced ActionScript knowledge that is left for the *ActionScript Cookbook*.

A combo box lets a user select one value at a time. A list, on the other hand, can potentially allow a user to select multiple options. In order to enable a list so that the user can choose more than one option at a time, set the multipleSelection parameter to true by choosing the list instance and then changing the parameter value using the Component Inspector panel or the Property inspector. When a list's multipleSelection parameter is set to true, the user can select and deselect multiple values by holding down the Ctrl or Command key while clicking on items in the list. Holding down Shift will allow the user to select consecutive items.

You can change the dimensions of either a combo box or a list by using the Property inspector to assign specific values for the width and height or by using the tools to scale and transform the instances. The only exception is that you likely don't want to change the height of a combo box from its default height of 22 pixels. The reason is that a combo box is designed to have a fixed height, and resizing it in the *y* direction will cause the artwork to appear distorted.

13.4   Adding a Checkbox Form Control

Problem

You want to add a checkbox to your Flash application.

Solution

Add an instance of the CheckBox component and set the parameters.

Discussion

The checkbox is one of the simplest of the form controls. All you need to do is drag an instance of the CheckBox component from the Components panel to the stage, give it an instance name via the Property inspector, and set some parameters.

The checkbox allows you to set three parameters using the Component Inspector panel or the Property inspector. In just about every case, you'll want to set the label parameter. The label parameter determines what text is displayed along with the checkbox. The labelPlacement parameter allows you to specify how the text should be displayed relative to the checkbox. And the selected parameter allows you to specify whether the checkbox is selected by default.

If you add a label that extends beyond the bounding box of the checkbox component, it will get cut off. You can adjust the dimensions of the checkbox to accommodate a longer label if that happens. Just select the instance and adjust the width property with the Property inspector. Or, if you prefer, you can use the tools to transform or scale the instance.

13.5   Adding a Radio Button Form Control

Problem

You want to add a radio button to your Flash application.

Solution

Add an instance of the RadioButton component and set the parameters.

Discussion

Radio buttons are typically used in groups, and they allow the user to select one option from the group. When the user clicks on one radio button, it gets selected and the others in the group get deselected. Adding radio buttons is almost as simple as adding checkboxes. The only additional thing you need to make sure of with radio buttons is that you specify a value for the groupName parameter.

To add a radio button to your application, drag an instance from the Component Inspector onto the stage. As with any component, give it an instance name in the Property inspector. You can then set the parameters for the instance using the Property inspector or the Component Inspector panel. You'll likely notice that radio buttons have the same three parameters as checkboxes. You can set those values appropriately.

In addition to the three parameters that they share with checkboxes, radio boxes also have a groupName parameter. The group name is important for several reasons. It is what tells Flash which radio buttons are grouped together so that it knows how to select and deselect radio buttons based on user interaction. All radio buttons with the same group name will automatically interact with one another in the way described earlier in this recipe. Another reason that the group name is important is that it allows you to later retrieve the selected value for a group. So for each radio button that you want to group together, make sure that you assign the same group name value.

Radio buttons also allow you to specify a data parameter. The data parameter for a radio button is very similar to the data parameter values for a combo box or list. The data value is hidden from the user, but it can be used programmatically if appropriate. If you specify a data value, that is the value that will be returned as the selected value for a radio button group. Otherwise, if you don't define the data parameter value then the label is used as the value.

As with checkboxes, if the label of your radio button extends beyond the bounding box of the component instance, it will appear cut off. You can resize the radio button using the Property inspector or any of the tools for scaling or transforming the instance.

13.6   Adding a Form Control for Gathering Numeric Input

Problem

You want to add a form control to your application that allows the user to input a number.

Solution

Use a numeric stepper. Alternatively, you can also use a combo box, list, text input, or input text field.

Discussion

The `NumericStepper` component is specifically designed to allow the user to select from a sequential range of numeric values. Adding a numeric stepper is quite simple. You can drag an instance of the component from the Components panel to the stage. Then, as with most components, you should give the numeric stepper an instance name using the Property inspector. If the default settings work for your application, you don't need to do anything else. Otherwise, you should set the parameters for the instance using the Component Inspector panel or the Property inspector.

Numeric steppers have four parameters that you are most likely to configure. The minimum and maximum properties determine the range of possible values for the numeric stepper. The `stepSize` parameter determines what increment is used between each step. The value parameter allows you to specify the default value. For example, if you want to allow the user to specify a numeric value from 0 to 100 in increments of 5 then you should set minimum to 0, maximum to 100, and `stepSize` to 5. It should be noted that the possible values are calculated starting from 0 and not from the value specified by the value parameter. For example, you might think that you could configure a numeric stepper to allow only odd numbers by setting the value parameter to 1 and the `stepSize` to 2. However, even though the initial value will be 1, the subsequent values will be 2, 4, 6, and so on. And if you scroll back down, the numeric stepper will land on 0, not 1 (assuming the minimum value is still set to 0).

Although the numeric stepper is specifically designed to allow users to select from a range of numbers, you can also choose to use a combo box or list for the same purposes, but a slightly different display. A combo box and/or list also allow you to define specific numeric values that are not necessarily part of a pattern that would work within a numeric stepper. For example, you might want to allow the user to select from the values 1,000, 2,300, 2,401, and 8,200. In such a case, a combo box or list would be much better suited than a numeric stepper.

You can also choose to use a text input or an input text field to allow the user to input a number without having to select from a predefined set of values. In such a case, you should disallow the user from inputting nonnumeric characters. You can accomplish that by setting the restrict parameter for a text input or the restrict property for a dynamic text field. You can access the restrict parameter for a text input via the Component Inspector panel (the parameter is not accessible from the Property inspector). The parameter allows you to specify characters to allow and/or disallow. In the case of allowing numeric input, allow all the digits as well as the dot if you want to allow floating-point number entries (numbers with decimal places). For example, to allow a user to enter any floating-point number, you should specify the value of 1234567890. for the restrict parameter.

If you are using a dynamic text field, you must use ActionScript to access the restrict property. The restrict property for a text field allows you to specify the same types of values as the restrict parameter for a text input. The following code allows a user to input any floating-point number into a text field with an instance name of tNumericInput:

```
tNumericInput.restrict = "1234567890.";
```

13.7   Adding a Clickable Button

Problem

You want to add a clickable button to a Flash application.

Solution

Create an instance of the Button component and set the parameters. Alternatively, use an instance of a button symbol.

Discussion

The Button component is specifically intended to be used as a button in your Flash forms. You can create a button by dragging an instance from the Components panel to the stage. You'll want to make sure to give the component an instance name via the Property inspector so that you can assign the appropriate actions to it later. Then, you can set the label parameter by way of the Property inspector or the Component Inspector panel, and your button is ready. The label parameter determines what text is displayed on the button instance.

You can also use a button symbol instance or even a movie clip symbol instance with a Flash form. In order to do so, create the button or movie clip symbol and then drag an instance onto the stage, assigning it an instance name as usual. You can read more about using buttons and movie clips in Chapter 9. Using your own button or movie clip symbol instance means that you can more readily customize the look of the button.

13.8   Adding a Button that Can Toggle

Problem

You want to add a button that the user can toggle to a selected or deselected state.

Solution

Add a `Button` component instance and set the toggle parameter to true.

Discussion

More often than not, buttons are used to trigger some action or actions. In such cases, a button like the one described in Recipe 13.7 is quite suitable. However, sometimes you want to use a button that can toggle between a selected and a deselected state. Such a button provides similar functionality to that of a checkbox, but with a slightly different interface.

It's actually quite simple to add a button that can be toggled to your Flash application. All you need to do is follow the directions for adding a `Button` component instance that are given in Recipe 13.7, and then set the toggle parameter to `true` rather than the default value of `false`. By default, the button will be deselected when the application starts. However, you can specify that it should default to the selected state by setting the selected parameter to `true`.

See Also

Recipe 13.7

13.9   Adding a Form Control for Collecting Date Information

Problem

You want to add a form control that allows the user to input a date (year, month, and day).

Solution

Use a `DateField` or `DateChooser` component (available only in Flash Professional). Alternatively, use a form control for allowing the user to input text and restrict the allowable characters.

Discussion

Flash Professional includes many components that are not part of the standard version, among which are the `DateField` and `DateChooser` components. These two components provide you with a convenient way of prompting a user to input a date value. A date chooser displays a calendar (one month at a time) from which the user can select a date. A date field is a slight variation on the date chooser. In fact, you'll notice that the date field actually includes a nested date chooser. However, a date field doesn't require you to display the calendar at all times. Instead, the nested date chooser is hidden except when the user is actively selecting a date. Otherwise, all that the user sees is a field (similar to a text input) with a small button to the right from which the user can open and close the nested date chooser. The date field is often more appropriate when space is a consideration.

You can create a date field or a date chooser by dragging an instance from the Component Inspector panel onto the stage and giving it an instance name via the Property inspector. Both component types have the same set of parameters that you can configure. The default parameter settings are likely suitable for most situations. However, you can adjust the following settings if appropriate:

dayNames

>This parameter determines the labels that are applied to the tops of each column, indicating the day names. By default, the values are single letters representing the English names of the days. Be aware that most fonts allow you to display only two characters in each column. However, if you prefer that Thursday be abbreviated as Th rather than simply T, for example, then you can make that change. Probably the most common reason to change the dayNames values is if you are publishing an application to another language in which the names of the days are not given in English. To change the values for dayNames, double-click in the Values column (the right column).

disabledDays

>By default, all days in the calendar are selectable. However, in some situations you may want some days of the week to be unselectable. For example, if you are prompting the user to select a date for a class that meets Monday through Friday, disable Saturday and Sunday. When a day of the week is disabled, the user will not be able to select from that column and the column will appear in the unselectable color (gray, by default). You can specify a list of days to disable by number. Each day of the week has a number to which it corresponds. Sunday corresponds to 0, Monday to 1, Tuesday to 2, and so on. To change the values for disabledDays, double-click in the Values column.

firstDayOfTheWeek

>The default setting for date field and date chooser is that Sunday is displayed in the first column. You can change which day of the week gets displayed in the first column by changing the firstDayOfTheWeek parameter value. The default value of 0 corresponds to Sunday. You can change the value to any integer value from 0 to 6 to change the order of the columns. For example, if you set the value to 1, then Monday will be displayed as the first column and Sunday will be moved to the last column. Though you can change which column is displayed first, you cannot re-sort the columns such that the days of the week do not appear in order.

monthNames

By default, the names of the months are spelled out in English. You can change the month names that are displayed by changing the values for the monthNames parameter. You may prefer that the months be abbreviated, all in caps, or in a language other than English.

showToday

By default the current date is highlighted on the calendar. You can set the showToday parameter to false if you prefer that the current date is not highlighted.

If you do not have Flash Professional, you can still prompt the user for a date value. However, the standard version does not provide any components specifically for that purpose. Instead, you can use a text input of an input text field. Because you'll be prompting the user for a date value in a specific format, you may want to restrict the allowable characters using the restrict parameter or the restrict property (see Recipe 13.6 for more details). For example, if you want the user to input the date value in the format of YYYY/MM/DD, set the restrict parameter of a text input to 0123456789/ so as to allow all numbers and the forward slash but no other characters.

When you use a date field or a date chooser component, Flash automatically collects the data in the ActionScript Date format. That helps to eliminate a lot of potential error. When you use a text input or an input text field, Flash collects the information as regular text. Although restricting the allowable characters is helpful, it does not force the user to input a valid date. In order to confirm that the user has input a valid date value, you will need to use ActionScript that is rather advanced and beyond the scope of this book. If you are using the FormController component that is discussed in Recipe 13.17 you can use its built-in validation to verify the data.

See Also

Recipe 13.6 and Recipe 13.17

13.10 Performing Actions When the User Clicks a Button

Problem

You want Flash to do something when the user clicks a button.

Solution

Add ActionScript that creates a listener object and registers the listener object with the button instance. Alternatively, if you've used a button symbol instance or a movie clip symbol instance, add an *onRelease( )* event handler method.

Discussion

For Flash to be responsive to the user's mouse clicks, you're going to need to write some ActionScript. The ActionScript you'll need to write is not particularly long, however. The details of the ActionScript you'll write depend, in part, on which type of button you've used.

If you've used a `Button` component:

1. Create a listener object.
2. Assign a *click( )* method to the listener object.
3. Register the listener object with the button instance.

A listener object is a code-based construct that basically sits around waiting (listening) for a component to do something. This *something* for which the listener is waiting is called an *event*. If the component performs the particular type of event for which the listener is configured, then the corresponding code on the listener object runs. Each type of component can dispatch different types of events. The button component dispatches an event called *click* when the user clicks it. The way that the listener object knows what code to run at that point is by looking for a method (a group of actions) called *click( )*.

That may all sound a bit confusing, but a simple example will illustrate that it really does not require too much code. First you need to create the listener object. The following line of code creates an object named oListener:

```
var oListener:Object = new Object( );
```

Next, define a method that corresponds to the event for which you want the object to listen. In this example, the listener should listen for a click event. Inside the curly braces of the method definition is where you should place the code that should run when the event is dispatched. In this example, Flash will call the *trace( )* statement to display a message in the Output panel during testing:

```
oListener.click = function(oEvent:Object):Void {
  trace("The button was clicked");
};
```

Then, register the listener object with the component instance for the particular type of event. Call the *addEventListener( )* method from the component instance and pass it two parameters: the name of the event as a string and a reference to the listener object. For example, to register oListener to listen for click events dispatched by a button named cbtSubmit, use the following code:

```
cbtSubmit.addEventListener("click", oListener);
```

That covers the basics of listener objects and handling component events. Even though the code may be unfamiliar to you at first, once you have learned it, you'll be able to reapply it to just about all of the components. That's because just about all of the components dispatch events and work with listener objects in the same way. The primary difference in different scenarios has only to do with the name of the event that is being handled.

If you've used a button symbol instance or a movie clip symbol instance, you still need to write some ActionScript code to perform some actions when the user clicks the button. However, the code you will need to write is quite different from the code for a Button component. You don't need to use listener objects at all. Instead, you should define an *onRelease( )* event handler method for the instance. Within the *onRelease( )* event handler method (between the curly braces) is where you can place all the code that you want to run when the user clicks on the button. The following example defines an *onRelease( )* event handler method for a button instance named btSend:

```
btSend.onRelease = function( ):Void {
  trace("You have clicked the send button");
};
```

The preceding example displays the message "You have clicked the send button" in the Output panel while testing the movie. You could replace the *trace( )* statement with any other ActionScript code that you want to run when the button is clicked, but in any case the rest of the syntax remains the same. You can read more details on working with button event handler methods in Chapter 9.

See Also

Recipe 13.7

13.11 Retrieving Text Field, Text Input, and Text Area Values

Problem

You want to retrieve the value from a text field, text input, or text area.

Solution

Use the instance's text property.

Discussion

Whether you are using a text field, text input, or text area, you can retrieve the value in the same way. Each of these text form controls has a text property that returns the current text value. For example, the following retrieves the text value from a text input with an instance name of ctiUsername and then saves it to a variable named sUsername:

```
var sUsername:String = ctiUsername.text;
```

Keep in mind that you'll most often want to retrieve the value from a text form control only after the user has clicked on a submit button. Therefore the ActionScript code should be placed within a *click( )* method on a listener object or within a button's *onRelease( )* event handler method. The following example uses a listener object registered with a button instance named cbtSubmit. When the user clicks on the button, the value that the user has entered into the ctiUsername text input gets displayed in the Output panel while you are testing the movie:

```
var oListener:Object = new Object();
oListener.click = function(oEvent:Object):Void {
  trace(ctiUsername.text);
};
cbtSubmit.addEventListener("click", oListener);
```

13.12 Retrieving Combo Box, Single-Select List, and Numeric Stepper Values

Problem

You want to retrieve the selected value from a combo box, a single-select list, or a numeric stepper.

Solution

Use the instance's value property.

Discussion

Combo boxes, single-select lists, and numeric steppers all have a property named value that returns the currently selected value from the component. With combo boxes and lists the value property returns the data value that corresponds to the selected item if the data value is defined. If no data value is defined for that item, it returns the label instead. Numeric steppers return the currently selected numeric value.

The following retrieves the value from a combo box named ccbProducts and saves it to a variable named sProductName:

```
var sProductName:String = ccbProducts.value;
```

In most cases, of course, you want to retrieve the selected value only when the user clicks on a button in the form to submit the data for processing. Therefore you should place the ActionScript code within a listener object's *click( )* method or a button instance's *onRelease( )* event handler method. The following example uses a listener object to display the value from a numeric stepper name cnsQuantity in the Output panel when the user clicks on a button component instance named cbtSubmit:

```
var oListener:Object = new Object();
oListener.click = function(oEvent:Object):Void {
```

```
    trace(cnsQuantity.value);
};
cbtSubmit.addEventListener("click", oListener);
```

13.13 Retrieving Values from Multiselect Lists

Problem

You have a multiselect list from which you want to retrieve all the selected values.

Solution

Use the instance's selectedItems property to retrieve an array of the selected items. If you want to extract the data or label values specifically, use a for statement to loop through all the elements of the returned array.

Discussion

If a List component instance is used as a single-select list, you can retrieve the selected value just as you can retrieve the value from a combo box (see Recipe 13.11 for more details). However, if you have configured the list to allow for multiple selections, you need to use slightly different ActionScript code to retrieve the selected values.

Lists have a property named selectedItems that returns an array containing all the information for the items that the user has selected. The elements of the array are each objects with label and data properties. In order to do something useful with that array, you will more than likely need to use a for statement to loop through each of the elements of the array and extract the label and/or data value.

The simplest way to understand this is to take a look at an example. Suppose that you have a list with the instance name of clProducts. The list has many items, each with a label value. If the user has selected three items from the list before you try to retrieve the values, the instance's selectedItems property will return an array with three object elements. You can then use a for statement to loop through the elements of the array, extract the label property values, and do something with those values. The following code takes those label values and displays them in the Output panel within the test player:

```
var aValues:Array = clProducts.selectedItems;
for(var i:Number = 0; i < aValues.length; i++) {
  trace(aValues[i].label);
}
```

In most scenarios, you will want to retrieve the selected values from a list only once users have signaled that they want to process the information from the form. Typically that is done by clicking on a submit button. The following code shows a listener object used to process the selected values from a list once a button is clicked:

```
var oListener:Object = new Object();
oListener.click = function(oEvent:Object):Void {
  var aValues:Array = clProducts.selectedItems;
  for(var i:Number = 0; i < aValues.length; i++) {
    trace(aValues[i].label);
  }
};
cbtSubmit.addEventListener("click", oListener);
```

See Also

Recipe 13.12

13.14 Retrieving Values from Checkboxes and Toggle Buttons

Problem

You want to retrieve the value from a checkbox or a toggle button.

Solution

Use the instance's selected property.

Discussion

Checkboxes and buttons that toggle provide basically the same type of functional-ity—they can be selected or deselected. Each of these two types of components has a property named selected that returns either true or false. In the case of a check-box, the selected property is true if the checkbox is checked and false if it is unchecked. The button that toggles returns true if the button is pressed in and false otherwise. The following code retrieves the current state of a checkbox named cchOptIn and writes it to the Output panel when the listener object's *click( )* method gets called:

```
var oListener:Object = new Object();
oListener.click = function(oEvent:Object):Void {
  trace(cchOptIn.selected);
};
cbtSubmit.addEventListener("click", oListener);
```

13.15 Retrieving Values from Radio Button Groups

Problem

You want to retrieve a value from a group of radio buttons.

Solution

Use the radio button group's `selectedData` property.

Discussion

As discussed in Recipe 13.5, radio buttons are typically used in groups. Therefore, you usually will want to retrieve the value from the selected radio button in the group. In order to do that, all you need to do is use the `selectedData` property of the radio button group.

Recall that when you create a radio button instance, you set the `groupName` parameter. The `groupName` parameter defines how the radio buttons are associated. Not only that, but it also creates a new ActionScript object with that same name. For example, if you create five radio buttons and assign each of them the group name of `rbgQuizQuestion`, Flash will automatically create an ActionScript object named `rbgQuizQuestion`. You can later use that ActionScript object to retrieve the value that has been selected for the entire group of five radio buttons. That object has a property named `selectedData` that will return the chosen value.

If you have defined a data parameter value for the radio buttons, the radio button group's `selectedData` property will return the data value for the selected radio button. However, if you have not defined the data parameter value for the radio buttons, the `selectedData` property will simply return the chosen radio button's label value.

In most scenarios, you will want to retrieve the selected radio button value only after the user has clicked a submit button or some other similar event indicating that the form data should be processed. The following code is an example in which the selected value from a radio button group named `rbgQuizQuestion` is displayed in the Output panel when the user clicks on a button:

```
var oListener:Object = new Object( );
oListener.click = function(oEvent:Object):Void {
  trace(rbgQuizQuestion.selectedData);
};
cbtSubmit.addEventListener("click", oListener);
```

See Also

Recipe 13.5

13.16 Retrieving Date Values

Problem

You want to retrieve a date from a date form control.

Solution

If you are using a date chooser or date field, use the instance's `selectedDate` property. Otherwise, use the `FormController` component to handle your form processing.

Discussion

The date chooser and date field components both have a `selectedDate` property that returns the date that the user has selected. The value that the property returns in either case is in the format of an ActionScript `Date` object. In most cases, you will want to retrieve the selected date only after users have indicated that they want to process the form data. Typically, that is done by clicking a submit button. The following code shows an example in which the selected date from a date chooser named `cdcCalendar` is retrieved and displayed when the user clicks a button:

```
var oListener:Object = new Object();
oListener.click = function(oEvent:Object):Void {
  trace(cdcCalendar.selectedDate);
};
cbtSubmit.addEventListener("click", oListener);
```

If you are not using a date field or a date chooser, but rather a text input or input text field, you can simply retrieve the information the user has input via the text property as discussed in Recipe 13.11. However, as was mentioned in Recipe 13.9, verifying that the information represents a valid date requires some advanced ActionScript code. Therefore, unless you are very familiar with ActionScript, you will likely find it much simpler to use a `FormController` component to manage your form.

See also

Recipe 13.9, Recipe 13.17

13.17 Submitting Form Data to the Server

Problem

You want to submit the form data to a server-side script for further processing.

Solution

Use the `FormController` component. Alternatively, you may write ActionScript code to retrieve the form data and submit it to the server using an ActionScript `LoadVars` object.

Discussion

Working with forms in Flash has been simplified by many of the components that Macromedia includes in the product. However, it is still a fairly ActionScript-intensive process to retrieve the form data and submit it to a script on the server.

Although the required ActionScript is not particularly difficult, it can appear some-what daunting to those who are new to writing code. And many may prefer a simpli-fied alternative even if they are comfortable writing ActionScript code. Thus the FormController component exists, a custom component that you'll find in the *Flash 8 Cookbook* components (downloadable from *http://www.rightactionscript/fcb*).

The FormController component works in the following manner: you create your form using the form controls discussed in the earlier recipes in this chapter, making sure to give each an instance name. Then create an instance of the form controller and, using the graphical user interface, provide the component instance with infor-mation about the elements of the form you want it to control. Additionally, you can assign a URL to which the information should be submitted and a button compo-nent instance that will be the submit button. The form controller handles the rest (although you'll still need to configure the server-side script).

If you've installed the *Flash 8 Cookbook* components, you can find the FormController component listed within the *Flash Cookbook* folder in the Compo-nents panel. Drag an instance of the form controller from the panel onto the stage. The component contains artwork that is visible during authoring time so that you can locate the instance on stage in order to set the parameters. However, during runtime the artwork is invisible. Therefore you can place the instance anywhere on stage and it still will not interfere with any other artwork when you view the *.swf* file.

The form controller has three parameters, all of which must have values for the com-ponent to operate correctly. The elements parameter is the way in which you tell the form controller which form controls (text inputs, combo boxes, etc.) it should con-trol. You can specify the values by double-clicking on the Values column to open the Values dialog box. After you have opened the dialog box, click the plus sign to add a new element for each form control that should be managed by the form controller. For each element, you need to set at least one value: the InstanceName value. The InstanceName is the name of the instance of the form control. For all form controls you should specify the instance name of the actual component or text field instance, with the exception of radio buttons. For radio buttons you should specify the name of the radio button group, and just once for the entire group of radio buttons. By default, the data for each form control is submitted to the server with a variable name that corresponds to the form control's instance name. For example, if you have a form control named ccbProducts, the value for that control will be submitted with the variable named ccbProducts. However, because the server-side script may expect very specific values other than what you have named the form controls, you can also spec-ify a FieldName value. The FieldName value determines the variable name by which the value is submitted to the server. Therefore, if you want the value from ccbProducts to be submitted with the variable name PRODUCT_ID, you can specify PRODUCT_ID as the FieldName value for that element. The Message and Validator values are also optional, and they are used for validating form data. The Type parameter defaults to Regular. For any form element that references a standard form control (e.g., text input, combo box), you should leave Type set to Regular. However, you can also create hidden form elements by setting Type to Hidden. A hidden form field does not require any form control on the stage. Rather, it is a way of passing extra values to a server-side script when the form is submitted. If you set Type to Hidden, you should also specify a Value. The Value is what gets passed to the server-side script when the form is submitted. For example, in the program you create in this chapter, the email subject line is passed to the server-side script by way of a hidden form element.

You should include each form control in the elements parameter value, with the exception of the submit button. The submitButton parameter is where you specify the instance name of the button component that you want to use to submit the form data to the server. All you need to do is create the button instance, give it an instance name, and assign that name to the form controller's submitButton parameter. The form controller will handle all the ActionScript code automatically—without you having to write any of it.

Additionally, you need to specify a value for the url parameter. The url parameter determines where you are going to submit the form data when the user clicks on the submit button. The value can be either a relative or an absolute URL.

After you've set up the form controls and the form controller, Flash will handle the details for you. Make sure you have the server-side script properly configured and that you are submitting the correct information. The FormController component submits the form data using HTTP POST as URL-encoded name-value pairs. That is the standard way in which form data is submitted on the Web with HTML pages, so scripts that are configured to accept form input from an HTML page should work with the form controller.

If you prefer to write your own ActionScript to submit your Flash form data, you can do so without too much complicated code. In fact, the code is really quite simple. However, depending on how much data you are sending you may find it can get a little lengthy.

The first thing you will want to do is to retrieve the form data. After you've retrieved the form values, you should next construct an ActionScript LoadVars object, assign the values to the object, and call the *send( )* method to send the data to the server.

You can construct a LoadVars object using the LoadVars constructor as part of a new statement and assigning the value to a variable. The following example creates a new LoadVars object and assigns it to a variable named lvFormData:

```
var lvFormData:LoadVars = new LoadVars( );
```

After you've constructed the LoadVars object, you should next assign all the values to custom properties of the LoadVars object. Each property should have the name under which you want the data to be submitted to the server-side script. For example, if you want a particular piece of information to be submitted to the server with the variable name of PRODUCT_ID, you should use the PRODUCT_ID property name:

```
lvFormData.PRODUCT_ID = 10;
```

After you've assigned all the values to custom properties, tell Flash to send the data to the server by calling the *send( )* method. The *send( )* method requires that you pass it a parameter indicating the URL to which to submit the data. The following code tells Flash to submit the data to a script named *updateData.php* on the same server (and same directory) as the SWF:

```
lvFormData.send("updateData.php");
```

The following code contains a complete example of the ActionScript code to handle submitting a sample Flash form to a script named *updateData.php*. The form has three form controls: a combo box named ccbProduct, a text area named ctaComments, and a numeric stepper named cnsQuantity. The values are submitted using variable names of PRODUCT_ID, COMMENTS, and QUANTITY, respectively. The form data is retrieved and sent after the user clicks on a button component instance named cbtSubmit:

```
var oListener:Object = new Object();
oListener.click = function(oEvent:Object):Void {
  // First, retrieve the form data and store it to three variables.
  var nProductId:Number = ccbProducts.value;
  var sComments:String = ctaComments.text;
  var nQuantity:Number = cnsQuantity.value;

  // Next create the LoadVars object.
  var lvFormData:LoadVars = new LoadVars();

  // Add the properties and values.
  lvFormData.PRODUCT_ID = nProductId;
  lvFormData.COMMENTS = sComments;
  lvFormData.QUANTITY = nQuantity;

  // Send the data to the script.
  lvFormData.send("updateData.php");

};
cbtSubmit.addEventListener("click", oListener);
```

 The preceding code could be simplified somewhat. The values could be retrieved from the form controls and assigned to the properties of the LoadVars object in one step instead of the intermediate step of assigning the values to variables. The extra step is added in the preceding code merely to clarify the process.

13.18 A Feedback Form

One of the most frequent information requests from Flash developers is how to create a form that gathers user feedback and then submits it to a server-side script, which then emails that information to a specified email address. In this short program, you will create a Flash form that does just that using the FormController component along with a combo box, text input, text area, and button form control. For the server-side script, you'll find several predefined scripts provided in the *.zip* file that contains the files accompanying the Flash Cookbook. You can find the *Flash 8 Cookbook* components at *http://www.rightactionscript/fcb*. One file is a PHP script named *sendEmail.php*. The other is a ColdFusion script named *sendEmail.cfm*. Select the script that your server supports and copy it to a directory that is accessible from the Web.

To build the application, complete the following steps:

1. Open a new Flash document and save it to your local disk as *FeedbackForm.fla*.

2. Open the Components panel, and locate the UI Components folder.

3. Drag an instance of the ComboBox component from the Components panel to the stage on the main timeline. Name the component instance ccbTo using the Property inspector.

4. With the combo box selected on the stage, open the Component Inspector panel and double-click on the Values column for the labels parameter. The combo box should allow the user to select from a list of departments such as Support, Sales, and Webmaster. When you've added the label values, click OK to close the Values dialog box.

5. Double-click on the values column for the data parameter in the Component Inspector panel. Each label needs to have a corresponding data value, so if you added three labels, you should also add three data values. The data values should be valid email addresses. If you happen to have multiple email addresses you can check, you may want to use those emails for testing purposes. If you have only one email address that you can check, use that same email address for each data value. When you've added the data values, click OK to close the Values dialog box.

6. Drag an instance of the TextInput component from the Components panel to the stage on the main timeline, arranging it just below the combo box instance. Assign the text input the instance name ctiEmail. The text input will be the field the user will use to input her return email address.

7. Use the Property inspector to set the text input's width to 200 pixels so that the instance will be able to accommodate even long email addresses without a part being cut off visibly.

8. Drag an instance of the TextArea component from the Components panel to the stage on the main timeline, assigning it an instance name of ctaComments.

9. Use the Property Inspector to set the dimensions of the text area to 200 × 200 so that the user can type in a decent amount of text before it scrolls.

10. Drag an instance of the Button component from the Components panel to the stage on the main timeline, assigning it an instance name of cbtSubmit.

11. With the button selected, open the Component Inspector panel and change the label parameter value to Send.

12. Drag an instance of the `FormController` component from the Components panel to the stage on the main timeline.

13. With the `FormController` instance selected, open the Component Inspector panel and double-click on the Values column for the elements parameter.

14. In the Values dialog box click on the plus-sign button to add a new entry. Assign values of `ccbTo` for the `InstanceName` and `toAddress` for `FieldName`.

15. Add another entry using the plus-sign button, and assign the values of `ctiEmail` for the `InstanceName` and `fromAddress` for `FieldName`.

16. Add another entry using the plus-sign button, and assign the values of `ctaComments` for the `InstanceName` and `message` for `FieldName`.

17. Add another entry using the plus-sign button, and assign the value of subject for `InstanceName` and `Message from Flash Form` for Value. Set the Type to Hidden.

18. Click OK in the Values dialog box.

19. In the Component Inspector panel, set the `submitButton` parameter to `cbtSubmit`.

20. Set the `url` parameter to the URL at which the PHP or ColdFusion script can be located.

21. Test the movie.

You should be able to fill out the form and click on the submit button. The data should be sent to the server-side script, and an email should be sent.

CHAPTER 14

Building Advanced Flash Forms

Chapter 13 introduced building user input forms in Flash. This chapter takes that topic a few steps further by introducing advanced form features, such as data validation, prepopulating and preselecting data in form controls, dynamically populating forms, and creating responsive form elements.

14.1 Performing Actions When the User Clicks a Checkbox or Radio Button

Problem

You want your Flash application to perform some actions when the user clicks a checkbox or radio button.

Solution

Define a listener object with a *click( )* method and register the listener with the checkbox or radio button group.

Discussion

By default, when the user clicks a checkbox or radio button, Flash doesn't take any immediate action. In many cases, that is the behavior that you want. However, it is possible to tell Flash that you want it to perform some actions when the user clicks the checkbox or radio button control. There are a variety of reasons why you may want to do that. For example, you may want a form to automatically submit its data when the user clicks the form control rather than using a button.

In order for Flash to know to do something when the user clicks the checkbox or radio button, you need to use a listener object. You can create the listener object using the Object constructor as part of a new statement and assigning the value to a variable. The following code is an example of how you can create a listener object named oListener:

```
var oListener:Object = new Object();
```

After you've created the listener object, define a *click( )* method for the object. Within the *click( )* method, place the ActionScript code that you'd like Flash to run when the user clicks the form control. The following code assigns a *click( )* method to oListener. Within the *click( )* method is a *trace( )* statement that will display the message "User clicked form control" when the user clicks the checkbox or radio button:

```
oListener.click = function(oEvent:Object):Void {
  trace("User clicked form control");
};
```

Then you need to register the listener with the form control. If the form control is a checkbox, you should register the listener with the checkbox instance. For example, the following code registers the oListener object with a checkbox named cchEULA:

```
cchEULA.addEventListener("click", oListener);
```

If you want to use the listener with radio buttons, you should register the listener object with the RadioButton group. For example, if you have a group of radio buttons to which you have assigned a groupName value of rbgMonitorResolution, you could use the following code to register oListener with the RadioButton group. All radio buttons in the group will then call the *click( )* method when clicked:

```
rbgMonitorResolution.addEventListener("click", oListener);
```

You may have noticed that in defining the *click( )* method for the listener object that I have declared the method such that it expects a parameter. In the example, I called that parameter oEvent. Flash automatically passes a parameter to listener object methods that contain information about the event and the object that initiated the event. The parameter is an object that has several properties, among which is the target property. The target property is a reference to the form control that dispatched the event. Therefore, you can use that reference in order to retrieve the value from the component instance. This step is especially useful if you have a single listener object registered for several components. The following example code registers a single listener object with three checkboxes: cchCar, cchPlane, and cchTrain. When the *click( )* method is called, it displays the name of the instance and the selected state for that component.

```
var oListener:Object = new Object();
oListener.click = function(oEvent:Object):Void {
  trace(oEvent.target._name + " : " + oEvent.target.selected);
};
cchCar.addEventListener("click", oListener);
cchPlane.addEventListener("click", oListener);
cchTrain.addEventListener("click", oListener);
```

See Also

Recipe 13.4 and Recipe 13.5

14.2 Performing Actions When the User Makes a Date Selection

Problem

You want Flash to perform some actions when the user chooses a value from a date chooser or a date field.

Solution

Define a listener object with a *change( )* method.

Discussion

Both the date chooser and date field dispatch a change event when the user selects a date value. Thus you can use a listener object to detect the change event and perform some actions when that occurs. For example, if you are using a date chooser to allow the user to select a date for which he or she wants to see a schedule, you may want the event to cause Flash to display some corresponding schedule information in a text area.

In the following code, a listener object is defined and registered such that when the user makes a selection from a date chooser named cdcSchedule, the selected date is displayed in the Output panel:

```
var oListener:Object = new Object();
oListener.change = function(oEvent:Object):Void {
  trace(oEvent.target.selectedDate);
};
cdcSchedule.addEventListener("change", oListener);
```

For more details on using a listener object as well as the parameter passed to the listener object's method, see Recipe 14.1.

See Also

Recipe 14.1, Recipe 13.9, Recipe 13.16

14.3 Creating a Jump Menu

Problem

You want to create a *jump menu*—a menu that causes some action to take place as soon as the user makes a selection.

Solution

Use a combo box or a list in conjunction with a listener object.

Discussion

The combo box and list components dispatch change events when the user makes a selection. Therefore, if you use a listener object to handle those events, you can have Flash perform some tasks as soon as the user chooses an item from the combo box or list. This type of functionality is often referred to as a *jump menu*.

In the following example, a listener object is registered with a combo box named ccbProducts. When the user makes a selection from the combo box, the value is displayed in the Output panel.

```
var oListener:Object = new Object( );
oListener.change = function(oEvent:Object):Void {
  trace(oEvent.target.value);
};
ccbProducts.addEventListener("change", oListener);
```

For more information regarding using listener objects, see Recipe 14.1.

See Also

Recipe 14.1, Recipe 13.12

14.4   Preselecting Date Control Values

Problem

You want a Flash form date control to initialize with a particular value selected.

Solution

Assign a Date object to the component instance's selectedDate property.

Discussion

The selectedDate property of a date field or date chooser component instance is a read/write property. That means that you can use it not only for retrieving a user-selected value, but also to programmatically assign a value. The selectedDate property must be in the format of an ActionScript Date object. Though you can create a Date object in a variety of ways, the simplest here is to use the Date constructor in a new statement, passing the constructor three parameters: the year, month, and date. The following example creates a new Date object that represents December 01, 2010, and assigns it to a variable named dSomeDay:

```
var dSomeDay:Date = new Date(2010, 11, 1);
```

You may notice that the month value for December is 11, and not 12. This is because the month indices for the Date class start with 0 instead of 1. Therefore, January is 0, February is 1, March is 2, and so on.

After you've created the date, you can assign it to the date chooser or date field's selectedDate property. The following example assigns the value from dSomeDay to the selectedDate property of a date field named cdfAppointment:

```
cdfAppointment.selectedDate = dSomeDay;
```

Of course, you could skip the intermediate step of assigning the date to a variable first and simply create the date while assigning it to the selectedDate property, as in the following statement:

```
cdfAppointment.selectedDate = new Date(2010, 11, 1);
```

When you assign a date to the selectedDate property of a date chooser, the calendar will display the month for that selected date and highlight the selected date. When you assign a date to the selectedDate property of a date field, the value is displayed in the text field. If the user clicks on the button to pick another date, the calendar will display the month for the selected date with the selected date highlighted.

See Also

Recipe 13.9, Recipe 13.16

14.5   Preselecting Menu Control Values

Problem

You want a Flash form to initialize with values already selected in a combo box or list.

Solution

For a combo box or single-select list, assign a value to the selectedIndex property. For a multiselect list, assign a value to the selectedIndices property.

Discussion

You can use the selectedIndex property to programmatically select a value from a combo box or list component instance. In order for that approach to work, of course, you'll need to know the index of the item you want to select. Each item in the combo box or list has a whole number index. The first item has an index of 0, the second has an index of 1, and so on. Therefore, if you know you want to programmatically select the third item in the combo box, you need only assign the value of 2 to the selectedIndex property. For example, if you have a combo box named ccbProducts, you can programmatically select the third item with the following code:

```
ccbProducts.selectedIndex = 2;
```

However, more often than not, you will know the value of the item you want to select rather than the index. If that occurs, you will need to use a for statement to loop through all the items of the combo box, checking each to see whether it matches the value you want to select. You can use the *getItemAt( )* method to retrieve a combo box item of a particular index. You can use the length property to retrieve the number of items in the combo box. So with that in mind, the following code shows an example in which the code loops through the items of a combo box named ccbProducts. When it finds an item with the label Flash, it sets the selectedIndex to that item's index.

```
// Loop from 0 until the length of the ccbProducts indices is reached.
for(var i:Number = 0; i < ccbProducts.length; i++) {

  // Check to see if the current item's label matches the value of Flash.
  if(ccbProducts.getItemAt(i).label == "Flash") {

    // If so, set the combobox's selected index to the item's index.
    ccbProducts.selectedIndex = i;
  }
}
```

Although the preceding code will work, it can be made more efficient by adding one extra line of code. As it stands, Flash will continue to loop through the remaining items in the combo box even after the matching item is found. However, that is a waste of processing time. When the match has been found, you can tell Flash to stop the loop by using a break statement. The following code is identical to the preceding example, except that it adds the break statement to make it more efficient:

```
for(var i:Number = 0; i < ccbProducts.length; i++) {
  if(ccbProducts.getItemAt(i).label == "Flash") {
    ccbProducts.selectedIndex = i;
    break;
  }
}
```

If you are using a single-select list, you can use the same basic code as when using a combo box. However, if you are using a multiselect list, you will need to use the selectedIndices property instead of the selectedIndex property. The selectedIndices property, as the name would suggest, allows you to specify multiple indices that should be selected. The property value should be in the for statement of an ActionScript array in which each of the elements is an index within the list that should be selected. For example, the following code assigns an array with four indices to the selectedIndices property of a list named clFavorites. When assigned, the list will display with the four corresponding elements selected.

```
clFavorites.selectedIndices = [2, 4, 7, 13];
```

For the selectedIndices property to work properly you must set the multipleSelection property to true as well.

As with combo boxes and single-selected lists, when you are preselecting values for multiselect lists, you are likely to know the value rather than the index of each item you want to select. Therefore you need to use a for statement to add index values to an array before assigning that array to the selectedIndices property of the list. The following code uses a for statement to loop through all the items of the list. For each item in which the label is either Flash Cookbook or ActionScript Cookbook, the corresponding index is added to an array using the array's built-in *push( )* method. Then, when the array has been populated, it is assigned to the list's selectedIndices property.

```
// Create a new array into which the indices should be stored.
var aIndices:Array = new Array( );

// Loop through all the elements of the list.
for(var i:Number = 0; i < clFavorites.length; i++) {

  // Check to see if the label of the list item is either Flash Cookbook or
ActionScript Cookbook.
  if(clFavorites.getItemAt(i).label == "Flash Cookbook" ||
      clFavorites.getItemAt(i).label == "ActionScript Cookbook")
  {

    // If the label is a match with either of the two titles then use the push( )
method to add
    // the corresponding index to the aIndices array.
    aIndices.push(i);
  }
}

// Assign the aIndices array to the selectedIndices property.
clFavorites.selectedIndices = aIndices;
```

See Also

Recipe 13.3, Recipe 13.12, Recipe 13.13

14.6 Validating Form Data

Problem

You want to validate form data before allowing the user to submit it to a server-side script.

Solution

Use the built-in data validation features of the `FormController` component.

Discussion

Data validation can be an important feature to include in your Flash forms. Often you may have required fields in a form that you want users to fill out before submitting the form data. If they don't fill out the form fields, you'll want to prompt them for that information before allowing them to continue. Furthermore, you may also want to verify that the data being entered matches certain criteria. For example, you may want to make sure that the value entered into a field looks like a valid email address. Or you may want to make sure that users have entered a valid number value.

Although you can write your own data validation scripts, it can require quite a lot of ActionScript code, and it is beyond the scope of this book. However, the `FormController` component (discussed in Chapter 13) provides built-in data validation features. Using the `FormController` component, you can make particular form elements required, and you can also verify that entered values match particular patterns such as email or number.

In order to use the data validation features, there are two requirements. You must include a component that can display any messages to the user in your Flash document's library, and you must specify the `Validator` and `Message` values in the `FormController`'s elements parameter for each of the form controls to which you want to apply data validation.

There are two types of components that the form controller can use in order to display messages to the user. If you are using Flash Professional, you can add the `Alert` component to your document's library. The Alert component is available only in the Professional version of Flash, however. Therefore, if you are using the standard version of Flash, you may use the `FCBAlert` component instead. The `FCBAlert` component is provided as part of the *Flash 8 Cookbook* component set (downloadable from *http://www.rightstart.com/fcb*). Regardless of which component you use, you add the component to the library in the same way: drag an instance of the component from the Components panel onto the stage. Then delete the instance from the stage. Although it may seem somewhat odd to create an instance only to delete it, doing so ensures that the component symbol is copied into the Flash document.

The form controller can apply data validation to specific form controls. For example, you may have some form controls to which you want to ensure that the user actually enters any value, some for which you want to ensure that the user enters a value of a specific type, and others for which you want no data validation. You can apply the data validation settings for each form control by way of the form controller's elements parameter. Each element listed allows you to specify a `Validator` and a

Message value. When no value is specified for Validator (which is the default set-ting), no data validation is applied to the form control. You may optionally specify any of the following values:

true

A value of true indicates that the user must enter or select some valid value for the form control. In the case of text fields, text inputs, and text areas, a value of true requires the user to enter some text. With checkboxes, the user is then required to select the checkbox (useful in situations where the user must check a box to accept a user agreement). For RadioButton groups, the user is then required to select one of the radio buttons in the group. When used with date form controls, the user must make a date selection. And when used with combo boxes and lists, the user must select at least one value in which the data is not equal to –1. The value of –1 allows you to add an initial item to your menus that does not count as a valid selection. For example, you may want a combo box's initial item to inform the reader as to what they are selecting (e.g., Select a Coun-try), yet not want that initial item to count as a valid selection. Therefore you can assign –1 to that item's data value.

email

Checks to make sure that the value that is entered follows the pattern for a valid email address. This validation does not ensure that email can be delivered to the address, but it does make sure the user has at least entered text that appears to be a valid email.

number

Checks to make sure that the value is a number.

Any regular expression

Regular expressions are beyond the scope of this book (for more, see Friedl, *Mastering Regular Expressions*, O'Reilly). However, if you are familiar with regu-lar expressions, you can use this feature to create a specific pattern that the value should follow. A repository of many regular expressions that you may find use-ful is *http://www.regxlib.com*.

For Message, you should specify the text that should appear to the user in the event that he attempts to submit the form without filling out one of the elements properly. For example, if you have a text input for which you have set Validator to email, you may want to use a Message value such as "Please ensure that you have entered a valid email address before submitting the form." The Message value appears in the Alert or FCBAlert window that opens automatically if a form control's data is not properly validated.

You may find it helpful to modify the email submission form application from Rec-ipe 13.18 so that it validates the information that the user enters. You can do so by completing the following steps:

1. Open the *.fla* file that you completed in Recipe 13.18 and save it with a different name, so that you don't overwrite your previous version.

2. Select the form controller component instance, and open the Values dialog box for the elements parameter by double-clicking in the values column within the Property inspector or the Component Inspector panel.

3. For the `ctiEmail` element, add a `Validator` of `email` and a `Message` of `Please enter a valid email address`.

4. For the `ctaComments` element, add a `Validator` of `true` and a `Message` of `Please enter your comments`.

5. Click OK to close the Values dialog box.

6. Test the movie.

CHAPTER 15

Customizing UI Components

The Flash UI components provide you with a set of functional controls that take mere minutes to implement. These components are great time-savers—consider how long it can take to create something as seemingly simple as a combo box. However, these components have the same default look. With just a little bit of knowledge and code, you can quickly customize these components. This chapter explains how to programmatically style your components and how to create new artwork for your components.

15.1 Applying Individual Component Styles

Problem

You want to change the styles for a single component instance.

Solution

Call the *setStyle( )* method for the component instance.

Discussion

Each of the UI components (combo box, checkbox, list, text input, and so on) has an ActionScript method named *setStyle( )*. Using *setStyle( )*, you can programmatically tell Flash to change many aspects of the component's appearance. There are many styles that you can change using the *setStyle( )* method, as discussed in the recipes throughout this chapter. However, regardless of which style you want to change, the same basic syntax applies:

```
componentInstanceName.setStyle(styleName, styleValue);
```

One of the styles that can be applied to all of the UI components is a style called themeColor. There are three preset values for themeColor (haloGreen, haloBlue, and haloOrange), as you can read in Recipe 15.5. The following code shows how you can apply a new themeColor value to a button component instance named cbtSubmit:

```
cbtSubmit.setStyle("themeColor", "haloOrange");
```

If you want to apply just one or two styles to a single component instance, the *setStyle( )* technique described in this recipe will be ideal. However, if you want to apply many styles to the instance, or if you want to apply the same styles to more than one component instance, consider the other techniques that are discussed in detail in the following three recipes.

15.2 Applying Styles to Component Groups

Problem

You want to apply the same style settings to more than one component instance, or you want to apply a lot of styles to a single component instance.

Solution

Create a new ActionScript style object, assign the style values, and then apply it to the component instance or instances.

Discussion

The *setStyle( )* technique discussed in Recipe 15.1 is great if you want to apply just a few styles to a single component. However, if you want to apply those same settings to other components, the first technique doesn't provide you with a very convenient way to do that. Furthermore, although you can apply as many styles as you want to a single component by calling the *setStyle( )* method many times, this approach is slightly inefficient. Each time the *setStyle( )* method is called for the component instance, it is redrawn. If you are applying 10 style settings, the component will be redrawn 10 times, even though it really needs to be redrawn only once—after all the settings have been made. Although there is no visible effect that the user can see, it is a rather inefficient use of processing.

Creating and applying an ActionScript style object resolves both of the aforementioned issues. By working with a style object, you can define the settings once, and then apply them to as many component instances as you want. Additionally, because a style object is defined and *then* applied to the component or components, no matter how many styles you set, the component or components will need to redraw only once.

To create an ActionScript style object, use the *CSSSTyleDeclaration* constructor in a new statement. In order to work properly with the components, the style object must be assigned to a property of the _global.styles object. (_global.styles is automatically created for you whenever you have added at least one component to your Flash document's library.) You get to make up the name of the property, though it is certainly recommended that you use a name that indicates what the style represents. For example, the following code creates a new style object and assigns it to a property named menuStyles:

```
_global.styles.menuStyles = new mx.styles.CSSStyleDeclaration();
```

 The CSSStyleDeclaration class is in the mx.styles package. Simply put, that means you must use the full name of mx.styles. CSSStyleDeclaration when calling the constructor. The only exception is if you have used an import statement to import the class previously. Classes, packages, and importing are beyond the scope of this book, however. So for a fail-safe technique, make sure you provide the full name, as shown in the preceding code.

After you have defined the new style object, define the style settings with the following syntax:

```
_global.styles.styleObjName.styleName = styleValue;
```

You can repeat that same syntax for as many styles as you want to set. The following example defines three style properties for the menuStyles style object. Those properties are themeColor, fontFamily, and fontStyle—style properties you can read about in the recipes in this chapter.

```
_global.styles.menuStyles.themeColor = "haloOrange";
_global.styles.menuStyles.fontFamily = "_typewriter";
_global.styles.menuStyles.fontStyle = "italic";
```

After defining the style settings, the next step is to apply the style object to the component or components for which you want the styles to take effect. You can do that using the *setStyle( )* method for each component. When you call the *setStyle( )* method in order to apply a style object's settings, you need call the method only once per component instance. The first parameter should be styleName, and the second should be the name of the style object in quotation marks and without the _global. styles prefix. For example, the following code applies the menuStyles object's settings to two component instances—ccbProducts and clPreferences:

```
ccbProducts.setStyle("styleName", "menuStyles");
clPreferences.setStyle("styleName", "menuStyles");
```

15.3   Applying Styles to Component Types

Problem

You want to apply the same style settings to all instances of the same component type within your Flash movie.

Solution

Define an ActionScript style object with the component class name.

Discussion

In some cases, you may want to apply particular style settings to all instances of a particular component. For example, you may want to apply one set of style settings to all radio buttons and another set of style settings to all text inputs. You can apply the same set of style settings to the entire component type by defining an Action-Script style object with the same name as the component class. For example, if you want to apply the same style settings to all radio buttons, you can define a style object with the name *RadioButton* (using the proper capitalization is important.) As with the style objects you create, in order to apply them to groups (as discussed in Recipe 15.2), you should assign the style object to the _global.styles object. Therefore, if you want to define a style object to determine the style settings for all the radio buttons in your Flash movie, your code will look like the following:

```
_global.styles.RadioButton = new mx.styles.CSSStyleDeclaration( );
```

After you've declared the style object as shown in the preceding code, you need only assign the values to the specific styles you want to set. In order to do that, use the *setStyle( )* by calling it from the style object. The following is an example in which the themeColor and fontFamily styles are set for all the radio buttons:

```
_global.styles.RadioButton.setStyle("fontFamily", "_typewriter");
_global.styles.RadioButton.setStyle("themeColor", "haloOrange");
```

If for no other reason than simply to keep you on your toes, the list component type will not work with the technique described thus far. Instead, you should use the already-defined style object named ScrollSelectList in order to manage list styles. Therefore, you should not reinitialize the preexisting ScrollSelectList object by assigning a new style object to it. That means you should *not* use the following line of code:

```
_global.styles.ScrollSelectList = new mx.styles.CSSStyleDeclaration( );
```

Instead, call the *setStyle( )* method from the object that has already been created automatically. For example, you can set the fontFamily and themeColor styles using the following two lines of code:

```
_global.styles.ScrollSelectList.setStyle("fontFamily", "_typewriter");
_global.styles.ScrollSelectList.setStyle("themeColor", "haloOrange");
```

Styles settings made on an individual component instance take precedence over settings made through a component class object, as described in this recipe.

15.4   Applying Styles Globally

Problem

You want to assign style settings to all component instances in your Flash movie.

Solution

Assign the settings to the _global.style object using the *setStyle( )* method.

Discussion

Flash automatically creates a style object that you can use to manage the styles of all component instances in your Flash movie. The name of the object is _global.style. It's a fairly common mistake for novices and experts alike to accidentally use the incorrect name by pluralizing _global.style as _global.styles. The _global.styles (plural) object is a container object that Flash uses to hold all the other style objects you might define (see Recipe 15.2 and Recipe 15.3). However, the _global.style (singular) object is an actual style object from which all component instances can inherit their style settings.

The _global.style object is created automatically for you by Flash, so there is no need to declare it anew as with many of the other style objects you need to create (see Recipe 15.2 and Recipe 15.3). Instead, all you need to do is use the *setStyle( )* method to assign new style settings. For example, the following code will set the themeColor and fontFamily styles for all component instances in your Flash movie:

```
_global.style.setStyle("fontFamily", "_typewriter");
_global.style.setStyle("themeColor", "haloOrange");
```

The global style settings will take effect for all component instances for which you have not otherwise applied settings for the same styles. The _global.style object has the lowest precedence of all other style objects. Therefore, if you have applied a themeColor setting to a component instance via a component class style object, a group style object, or on the instance itself, the global themeColor style setting will not be inherited by that instance.

15.5   Working with Color Styles

Problem

You want to apply a color style setting to a component or components.

Solution

Assign a value to the appropriate style using either a numeric value or one of the predefined color strings.

Discussion

There are a handful of styles that deal with color. Each of the color styles is discussed in slightly more detail in the appropriate recipe later in this chapter as they apply to specific components. However, regardless of which color style you are setting, you have two options for the value: one of the predefined color string values, or a numeric value (typically in hexadecimal format). The following color strings are recognized by Flash:

Color string	Hexadecimal value
Black	0x000000
Blue	0x0000FF
Cyan	0x00FFFF
Green	0x00FF00
Magenta	0xFF00FF
Red	0xFF0000
White	0xFFFFFF
Yellow	0xFFFF00

For example, if you want to apply a red value to the `color` style globally, you can use the following line of code:

```
_global.style.setStyle("color", "red");
```

If you want to use a color value other than one of the predefined color strings, you can use numbers instead. Typically, you'll work with the numbers in hexadecimal format. In ActionScript, hexadecimal numbers are prefixed with 0x. For example, the hexadecimal representation for red is 0xFF0000. The following line of code is, therefore, the equivalent to the previous example:

```
_global.style.setStyles("color", 0xFF0000);
```

Unless you happen to already know the hexadecimal value for the colors you want to use, you likely could use a little assistance from the computer. One simple way to get the hexadecimal value of a particular color within Flash is to use the Color Mixer panel. Open the Color Mixer panel (Window → Design Panels → Color Mixer) and select a color. The hexadecimal value is displayed in a text field in the lower-left corner of the panel. You can then copy that text field and paste the value into the appropriate part of your code in the Actions panel. Notice, however, that in the Color Mixer panel, Flash prefixes the value with a #. So make sure to make the appropriate change. For example, if you select a color in the Color Mixer panel for which Flash displays #634181 in the text field, you should copy just the 634181 portion, and then change that to 0x634181 in your ActionScript code.

Any style in which the name ends with either `Color` or `color` (e.g., `borderColor`) is a color style. So you can use the color strings or numeric values with those styles.

Additionally, there is one color style, themeColor, that accepts three extra color string values. With themeColor, you can use the regular color strings, numeric values, or one of the following three extra color strings: haloGreen, haloBlue, haloOrange.

15.6 Working with Font and Text Styles

Problem

You want to apply styles to components that affect the text and font.

Solution

Use predefined styles in Flash to change aspects of the text.

Description

Flash uses text in many different ways throughout the components. For example, text appears on buttons, as labels next to check boxes and radio buttons, and it is used to populate combo boxes and lists. But regardless of how Flash uses the text within a specific component, you can use the same group of styles. The styles are as follows:

color
> The color of the text.

embedFonts
> Whether or not (true or false) to embed the font in the *.swf* so that the text will render consistently on computers.

disabledColor
> The color of disabled text.

fontFamily
> The name of the font face. You can also specify one of the font groups: _sans, _serif, or _typewriter.

fontSize
> The point size of the font.

fontStyle
> Either normal or italic.

fontWeight
> Either normal or bold.

marginLeft
> The number of pixels for the right margin.

marginRight
> The number of pixels for the left margin.

textAlign
> Specifies how the text should align—left, center, or right.

textDecoration
> Either normal or underline.

For example, if you want to globally make the text in the components red using the _typewriter font group, you can use the following code:

```
_global.style.setStyle("color", "red");
_global.style.setStyle("fontFamily", "_typewriter");
```

If you want to use an embedded font, make sure you've done the following:

1. Set the embedFonts style property to true.

2. Embed the font in the .swf file.

3. Set the fontFamily style property to the name of the embedded font.

You can embed a font in your .swf file either by adding a dynamic text field instance off the stage in which you've embedded the font or by using a font symbol. Both techniques are discussed in more detail in Recipe 8.14.

15.7 Working with Border and Background Styles

Problem

You want to apply styles to the border and background of a component or components.

Solution

Use the backgroundColor, borderColor, or borderStyle style property.

Discussion

You can set the background and border colors for components using the appropriate styles. For the background, just assign a value to the backgroundColor property. For example, the following code applies a red background to a list named clProducts:

```
clProducts.setStyle("backgroundColor", "red");
```

The background color is one of the styles that does not inherit properly when you apply it globally. That means that it will not take effect for some types of components if you use the following line of code:

```
_global.style.setStyle("backgroundColor", "red");
```

It does inherit correctly for some types of components, such as the combo box, numeric stepper, window, date chooser, and date field. However, it does not properly inherit for other component types, such as list, text input, and text area. One solution is to apply the styles to each component instance, or perhaps each component class. However, that could prove rather unnecessarily tedious. Instead, as a workaround, you can apply the style settings globally as normal. But in addition, define the class style objects for the necessary classes. By just defining the class style object, the global styles will then inherit properly. The following is an example in which you can apply the backgroundColor style globally. If your document contains a combo box, a list, a numeric stepper, and a text area, the combo box and numeric stepper automatically inherit the style setting properly. However, because the list and text area components do not properly inherit the styles, you need to define the corresponding class style objects. Remember, as discussed in Recipe 15.3, you should not define the class style object for components such as List and Tree. Instead, you should define the class style object for their parent class—ScrollSelectList:

```
_global.style.setStyle("backgroundColor", "red");
_global.styles.TextArea = new mx.styles.CSSStyleDeclaration();
_global.styles.ScrollSelectList = new mx.styles.CSSStyleDeclaration();
```

The borders for each of the components utilize the same set of styles. That includes the borders of text inputs, text areas, lists, date fields, checkboxes, etc. The number of border style properties depends on which theme you are using. Figure 15-1 shows the parts of the border and their corresponding style properties for a default inset border for the Halo theme.

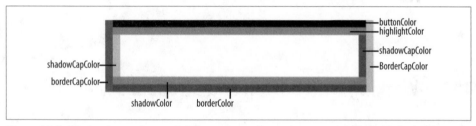

Figure 15-1. The border sections and their corresponding style properties for the Halo theme

Alternatively, if you are using the Sample theme, or a derivative of that theme, the border styles map to the components differently. Figure 15-2 shows the parts of the border and their corresponding style properties for a default inset border for the Sample theme.

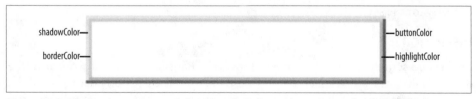

Figure 15-2. The border sections and their corresponding style properties for the Sample theme

As with the backgroundColor style property, some of the border style properties don't inherit properly on some components. In particular, the borderColor property doesn't seem to get applied to list components (as well as the related datagrid and tree components) when used globally. You can use the same technique as is described for getting backgroundColor to work correctly: define the correct class style object. For the list component, define the ScrollSelectList class style object as follows:

```
_global.styles.ScrollSelectList = new mx.styles.CSSStyleDeclaration( );
```

You can also affect how the border is displayed. By default, the border for most components is displayed as in inset border. Inset borders give the appearance that the content they frame is recessed (for the Halo theme, but it is the inverse for the Sample theme). You can control the how the border is displayed using the borderStyle style property. The default value is inset. But you can also specify outset, solid, or none. An outset border is the inverse of the inset border. A solid border displays a solid rectangular border around the component using the borderColor style property value to determine the border color. Solid borders give a two-dimensional appearance to the component(s). And if you assign a value of none to the borderStyle style property, the component(s) will not have a visible border.

```
_global.styles.setStyle("borderStyle", "none");
```

The text input and text area components do not properly inherit the borderStyle property when it is applied globally. You can handle that in one of the usual ways.

You cannot change the borderStyle setting for a button component.

15.8 Working with Button and Scrollbar Styles

Problem

You want to apply style settings for buttons and scrollbars.

Solution

Use a theme other than the Halo theme. Use the buttonColor style property for the button face and the border styles for the button border. Use scrollTrackColor style property for the scroll track.

Discussion

Button and scrollbar styles are some of the styles that simply will not work with the default Halo theme. Instead, you need to use the Sample theme or a derivative of the Sample theme. For more information about using a different theme with the components, see Recipe 15.12.

After you've added a non-Halo theme to your Flash document, you can use the following style properties to change the appearance of buttons and scrollbars:

buttonColor

> Changes the color of button faces and the outer portion of the upper-left border for buttons. Also changes the outer highlight for borders in general, including text input, text area, and so on.

highlightColor

> The inner portion of the upper-left border for buttons.

shadowColor

> The inner portion of the lower-right border for buttons.

borderColor

> The outer portion of the lower-right border for buttons.

scrollTrackColor

> The color of the scroll track for scrollbars.

Not only are actual button components considered buttons, but so are the portions of combo boxes, scrollbars, numeric steppers, and other components that allow the user to click or drag some element. Most buttons inherit styles properly. However, actual button components do not. Instead, you need to either apply the styles directly to the instance or class style object, or you can apply them globally and just define the class style object as discussed in Recipe 15.7.

15.9   Working with List Styles

Problem

You want to apply style settings to list components.

Solution

Use the styles specific to the list components, including alternatingRowColors, rollOverColor, selectionColor, selectionEasing, textRollOverColor, textSelectedColor, selectionDisabledColor, selectionDuration, and useRollOver.

Discussion

There are quite a few styles that are specific to list components, primarily because they deal with the colors of the list elements as they are moused over and selected. Most of those properties are color properties:

rollOverColor

> The color of a row when the user moves the mouse over it

selectionColor

> The color of a row when it has been selected

textRollOverColor

> The color of the text in a row when the user moves the mouse over it

textSelectedColor

> The color of the text in a row when it has been selected

selectionDisabledColor

> The color of a row when it is selected and the entire list has been disabled (the enabled property set to false)

Additionally, you can assign a group of color values such that the background colors of the rows are different from the adjacent rows. For example, if you assign the colors of red and yellow, the row colors will alternate between red and yellow. If you assign the colors of blue, green, and magenta, the row colors will repeat that pattern. In order to accomplish this, assign an array of colors to the alternatingRowColors style property. You can use any valid syntax to create the array. However, often the most convenient way is to use array literal notation in which the array definition is denoted by a comma-delimited list between square brackets. The following is an example that assigns the colors red and yellow to the alternatingRowColors style property globally:

```
_global.style.setStyle("alternatingRowColors", [0xFF0000, 0xFFFF00]);
```

The alternatingRowColors style property is the one color style property that does not allow you to use the color strings. You must specify numeric values for the colors.

You can also tell Flash that you would prefer it did not show a rollover color on rows: assign a value of false to the useRollOver style property. For example:

```
_global.style.setStyle("useRollOver", false);
```

One additional feature that you can adjust for lists using styles is the animation when a row is selected. If you watch carefully when you select a row in the list, you'll notice that the highlight on the row that is selected quickly opens from the center outward. If another item had previously been selected and becomes deselected, the row closes in the reverse direction as it opened. You can use the selectionEasing and selectionDuration style properties to determine how the rows animate when selected and deselected. You can assign the selectionEasing style property a reference to one of the easing functions listed in Recipe 11.3. The selectionDuration property specifies the duration over which the row animates. The value should be given in milliseconds. You can convert from seconds to milliseconds by multiplying by 1,000. Therefore, if you want the rows to animate over the course of one second, use the following code:

```
_global.style.setStyle("selectionDuration", 1000);
```

15.10 Working with Combo Box Styles

Problem

You want to apply style settings to a combo box.

Solution

Use the same style properties as a list component, plus the additional properties openDuration and openEasing.

Discussion

Combo boxes use many of the same style properties as list components, largely because the drop-down portion of the combo box is actually a list instance. Therefore, you can style the drop-down portion of a combo box in the same way you style a standard list.

In addition to the list style properties and the standard style properties, combo boxes have two extra style properties: openDuration and openEasing. These two properties affect how the combo box expands and collapses. The openDuration property allows you to specify how many milliseconds the open or close animation takes, and the openEasing property allows you to specify *how* the combo box expands and collapses. Assign a numeric value to the openDuration property. For example, the following code specifies that the opening and closing of combo boxes should take one second:

```
_global.style.setStyle("openDuration", 1000);
```

You can assign any easing function reference to the openEasing style property. You can find a list of the built-in easing functions in Recipe 11.3. The following code assigns a standard ease out to combo boxes globally:

```
_global.style.setStyle("openEasing", mx.transitions.easing.Regular.easeOut);
```

15.11 Working with Radio Button, Checkbox, and Arrow Styles

Problem

You want to apply style settings to radio buttons, checkboxes, and/or the arrow on a button (as found in a scrollbar or combo box).

Solution

Use the symbolColor and associated style properties.

Discussion

Before you can programmatically style the dots in radio buttons, the checks in checkboxes, or the arrows on scrollbars and combo boxes, you have to use the Sample theme or a custom theme based on the Sample theme. The default Halo theme does not work properly with the style properties that style those elements. For more information regarding using another theme, see Recipe 15.12.

After you have applied the Sample theme (or a theme based on the Sample theme), you can use the following style properties:

symbolColor
> The color of the radio button dot, checkbox check, or scrollbar arrow

symbolDisabledColor
> The color of the radio button dot, checkbox check, or scrollbar arrow when the component instance is disabled

symbolBackgroundColor
> The background color for radio buttons and checkboxes

symbolBackgroundDisabledColor
> The background color for radio buttons and checkboxes when the component instance is disabled

symbolBackgroundPressedColor
> The background color for radio buttons and checkboxes when the user is clicking on the component instance

15.12 Using Different Artwork Themes

Problem

You want to use a different artwork theme for your components.

Solution

Open the *.fla* file containing the theme artwork symbols, and drag them into your *.fla* file.

Discussion

The UI components that ship with Flash 8 use the Halo theme by default. However, you can change the theme that the components use by copying a set of symbols from a theme *.fla* file to your *.fla* file. A theme is simply the set of movie clip and graphic symbols that the components use. The Halo theme is compiled into the components as the default theme. However, if you create the appropriate movie clip and graphic symbols in your *.fla* file, they will override the default versions.

The simplest way to apply a theme is to use one of the themes that ships with Flash. There are two built-in themes: Halo (the default) and Sample. You don't need to explicitly apply the Halo theme, because it is compiled into the components by default. However, to apply the Sample theme, do the following:

1. Open the *.fla* file for which you want to apply the theme.
2. Choose File → Import → Open External Library.

3. In the Open as Library dialog box, navigate to the *SampleTheme.fla* file located in the *Flash 8/en/Configuration/ComponentFLA* directory, and then click the Open button.

4. Make sure you have the library for your *.fla* file open. You should be able to see both the library for your *.fla* file and the library for *SampleTheme.fla*. By default, Flash 8 displays only one Library panel. However, you can click the "New library panel" button on the upper right of the library to open a new panel. You can then select a different library from the drop-down menu in each panel.

5. Drag the *Flash UI Components 2* folder from the *SampleTheme.fla* library to the library of your *.fla* file.

Even though you won't see the live preview update on the stage during authoring time, you'll see the new theme applied once you export the *.swf* file.

You can create your own themes as well. To do so, start with either the *HaloTheme. fla* or *SampleTheme.fla* file, and save it as a new *.fla* file. Then, modify the artwork in the symbols. Keep in mind that the Halo and Sample themes use slightly different sets of style properties. Therefore, choose the starting *.fla* file accordingly. For example, if you want your custom theme to support the symbolColor style property, you should use *SampleTheme.fla* as your starting document. When you've created your custom theme files, you can follow the same steps as you used to apply the Sample theme in order to apply your custom themes.

CHAPTER 16

Loading Images and Flash Content

Typically your first Flash applications are likely to be fairly small in scope. But the scope of projects will grow as your skill set grows, and then it becomes important to take into consideration how you can best manage the content. This chapter explains how to load content and even how to share common content amongst multiple files. There are several primary benefits from these processes:

Loading content means better manageability

There are plenty of examples that illustrate this point. Consider an example of a gallery of animations. When the gallery contains one or two animations, it is reasonable to manage whilst all the content is within a single file. But as the number of animations grows, it becomes less and less reasonable to have them all contained within a single file. Each time you want to add a new animation you have to open the same *.fla* file and add new content. That process would not only be unmanageable for a single person, but is notably less manageable for a team of people. Instead, a much more feasible solution is to have a single file that displays the animations while each animation is its own file.

Loading external content makes it much simpler to use dynamic content

For example, if you have a Flash application that allows the user to search and view products, you may want to consider loading the product images from external *.jpg* files rather than embedding them in the *.swf* file. This has several advantages. If the image needs to change, it is much simpler to switch out the *.jpg* file than to update the symbol in the *.fla* and re-export/publish the *.swf*. Also, if the other content is generated from a database or other external source, keeping the images external makes the application much simpler to design as well.

Loading external content keeps the initial download for web applications relatively small

Because of this, you can load content on demand or preload the content. For example, if your application consists of an image gallery section, you may not want to force all users to download all the images if they aren't necessarily going to view them. Instead, you can load the content as it is requested.

Flash has long been able to load external SWF content and, since Flash Player 6, Flash has been able to load nonprogressive JPG content. Starting with Flash Player 8, you can load JPG content (progressive and nonprogressive), GIF content, and even PNG content. If you attempt to load unsupported image content, Flash will silently fail.

16.1   Loading External SWF/Image Content

Problem

You want to load an external *.swf* or *.jpg* file into your Flash application during runtime.

Solution

Use the Macromedia v2 Loader component.

Alternatively, for a smaller file size, use the custom *Flash 8 Cookbook* Loader component.

For the smallest file size, use the MovieClipLoader ActionScript solution.

Discussion

In Flash, you'll find an included Loader component that facilitates loading external content without you having to delve into ActionScript. You can find the Loader component in the User Interface section of the Components panel. To use the Loader component:

1. Drag an instance of the Loader component from the Components panel to the stage, and name the component instance in the Property inspector. (You are not required to name the component instance for it to work, but doing so is a good practice, and facilitates using the instance in conjunction with other types of components such as the ProgressBar.)

2. Make sure the new Loader instance is selected, and locate the component instance's parameter settings. You can opt to change the parameter settings either in the Parameters tab of the Property inspector or within the Component Inspector panel. In the case of the Loader component, the Component Inspector panel gives you superfluous parameter settings that you won't likely have any reason to use, so the only practical difference between using the Property inspector or the Component Inspector panel is that of which one you prefer.

3. Leave the autoLoad parameter set to true. If you set the value to false, the Loader will not load the content until triggered by ActionScript, and that is not a way in which you are likely to use the Loader component. If you want to use Action-Script, it's advisable to use an entirely ActionScript-based solution rather than using the Loader component.

4. Set the `contentPath` parameter value to the URL that points to the content you want to load. The URL can be either absolute or relative. For example, if you want to load a JPG from another domain, you should use the absolute URL, such as *http://www.rightactionscript.com/samplefiles/image1.jpg*. On the other hand, if you want to load something from the same computer as that from which the Flash application is being served, you can specify a relative URL, such as *image.jpg*.

5. Set the `scaleContent` parameter value based on the type of scaling behavior you want. If you want the content to maintain its original dimensions regardless of the width and height of the `Loader` component instance, then set `scaleContent` to `false`. If you want the loaded content to scale to fit within the width and height of the `Loader` component instance, set `scaleContent` to `true`.

6. If you set `scaleContent` to `true`, resize the `Loader` component instance to the dimensions within which you want the content to scale. Flash will maintain the original aspect ratio of the content, so the scaled content will not always match the exact dimensions of the `Loader` component instance. For example, if you set the `Loader` instance's dimensions to 100×100 pixels, and the content's original dimensions are 200×100 pixels, the scaled content will have dimensions of 100×50 pixels. If the aspect ratios of the content and the `Loader` component instance don't match, the scaled content will center itself within the dimensions of the `Loader` instance.

One of the issues that you may notice with the Macromedia `Loader` component is that it alone adds 27KB to an *.swf* file's size. Depending on the type of project on which you are working, 27KB may or may not be an unacceptable file size increase just for the convenient means of loading external content. If a 27KB increase is not acceptable for your project, then don't worry. There are other options.

You can use an alternative `Loader` component from the *Flash 8 Cookbook* component set (downloadable from *http://www.rightactionscript.com/fcb*). After you've downloaded the component, follow the directions in the Preface to install it. When you've successfully installed the component, you'll find it in the Components panel in the FlashCookbook section. You can use the FlashCookbook `Loader` component in any situation in which you would use the Macromedia `Loader` component. And they have the same settings. The primary differences are that the Flash Cookbook `Loader` aligns the loaded content to the upper left and it only adds 3KB to an *.swf* file instead of 27KB.

If you are particularly interested in loading external content without the overhead of any component, you can do so using ActionScript. The `MovieClipLoader` class provides a convenient API (application programming interface—the properties and methods of the class) for loading content and monitoring the load progress. One of the benefits of using `MovieClipLoader` is that you can load content completely programmatically without having to rely on a component. Thus your application needn't be bogged down with the overhead of either of the Loader components previously mentioned. The process involved in working with MovieClipLoader is not particularly complicated, but there are two steps, and various options are available. The first step is to create the movie clip object into which the content should be loaded. For reasons that are beyond the scope of this book, it is advisable that should you want to load image content, you create a movie clip nested within another movie clip into which you can load the content. For simplicity, we'll provide the same instructions for both scenarios. Adding a nested movie clip is unnecessary when loading SWF content, but it will not hurt anything.

Additionally, you have the option of creating the movie clips as symbols in the library that you add to the stage at authoring time, or you can create the movie clips programmatically. The latter has the benefit of being fully scripted, and thus facilitates much more dynamic applications, but in many simple cases it is not a necessity.

To create an authoring time movie clip for loading content, complete the following steps:

1. Create a new movie clip symbol in the library. You can give the symbol a name you choose, but a suggested name is Empty Nested Loading Clip. Select the upper-left corner as the registration point.

2. Create another new movie clip symbol in the library. A suggested name for this second movie clip symbol is Loading Clip. Select the upper-left corner as the registration point.

3. Add an instance of Empty Nested Loading Clip (the first movie clip symbol) to Loading Clip (the second movie clip symbol). Make sure that the instance is aligned to 0,0.

4. Name the instance of Empty Nested Loading Clip that you just created, using the Property inspector. Give it an instance name of mContent.

5. Add an instance of Loading Clip to the stage at the point in the timeline where you will be issuing the ActionScript statements to load the content.

6. Give the object an instance name using the Property inspector. You can name the instance as you want, but for the purposes of this example we'll use the instance name mHolder.

If you want to load content with a solution that is entirely ActionScript-based, create a movie clip programmatically. To create a programmatic movie clip for loading content, add the following ActionScript code to the keyframe at which you will be issuing the statements to load the content:

```
this.createEmptyMovieClip("mHolder", this.getNextHighestDepth());
this.mHolder.createEmptyMovieClip("mContent", this.mHolder.getNextHighestDepth());
```

After you've created the movie clip—either at authoring time or by programmatic means—you have completed the first part. The second part involves a few lines of

ActionScript code that instruct Flash to then load the content into the movie clip you created in the first part.

Complete the following steps in order to load content into your Flash application using the `MovieClipLoader` class:

1. Select the keyframe on the timeline at which point you want to initiate the loading of the content and open the Actions panel to add ActionScript code. If you created the movie clip from part one programmatically, make sure you move the cursor to the line following that code. You'll want to ensure that the code to load the content comes after the code that creates the movie clip.

2. Add the following code (making sure to replace *URLToContent* with the URL to the content you want to load):

```
var mlLoader:MovieClipLoader = new MovieClipLoader();
mlLoader.loadClip("URLToContent", this.mHolder.mContent);
```

 The second parameter for the *loadClip( )* method is a reference to the movie clip into which you want to load the content. If you named the movie clip instances differently from the examples given in the first part of the recipe, you will need to change the reference in the parameter accordingly.

See Also

Recipe 1.13, Recipe 16.4

16.2   Loading External SWF/JPEG Content into a Draggable Window

Problem

You want to load an external *.swf* file or image into a draggable window at runtime.

Solution

Use the custom *Flash 8 Cookbook* `Window` component.

Discussion

Loading content into a draggable window has the same benefits as loading content into a `Loader` component discussed in Recipe 16.1, but with the added benefit that the user can move the loaded content around the screen. The Macromedia v2 `Window` component does not correctly accomplish this task at the time of this writing. Due to a bug in the component, the content may or may not be correctly masked. You may want to check to see if Macromedia has updated the Window component so as to fix the malfunctioning. However, you can download and use the custom *Flash 8 Cookbook* Window component instead. The *Flash 8 Cookbook* Window component looks and functions much like the Macromedia Window component, utilizing the same parameters. That means that if Macromedia does correct the error in their Window component and you later decide that you would prefer to use the Macromedia version, you will not need to learn new information to work with their component.

When you've downloaded and installed the *Flash 8 Cookbook* Window component (see the Preface), you can use the Window component in your Flash applications. To do so, complete the following steps:

1. Drag an instance of the *Flash 8 Cookbook* Window component from the Components panel onto the stage and name the instances using the Property inspector. Naming the instance is optional, but it is a good practice and facilitates using the component in conjunction with others, such as a ProgressBar.

2. With the Window component instance selected, open either the Component Inspector panel or the Parameters tab within the Property inspector. Either one will allow you to configure the parameters for the component instance.

3. Set the autoSize parameter based on the type of behavior you want for the Window. If the value is false (default), the Window will mask the loaded contents. For example, if you leave the Window instance's dimensions at 100×100 pixels and load an image that is 200×200 pixels, the default behavior is that only the upper-left 100×100 pixels of the image will display. If you set the autoSize parameter to true, the Window instance will automatically resize to match the dimensions of the content it loads.

4. Set the autoClose and closeButton parameters based on the type of behavior you want for the Window. The closeButton parameter determines whether the close button is visible in the Window instance. The default value of false means that the close button does not appear. A value of true will make the close button appear. The autoClose parameter has an effect only if the closeButton parameter is set to true. In the case that the close button is visible, the autoClose parameter determines the behavior of the close button. The default setting of false for the autoClose parameter means that the close button dispatches a programmatic close event when the button is pressed, but nothing more. If you set the autoClose parameter value to true, the Window still dispatches the programmatic event, but it also automatically closes.

5. Set the contentPath parameter. The contentPath value should be the URL to the content you want to load into the Window. The URL can be either an absolute or a relative address.

6. Set the scaleContent parameter. If scaleContent is set to true, the content will scale to fit within the Window instance.

7. Set the title parameter. The title parameter determines what, if any, text should appear in the title bar.

8. If you did not set autoSize to true, you can resize the Window component instance to the dimensions you want. You can resize the instance either using the Property inspector or by using the Free Transform tool.

See Also

For more information on the benefits of loading content at runtime as well as the types of content that can be loaded, see Recipe 16.1.

16.3 Loading External SWF/JPEG Content into a Scroll Pane

Problem

You want to load external SWF or JPEG content into a scroll pane.

Solution

Use the *Flash 8 Cookbook* ScrollPane component.

Discussion

When you want to load an external *.swf* or *.jpg* file into your Flash application, but you want to display it in an area with smaller dimensions than the content, you can use a *Flash 8 Cookbook* ScrollPane component. As with the Macromedia v2 Window component, the Macromedia v2 ScrollPane has a bug that prevents it from correctly masking loaded content with consistency.

When you have downloaded and installed the *Flash 8 Cookbook* ScrollPane, you can use it in your Flash application by completing the following steps:

1. Drag an instance of the ScrollPane component from the Components panel onto the stage and give the instance a name using the Property inspector. As with the Loader and Window components, naming the ScrollPane is optional, but recommended. Naming the instance allows you to use it in conjunction with other components, such as a ProgressBar.

2. With the ScrollPane component instance selected, open either the Component Inspector panel or the Parameters tab within the Property inspector. Either one will allow you to configure the parameters for the component instance.

3. Set the contentPath parameter of the ScrollPane instance to the URL of the content you want to load. As with the Loader or Window components, the URL can be relative or absolute.

4. Resize the ScrollPane instance as appropriate. You can resize the instance using the Property inspector or the Free Transform tool.

Remember that when loading image content, Flash can only load nonprogressive JPEG content. If you attempt to load other types of images, Flash will silently fail.

See Also

For more information on the benefits of loading external content at runtime, see Recipe 16.1.

16.4   Determining Load Progress

Problem

You want to monitor the load progress for content you are loading with MovieClipLoader, Loader, Window, or ScrollPane.

Solution

Use the Macromedia v2 ProgressBar component.

Alternatively, for a smaller file size, use the *Flash 8 Cookbook* ProgressBar component.

If you want a completely programmatic solution, and you have used MovieClipLoader to load the content in the first place, you can use a listener object with MovieClipLoader to monitor the load progress.

Discussion

When you are loading SWF and/or JPEG content into your Flash application, one important consideration is the time it will take to load the content. Most often, you want to make sure the user is notified as to what is going on as content loads. For example, if you are loading a 50KB *.swf* file and the user is connecting to your application over a dial-up connection, the content will not appear right away. In the interim, you want to make sure that the user at least knows that the content is loading. Otherwise he or she may be led to think that an error has occurred.

Macromedia provides a ProgressBar component that you can use to monitor the load progress and display that progress to the user. To use the Macromedia ProgressBar with a Loader, ScrollPane, or Window component instance, complete the following steps:

1. Add a ProgressBar instance to the stage by dragging it from the Components panel (you'll find it in the *UI Components* folder) to the stage at the point where you want it to appear. Name the instance via the Property inspector. As with naming other component instances, this not required for the ProgressBar instance to function, but it will facilitate features such as hiding the ProgressBar when the content has loaded.

2. With the `ProgressBar` component instance selected, open either the Component Inspector panel or the Parameters tab within the Property inspector. Either one will allow you to configure the parameters for the component instance.

3. Assign the instance name of the component for which you want to monitor the load progress. Assign the value to the `ProgressBar` instance's source parameter. For example, if you want the `ProgressBar` to monitor the load progress of a `Window` component instance to which you have given the instance name `cwImage`, you should type the name `cwImage` in the field for the `ProgressBar` instance's source parameter.

If you are using the `ProgressBar` to monitor content loaded with `MovieClipLoader`, you can still use the `ProgressBar` component, but you need to make a few slight adjustments. The components, such as `Loader`, `ScrollPane`, and `Window`, dispatch events notifying any listening objects (such as a `ProgressBar`) as the content loads. However, content loaded with `MovieClipLoader` does not work in that way. Instead, the `ProgressBar` has to continually request the load progress from the movie clip into which the content is loading. In order to use a `ProgressBar` component in this manner, first complete the first two steps from the previous list, and then complete the following two steps in addition:

1. Assign the instance name of the movie clip into which the content is being loaded to the source parameter of the `ProgressBar`. For example, if you are loading the content into `mHolder.mContent`, then assign the value of `mHolder.mContent` to the source parameter via the Component Inspector or Parameters tab in the Property inspector.

2. Set the mode parameter for the `ProgressBar` to polled instead of event. The event mode is used for monitoring progress of objects that dispatch events such as the components. The polled mode is used for objects such as movie clips.

One thing that you may notice about the Macromedia v2 `ProgressBar` is that it alone adds 27KB to the file size of an *.swf* file. A `ProgressBar` component that is 27KB is, for many web-based projects, rendered useless. It is likely useful for web-based projects only if the audience has broadband connections and the content being loaded is quite large. Otherwise, the `ProgressBar` component needs to be smaller in file size to be effective. The *Flash 8 Cookbook* `ProgressBar` functions much like the Macromedia v2 `ProgressBar`, but it is significantly smaller in file size. If that is an issue for your project, you can consider downloading and using the *Flash 8 Cookbook* `ProgressBar` instead of the Macromedia version. The *Flash 8 Cookbook* `ProgressBar` works in the same way as that outlined in the preceding instructions.

 The `ProgressBar` component has several parameters that are not mentioned in this recipe because they have to do with customizing the way in which the information is displayed within the `ProgressBar` instance. You can read more about the parameters in the Help panel within Flash.

If you want a completely programmatic solution for monitoring load progress, and if you are using MovieClipLoader to load the content, you can use some ActionScript code instead of a ProgressBar component. It is important to understand that with a completely programmatic solution, you will be responsible for providing any graphical content that you want to display to the user. The ProgressBar displays both a graphical and textual load indicator by default. With a completely programmatic approach, you will need to supply either of these elements.

Before looking at how to coordinate any graphical elements with the programmatic solution, let's first look at the basic way in which you can use ActionScript to monitor the progress of loading content. The code-based solution works by way of a listener object. A listener object is an object that you register with, in this case, the MovieClipLoader instance that is managing the loading. The MovieClipLoader instance then dispatches events to the listener object that tell the listener when certain types of things have occurred. The event we'll look at in this recipe is the progress event. Each time more bytes of data are loaded, the MovieClipLoader dispatches the event and calls the *onLoadProgress( )* method on the listener object. You can define the *onLoadProgress( )* method such that you can tell Flash to perform certain tasks each time more bytes are loaded. For example, you could tell a graphical load indicator to update to reflect the amount of data that has loaded. If that sounds somewhat complicated, don't worry: it's actually much simpler than it sounds. Let's look at the steps, and examine each of them a little more carefully:

1. Create the MovieClipLoader object and tell it to start loading the content. You can read more about how to do that in Recipe 16.1.

2. Create a listener object. A listener object can actually be many different types of objects, and there are many different ways in which you can most effectively use listeners. However, for simplicity and clarity we'll only look at creating a listener object from the Object class. Therefore, in this example you can create a listener object with the following line of code:

   ```
   var oMlListener:Object = new Object( );
   ```

3. Add an *onLoadProgress( )* method to the listener object. The *onLoadProgress( )* method is the method that gets called each time more bytes get loaded. The MovieClipLoader object that calls the method automatically passes it three parameters—a reference to the movie clip into which the content is being loaded, the number of bytes loaded, and the number of bytes total. Within the *onLoadProgress( )* method is where your custom code will go. We'll get to that in the next step. First, in order to add the method to the listener, use the following code:

   ```
   oMlListener.onLoadProgress = function(mContent:MovieClip, nBytesLoaded:Number,
   nBytesTotal:Number):Void {

   };
   ```

4. Within the *onLoadProgress( )* method, specify the code that you want Flash to run each time there is load progress. We'll look at some more details with regard to this step in a moment, but as an example, the *onLoadProgress( )* method could be defined as follows, such that the number of loaded bytes is displayed in a text field named tLabel. (The code shown is similar to the preceding code, with the new code shown in boldface.)

```
oMlListener.onLoadProgress = function(mContent:MovieClip, nBytesLoaded:Number,
nBytesTotal:Number):Void {
  tLoadIndicatorLabel.text = nBytesLoaded + " bytes loaded";
};
```

5. Now that you've defined the listener object, you need to register it with the MovieClipLoader. In order to do that you should call the *addListener( )* method from the MovieClipLoader instance and pass it a reference to the listener. Assuming that you named your MovieClipLoader instance mlLoader and your listener object is named oMlListener, your code would look like the following:

```
mlLoader.addListener(oMlListener);
```

When you understand the basic way in which programmatic load progress monitoring works, the only other step is to coordinate that with graphical and/or textual elements that update to display the load progress to the user. One of the most common graphical elements is a load indicator bar that fills from left to right, just as with the ProgressBar component. You can achieve that same result by updating the _xscale property of a movie clip with horizontal bar artwork placed within it from within the *onLoadProgress( )* method of the listener object. For example, assuming that you have created a movie clip instance named mLoadIndicator on the same timeline from which you have defined oMlListener, the following *onLoadProgress( )*method definition will update the scaling of mLoadIndicator so that it coordinates with the load progress:

```
oMlListener.onLoadProgress = function(mContent:MovieClip, nBytesLoaded:Number,
nBytesTotal:Number):Void {
  mLoadIndicator._xscale = nBytesLoaded/nBytesTotal * 100;
};
```

See Also

Recipe 16.1

16.5   Hiding a Progress Bar When Content Has Loaded

Problem

You want to determine when content has completed loading so that you can tell Flash to hide the progress bar.

Solution

If you are using the *Flash 8 Cookbook* `ProgressBar`, set the `autoHide` parameter to true.

Otherwise, if you are using the Macromedia v2 `ProgressBar`, add a listener object, and when the *complete( )* method is called, have Flash set the `ProgressBar` instance's visible property to `false`.

Alternatively, if you are using a custom load indicator as discussed at the end of Recipe 16.4, add a listener object to the `MovieClipLoader` object, and when the *onLoadInit( )* method is called, have Flash set the movie clip and/or text field's `_visible` property to false.

Discussion

Typically, when content has completed loading, you will want to hide the `ProgressBar` or other graphical indicator that you have used to display the load progress to the user. If you are using the *Flash 8 Cookbook* `ProgressBar`, all you need to do is set the `autoHide` parameter to `true`. Then, when the percent loaded has reached 100%, the instance will automatically hide.

If you are using the Macromedia v2 `ProgressBar`, your job is a little more complex. In order to accomplish this task, you'll need to use a little bit of ActionScript. But you needn't worry: the ActionScript is fairly short and simple.

If you want to hide a `ProgressBar` component instance after the content has loaded, complete the following steps:

1. Create an event listener object. As with the other types of listener object discussed in this book, there are many different types of objects that could be used, but for the purposes of keeping the example simple and functional, I will use an instance of the `Object` class. Therefore, to create the object, use the following code as an example:

   ```
   var oLoadedListener:Object = new Object();
   ```

2. When the content has loaded, the `ProgressBar` will dispatch a complete event and the listener object's *complete( )* method is automatically called. Therefore, you'll want to add a *complete( )* method to the listener. The following code shows how to add the method to the listener object (we'll look at the code that goes within the method in the next step):

   ```
   oLoadedListener.complete = function(oEvent:Object):Void {

   };
   ```

3. Within the *complete( )* method, set the `ProgressBar` instance's visible property to `false`. You can reference the `ProgressBar` instance in one of several ways. The

complete( ) method is passed a parameter that has a reference to the `ProgressBar`. You can retrieve that reference by way of the target property of that parameter. Therefore, you should define the code within the *complete( )* method as follows. (The code shown includes the code from the previous step, with the new code shown in boldface.)

```
oLoadedListener.complete = function(oEvent:Object):Void {
    oEvent.target.visible = false;
};
```

4. The remaining step is to add the listener object as a listener for the `ProgressBar` instance. You should call the *addEventListener( )* method from the `ProgressBar` instance in order to do that. Assuming that you have named the `ProgressBar` instance pbIndicator, then you can use the following code to register a listener object named oLoadedListener to listen for the complete event.

```
pbIndicator.addEventListener("complete", oLoadedListener);
```

If you are using a custom (non-`ProgressBar`) load indicator in conjunction with `MovieClipLoader`, you can hide the indicator with the following steps:

1. If you haven't already, complete steps 1 through 5 from the discussion of using `MovieClipLoader` to monitor load progress in Recipe 16.4.

2. Add an *onLoadComplete( )* method to the listener object. The *onLoadComplete( )* method is automatically called when the content has loaded completely. The following code shows the basic method declaration (I'll discuss the content of the method in the next step):

```
oMlListener.onLoadComplete = function(mContent:MovieClip):Void {

};
```

3. Within the *onLoadComplete( )* method definition, set the _visible property to false for any and all load indicator movie clips and/or text fields that you have used. For example, if you have a load indicator bar movie clip named mLoadIndicator and a text field named tLoadIndicatorLabel, than you can use the following *onLoadComplete( )* declaration (new code shown in boldface):

```
oMlListener.onLoadComplete = function(mContent:MovieClip):Void {
    mLoadIndicator._visible = false
    tLoadIndicatorLabel._visible = false;
};
```

See Also

Recipe 16.4

16.6 Optimizing Download Time by Sharing Content Among Movies

Problem

You are loading multiple *.swf* files into a single application using one of the techniques discussed in this chapter, and two or more of the *.swf* files happen to share one or more common elements, such as a movie clip, a sound, a bitmap, or a font. Rather than loading the same element multiple times, you want to load the element once and share it amongst the multiple *.swf* files.

Solution

Use a shared library.

Discussion

Shared libraries are a good way to reduce overall download size when the same element or elements are used across multiple *.swf* files in a single project. For example, if you have several *.swf* files that use the same embedded font, and if you embed the font in each of those files, you could be adding 10, 15, or even 20KB to the file size of each. Obviously that is not the greatest solution, because if you use that font in five *.swf* files in the same project, you could be adding 40 to 80KB to what the user has to download unnecessarily. Instead, what you can do is place the font in a shared library, link each of the *.swf* files to the shared library, and then require that the user only download the font once. The same idea applies not only to fonts, but to other types of elements including movie clips, buttons, graphics, bitmaps, and sounds.

There are essentially two steps when working with a shared library: creating the shared library and linking the *.swf* files to the shared library. Each of these steps is quite simple. To create the shared library:

1. Open a new *.fla* document, and save it to the same directory as the other files for your project.

2. Add the shared symbols to the library:

   - For movie clip, button, or graphic symbols, you may either create the symbol from scratch or copy the symbol from the library of another *.fla* file.

   - For sound and bitmap symbols, you may either import the symbol or copy the symbol from the library of another *.fla* file.

   - For font symbols, you may either create a new font symbol or copy a font symbol from the library of another *.fla* file. To create a new font symbol, choose the New Font option from the library's menu and follow the prompts in the dialog box.

3. Open the linkage settings for a symbol in the shared library. You can open the linkage settings by right-clicking/Command-clicking the symbol in the library and choosing Linkage from the context menu.

4. Check the Export for runtime sharing checkbox. The Export in first frame checkbox will automatically be selected. You can leave it checked.

5. In the URL field, enter the name of the *.swf* file as you plan to export it. For example, if you intend to export the *.swf* for the shared library as *sharedAssets. swf*, enter that value in the URL field.

6. Click the OK button to close the dialog box.

7. Repeat steps 3 through 6 for each symbol in the shared library.

8. Export the *.swf* file for the shared library document. Make sure to name the file with the same name you set in the URL field for each of the symbols' linkage settings.

To link the shared assets from the shared library to the libraries of the other documents that will use them:

1. If the shared library Flash document is not already open, open it and make sure that the library is opened.

2. Open a Flash document that will use the use the shared symbol(s), and make sure that its library is opened.

3. You should be able to see the libraries for both documents at the same time. Drag all of the linked symbols from the shared library to the library of the Flash document that will use them. If you already have any symbols with the same names in the document, Flash will prompt you for what to do. In such a case, choose the "Replace existing component" option. When you drag a symbol from the shared library into another Flash document's library, Flash knows to link to the shared library asset rather than export the symbol in the *.swf* file.

4. Use the linked symbols:

   • For movie clip, button, graphic, bitmap, and sound symbols, use the symbols as you would if they were normal symbols. For example, you can drag a linked movie clip symbol onto the stage. If you replaced any existing symbols when completing step 3, you should not need to make any additional changes with respect to how the existing instances of those symbols are used.

   • For font symbols, you should make sure that for any text fields in which you want to use the shared font, you have selected the shared font name from the Font menu in the Property inspector. The font will show up in the list with the font symbol name followed by an asterisk. Thus if you named the font symbol NeatFont Shared, then the option will show up in the Font menu as NeatFont Shared *. Static text embeds the font by default, but if you are using the shared font with a dynamic or input text field, make sure to embed the font following the instructions in Recipe 8.14. Although it is possible to use shared fonts with text fields created with ActionScript code, it is beyond the scope of this book to describe how to do that (see the *ActionScript Cookbook*, O'Reilly, for more information).

5. Repeat steps 2 through 4 for each Flash document that will use the shared assets.

When you publish your project, you must make sure to include the shared library .swf with the other .swf files.

See Also

Recipe 8.14

CHAPTER 17

Working with Sound

Sound is an integral part of many Flash movies, and working with sound effectively is an important skill for Flash developers. In this chapter are recipes covering all aspects of working with sound in Flash.

17.1   Importing Sounds

Problem

You want to import a sound file into your Flash document.

Solution

Use the File → Import → Import to Library feature to import the sound to the document's library.

Discussion

You can import a variety of sound formats into Flash. Exactly which formats you can import depends on factors such as your operating system and whether you have QuickTime (Version 4 or higher) installed on your computer. Table 17-1 lists a matrix that shows you what kinds of formats you can import.

Table 17-1. Sound formats for importing

	Macintosh	Windows	Macintosh with QuickTime	Windows with QuickTime
WAV	No	Yes	Yes	Yes
AIFF	Yes	No	Yes	Yes
MP3	Yes	Yes	Yes	Yes
Sound Designer II	No	No	Yes	No
QuickTime movie (sound only)	No	No	Yes	Yes

Table 17-1. Sound formats for importing (continued)

	Macintosh	Windows	Macintosh with QuickTime	Windows with QuickTime
Sun AU	No	No	Yes	Yes
System 7 sounds	No	No	Yes	No

You can use any sound in an importable format. For example, you might have purchased a CD-ROM with a library of sounds. Assuming that those sound files are in an importable format, you can use those. Or perhaps you want to create your own sounds—not only for sound effects, but also for voice-overs. Almost all sound recording/editing programs allow you to export or save the sound in one of the formats that Flash can import.

To import a sound into your Flash movie:

1. Select File → Import to Library.
2. When the Import to Library dialog box opens, browse to the sound file you want to import, select it, and click on the Open button. This action will import the sound into the Flash document's library.

When you have successfully imported a sound file into your Flash document, you should be able to see it in the library. An imported sound shows up as a library symbol with a speaker icon next to it. When you select the library symbol from the library list, the waveform appears in the top library pane along with two buttons. You can use the arrow button to preview the sound, and you can use the square button to stop a playing sound.

Of course, importing a sound is not of much use on its own. Although it is a crucial step, importing a sound merely places it in the library. It does not automatically add the sound to a timeline for playback. You'll need to add the sound to a timeline on your own. For more information on how to accomplish that, see Recipe 17.3.

See Also

Recipe 17.3

17.2 Updating Imported Sounds (When the Source File Has Been Modified)

Problem

You have modified the source for an imported sound, and you want to update the Flash movie to reflect these changes.

Solution

Use the Update feature within the library.

Discussion

If you have already imported a sound into your Flash document's library, and then modified the original sound file outside of Flash, it is not automatically updated in your Flash document. However, don't rush into deleting the sound from the library and reimporting it. There is an easier and more efficient way to solve this problem:

1. Select the sound from the library and then choose the Update feature from the library menu or from the right-click/Control-click menu.

2. The Update Library Items dialog box will open. From the dialog box, check the box next to the associated external sound file and click the Update button.

3. It may take Flash a few moments to update the sound, but when it is finished, click the Close button.

When you have updated a sound in the library, the change will be reflected in all instances of the sound on any timeline throughout the movie. As you can see, updating the sound is a huge time-saver when compared with deleting the symbol and replacing it.

When you update an imported sound, Flash will try to replace the current sound with the contents of the external sound file with the same name and location as the one that was originally imported. This means that if you originally imported a sound from *C:\sounds\voiceover.mp3*, Flash will look to the same location for the new contents. If you don't have a file with the same name at the same location, Flash will be unable to update the sound.

See Also

Recipe 17.1 for information on adding sounds to a movie. Also see Recipe 17.3 for information on adding instances of the sound to timelines in the movie.

17.3   Adding a Sound to a Timeline for Playback

Problem

You want to add an imported sound to your movie's timeline.

Solution

Create a new layer within the timeline into which you want to add the sound, create a new keyframe if necessary, and with the keyframe selected, drag the sound from the library onto the stage.

Alternatively, instead of dragging the instance from the library onto the stage, you can select the keyframe, and select the sound you want to add from the Sound menu in the Property inspector.

Discussion

Obviously, before you can add a sound to a timeline for playback, you need to import the sound into the movie. See Recipe 17.1 for more information on that process. After you have imported a sound, you can add it to any keyframe by selecting that keyframe and then dragging the sound symbol from the library and dropping it on the stage. It is a good practice to always create a new layer for each sound in your timeline. Here is the step-by-step process for adding an imported sound to the movie:

1. Create a new layer in your timeline to which you want to add the sound.

2. Name the layer with a name that describes the sound you are adding to it. For example, if the sound is a narration, you could name the layer Narration Sound.

3. If you want the sound to start on a frame other than the first frame, add a keyframe at the frame from which you want the sound to start playback.

4. Select the keyframe to which you want to add the sound.

5. Open the library, and drag an instance of the sound symbol onto the keyframe in the timeline. If you do this successfully, the sound will be added to the corresponding keyframe. If you have enough blank frames after the keyframe, you should see the sound's waveform appear within the timeline on that keyframe. If you don't have enough blank frames after the keyframe, you can still verify that the sound was added by checking the Sound menu in the Property inspector for that keyframe.

As an alternative to dragging and dropping the sound onto the stage, you can also choose the sound you want to add to a keyframe from the Sound menu in the Property inspector. To do this, follow steps 1 through 4 from the preceding list, and then in the Property inspector choose the sound you want to add from the Sound menu.

When you add a sound to a keyframe, the synchronization defaults to Event. You can also select from other types of synchronization options if Event does not meet your movie's needs. Synchronization can affect how the sound plays back as well as how the Flash movie plays, and it is an important topic. See Recipe 17.4 and Recipe 17.10 for more information on how to synchronize your sounds.

See Also

Recipe 17.4 and Recipe 17.10 for more information on how to synchronize sounds. Also, see Recipe 17.5 for more information on how to place a sound in a button timeline so that the playback occurs when the user clicks on the button.

17.4   Synchronizing Sounds to Animation

Problem

You want to make sure that your sound remains synchronized with the animation.

Solution

Use the Stream setting for synchronizing your sound.

Discussion

Flash sounds can be synchronized a variety of ways, and each way has its own benefits. The streaming synchronization option is ideal when you want to make sure that that the Flash animation stays in step with the audio. When you select the Stream option for sound synchronization, Flash makes sure that the movie's timeline plays back along with the sound. If Flash cannot draw the frames fast enough, it will automatically drop frames to keep up with the sound. This is important if you have a single, long sound that acts as a narration or soundtrack that needs to be in sync with the visual elements.

Flash sounds default to the Event synchronization, so if you want your sound to synchronize using the Stream option, you need to explicitly tell Flash to do this. Select the keyframe that contains the sound, and in the Property inspector, select Stream from the Sync menu. That is all there is to it.

Setting a sound to synchronize using the Stream setting is a simple process; however, there are a few things you should be aware of with sounds set to this synchronization type. First of all, unlike sounds set to synchronize as Event or Start, those set to Stream play only as long as there are enough frames in the layer in which the sound has been placed. So when you use stream sounds, make sure that you have created enough regular frames (non-keyframes) on the same layer, directly following the keyframe with the sound. You will be able to see where the sound ends, because Flash places a waveform in the timeline for your convenience. Another thing to be aware of is that it is inadvisable to choose to loop these types of sounds. See Recipe 17.8 for further discussion.

17.5   Playing a Sound with a Button

Problem

You want to add a sound to a button so that when the user clicks the button, the sound is played.

Solution

Add the sound to the Down keyframe of the button's timeline.

Discussion

You can add a sound to a button such that it is played when the user clicks the button. In order to accomplish this, you need only to add the sound to the Down frame of the button's timeline. Here are the steps to follow in order to accomplish this:

1. Edit the button symbol.

2. Add a new layer to the button's timeline, and name the new layer sound.

3. If you have not yet defined over and down states for your button, do so now. Or just add regular frames to the default layer up through and including the Down frame. This step ensures that Flash will still know how to display the button when the user mouses over it and/or clicks on it.

4. Add a new keyframe to the sound layer at the Down frame.

5. Add the sound to the new keyframe. There are two ways you can do this: by dragging the sound from the library onto the stage or by using the Sound menu in the Property inspector.

6. If you read Recipe 17.4, you know about how the Stream synchronization setting works. However, in the case of a button, you are adding the sound to a single frame, and the Stream setting will not work because it will not allot enough frames for the sound to play. You should choose the Event or the Start options from the Sync menu in the Property inspector. These two types of synchronization are almost the same. In each case, the sound begins playing independently of the timeline and continues to play until the sound ends or until you specifically issue a command to stop the sound. The only difference is that when you choose Event, if the user clicks the button repeatedly, the sound will play each time even if the previous sound has not yet completed. With the Start setting, the sound will begin playing only if the previous sound has finished.

After you have added a sound to a button, you may want to also take a look at Recipe 17.10, for a discussion of how to use buttons not only to start the playback of a sound, but also to stop the playback of that sound.

See Also

Recipe 17.10

17.6   Applying Effects to Sounds

Problem

You want to apply effects such as panning and fading to your sounds.

Solution

Select the keyframe with the sound, and choose from the Effect menu.

Discussion

You can add envelope effects to your sounds in Flash by choosing from the Effect menu. First, select the keyframe to which you have applied the sound. Then, in the Property inspector locate the Effect menu, and choose the effect that you want to apply.

Flash offers you seven presets to choose from in the Effect menu:

None
> This preset is the default value, and it plays both the right and left channels at 100% volume.

Left Channel
> This preset plays the sound from the left channel only.

Right Channel
> This preset plays the sound from the right channel only.

Fade Left to Right
> This preset plays the sound such that it begins playing completely in the left channel, and ends playing completely in the right channel.

Fade Right to Left
> This preset plays the sound such that it begins playing completely in the right channel, and ends playing completely in the left channel.

Fade In
> This preset plays the sound such that it begins with the volume at zero, and it gradually fades in the sound until it reaches full volume by the time one-quarter of the sound has played.

Fade Out
> This preset plays the sound such that it begins at full volume and plays at full volume for the first three-quarters of the duration of the sound. Then, over the last quarter, the volume gradually decreases until it reaches zero at the end of the sound.

Additionally, you can create a custom sound envelope effect by choosing the Custom option from the Effect menu, which will cause the Edit Envelope dialog box to display.

The top waveform represents the left channel, and the bottom waveform represents the right channel. You can use the mouse to grab and drag any existing envelope handles on either channel to adjust the volume. You can add more points (up to eight total) by clicking on the volume envelope line. You can also remove envelope handles by dragging them off of the waveform.

You may find that the envelope effects in Flash can be quite useful to you in many situations. For example, it is a great way to quickly add a basic fade to a sound. However, for more complex effects, you will need to use a third-party audio editor in order to add effects. For example, you cannot add distortion, pitch, or equalizer effects using the Flash envelope tool. And even though you could, theoretically, add a phase effect within Flash by creating a custom envelope in which the panning is shifted quickly from one channel to the other and back, over and over, the process would be tedious. You would be much better served to use a third-party editor that can process the entire sound and add a phase effect with a few clicks of the mouse.

Also, be aware that when you add an envelope effect to a sound in Flash, you are adding that effect to the instance only: other instances of that same sound will not have the same effect applied to them. And if you remove the instance to which you have applied the effect and then add the sound to the keyframe again, you will need to also reapply the effect.

See Also

One of the ways that the envelope effects can be employed most often in your Flash movies is to set in and out points for sounds. For more information on this topic, see Recipe 17.7.

17.7   Changing the In and Out Points of a Sound

Problem

You want to change the points within a sound at which it begins and ends playing.

Solution

Open the Edit Envelope dialog box for the sound, and adjust the Time In and Time Out controls.

Discussion

Flash allows you to modify the in and out points for a sound by adjusting the Time In and Time Out controls within the Edit Envelope dialog box. Use the mouse to drag them to the points at which you wish the sound to start and end. When Flash plays the sound, it begins to play it immediately at the in point, and it stops it immediately at the out point. The SWF's file size is affected by the in and out points as well. Flash only exports the sound that is actually used in the movie, so if you adjust the in and out points to play less of the sound, the resulting SWF has a smaller file size.

If you find it convenient, you can import a single sound file into your Flash movie, and use the in-and-out point settings to create multiple sound instances within the movie—each containing different parts of the total sound. For example, you might happen to have a single MP3 file containing a voice-over that you have recorded. However, in your Flash movie you want to apply different parts of the voice-over to different sections, and you don't have a third-party editor that allows you to break the sound into multiple MP3 files before importing to Flash. In such a scenario, you could use the in and out points of the envelope settings to create multiple instances of the sound, but with each playing only a particular part.

See Also

Recipe 17.6

17.8   Looping Sounds

Problem

You want to loop the playback of a sound.

Solution

Set a Loop value for the sound in the Property inspector.

Discussion

Flash allows you to loop sounds within your movies. This can be a great benefit to you, because you can create longer soundtracks without increasing your movie's file size. You can import a short sound file, add it to a keyframe as in Recipe 17.3, and then set the number of times you want it to loop. You can loop a sound only in whole number increments. For example, you can loop a sound three times, but not three-and-a-half times. And if you attempt to enter a non-integer value, Flash will prompt you to fix your entry.

In order to set the number of times to loop a sound, select the keyframe into which you have placed the sound, and then locate the Loop field in the Property inspector. By default, the loop value is 0. A value of 1 or less (including negative numbers) results in the sound playing once. Otherwise, the sound plays the number of times you specify, without any pause in between. The valid range of values for the loop value extends up to 2,147,483,647. If you enter a value greater than that, Flash will automatically reassign a value of 2,147,483,647.

Generally, looping works best with sounds that you have synchronized using either the Start or Event setting. Because of the way that the Stream synchronization works, Flash requires that you first create enough frames in order to play the sound. In most looping scenarios, this is not something you want to have to deal with. After all, usually you want looping sounds to continue to play regardless of whether the playhead is moving. Another problem with trying to loop sounds set to Stream is that the Flash movie's file size will increase.

Also, although looping sounds offer a way for you to add continuous sound to your movie, it is a technique that has been overdone and has become cliché. Don't let this completely deter you from implementing this technique—if done carefully and with some careful consideration, it can have a nice effect. But a single, four-beat loop that continues for hours can often have the effect of aggravating users. If you are unsure of the effect of your musical selection, at least give the user the option to stop the sound. See Recipe 17.10 for more information on how to achieve this.

See Also

Recipe 17.3. Also see Recipe 17.10 for more information on how to stop a looping sound or how to restart it after it has been stopped.

17.9 Compressing Sounds in Your Movie (Optimizing Quality and File Size)

Problem

You want to add compression to the sounds in your Flash movie to optimize both the quality of the sounds as well as the file size of the exported movie.

Solution

Adjust the compression settings for each sound and/or the global compression settings for the movie.

Discussion

How you choose to compress and export the sound in your Flash movies makes a tremendous difference in the quality and file size of the resulting movie. And Flash gives you quite a lot of control over how you want to handle the sounds. You can affect the compression for each sound individually, and you can also apply movie-wide, global sound compression settings. You can apply settings to each sound individually in order to assure that you maximize the quality of your sounds while also minimizing the required file size. Because each sound is generally quite different from another, no one setting will necessarily work best for all sounds. For example, you can generally apply much more compression to sounds that are voice-only than you can to sounds that include music.

In order to apply compression settings to each sound individually:

1. Locate the sound symbol in the library, and open the Sound Properties dialog box for that symbol. You can do this either by selecting Properties... from the

menu that appears when you right-click/Control-click on the symbol in the library. Or you can select the symbol by clicking on it once in the library, and then choose Properties... from the library menu.

2. In the Sound Properties window, you will see a Compression menu in the Export Settings portion at the bottom. If the sound you initially imported was an MP3 file, the MP3 compression option will already be selected, and the Use Imported MP3 Quality checkbox will be checked. Otherwise, if the original sound file was of a different format, the Default compression option is selected by default.

3. Select the compression type you want to apply to the sound:

   Default
   > The default compression uses the movie-wide, global sound compression settings.

   ADPCM
   > This compression type was used in Flash 4 and earlier before Flash movies could use MP3 compression. Unless you are authoring to Flash 4 or earlier, use MP3 compression instead.

   MP3
   > MP3 compression became available in Flash 5, and it offers the highest compression with the highest sound quality.

   Raw
   > This setting allows you to export the sound without compression. You can still adjust the sample rate and convert stereo tracks to mono to decrease the file size somewhat. Exporting without compression is not recommended for the Web.

   Speech
   > This compression is a special compression optimized for voice-only audio. In almost all cases, it is preferable instead to use MP3 compression.

4. Choose the compression settings and/or sampling rate. Depending on what compression type you select, you can choose from different compression options and/or sampling rate options. The higher the value that you choose for the bit rate (which is the compression setting), the higher the sound quality will be, but the file size also will increase.

5. With MP3 compression, you can also choose a Quality setting. This setting affects the speed at which the sound is compressed when you export the movie. The Fast value means that the sound exports faster, but with less sound quality. Likewise, the Medium setting offers medium export speeds and sound quality, and the Best setting offers the longest export speeds and the highest sound quality. Therefore, while testing use Fast, but for your final export use Best. The Quality setting does not affect file size.

6. Test the sound. When you have selected the compression type and settings, click on the Test button within the Sound Properties window to play back the sound once as it will sound in the exported movie. If you want to stop the sound before it has reached the end, click the Stop button.

7. If the sound is as you want it, then click the OK button. Otherwise, adjust the compression settings and test the sound until it is to your liking. Then click OK.

When you export your Flash movie, each Event or Start synchronized sound exports with its individual settings. However, for a given Flash movie, there can be only one sound *stream*. Therefore, Flash automatically mixes all your streamed sounds into a single stream, and applies a single compression setting to the whole stream. Flash determines what settings to use by applying the settings from whichever streamed sound has the highest settings. When discussing the highest settings, I am referring to the settings that result in the largest file size.

By setting the compression and export options for each sound in your library, you can create the most effective results it terms of optimized sound quality and file size. However, there are also reasons to apply global sound settings. For one thing, if there are many (or all) sounds in your movie to which you want to apply the same setting, it is more efficient to leave each of the individual sounds' compression types set to Default, and apply a global setting.

To set the global sound settings:

1. Open the Publish Settings dialog box. You can do this by choosing File → Publish Settings.

2. Within the Publish Settings window, make sure that you have selected the Flash tab.

3. Near the bottom of the window are two options: Audio Stream and Audio Event. If you click the Set button next to these options, you can set the default compression values for all sounds set to Stream or to Event (including Start).

4. When you click the Set button, Flash opens the Sound Settings dialog box. The compression settings in this window are the same as the compression settings in the Sound Properties window. Choose the settings you want to apply, and click OK.

Because Flash applies different settings to stream and event sounds, make sure to modify the global settings for both Stream Audio and Event Audio. And remember that the global settings are only applied to sounds that have default compression applied to them individually. Otherwise, the individual sound compression settings take precedence over the global settings.

Another good reason to apply global sound settings is that you can choose to override the individual sound compression settings. This approach is particularly useful if you want to quickly export a movie with different sound settings without having to modify each individual sound's properties. For example, if you have applied settings to your movie in order to optimize it for the Web, but you want to also quickly export a version with higher sound quality for a CD-ROM, you can choose to do so with a single checkbox option. In the Publish Settings window, check the Override Sound Settings option, and Flash will automatically apply the global sound settings to all sounds.

17.10 Starting and Stopping Sounds with Buttons

Problem

You want users to be able to start and stop a sound using buttons.

Solution

Create two buttons. On the Down frame of each button, add the same sound. On the Start button, synchronize the sound to Start. On the Stop button, synchronize the sound to Stop.

Discussion

Flash offers a convenient way to start and stop sounds by using the Start and Stop synchronization settings, respectively. You can readily create buttons that start and stop a sound when you know how to use the Start and Stop synchronization settings properly:

1. Create a button symbol, and place an instance on the stage. This button will be the start button.
2. Edit the start button, and add the sound to its timeline on the Down frame.
3. Make sure to set the sound's synchronization to the Start option.
4. Return to the main timeline.
5. Create a second button symbol, and place an instance on the stage. This button will be the stop button.
6. Edit the stop button, and add the sound to its timeline on the Down frame.
7. Change the sound's synchronization setting to Stop. This will cause Flash to stop playing all instances of that particular sound.

That is all there is to starting and stopping a sound with buttons. When you click on the start button, the sound should begin to play, and when you click on the stop button, the sound should stop.

You can use the Stop synchronization setting to stop a sound whether it was started by the playhead entering a timeline keyframe or by the user pressing a button. Regardless of the way in which the sound was started, the Stop synchronization stops all instances of that particular sound that are playing.

17.11 Stopping All Sounds

Problem

You want to stop all sounds.

Solution

Use the *stopAllSounds( )* function.

Discussion

Recipe 17.10 shows you how to stop individual sounds. You can also stop *all* sounds using the *stopAllSounds( )* function. When this function is invoked, all sounds that are playing are immediately stopped. It doesn't matter if the sounds were started with a button or from the playhead entering a timeline keyframe.

```
stopAllSounds();
```

If you want to use a button to stop all sounds, you can place the function call within an event handler method.

```
btn.onRelease = function() {
  stopAllSounds();
}
```

Or, if you want to stop all the sounds when the playhead enters a certain frame, you can add the function to that keyframe.

17.12 Manually Synchronizing Sounds and Visuals

Problem

You want to synchronize your animation to a soundtrack.

Solution

Display the timeline in Preview or Preview in Context mode so that you can more easily see the waveform, and then use the mouse to adjust keyframes so that they properly synchronize with your soundtrack.

Discussion

As discussed in Recipe 17.4, use the Stream synchronization setting when you want to ensure that Flash will keep your animation and audio in sync. After you have added your sound to its own layer, as described in Recipe 17.3, display the timeline in either Preview or Preview in Context mode. You can select these settings from the Frame View menu. You can open the Frame View menu by clicking the Frame View button in the upper-right corner of the timeline panel.

Both the Preview and Preview in Context settings display the timeline in an enlarged format so that it is easier to see the waveform of your sound. In addition to showing the waveform in a larger format, both of these Frame View settings cause Flash to display each frame's contents within the timeline. The difference between the two settings is that Preview displays all visual contents as an exact fit within each frame in the timeline, while the Preview in Context mode displays the contents in the context of the entire stage. In the three keyframes in the timeline there are three shapes: a circle, a square, and a triangle. In Preview mode, the entire frame is filled with the shape. In Preview in Context mode, you can see the shapes in the context of the stage, and you can see that the circle appears to the left side, the square to the right, and the triangle near the center. Which mode you choose is entirely up to you and what you prefer.

When you have your sound added to the timeline and you have chosen to display the timeline in Preview or Preview in Context mode, you are ready to synchronize your visual and audio elements. Add animation to the movie as normal, but with the enlarged timeline view, you can more easily see how to sync all the elements.

CHAPTER 18

Working with Video

Flash Player 8 can deliver better video quality than Flash Players 6 and 7 could. With the new On2 VP6 codec that is part of the Flash Player 8 plug-in, you can encode your video content to display better detail, better color, and smoother motion. You still have the option to use the Sorenson Spark codec with any Flash Player 6, 7, or 8 content, and you'll learn later in this chapter how to choose the appropriate codec for your Flash production.

Regardless of how you deploy web-based video, there are a few principles of video that you should understand. Most video files, even after heavy compression, are substantially larger than other files loaded into a web browser, such as HTML, XML, CSS, or other Flash content. One of the most critical factors of a video file is its bit rate, also referred to as a *data rate*. The data rate of a video file determines how much data (in bits or kilobits per second) is required to sustain smooth playback of the video. Every computer or device connected to the Internet has a connection speed, or available bandwidth, which determines how fast content over the Web can load and display in a browser.

The data rate of any given Flash Video file is fixed, and can be allocated across a variety of video properties, including *frame rate* (how smooth the motion appears within the content), *frame size* (how large the video displays on the screen), and *quality* (how much compression is applied to each frame of video). You can use the data rate of a video file to favor any one of these properties, depending on your content. For example, a video clip of a person delivering a lecture could afford to use a slower frame rate, and a clip of cars racing could use a higher frame to retain the smoothness of motion. A clip with a slower frame rate could use the remaining data rate for a higher quality image (or less compression) or a larger frame size.

In addition to data rate, video content can also be buffered in the playback environment. *Buffering* is the process of storing a specific amount (in units of time) of video in the player before playback can begin or resume. You can set the buffer time for video playback with the Flash Player, using ActionScript or parameters of video components.

With these factors in mind, you should plan how you want the user to experience the playback of the file:

- Does everyone get the same video file, regardless of his or her connection speed to your server?

- Will each user need to wait for the entire clip to download before playback, or will you use a specific buffer time to enable the video to begin playback sooner?

- If you offer several data rates for the same video content (that is, you create two or more Flash Video files, each with a unique data rate), can the user choose which one to play or do you script your Flash movie to pick the best clip for that user's available bandwidth? Does each clip have the same frame size or will the user interface layout change depending on which clip is played?

The answers to these questions are largely up to you. In order to make the right decisions, you need to know more about the specifics of Flash Video. This chapter helps you better understand how to encode, deploy, and optimize your Flash Video (FLV) content. You also learn how to create embedded cue points, a capability found within the Flash 8 Video Encoder that ships with Flash Professional 8. It is possible to embed video content into a Flash file directly. However, progressive and streaming FLV are preferable in nearly all cases, and therefore this chapter discusses FLV solutions only.

18.1 Encoding Video

Problem

You want to encode video for playback on a web page (HTML document) or within a larger Flash framework or application.

Solution

Use the Flash 8 Video Encoder that ships with Flash Professional 8 to create Flash Video (FLV) files, or use a third-party Flash Video compression utility such as Sorenson Squeeze or On2 Flix.

Discussion

Regardless of which encoding application you use, the process of converting a source video file into a Flash Video file involves a similar approach, including the following steps:

1. Choose a compression preset (or profile) that best suits the quality and data rate that you want to deliver to your audience.

2. Adjust the settings within the profile to fine-tune the output (optional).

3. Compress the video.

If you use the Macromedia Flash 8 Video Encoder, the profiles are split into two categories: Flash 7 and Flash 8. These profile names imply "Flash Player 7" and "Flash Player 8," respectively. The Flash 7 profiles use the Sorenson Spark codec, while the Flash 8 profiles use the new On2 VP6 codec. Refer to Table 18-1 to help you determine which codec you should use.

Table 18-1. Codec selection

Target factor	Sorenson Spark	On2 VP6
Earlier Flash Players, including Flash Player 6 or higher	Yes	No
Flash Player 8 or higher	Yes	Yes
Slower computers and processors, including Pentium III or earlier and PowerMac G3 processors	Yes	No
High image quality and more dynamic color range	No	Yes
Smaller file size for equivalent data rate	No	Yes
Shorter wait time during the encoding process	Yes	No
Frame sizes up to 640 × 480	Yes	Yes
Frame sizes beyond 640 × 480	Yes	No
Data rates up to 1 Mbps	Yes	Yes
Data rates beyond 1 Mbps	Yes	No
Streaming file for Flash Communication Server MX 1.5	Yes	No
Streaming file for Flash Media Server 2.0	Yes	Yes
Alpha channel for content masking	No	Yes

For most Flash Player 8 compatible movies, you will likely want to use the new On2 VP6 codec, because the image quality is superior to what you can achieve with the Sorenson Spark codec. To view a comparison of video content encoded with each codec, visit *http://www.flashsupport.com/bonus/codec_comparison*.

Another new feature supported only in the On2 VP6 codec is an alpha channel. An *alpha channel* is a mask (or matte) for the video display area, and enables you to layer (or composite) video content on top of other Flash content. For example, you can create an alpha channel around a clip of a person's body walking, and then layer that clip on top of a different graphical background in Flash. However, you can't create an alpha channel for FLV files using any encoding utility. For most video content, you need to use an application such as Adobe After Effects to remove (or key out) the area that will act as a mask. You must use QuickTime source video files to store alpha channel data that can be recognized by Flash Video encoding utilities. Later in this recipe, you will see how to encode a video file already containing a mask with the Flash 8 Video Encoder.

You can find royalty-free video content to practice encoding at the Prelinger Archive (*http://www.archive.org/details/prelinger*).

To encode a video file with the Flash 8 Video Encoder:

1. Open the Flash 8 Video Encoder application, and click the Add button.

2. In the Open dialog box, browse to the location where your video file exists, select the file, and click the Open button to add the file to the Source File list.

3. To specify the encoding settings for the newly imported clip, select the file in the Source File list and click the Settings button. Using Table 18-1 as a guide, choose a Flash 7 or Flash 8 profile in the Flash Video Encoding Settings dialog box. When you've picked a profile that encodes with your preferred codec, determine which data rate matches the needs for your content and audience. I recommend starting with one of the Medium Quality profiles, as the image quality for this data rate (400 Kbps) retains adequate detail for most video content.

4. By default, the encoder will create a new FLV file that uses the same name as the original source file, in the same location as the source file. Make sure that you have adequate file space remaining on the hard drive where your source file exists, to store the FLVs produced by the encoder application. If you want to use a different filename for the FLV, type a new name in the Output filename field in the Flash Video Encoding Settings dialog box.

5. To fine-tune the selected profile's settings, click the Show Advanced Settings button. In the Encoding tab, you may want to change the Frame rate setting to more adequately suit the needs of your video clip. If the clip shows subject matter that moves across more than 30% of the video frame, you should use the "Same as source" setting so that frames are not thrown out during the encoding process. If the clips feature subject matter that stays within the same place of the video frame, such as a talking head, you can choose a slower frame rate, such as 24 or 15 fps, to achieve a better quality of image. You can also reduce the frame size of the video image to improve image quality per frame. Select the "Resize video" button to enter a new width and height for your video, such as 320×240 or 160×120. I recommend that you use the default value for the keyframe placement setting, Automatic, as this value enables the encoder to add keyframes whenever a significant change occurs within the video frame. Also, don't overlook the audio data rate setting. For narration or human speech, you can use values as low as 32 Kbps. For more high-fidelity soundtracks, such as music, you should use a higher data rate, such as 96 Kbps.

6. If you need to crop the video frame or edit the in or out point of the video clip, you can select the Crop and Trim tab to perform these tasks. You can change the beginning (or in point) by dragging the leftmost triangle marker under the video

preview, and you can change the ending (or out point) by dragging the right-most triangle marker.

7. When you are finished adjusting the settings, click OK to return to the default window of the Flash 8 Video Encoder. You can continue to add other video files, choosing and adjusting a different profile for each newly added clip. Click the Start Queue button to begin the process of encoding the files you added to the Source File list. The application displays the progress of the encoding procedure in the lower pane. When the encoding process has finished, you will find new FLVs in the same location(s) as your source clips or the location you specified.

To encode video containing an alpha channel in Flash 8 Video Encoder, complete these steps:

1. Follow steps 1 through 6 from the preceding section, choosing a source video file that contains an alpha channel. You can download a sample QuickTime movie from *http://www.person13.com/fcb*. This file contains an alpha channel built in Adobe After Effects.

2. In the Flash Video Encoding Settings dialog box, you must choose a Flash 8 pro-file. Because alpha channels require space within the data rate, you should use a medium- or high-quality profile to retain image quality for the unmasked areas of the video clip. In the advanced settings area of the dialog box, select the "Encode alpha channel" checkbox below the "Video codec" combo box.

3. Follow step 7 from the previous section, producing a new FLV from the source video file.

There are several additional Flash Video encoders that can compress video content with either the Sorenson Spark or On2 VP6 codec. Sorenson Squeeze, available from *http://www.sorensonmedia.com*, is the only encoding utility that can compress FLVs (or FLV content within SWFs) with the Sorenson Spark Pro codec. The Pro codec offers more compression options, such as image smoothing and playback scalability. Image smoothing attempts to smooth out blocky areas of low data-rate video content. (You shouldn't use image smoothing for bit rates that are 384 Kbps or higher.) The playback scalability option, when used during the encoding process, enables the playback decoder to more evenly drop frames when the FLV is played on slower computers or devices. For example, if you have a 30 fps FLV and the playback environment can only process the video stream at 15 fps, the playback experience will be much better with the playback scalability option enabled. Without this option, the decoder will drop frames and pause the video frame until the next keyframe is reached.

In addition to these two encoding options, Squeeze also enables you to specify CBR (constant bit rate) or VBR (variable bit rate) encoding for your FLV. All encoding performed by Macromedia Flash 8 Video Encoder is CBR, which means that the data rate of the resulting FLV is fixed throughout the entire file, regardless of the content within the video clip. As such, if you have two source video files that are 60 seconds long and you use the same compression settings on each clip, the two FLV files will have the same file size. However, with VBR encoding, the encoder can analyze the video content more thoroughly, usually in a two-pass scenario where the encoder examines the content without trying to compress it on the first pass, and then uses that analysis to aid in the second pass when it produces the FLV. During VBR encoding, the encoder can maximize the data rate (that is, use the entire data rate you've specified) for every frame that requires that much data, and minimize the data rate (that is, drop the data rate) for frames that don't contain as much detail. The final file size of a VBR-encoded file can vary for files of the same duration, depending on the content of that video.

Another popular Flash Video encoder is On2 Flix Pro. This application was originally created by Wildform, and can create more than just FLV files from your source video files. Flix can also generate vector-based SWF conversions of your video content, enabling you to create multitone palettes that resemble creative filters in Photoshop or After Effects. You can also control color, saturation, and hue values of any encoded content, including FLVs. Table 18-2 contains a feature comparison of the three encoders discussed in this section.

Table 18-2. Comparison of encoders

Feature	Macromedia Flash 8 Video Encoder	Sorenson Squeeze 4.2	On2 Flix Pro
Encode with Sorenson Spark Basic	Yes	Yes	Yes
Encode with Sorenson Spark Pro	No	Yes	No
Encode with On2 VP6	Yes	Yes	Yes
Encode with VBR compression	No	Yes	Yes
Video filters	No	Yes	Yes
De-interlacing	No	Yes	Yes
Alpha channel data-rate control	No	Yes	Yes
Batch processing	Yes	Yes	Yes
Compression profiles for batch jobs	No	Yes	Yes
Watch folder	No	Yes	Yes

18.2   Deploying Video

Problem

You want to deploy video for a project.

Solution

Determine if you want to serve Flash Video from a standard web server, over HTTP, or from a Flash Video streaming server, over RTMP, and then upload the *.flv* file(s) to the server.

Discussion

Content distributed over the Internet can use a variety of protocols, ranging from common protocols such as FTP and HTTP to more obscure protocols. Most content that the Flash Player plug-in uses is distributed over HTTP. Just about every major web video format can be loaded to a web browser (or plug-in/player application) in two ways:

Progressive download (HTTP)
> The easiest and most economical approach to deploy web video is to upload your video content to a web server, just as you would any other file (e.g., HTML, GIF, JPEG) for display in a web browser. For Flash Player 7 and higher, you can load Flash Video (*.flv*) files directly into your Flash movie interface (*.swf* file). The major drawback to this approach is that the entire *.flv* file is downloaded and cached to the user's machine, and the user can only seek to points in the video that have already downloaded. Also, unless you're using a dedicated web server just for FLV content serving, bandwidth from your server may be taxed serving other site assets (HTML, image files, and so on) to other users visiting the site.

Streaming delivery (RTMP)
> Another method of delivering video content over the Internet is to use a real-time streaming server. Web video formats such as Real Video and Apple Quick-Time use RTSP (Real-Time Streaming Protocol) to send the data from the streaming server to the client. Flash Player 6 and higher can use an equivalent protocol, RTMP (Real-Time Messaging Protocol), to receive streaming video from a Flash Communication Server or Flash Media Server.

Refer to Table 18-3 to help you determine which deployment method best suits the Flash Player version you want to require from your target audience. Keep in mind that streaming delivery requires your Flash Video content to be hosted on a Flash Communication Server, Flash Media Server, or Flash Video Streaming Service account. By far the most economical solution is a progressive download solution, but streaming delivery has its advantages, as shown in Table 18-4.

Table 18-3. Flash Player support for Flash Video

Factor	Flash Player 6	Flash Player 7	Flash Player 8
Progressive download	SWF	FLV, SWF	FLV, SWF
Streaming delivery	FLV	FLV	FLV

Table 18-3. Flash Player support for Flash Video (continued)

Factor	Flash Player 6	Flash Player 7	Flash Player 8
Sorenson Spark	Yes	Yes	Yes
On2 VP6	No	No	Yes

Table 18-4. Flash Video delivery considerations

Factor	Progressive download	Streaming delivery
Cost-prohibitive (requires licensing or additional hosting costs)	No	Yes
Protected content	No	Yes
Faster seek times for longer video content	No	Yes
Offline use	Yes	No
Live video streams	No	Yes
Enhanced server-side control of content	No	Yes
More likely to be blocked by firewalls or proxies	No	Yes

To deploy Flash Video files to your web server, do the following:

1. Determine how you will format your Flash Video content, as either embedded within a Flash movie (SWF) or as a Flash Video file (FLV).

2. Create a Flash movie that acts as a video playback user interface for the video content. The video content is loaded separately, at runtime, into this movie. You'll learn more about using the FLVPlayback component as a video controller later in this chapter.

3. Upload your video controller movie (SWF) and video content (SWF or FLV) to your web server, in addition to the HTML document containing the <object> and <embed> tags for the video controller movie.

To deploy Flash Video to a Flash Communication Server or Flash Media Server, do the following:

1. Encode your video content as Flash Video files (FLV).

2. Create a Flash Player 6 or higher compatible movie (SWF) that acts as a video controller for the content. The FLV will stream into the Flash Player and be displayed in this Flash movie.

3. Create an application folder with a unique name on your Flash Communication Server or Flash Media Server. Inside of this new application folder, make a new folder named *streams*. Within this *streams* folder, create a folder named *_definst_*. Upload your .flv file(s) to this last folder.

4. Upload your video controller movie (SWF) and HTML document for the controller to your web server.

18.3   Playing Flash Video

Problem

You want to play streaming or progressive-download Flash Video content.

Solution

Code your own playback interface or use the FLVPlayback component.

Discussion

You can display Flash Video in your Flash projects by building your own interface and writing ActionScript to load the video. The general process to building a simple Flash Video player involves these steps:

1. Add a Video object to the library of your Flash document, and place an instance of that Video object on the stage.

2. In the Actions panel, create `NetConnection` and `NetStream` objects. If your Flash Video resides on a web server, specify the URL to the *.flv* file in the *NetStream. play()* method. If your Flash Video resides on a Flash Communication Server, Flash Media Server, or Flash Video Streaming Service (FVSS) provider account, specify the RTMP location of the application in the *NetConnection.connect()* method and the FLV (without the *.flv* extension) in the *NetStream.play()* method.

3. Add `Button` or `MovieClip` instances to act as play, stop, or pause buttons that control the playback of the video file.

To build a simple playback for progressive-download FLV files, follow these steps:

1. Create a new Flash document in Flash 8.

2. In the Library panel, click the Options menu in the top right corner and choose New Video. In the Video Properties dialog box, set the Type option to Video (ActionScript-controlled). Name the symbol whatever you prefer, and click OK.

3. Rename layer 1 to Video. On frame 1 of this layer, drag an instance of the Video object from the Library panel to the stage. In the Property inspector, name the instance vWin. Change the width and height of the instance to match that of the *.flv* file that you will play.

4. Create a new layer named Actions, and place this layer at the top of the layer stack. Select frame 1 of this layer, and open the Actions panel. Add the following code, substituting the FLV filename with the location and name of your FLV:

```
var nc:NetConnection = new NetConnection();
nc.connect(null);

var ns:NetStream = new NetStream(nc);
ns.play("http://www.flashsupport.com/video/sample.flv");
```

```
    var vWin:Video;
    vWin.attachVideo(ns);
```

5. Save the Flash document, and test it (Control/Command-Enter). The Flash Video content should play in the vWin instance.

6. Go back to the Flash document, and create a new layer named Buttons. Open the Window → Common Libraries → Buttons library, and expand the playback rounded folder. With frame 1 of the buttons layer selected, drag instances of the rounded green pause, rounded green play, and rounded green stop buttons to the stage below the *vWin* instance. In the Property inspector, name these new instances *btPause*, *btPlay*, and *btStop*, respectively.

7. Select frame 1 of the actions layer, and open the Actions panel. Add the following actions to the script:

```
    var nDuration:Number;

    ns.onMetaData = function(oData:Object):Void {
        nDuration = oData.duration;
    };

    var btPause:Button;
    var btPlay:Button;
    var btStop:Button;

    btPause.onRelease = function():Void {
        ns.pause();
    };

    btPlay.onRelease = function():Void {
        if(ns.time < Math.floor(nDuration) ){
            ns.pause(false);
        } else {
            ns.seek(0);
        }
    };

    btStop.onRelease = function():Void {
        ns.seek(0);
        ns.pause(true);
    };
```

8. Save the Flash document, and test the movie. Click each button to test its functionality.

To play streaming Flash Video content, modify the code on frame 1 of the Actions layer to connect to the Flash Communication, Flash Media Server, or Flash Video Streaming Server provider account. The following sample code connects to the Flash Communication Server account provided by Influxis (*http://www.influxis.com*):

```
    var nc:NetConnection = new NetConnection();
    nc.connect("rtmp://fcs.iknowbetter.com/free/");
```

```
var ns:NetStream = new NetStream(nc);
ns.play("sample");
```

To play Flash Video with the FLVPlayback component, follow these steps:

1. Create a new Flash document in Flash Professional 8.

2. Rename Layer 1 to cfp, short for component FLVPlayback.

3. Open the Components panel (Window → Components), and from the *FLV Playback—Player 8* folder, drag an instance of the FLVPlayback component to the stage.

4. With the instance selected, open the Property inspector and name the instance cfp.

5. You can set the parameters for the instance in the Parameters tab of the Property inspector or specify them in ActionScript. Click the Parameters tab, and click the contentPath field to open the Content Path dialog box. There, you can type the name of the FLV you want to play, as a relative URL (for example, *sample.flv*, */videos/sample.flv*), or a fully qualified HTTP or RTMP URL. You can use *http://www.flashsupport.com/video/sample.flv* to test the functionality of the component.

6. You can also choose a player skin for the component in the Parameters tab. Scroll down to the skin field, and double-click the value. In the Select Skin dialog box, you can choose from 32 pre-built skins. The player skin is a separate Flash movie (*.swf* file) that is automatically copied to the same location as your local published Flash movie for the current document. The skin file must be uploaded to the same parent folder on your web server as the published Flash movie.

7. Save the Flash document, and test it (Control/Command-Enter). The Flash Video content automatically downloads and plays in the display area of the FLVPlayback component. Depending on the skin you selected, you can control a variety of playback options, from play, pause, stop, forward/back, and seek buttons to a scrub bar and a mute on/off button.

18.4   Customizing the FLVPlayback Component

Problem

You want to customize the look and feel of the FLVPlayback component.

Solution

Use the custom UI components that ship with Flash Professional 8.

Discussion

If the 32 skins that ship with Flash Professional 8 don't suit your particular preferences for playback controls, you can pick and choose from a variety of components
in the FLV Playback Custom UI folder of the Components panel to build your own
user interface for the FLVPlayback component. Using ActionScript, each aspect of
the FLVPlayback component's user interface can be set to the appropriate custom UI
component.

To build a simple playback interface consisting of a play/pause toggle button and a
volume bar, perform the following steps. In the process, you'll learn how other playback controls can be exposed and set in ActionScript.

1. Create a new Flash document in Flash Professional 8.

2. Rename Layer 1 to cfp, short for component FLVPlayback.

3. Open the Components panel (Window → Components), and from the *FLV
   Playback—Player 8* folder, drag an instance of the FLVPlayback component to
   the stage.

4. With the instance selected, open the Property inspector and name the instance
   cfp. In the Parameters tab, double-click the skin value and choose None in the
   Select Skin dialog box. You do not need to use a skin *.swf* file for this example,
   because you will build your own UI.

5. Add a new layer named Controls. On frame 1 of this layer, drag an instance of
   the PlayPauseButton and VolumeBar components from the *FLV Playback Custom
   UI* folder of the Components panel to the stage. Place the instances below the
   cfp instance.

6. In the Property inspector, name the PlayPauseButton instance cppb and the VolumeBar instance cvb.

7. Create a new layer named Actions, and place the layer at the top of the layer
   stack. Select frame 1 of the Actions layer, and open the Actions panel. Add the
   following code. After you declare the variable names, notice the code hint menu
   displayed after you type cfp in the Actions panel. All of the public properties for
   the FLVPlayback component are displayed. All the other playback control
   parameters can be found in this list, including playButton, bufferingBar, and
   backButton—just to name a few.

   ```
   var cfp:mx.video.FLVPlayback;
   var cppb:MovieClip;
   var cvb:MovieClip;

   cfp.playPauseButton = cppb;
   cfp.volumeBar = cvb;
   ```

8. Save the Flash document, and test it (Control/Command-Enter). You can now
   control the playback of the video content with the play/pause button and the
   volume with the volume slider.

18.5 Adding Cue Points/Captions

Problem

You want actions within your Flash movie (SWF) to synchronize with the playback of Flash Video content. For example, you want to add captions within Flash that synchronize with the video.

Solution

Add cue points when encoding the video with the Flash 8 Video Encoder. Optionally, use an application like Captionate to add and edit markers and captions for *.flv* files.

Discussion

Cue points are markers that trigger events at specific playback times. There are many reasons you might want to set cue points for Flash video. For example, you might want to synchronize the playback of an FLV and an SWF. A common use of cue points is adding captions to a video presentation.

There are several ways you can go about adding cue points. One option is to use the cue points feature of the Flash 8 Video Encoder. Flash 8 Video Encoder is included with Flash 8 Professional, and it has a cue point feature that allows you to add cue points to the video before encoding. The program then adds the cue points to the FLV file.

To add cue points from the Flash 8 Video Encoder, complete the following steps.

1. From the Flash 8 Video Encoder window, click the Add button to add a file to the encoding queue.

2. Select the file from the queue list, and click the Settings button on the right.

3. The Flash Video Encoding Settings window opens. Make sure that it displays a preview of the correct video on the right side of the window. You ought to be able to move the playhead (the arrow above the playback bar) and scrub the video.

4. Click the Show Advanced Settings button.

5. From the advanced settings portion of the window, select the Cue Points tab.

6. Scrub the video to the point at which you want to add a cue point.

7. Click the + button in the Cue Points tab. That causes the encoder to add a new cue point to the list.

8. The default cue point name is New Cue Point. You can change the cue point name. The cue point name is sent to the event handler method when the cue point is dispatched.

9. Add parameters for the cue point if appropriate. Parameters are name-value pairs that you want to send to Flash with the cue point. For example, you might want to encode captions for several languages. In that case, you can use the language names as the parameter names, and the captions as the parameter values.

10. Repeat steps 7 and 8 as necessary.

11. Export the FLV. The cue points are embedded in the *.flv* file.

Note that the Flash 8 Video Encode allows you to specify the cue point as either Event or Navigation. Which value you select doesn't affect how the cue points work. In practical terms, there is no benefit in trying to distinguish between Event and Navigation events.

When Flash plays back the FLV, the cue points trigger events that automatically call the *onCuePoint()* method of the NetStream object used to play back the video. As with the event handler callback methods of many data types, it is your responsibility to define the method. When the *onCuePoint()* method is called, Flash automatically passes it a cue point event object as a parameter. The cue point event object contains properties called name, time, type, and parameters corresponding to the values you set for the cue point before encoding the FLV. The parameters property is an associative array in which the keys correspond to the names you specified for the name-value pairs in the parameters list for the cue point in the Flash 8 Video Encoder. The following code illustrates how you can use cue points to display captions in several languages. The code assumes that tCaptions is a text field and that you've encoded the FLV with cue point parameters named english and dutch.

```
nsExample.onCuePoint = function(oCuePoint:Object):Void {
  tCaptions.text = oCuePoint.parameters.english;
  tCaptions.text += "\n" + oCuePoint.parameters.dutch;
};
```

Optionally, if you are using an FLVPlayback component to play the video, you can listen for cuePoint events dispatched by the component instance. The event objects passed to the listener method for a FLVPlayback have a property called info that references the same properties as event objects passed to *onCuePoint()*.

```
var oListener:Object = new Object();
oListener.cuePoint = function(oCuePoint:Object):Void {
  tCaptions.text = oCuePoint.info.parameters.english;
  tCaotions.text += "\n" + oCuePoint.info.parameter.dutch;
};
flvpFlashTraining.addEventListener("cuePoint", oListener);
```

 Although the cue points feature for the Flash 8 Video Encoder appears to be helpful, it has a major flaw. You cannot edit cue points after you've encoded the FLV.

Captionate (*http://buraks.com/captionate/*) is a program that is designed to add and edit captions for FLV files. Captionate uses proprietary metadata for captions, and it does not allow you to edit cue points added with the Flash 8 Video Encoder. If you use Captionate, encode the FLV file normally, and then use Captionate to add captions. You can use Captionate to edit captions added via Captionate.

To use Captionate to add captions:

1. Select File → Open from the Captionate menus.
2. Select the *.flv* file to which you want to add captions, and click Open.
3. Open the Video Preview window by selecting View → Video Preview Window.
4. Use the video scrubber control in the main Captionate window to scrub the video to the point at which you want to add a caption.
5. In the Captions tab, specify the caption text in the Caption Text text area, and click Add Caption. That action adds the caption to the caption list. Note that you can edit the caption text from the caption list.
6. Repeat steps 4 and 5 as necessary.
7. If appropriate, add a new language track by clicking the New Language Track button at the top of the captions list.
8. Toggle between languages in the Language Track drop-down menu at the top of the captions list.
9. If appropriate, assign values to the caption text for each caption in the new language.
10. Save the file. Saving the file adds the captions to the FLV.

Captionate captions cause Flash to dispatch events that automatically call a method of the NetStream class called *onCaption()*. As with *onCuePoint()*, you must define the *onCaption()* method for the NetStream object. The *onCaption()* method is automatically passed a caption event object as a parameter. The caption event object is an array of language track values for that caption. The order of the elements in the array corresponds to the order of the language tracks.

```
nsExample.onCaption = function(aCaption:Array):Void {
  tCaptions.text = oCaption[0];
  tCaptions.text += "\n" + oCaption[1];
};
```

Captionate also dispatches an event that calls *onCaptionInfo()*, which notifies Flash as to the details of the language tracks. Captionate allows for more sophisticated caption data such as assigning a speaker (as in a person speaking) to each caption. You can read about each of the events in the Captionate help window.

18.6 Detecting Bandwidth

Problem

You want to determine the bandwidth capabilities of a user's computer.

Solution

Download a file using *MovieClipLoader*. Determine the amount of time it takes to download the file.

Discussion

Not all users have the same bandwidth capabilities. Users in many parts of the world still have dial-up access with 56k modems. And even for those users with broadband connections, actual bandwidth capabilities can vary greatly. Users on DSL networks might have speeds of 384 Kbps, 768 Kbps, or 1.5 Mbps, for example. Network traffic can also play a role. The more users are on a network, the less bandwidth is likely to be available to each user.

Video can require significant bandwidth capabilities when encoded at higher bit rates. Depending on your audience you might want to consider encoding videos at several bit rates. For example, you might encode a video at 800 Kbps, 400 Kbps, 200 Kbps, and 56 Kbps. In that case, each video will have four FLV files—one for each bitrate. You can name the files using a naming scheme such as *videoName_bitrate*. For example, you might have four FLV files named *welcome_800.flv*, *welcome_400. flv*, *welcome_200.flv*, and *welcome_56.flv*.

In order to present the user with the optimal video configuration, you'll want to know the user's bandwidth settings. If the user is capable of downloading data quickly, you'll want to allow the user to view video encoded at high bit rates (and therefore high quality). A user with low bandwidth capabilities may or may not want to view a video encoded at a high bit rate if it takes a long time for her to download the file. There are several ways you can optimize the video configuration for a user.

It is generally a good idea to allow users to make decisions about things involving quality and download times. A very direct way to ensure that users have the video configuration they want is to allow them to select the configuration manually. For example, you can allow the user to select a bit rate from a combo box or list. In that case, you don't need to detect the user's bandwidth because the user is selecting the bit rate manually.

Allowing the user to select a bit rate directly has the advantage of ensuring that the user is in control. However, it's possible that such a direct approach may be inappropriate for your audience. If your audience is not technically savvy, they may not know which option to select. Furthermore, automatic bandwidth detection gives the user the sense that the application is sophisticated and smart.

Automatic bandwidth detection requires that you download a file using *MovieClipLoader* and determine the amount of time required. You can then determine the approximate bandwidth capabilities by dividing the file size by the amount of time. You'll want to download a file that is not likely able to be decompressed by Flash Player (and therefore return incorrect bandwidth settings). Image files (JPEG, PNG, and so on) often work well. The smaller the file, the faster the download and the shorter the wait for your users. However, the less the user has to download, the less accurate the bandwidth detection as well. If the user has to download only 25 KB, then minor network traffic or CPU stutters could throw off the detection significantly. It's generally advisable to use a file that is at least 100 KB. Consider than a user with 768 Kbps DSL will be able to download a 100KB file in approximately one second. A user with a 56k modem can download that file in approximately 16 seconds. Sixteen seconds is about as long as you'd want to make a user wait for bandwidth detection. If you detect a user at 56k modem speeds you can download the file just once. If you detect the user at speeds higher than 56k modem speeds, consider downloading the file a few additional times and average the detected bit rates in order to have a more accurate result. For example, if the user has 384 Kbps DSL, it will take approximately eight seconds to download a 100KB file four times.

To detect the bandwidth, you'll want to use a few variables. You'll want to use variables to store the download start time, the total bytes downloaded, the total download time, and the number of times downloaded. You can initialize the variables for total bytes, download time, and times downloaded each to 0:

```
var nStartTime:Number;
var nTotalBytes:Number = 0;
var nTotalDownloadTime:Number = 0;
var nTimesDownloaded:Number = 0;
```

You'll also want to declare a variable to store the detected bandwidth:

```
var nDetectedBandwidth:Number;
```

You'll need to define a movie clip into which to download the file. You can use *createEmptyMovieClip()* to accomplish that. If you're downloading an image file, it's advisable that you add a movie clip nested within a movie clip. When you download an image file, it overwrites movie clip functionality. If you add a movie clip nested within a movie clip, you can overwrite the nested movie clip each time you want to download the file again. In that case, add the nested movie clip with a depth of 1. You'll create the nested movie clip in a function called *testBandwidth()* in just a few minutes.

```
this.createEmptyMovieClip("mBandwidth", this.getNextHighestDepth());
```

Use *MovieClipLoader* to make the download request. Construct a *MovieClipLoader* as follows:

```
var mlBandwidth:MovieClipLoader = new MovieClipLoader();
```

Register a listener object with the *MovieClipLoader* instance to detect events such as the download starting and completing. Construct a listener object using the *Object* constructor:

```
var oBandwidthListener:Object = new Object( );
```

Then, define *onLoadStart()* and *onLoadComplete()* methods for the listener object. The *onLoadStart()* method ought to assign the current timer value to the start time variable. The *getTimer()* global function returns a timer value in milliseconds since the Flash Player started running:

```
oBandiwidthListener.onLoadStart = function(mClip:MovieClip):Void {
   nStartTime = getTimer( );
};
```

The *onLoadComplete()* method should determine the difference between the current timer value and the start time and add that value to the total download time. It also should add the bytes downloaded to the total bytes downloaded. You can retrieve the bytes downloaded from the *getBytesTotal()* method of the movie clip reference passed to the method. Increment the times downloaded by 1. Then determine the detected bandwidth by multiplying the total bytes by 8 to convert bytes to bits (there are 8 bits in a byte) and dividing by the total time. If the detected bandwidth is near 56k modem speeds, you can exit the bandwidth detection. If the number of times downloaded has reached the maximum number of download times, you can exit the bandwidth detection. If the detected bandwidth is higher than 56k modem speeds and you still haven't reached the maximum number of downloads, download the file again.

```
oBandwidthListener.onLoadComplete = function(mClip:MovieClip):Void {
   nTotalDownloadTime += getTimer( ) - nStartTime;
   nTotalBytes += mClip.getBytesTotal( );
   nTimesDownloaded++;
   var nBandwidth:Number = nTotalDownloadTime * 8 / nTotalBytes;
   if(nBandwidth < 150 || nTimesDownloaded >= 4) {
     if(nBandwidth < 200) {
       nDetectedBandwidth = 56;
     }
     else if(nBandwidth < 400) {
       nDetectedBandwidth = 200;
     }
     else if(nBandwidth < 800) {
       nDetectedBandwidth = 400;
     }
     else {
       nDetectedBandwidth = 800;
     }
     // Call a function that starts the video.
   }
   else {
     testBandwidth( );
   }
};
```

Next, define the *testBandwidth()* function. The function defines the nested movie clip and calls the *loadClip()* method of the *MovieClipLoader* method. Because you are downloading the file specifically to determine bandwidth, you'll want to ensure that the file is never retrieved from the browser cache, so use a unique URL each time you make the request. You can accomplish that by appending a query string with a unique number to the URL. You can use the *getTime()* method of a new Date object to generate the unique number:

```
function testBandwidth( ):Void {
  mBandwidth.createEmptyMovieClip("mImage", 1);
  mlBandwidth.loadClip("http://www.server.com/file.jpg?id=" + (new Date()).getTime( ),
mBandwidth.mImage);
}
```

To start the bandwidth detection, call *testBandwidth()*.

As noted previously, it's generally advisable to allow the user to have control. Even if you use automatic bandwidth detection, consider allowing the user to override the detected settings. In the scenario presented in this recipe, you can accomplish that by allowing the user to manually override the value of nDetectedBandwidth.

18.7   Optimizing Video Playback

Problem

You want to ensure that the user gets the optimal video playback for his computer's bandwidth.

Solution

Create several Flash Video files (FLV), each with a specific data rate, for each piece of content.

Discussion

As discussed in the previous recipe, publishing several Flash Video files for a wide range of bit rates (or data rates) can enable you to offer your content to just about anyone watching your content. Two important factors to keep in mind with video playback over networks, including the Internet, are:

Delay
    Is the user waiting too long for the video content to buffer, or does the video play nearly instantaneously?

Quality
    Is the image quality of the content acceptable to the user? Is too much information lost if the image is severely compressed?

Some content can be highly compressed yet retain the information that made video the acceptable medium for communicating the content. For example, the visual of an avatar guiding you through the steps to use an online form doesn't necessarily need to be a high-quality image—as long as the audio track has sufficient quality to be intelligible by the user. Nor would such video content be conducive to user selection of the data rate—the playback of a video "guide" on a web site should be rather transparent and unobtrusive. Other content, however, may not be able to sacrifice image quality (or user choice) so easily. A movie trailer, for example, is usually watched by avid filmgoers, who appreciate detail, facial recognition of popular actors and actresses, and so on. Highly compressed audio and video information in this situation wouldn't necessarily yield satisfactory results with the target audience.

The previous recipe demonstrated how you can check the user's available bandwidth. In order to utilize that information effectively, you should compress your Flash Video content across several bit rates. By far the easiest compression utility to use for the generation of multiple data rates is Sorenson Squeeze. You can download a trial version of Sorenson Squeeze at *http://www.sorensonmedia.com*. Follow these steps to create several FLV files for your video clip:

1. Open Sorenson Squeeze. A new project is automatically created when you open the application.

2. From the Format & Compression Settings pane, expand the Macromedia Flash Video (*.flv*) grouping. Within the grouping, you'll find several data rate-specific presets, ranging from 56 Kbps to DVD-Video quality. The Flash Video presets are divided between Flash Player 6/7 compatible formats using Sorenson Spark and Flash Player 8 formats. All Flash Player 8 formats use the *VP6_ prefix* in the preset name. I recommend you use all seven Internet-ready presets, which include 56K, 112K, 256K, 384K, 512K, 768K, and 1 Mpbs, for the widest range of content distribution. Of course, you can elect to use only a few data rates depending on your server's storage capacity and bandwidth limitations. Drag each preset you wish to use to the Job pane on the right. Once you add all of the data rates you wish to use, you're ready to import clips.

 Each Sorenson Squeeze preset may use a different frame size. As such, you may want to edit each applied preset to have a consistent frame size, depending on the layout of the Flash movie that will display the video content. Otherwise, you could opt to scale all content to the largest frame size used by the highest data-rate preset. For example, if you encode a Flash Video file to 480×360 with the 1 Mbps_Stream preset, you could have all other data rates scale to the 480×360 frame size to keep a consistent layout with your Flash movie playing the content.

3. Click the Import File button in the Input pane at the top-left corner of the application window, or choose File → Import Source. Browse to one or more files that

you want to encode with the selected presets. Once the files are imported, the presets in the Job pane will be copied to each content clip. You can choose to edit any of the presets individually for each clip you have added, or apply additional filters (in the Filters pane) to each clip to adjust contrast, brightness, and audio levels.

4. Click the Squeeze It button in the lower right to begin the encoding process. Depending on the number of presets you have selected, the encoding process could take several hours to complete.

When you have encoded several data rates for your video content in Squeeze (or your preferred encoding application), you're ready to deploy a system that plays the appropriate *.flv* file for the user's available bandwidth. You can create your own ActionScript code that takes the user's detected bandwidth and picks the correct encoded FLV to play, or you can use the FLVPlayback component with a SMIL document.

SMIL, which stands for Synchronized Multimedia Integration Language, was developed by the W3C as a markup language to specify how text, audio, images, and video should be displayed in an interactive presentation. The most popular video player that uses SMIL is Real Systems' Real One Player, but it can also be consumed by other players such as Apple QuickTime and now Macromedia Flash Player. SMIL is just a specific schema to use with XML, and is very easy to use. You can specify the location, size, and number of data rates available for your Flash Video content, as shown in the following example:

```
<smil>
   <head>
      <meta base="http://www.flashsupport.com/video/" />
      <layout>
         <root-layout width="320" height="240" />
      </layout>
   </head>
   <body>
      <switch>
         <video src="sample_1Mbps_Stream.flv" system-bitrate="1000000" />
         <video src="sample_768K_Stream.flv" system-bitrate="768000" />
         <video src="sample_512K_Stream.flv" system-bitrate="512000" />
         <video src="sample_384K_Stream.flv" system-bitrate="384000" />
         <video src="sample_256K_Stream.flv" system-bitrate="256000" />
         <video src="sample_112K_Stream.flv" system-bitrate="112000" />
         <ref src="sample_56K_Dial_Up_Stream.flv"  />
      </switch>
   </body>
</smil>
```

The <head> section specifies the location of the video content, as a relative or absolute folder path on your web server (HTTP) or application URI on your Flash Communication Server/Flash Media Server (RTMP). The <body> section lists each FLV data rate, from highest bit rate to lowest. The last *.flv* file does not need to indicate its data rate, and will be chosen from the list as the default stream if the user's available bandwidth is lower than the second-to-last data rate listed.

If you use progressive Flash Video files (delivered from a standard web server), indicate the available bandwidth to the FLVPlayback component in ActionScript. If you serve the video content from a Flash Communication Server or Flash Media Server, you can upload the *main.asc* document included with Flash Professional 8's installation files to your application folder. This document has the necessary server-side handlers to communicate the available bandwidth directly to the FLVPlayback component at runtime. You can find the *main.asc* file in the *Samples and Tutorials\ Samples\Components\FLVPlayback* folder.

 The FLVPlayback component that shipped with Flash Professional 8 does not consume SMIL data correctly. As such, you need to reorder your content from lowest to highest, or use a corrected version of the component. You can find a fixed version of the component at *http:// www.flashsupport.com.*

To use SMIL data with the FLVPlayback component:

1. Create a new Flash document in Flash Professional 8.

2. Rename Layer 1 to cfp, short for component FLVPlayback.

3. Open the Flash document included in the fixed version download, and copy the FLVPlayback component from that document's library to your new document's stage.

4. Name the new instance cfp in the Property inspector.

5. Create a new layer named actions. On frame 1 of the Actions layer, open the Actions panel. Add the bandwidth detection code presented in the last recipe. After you have determined the bandwidth, set the bit rate value of the cfp instance and then load the SMIL document. If you're playing Flash Video from a Flash Communication Server or Flash Media Server, you should not include the bandwidth detection code or specify the bit rate value.

   ```
   cfp.bitrate = nDetectedBandwidth;
   cfp.contentPath = sample.smil;
   ```

6. Save the Flash document, and test the movie (Control/Command-Enter). When the SMIL data loads into the Flash movie, the FLVPlayback component chooses the appropriate *.flv* file to download, buffer, and play.

CHAPTER 19

Using Data

There was a time when Flash was used exclusively for timeline-based animations. However, many current Flash applications—even simple ones—load and send data to and from external resources. For example, a simple web site built in Flash might display news. In order to keep the news fresh, it's important to be able to load the text from an external resource, such as a text file or from a PHP page that retrieves the data from a database. If you have a comments form, you'll need to send data to a script. There are many potential uses of such data in Flash applications.

To work with data most effectively, you'll need to use ActionScript. In a few cases, the ActionScript will be relatively simple. For example, if you want to load variables from an external resource, the solution involves ActionScript as discussed in Recipe 19.1. However, there are also mechanisms for working with data in basic ways that do not require ActionScript. In this chapter, you'll read about solutions that use simple and/or minimal ActionScript. Non-ActionScript solutions are discussed where appropriate.

19.1 Loading Variables

Problem

You want to load variables at runtime.

Solution

Use a LoadVars object. Call the *load()* method.

Discussion

There are many reasons you might want to load variables at runtime. Loading variables at runtime makes applications more dynamic than they would be if you had to hardcode all values into the file. For example, if your application displays a new quote or snippet of text every week or month, you will find that loading the quote or text snippet at runtime is preferable to hardcoding the value. If you hardcode the value, you have to reexport the file every time you want to update the value. However, if you load the data at runtime you can simply update a text file or database field, and the data that's loaded into the Flash file is also updated.

You can load runtime variables from any source that can return URL-encoded text. URL-encoded text looks like a query string from a URL. URL-encoded text is composed of name-value pairs delimited by ampersands (&). Each name and value is delimited by an equals sign. For example, the following URL-encoded string defines two variables, color and area:

```
color=red&area=100
```

You can store URL-encoded data in a static text or HTML file, or you can output URL-encoded data from any valid resource, such as a PHP page or a ColdFusion page. Regardless of where the data resides, you use the same basic ActionScript code to load the data. You can use a LoadVars object to load URL-encoded data from an external resource. The first step is to construct the object as follows:

```
var lvSampleData:LoadVars = new LoadVars();
```

Then you need to define an *onLoad()* event handler method for the LoadVars object. The data isn't loaded immediately when it's requested. That means that Flash needs a way to receive a notification when the data is loaded—whether that takes milliseconds or seconds. The *onLoad()* event handler method is the way in which Flash receives the notification. When the data loads, Flash will automatically call the *onLoad()* method you define. The following example defines an *onLoad()* method for a LoadVars object called lvSampleData:

```
lvSampleData.onLoad = function(bSuccess:Boolean):Void {
  trace("data loaded");
};
```

Note that the *onLoad()* method is automatically passed a Boolean parameter indicating whether Flash was able to parse the data. The *onLoad()* method is always called as long as Flash was able to load data. Therefore, the Boolean parameter does not tell you whether the data loaded. Rather, it tells you whether Flash was able to parse the data into variables. If the parameter is true, each of the variables from the URL-encoded data is parsed into a property of the LoadVars object with the same name. For example, if you load the sample URL-encoded data (color=red&area=100), the LoadVars object will have properties called color and area. The following *onLoad()* method traces the values of those two properties.

```
lvSampleData.onLoad = function(bSuccess:Boolean):Void {
  if(bSuccess) {
    trace("color = " + this.color);
    trace("area = " + this.area);
  }
  else {
```

```
        trace("There is an error with the data.");
    }
};
```

After you've constructed the LoadVars object and defined the *onLoad()* event handler method, the next step is to tell Flash to load the data from the external resource. You can accomplish that by calling the *load()* method of the LoadVars object. The *load()* method requires one parameter specifying the URL of the resource. The following loads data from a file called *variables.txt* in the same directory as the SWF:

```
    lvSampleData.load("variables.txt");
```

When the *load()* method is called, Flash initiates a request to the specified resource. It then continues to run any code that follows and (if applicable) play back the timeline. When a response is returned, the *onLoad()* method is called. That means that you should not assume that the data will have loaded immediately following the call to the *load()* method. Any code that requires the values loaded from the external resource needs to be placed within the *onLoad()* method or within a function that is called by the *onLoad()* method.

This recipe describes how to load variables from URL-encoded data in external resources, such as HTML files, text files, PHP files, and so on. Generally, this works best when the values for the variables are fairly simple and short. The example values of red and 10 are good examples. When you want to load large blocks of text, it is generally much more convenient to load the data in the manner described in Recipe 19.3.

19.2   Sending Variables

Problem

You want to send variables to the server at runtime.

Solution

Use a LoadVars object. Call the *send()* method. Note that the *send()* method doesn't send values and always opens the response in a browser window. Optionally, to both send and load variables or to send variables transparently use the *sendAndLoad()* method.

Discussion

You can send variables to a script by way of the *send()* method of a LoadVars object. Sending data is useful when you want to record user or application events on the server. For example, when the user submits a form, you may want to send the data to a script running on a server.

The first step is to construct a new `LoadVars` object, as in the following example:

```
var lvDataSender:LoadVars = new LoadVars();
```

You then need to define values for custom properties of the object. Each property ought to have the name of the variable you want to send to the script. For example, the following code defines two custom properties for `lvDataSender` and assigns the values from two text input components called `ctiCity` and `ctiState`:

```
lvDataSender.city = ctiCity.text;
lvDataSender.state = ctiState.text;
```

When you've defined the custom properties, call the *send()* method. The *send()* method requires at least two parameters, specifying the URL of the resource to which you want to send the data (generally a script on a server) and the name of the window in which to open the response. The window name parameter is the name of an existing window, the name of a new window, or one of the following:

`_blank`
> A new window

`_self`
> The current frame

`_parent`
> The parent frame

`_top`
> The top-level frame

 The *send()* method always opens the response in a browser window. If you don't want to open the response in a window, use the *sendAndLoad()* method.

The following example sends the variables to a script called *form.cgi* running in the same directory as the SWF. It opens the response in a new window.

```
lvDataSender.send("form.cgi", "_blank");
```

By default, the variables are sent using the GET method. The `LoadVars` class enables either GET or POST. If you want to specify the method, you can do so with a third parameter to the *send()* method. The parameter must be a string with the value of GET or POST. The following sends the data using POST:

```
lvDataSender.send("form.cgi", "blank", "POST");
```

The *send()* method always opens the response in a browser window. That may be appropriate in some cases. However, there are many cases in which you want the sending or data to be transparent to the user. The *sendAndLoad()* method sends (and loads) data transparently, and it does not open the response in a browser window. Much of how the *sendAndLoad()* method works is very similar to how the *send()* method works. You must still construct a `LoadVars` object and define custom properties. Additionally, when you call the *sendAndLoad()* method, you must pass it a parameter specifying the URL of the resource to which you want to send the variables. However, because the *sendAndLoad()* method does not open the response in a browser window, you do not need to specify a window name. Rather, you must specify a LoadVars object that handles the response. The response LoadVars object is an object for which you've defined an *onLoad()* (or *onData()* (see Recipe 19.3) event handler method, as described in Recipe 19.1. The following example uses the same city and state variables and sends them to a script (*form.cgi*). However, it uses *sendAndLoad()*, and when the response is returned, the *onLoad()* method of lvReceipt is called:

```
var lvDataSender:LoadVars = new LoadVars();
lvDataSender.city = ctiCity.text;
lvDataSender.state = ctiState.text;
var lvReceipt:LoadVars = new LoadVars();
lvReceipt.onLoad = function(bSuccess:Boolean):Void {
  trace("server response");
};
lvDataSender.sendAndLoad("form.cgi", lvReceipt);
```

The *sendAndLoad()* method sends data via GET by default. As with the *send()* method, you can optionally pass the *sendAndLoad()* method a third parameter specifying whether to use GET or POST.

> The Test Player always sends data using GET even if you specify POST. If you want to test sending data via POST, you must test in a browser.

19.3 Loading Text

Problem

You want to load a block of text at runtime.

Solution

Use a LoadVars object. Use an *onData()* event handler method.

Discussion

Although you can load a large block of text as the value of a variable in the manner described in Recipe 19.1, it's frequently more convenient to load the text slightly differently. When a response is returned from a *load()* or *sendAndLoad()* method call, Flash automatically calls the *onLoad()* event handler method for the LoadVars object handling the response. However, there are a few steps that occur before the *onLoad()* method is called. First, the *onData()* event handler method is called. The *onData()* method is defined (by default) to parse the loaded data into properties of the

LoadVars object and then call the *onLoad()* method. Therefore, if you use the default behavior, you must load only URL-encoded data, or you will have no way to retrieve the data that was loaded, because Flash will not be able to correctly parse the data unless it is property encoded. However, if you override the default behavior, you can retrieve the data that's loaded before it's parsed. That means that you can load a block of (non-URL-encoded) text and assign it to a variable or display it in a text field, and so on.

You can override the *onData()* method by assigning a new anonymous function to the onData property. The *onData()* method is automatically passed a string parameter that contains the data that was loaded. The following example constructs a new LoadVars object, defines an *onData()* method that traces the loaded data, and loads the data from a text file:

```
var lvExample:LoadVars = new LoadVars( );
lvExample.onData = function(sText:String):Void {
  trace(sText);
};
lvExample.load("example.txt");
```

When you override the *onData()* method, the default behavior does not occur. That means that when you define a new custom *onData()* method, it no longer attempts to parse the loaded data and call *onLoad()*. If you define both an *onLoad()* and an *onData()* method, only the *onData()* method is called by default.

19.4   Loading XML Data with Components

Problem

You want to load XML data without having to write much ActionScript.

Solution

Use the XMLConnector component.

Discussion

XML stands for eXtensible Markup Language, which is a way of formatting data contextually for communication to and between applications. For example, an XML document may contain data you want to use within your application to populate components, URLs of images, and more. XML is formatted in a hierarchical style using tags that look similar to HTML tags. However, unlike HTML, the names of XML tags are arbitrary. Tags may be nested. In such cases you can describe the relationships between tags, or elements, as child, parent, and sibling. The following example has a parent element called book with two child nodes (that are siblings of one another) called title and authors:

```
<book>
  <title>ActionScript Cookbook</title>
  <authors>Joey Lott</authors>
</book>
```

ActionScript has an intrinsic XML class that enables you to work with XML. Although it would be misleading to suggest that working with ActionScript and XML is exceedingly difficult, there is a reasonably steep learning curve for the average Flash developer. If you want to work extensively with XML, it would be to your advantage to learn about using the ActionScript XML class, as it is a much more robust way of working with XML than a non-ActionScript solution. However, if your goal is to use XML in fairly simple ways (populating simple forms, for example) and you don't want to have to use ActionScript, you can use the XMLConnector component. That is the subject of this recipe.

The XMLConnector component is available in Flash Professional, and it allows you to utilize XML with little or no ActionScript. It can load XML from external sources as well as compose and send XML to a script. To use the XMLConnector component, the first step is to add an instance to the stage. You can accomplish that by dragging an instance from the Components panel (in the *Data* folder) to the stage. Then, as with most component instances, assign an instance name to the component on the stage by way of the Property inspector.

 The component has an icon that appears on the stage during authoring time. However, when you compile, the icon does not appear in the exported SWF.

After you've added an XMLConnector instance and given it an instance name, the next step is to set the necessary parameters in the Component Inspector panel. With the instance selected, open the Component Inspector panel (if it's not already visible). You'll need to set the following parameters:

URL
> The URL of the XML resource you want to load. The URL could be to an XML file or any resource that outputs XML (such as a PHP page).

direction
> When loading XML, set the direction to receive.

The remainder of the parameters can be left at their default values.

Next, you need to tell Flash when to load the XML. You can accomplish that by way of one line of ActionScript. You need to call the *trigger()* method of the XMLConnector component instance. For example, if the component instance is called cxcExample, the following code tells Flash to load the XML from the URL you specified in the parameters:

```
cxcExample.trigger();
```

Where you place the code depends on when you want to load the XML. If you want to load the XML when the application starts (assuming that you've placed the component instance on the first keyframe of the main timeline), you can place the ActionScript on the first keyframe of the main timeline. If you want to load the XML when the user clicks a button, you can place the code within an event handler method, as in the following example:

```
btLoadData.onPress = function( ):Void {
  cxcExample.trigger( );
};
```

The XML data loads and is parsed by the XMLConnector component instance. In order to do something useful with the data, you'll likely want to use the built-in data-binding feature of Flash in order to display the data in components. You can read more about data binding in Recipe 19.7. However, before you can properly use data binding with an XMLConnector component, you have to tell it what schema to use. The schema is the structure of the XML data. The XMLConnector uses that schema to enable data binding so that you can tell Flash which elements from the XML data ought to get displayed in which components. If the idea of telling the XMLConnector what schema to use sounds daunting to you, don't worry. It's as simple as a few clicks of the mouse.

Assuming that you are loading the XML from a static document, you can simply do the following:

1. Select the XMLConnector component instance.
2. Open the Component Inspector panel.
3. Select the Schema tab.
4. Select the results:XML option from the list.
5. Click on the Import icon in the upper-right corner of the Schema tab.
6. A dialog box will appear. It prompts you to select a file. Select the XML document, and click the Open button.

When you've completed the preceding steps, the XML schema will appear in the Schema tab list nested under results:XML. If you are loading the XML from a dynamic resource such as a PHP page, open that resource in a web browser. Save a copy of the XML data as an XML document on your local disk. Then complete the preceding steps. You'll still load the data from the dynamic resource. Importing the schema merely tells Flash what the structure of the XML document looks like. It doesn't actually load the data into your Flash application at that time.

You can download a working example file from *http://www.rightactionscript.com/fcb*.

19.5 Calling Web Service Methods with Components

Problem

You want to call a web service method without having to write much ActionScript.

Solution

Use the `WebServiceConnector` component.

Discussion

Web services are systems that are designed so that they can be called from remote computers over a network. Typically, web services are called over HTTP much like a standard web page request. That means that you can run applications or parts of applications by making HTTP requests. The benefit is that applications can be deployed over a network, and more sophisticated applications can be built by utilizing remote services. For example, Amazon.com has a public web service program. You can build an application that calls methods from the Amazon.com web service. That way your application can leverage the functionality of Amazon.com without having to reinvent the wheel.

Because applications can be built using many different technologies (such as Java, PHP, .NET, and C), there needs to be a standard way in which diverse applications can communicate. There are many standards utilized by web services. However, the standards that are most commonly used are WSDL and SOAP. WSDL (Web Services Description Language) describes the public interface for a web service. That means that a WSDL document describes the methods you can call for a web service. SOAP (which is currently no longer considered to be an acronym) is an XML-based messaging format used to send requests and responses. In practical terms, a WSDL document is the resource you point to when you want to call a web service method and you use SOAP packets to send requests and receive responses.

Flash has no native web service features. Flash Player does not natively understand SOAP. That means that calling web services from Flash could potentially be a challenging task. However, Flash Professional ships with a component called `WebServiceConnector` that enables you to call web service methods with little to no ActionScript. The `WebServiceConnector` component utilizes a library of functionality written in ActionScript that is capable of writing and reading SOAP packets and sending and receiving them using the native XML class. All the functionality is encapsulated for you, so that you can utilize the features by simply setting some parameters for a component instance.

To use `WebServiceConnector`, you must first add an instance to the stage. You can do so by dragging an instance from the Components panel (from the *Data* folder) to the stage. As with most components, you should assign an instance name to the component instance. When you've added an instance and assigned an instance name, you next need to assign values to a few parameters. To do so, select the component instance and open the Component Inspector panel. From the panel, assign values to the following parameters:

WSDLURL
> The URL to the WSDL resource.

operation
> The name of the web service method to call. When you've assigned a valid WSDLURL value, Flash will retrieve a list of valid operations from the WSDL and populate the operation drop-down menu.

The remaining parameters can generally be left with the default values.

After you've selected a valid operation, the component schema will auto-populate. That is necessary for proper data binding so that you can associate specific parameters or results values with specific components. You can read more about data binding in Recipe 19.7.

As with the XMLConnector component, you have to tell Flash when to send the web service request. You can accomplish that task with one line of ActionScript. The WebServiceConnector component defines a method called *trigger( )* that does just that. When you call the *trigger( )* method of the WebServiceConnector instance, Flash makes the SOAP request packet, sends it to the web service, and awaits a response.

You can download a working example file from *http://www.rightactionscript.com/fcb*.

19.6 Calling Flash Remoting Methods with Components

Problem

You want to call a Flash Remoting method without having to write much Action-Script.

Solution

Use the RemotingConnector component.

Discussion

Flash Remoting is a technology that enables incredibly effective and efficient client-server communications with Flash applications. Flash Remoting works in a manner similar to that of web services in many respects. It allows Flash clients to call methods of services that may be written in Java, PHP, .NET, or other languages. However, Flash Remoting uses a binary messaging format called AMF that is native to Flash Player. Thus Flash Remoting is often significantly faster than web services.

Flash Remoting requires a server-side gateway that is capable of receiving the AMF requests, delegating the requests to the appropriate services, and returning the AMF responses. ColdFusion ships with a Flash Remoting gateway by default. So does JRun. Macromedia also sells Flash Remoting gateway products for J2EE application servers and .NET. You can learn more about the Macromedia Flash Remoting products at *http://www.macromedia.com/software/flashremoting*. In addition, there are non-Macromedia Flash Remoting gateway products. WebOrb (*http://www.themidnightcoders.com*) is available in both standard (free) and professional editions. WebOrb is available in both J2EE and .NET versions. FLAP (*http://www.simonf.com/flap*) is an open source product for Perl and Python. AMFPHP (*http://www.amfphp.org*) is an open source product for PHP. And OpenAMF (*http://www.openamf.org*) is an open source product for J2EE.

Although to utilize Flash Remoting fully it's recommended that you use Action-Script, the necessary ActionScript may involve a relatively steep learning curve for a Flash developer with little ActionScript experience. For basic Flash Remoting operations, you can use the `RemotingConnector` component that requires little to no Action-Script. The `RemotingConnector` component is the focus of this recipe.

The `RemotingConnector` component does not ship with Flash. However, if you have Flash Professional, you can download the `RemotingConnector` component for free from *http://www.macromedia.com/software/flashremoting/downloads/components*. When you've installed the component, it will be available from the *Data Components* folder of the Components panel.

The first step is to add an instance of `RemotingConnector` to the stage. You can drag an instance from the Components panel to the stage, and then assign the component an instance name. After you've assigned an instance name, you can assign values to parameters. To do so, select the instance and open the Component Inspector panel. Then assign values to the following parameters:

`gatewayUrl`
> The URL to the gateway. The gateway is the server resource that parses AMF and delegates the requests to the appropriate services. It's a servlet, ASP.NET page, PHP page, and so on, and it's always the same regardless of what service you are requesting.

`serviceName`
> The name of the service you are requesting. Generally, it's the fully qualified class name.

`methodName`
> The name of the method from the service that you want to call.

Unlike the WebServiceConnector component, the RemotingConnector component doesn't automatically populate the schema. That means that you have to correctly define the schema. With the RemotingConnector component, you generally have to define the schema by way of the add and delete field buttons in the Schema tab. From the Component Inspector panel, select the Schema tab. Then use the add and delete buttons in the upper-left corner of the tab. The button on the far left adds a new top-level field. Generally that is unnecessary, as Flash Remoting operations consist of requests (params) and responses (results). You can use the second button to define new fields nested under params and/or results. For example, if a Flash Remoting method requires two parameters, you would want to define two fields nested under params. For each field you can use the name/value portion of the panel to define the correct name and data type.

As with the XMLConnector and WebServiceConnector components, you need to tell Flash when to make the Flash Remoting request. You can accomplish that with the *trigger()* method. The RemotingConnector class defines a *trigger()* method that you can call from the instance. Place the ActionScript code on the first keyframe if you want to make the call as soon as the application starts. Place the code within a button event handler method if you want to make the call when the user clicks a button.

You can download a working example file from *http://www.rightactionscript.com/fcb*.

19.7   Displaying Data with Components

Problem

You want to display data in a component when it is loaded from XML, a web service, or Flash Remoting, and you don't want to have to write any ActionScript.

Solution

Use data binding.

Discussion

Frequently an XMLConnector, WebServiceConnector, or RemotingConnector call returns data that you want to display to the user. You can certainly use ActionScript to accomplish that task. However, given that the primary purpose of the components is to keep you from having to write ActionScript to work with data, it would seemingly defeat the purpose to have to write ActionScript to display the data. Instead you can use a feature called data binding.

Data binding associates a field from the component schema with a component. For example, if a web service call returns a string, you can associate the return value with a text area component and Flash will automatically display the value in the component as soon as it is returned.

To work with data binding, use the Bindings tab from the Component Inspector panel. In the upper-left corner of the Bindings tab, you'll see two buttons: Add binding and Delete binding. Click the Add binding button to add a new association, by opening the Add Binding dialog box. The dialog box displays the component schema. It's important that you've defined the correct schema before you add a binding. From the dialog box, select the field from the schema that you want to associate with a component. When you click OK, the dialog box will close and the new binding is added to the list in the Bindings tab. When you select the item from the list the name/value portion of the panel displays the binding details. You always need to define the following parameters:

direction

> The direction defines how the data moves from component to component. If you select in, the data moves from the associated component to the current component. If you select out, the data moves from the current component to the associated component. If you select in/out, the data moves both ways—if the data changes in either component then the data is updated in both.

bound to

> When you double-click on the value column, the Bound To dialog box opens, and you can select from the existing components that you want to associate with the current component. You are requested to select a component and a property of the component (or a field of the component's schema).

When you add a binding to a component, a corresponding binding is added to the associated component. For example, consider the case in which you have a WebServiceConnector called cwscExample and a TextArea component called ctaExample. When you add a new binding to cwscExample that binds the results field to the text property of ctaExample with a direction of out, a corresponding binding is added to ctaExample. In the ctaExample binding, the binding is for the text property. It is bound to the results field of cwscExample with a direction of in.

The example files available from *http://www.rightactionscript.com/fcb* demonstrate data-binding features.

19.8   Formatting Data with Data Binding

Problem

You want to format data that is displayed via data binding.

Solution

Use a formatter.

Discussion

Although standard data binding may work in many cases, there are at least as many cases in which you'll want to display the data in a slightly different manner than what is returned. For example, you may use an `XMLConnector` component to load the following XML document:

```
<book>
  <title>ActionScript Cookbook</title>
  <authors>Joey Lott</authors>
</book>
```

If you want to display both the title and the authors in a text area component, you'll have to apply formatting that tells Flash how to display the data.

When you assign values to the settings of a binding in the Bindings tab of the Component Inspector panel, there are two parameters for formatting called formatter and formatter options. The formatter parameter is set to none by default, and when the formatter parameter is set to none the formatter options is grayed out. However, you can apply formatting by selecting a new value for the formatter parameter. The options are as follows:

Boolean
: Converts strings to Boolean values.

Compose String
: Allows you to make a string value that is composed of a combination of string literal values and field values.

Custom Formatter
: The custom formatter option requires advanced ActionScript to implement, and it is not discussed in detail in this book.

Date
: When a date value is returned, you can format that value in a user-friendly format.

Rearrange Fields
: Use the rearrange fields formatter when you want to compose a new object utilizing the values from the original object. The original value must be an object, and the target must also require an object.

Number Formatter
: Defines how many fractional digits to display.

Each formatter type allows you to define different formatter options:

Boolean
: Specifies which string values should get converted to the Boolean values `true` and `false`.

`Compose String`

A string that can use string literal text as well as fields from the original value. Use `<fieldName>` to indicate field placeholders. For example, if you apply a binding for a schema field with nested fields `title` and `authors`, you can use the following template:

The title is `<title>` and the author(s) is/are `<authors>`.

`Date`

You can compose a string in which MM stands for the month, DD stands for the date of the month, YY stands for the year in two-digit format, YYYY stands for the year in four-digit format, HH stands for the hours, NN stands for the minutes, and SS stands for the seconds.

19.9 Sending Data Using Data Binding

Problem

You want to send data to the server when making a service call, but you don't want to have to write much ActionScript.

Solution

Use data binding to send data from components to the service.

Discussion

In Recipe 19.7, you learned how to use data binding to display data that is returned from a connector component call. You can also use data binding to determine what values to send to a service via a connector component. For example, a web service method may require a parameter. You can use data binding to tell Flash to retrieve the value for that parameter from a component.

The majority of data binding is the same regardless of whether you're displaying returned data or sending data from components. Refer to Recipe 19.7 for details on data-binding basics. When you are sending data as parameters via data binding, you'll want to add bindings from component properties to the connector component's params field or fields nested under the params field. There are a few additional considerations, discussed in this recipe.

When you are sending data as parameters, you most frequently won't need to format or encode the data. For example, if you allow the user to select a book from a list of books in a combo box and then send that to a Flash Remoting service as a parameter, you may not need to encode or format that data. Likewise, if you want to send a date parameter from a `DateChooser` or `DateField` component, you won't need to encode or format that value. However, there are cases in which your application requires greater sophistication. For example, if the combo box of books consists of elements that have id and title properties and you want to send a string in the format of id, title, you'll need a formatter. Likewise, if you want to allow the user to specify a date as a string in a text input component, you'll have to encode that as a Date object if that's what the service method requires. You can accomplish formatting and encoding via the Schema tab of the Component Inspector panel.

Formatting from the Schema tab works very much like formatting from the Bindings tab, as discussed in Recipe 19.8. From the Schema tab, select the field for which you want to apply the formatting. Then select the correct formatter from the formatter parameter menu, and apply the correct formatter options.

Encoding allows you to convert values before they are sent. For example, if you ask the user to specify a date value in a text input component in a particular format (such as MM/DD/YYYY) and the service method requires a Date object, you'll have to encode the string as a Date object. In such a case, use the Date encoder and specify MM/DD/YYYY for the encoding options.

The distinction between formatting and encoding may not be immediately obvious. Specifically, it may be unclear why both the formatter and encoder drop-down menus have Boolean, Date, and Number (Formatter) options. Think of formatters and encoders as having opposite effects. Where a formatter converts a Boolean, date, or number to a string, the encoder converts from a string to a Boolean, date, or number.

CHAPTER 20

Building Preloaders

Flash movies begin playback as soon as the first frame is loaded. This default behavior generally works well with compact Flash vector graphics. However, when you use other kinds of assets—notably, bitmap graphics, sound, video, and/or Flash components—Flash's default behavior can lead to stuttered, delayed, and broken playback. The cause of the unacceptable playback is that Flash is forced to try to play frames back that haven't been loaded yet.

For example, imagine a movie that has a frame rate of 12 frames per second. On frame 12, a keyframe contains a bitmap graphic that is 36 kilobytes in size. Even assuming that there is no other content in the movie, to display this frame at the proper time, Flash would have to download at a rate of 36 kilobytes per second, or 3 kilobytes for every frame. But a user on a modem may be able to download only 2–4 kilobytes per second. In this case, the playhead would reach frame 12 before its contents were loaded, and Flash would stop playback and wait for the content to load. Obviously, the lower the user's bandwidth, the more pronounced the problems are; thus, modem users are much more likely to experience poor playback than users on a corporate intranet.

Flash has a built-in tool, the Bandwidth Profiler, which can be used to simulate the playback of a movie at different connection speeds. For example, you can have Flash play back the movie assuming that the movie downloads at a rate of 4.7 kilobytes per second, which is roughly equivalent to the operating speed of a 56K modem. This simulation reveals whether problems in playback are likely and, if so, where in the timeline they're likely to happen.

Flash lacks a simple setting to tell it not to begin playback until the movie can stream properly. However, you can create equivalent functionality by creating a preloader. A *preloader* prevents Flash from playing the movie until part or all of the SWF has already downloaded. The most basic preloader holds the playhead on frame 1, which contains a message such as, "Loading..." until the necessary amount of content has loaded; then the movie begins normal playback.

One problem with a simple loading screen is that users have no idea how long they have to wait. If a simple loading screen is on the monitor without change for 30 seconds, users may suspect that the movie is broken and leave the site. Fortunately, you can add feedback that communicates the preload progress to the user, in the form of a numeric percentage that increases as the content is preloaded or in the form of a progress bar. This chapter contains recipes for both of these types of preloader.

You can check how much content has loaded into the Flash player using two movie clip methods called *getBytesLoaded()* and *getBytesTotal()*. Respectively, these two methods return the number of bytes that have been downloaded and the number of bytes overall that are required for the whole movie. You can divide the former by the latter to determine what percentage of the file has downloaded.

20.1   Determining How a Movie Will Download

Problem

You want to test the playback of a movie simulating different connection speeds, identify frames with assets too large to play back progressively, and/or determine whether you need a preloader.

Solution

Use the Bandwidth Profiler.

Discussion

The Bandwidth Profiler is available within the testing environment in Flash. That is, it is accessible when you test a movie by choosing Control → Test Movie. To access it, choose View → Bandwidth Profiler. The top half of the test player displays the Bandwidth Profiler.

The Bandwidth Profiler analyzes the file size of assets needed to download in each frame and plots the file size as bars on a graph. The values on the left side of the bar vary based on the size of the assets in the movie. The bottom line on the graph, or stream limit, shown in red, represents the dividing line between movies that will stream acceptably and those that may have problems during playback. If any frame has a column extending beyond the stream limit, the movie is unlikely to play back acceptably. Figure 20-1 shows a movie with bitmaps placed every fourth frame. All of these frames extend far beyond the stream limit; this movie would need a preloader to ensure acceptable playback.

The value of the stream limit is relative to the connection speed and frame rate. That is, if you have Flash simulate playback for a 56K modem at 12 frames per second, the

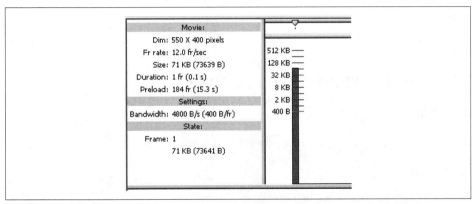

Figure 20-1. A movie needs a preloader when it contains frames that exceed the red line

line will appear at 400 bytes. However, if you change the playback simulated setting to a 28.8 modem, the line will appear at 200 bytes. If you increase the frame rate to 24 frames per second for a 28.8K modem, the line appears at 100 bytes because the content would essentially have to download twice as fast as it did when the frame rate was 12 frames per second in order to keep up with the playback.

You can change the connection speed by selecting it from the View → Download Settings menu. Built-in options range from 14.4K modems to T1 connections. You can also create your own custom settings by selecting the Customize option from that same menu.

In addition to seeing the graph depicting how a movie will download, you can have Flash simulate the download for a given bandwidth. Specify the connection speed in the View → Download Settings menu, and then select View → Show Streaming, or press Control-Enter (Windows) or Command-Return (Macintosh). Flash plays back the movie at the specified rate, pausing to simulate frames that have not yet downloaded.

The Bandwidth Profiler has two practical limitations:

- The Bandwidth Profiler can estimate how well a movie will stream only for a given setting. Other factors, such as network congestion, the quality of the phone line (for modem users), and demands on the server also affect how quickly content is downloaded.

- When Show Streaming is active, Flash simulates the download of the current *.swf* file. It also simulates the download of assets (JPEG, GIF, PNG, or MP3) that is loaded at runtime using MovieClipLoader or Sound if the assets are loaded using a relative URL. However, it will not correctly simulate the download of any *.flv* files, or simulate the download of any assets that use an absolute URL.

See Also

Recipe 20.2

20.2   Building a Simple Preloader

Problem

You want to create a basic preloader, which will ensure smooth playback of a movie.

Solution

Attach a preloader script to the first frame of the movie.

Discussion

To add a simple preloader to any movie, attach the following script to the first frame of the timeline:

```
stop( );
var nPreloaderInterval:Number = setInterval(this, "checkPreloader", 100);

function checkPreloader( ):Void {
  var nLoadedBytes:Number = this.getBytesLoaded( );
  var nTotalBytes:Number = this.getBytesTotal( );
  if(nLoadedBytes >= nTotalBytes) {
    clearInterval(nPreloaderInterval);
  play( );
  }
}
```

This script stops the playhead in the first frame, preventing further playback, until the preloader has verified that the entire SWF has loaded. It then uses an interval function to poll the SWF for the download progress every 100 milliseconds or so. When the number of downloaded bytes equals the total number of bytes, it knows that the file has downloaded entirely. At that point, it stops the interval and plays the timeline.

From a functional standpoint, this script accomplishes what it sets out to: it guarantees the smooth playback of the movie. However, it communicates none of this to the user. That is, while the script is busy determining whether the movie has fully loaded, the user sees only the content on frame 1. At a minimum, you should also put a message in frame 1 that indicates that the movie is loading and will begin playback when it has loaded. Users will have no way of knowing how long they will have to wait, but at least they won't initially assume the movie is broken. Place the contents of the main movie beginning on frame 2 or another frame, which you can specify by substituting a *gotoAndPlay( )* action in place of the *play( )* action.

To test the functionality of the preloader, add it to a Flash document with a large bitmap, sound, or other asset on frame 2 or later and test the movie (Control → Test Movie). Be sure to choose View → Show Streaming for the full effect.

See Also

Recipe 20.1, Recipe 20.3, Recipe 20.4

20.3 Building a Preloader that Displays Load Percentage

Problem

You want to build a preloader that continually updates a display of the percent loaded.

Solution

Divide *getBytesLoaded()* by *getBytesTotal()*, multiply the output by 100, and use a dynamic text field to display the output.

Discussion

The basic preloader script discussed in the previous recipe serves as the foundation for this preloader script. With the preceding script, nothing happens until the movie is fully downloaded, at which time the `if` statement checking load status evaluates to true, a *play()* action is executed, and the preloader movie clip is removed.

In this variation of the script, I've added a line of code (shown in boldface) that outputs the percent that has loaded to a dynamic text field on the stage:

```
stop( );
var nPreloaderInterval:Number = setInterval(this, "checkPreloader", 100);

function checkPreloader( ):Void {
  var nLoadedBytes:Number = this.getBytesLoaded( );
  var nTotalBytes:Number = this.getBytesTotal( );
  tProgress.text = Math.round(nLoadedBytes / nTotalBytes * 100) + "% downloaded";
  if(nLoadedBytes >= nTotalBytes) {
    clearInterval(nPreloaderInterval);
    play( );
  }
}
```

In addition to adding the script, you need to add the dynamic text field to the stage in frame 1. Create a dynamic text field, and give it an instance name of tProgress.

See Also

Recipe 8.2, Recipe 20.2

20.4 Using a Progress Bar to Create a Graphical Preloader

Problem

You want to create a preloader that displays a progress bar indicating how much of the movie has loaded.

Solution

Modify the script from Recipe 20.2 to update the _xscale property of a movie clip.

Discussion

Although simply displaying a text-based progress indicator to the user (as in Recipe 20.3) may work for some applications, you'll more frequently want to display the progress in some sort of visual, animated manner. The most common such indicator is the progress bar. The progress bar, as the name suggests, is a rectangular shape (the bar) that indicates the progress as the file downloads. Although you can certainly make more elaborate sorts of indicators, the progress bar is the standard, and the basic principals in creating a basic progress bar apply to any progress indicator.

The script in Recipe 20.2 takes care of the majority of the work in creating any sort of basic preloader—graphical or not. So you'll want to use the same script when adding a progress bar. However, you'll want to then add just one line of code (shown in boldface):

```
stop( );
var nPreloaderInterval:Number = setInterval(this, "checkPreloader", 100);

function checkPreloader( ):Void {
var nLoadedBytes:Number = this.getBytesLoaded( );
var nTotalBytes:Number = this.getBytesTotal( );
mProgressBar._xscale = nLoadedBytes / nTotalBytes * 100;
if(nLoadedBytes >= nTotalBytes) {
  clearInterval(nPreloaderInterval);
  play( );
}
}
```

The new line of code tells Flash to adjust the scale in the x-direction for a movie clip called mProgressBar such that it corresponds to the percentage of the file that has downloaded. Therefore, in order for the code to be effective, you must add a movie clip instance to the stage with an instance name of mProgressBar. That movie clip ought to contain rectangular artwork that is left-aligned (meaning that the left edge of the rectangle shape is positioned at 0).

20.5 Creating Preloaders for Files with Exported Symbols

Problem

Your have a file that exports movie clips for ActionScript, and you want to add a preloader.

Solution

Use the same preloader principles discussed earlier in this chapter. In addition, uncheck the "Export in first frame" option for each exported movie clip within the library.

Discussion

As you learned in Recipe 11.17, you can tell Flash to export a movie clip symbol even if it is not used at authoring time. That enables you to programmatically add instances of the movie clip using ActionScript. With a few simple movie clips exported for ActionScript, you won't likely notice any effect on the preloader. However, with many complex (particularly bitmap) movie clips that are exported for ActionScript, you may start to notice that the preloader doesn't appear immediately. It's possible that the preloader may not even appear until most of the file has downloaded. This is due to the default setting for movie clips exported for ActionScript—they are set to export on the first frame. Thus every exported movie clip must download before Flash will play back even the first frame.

There is a relatively simple solution, however. Although the default setting is such that Flash-exported movie clips are exported on the first frame, you can tell Flash to use an alternate frame instead, with the following steps:

1. Uncheck the "Export in first frame" option for each movie clip symbol. You can access the option from the Linkage properties dialog box. By default, the "Export in first frame" option is checked when you check the "Export for ActionScript" option. However, when the "Export for ActionScript" option is selected, you can independently toggle the state of the "Export in first frame" option.

2. Place instances of the movie clips on the stage at authoring time. That way Flash knows what frame to use in order to export the symbol.

The second step may seem counterintuitive. However, it is simply the way in which you communicate to Flash where to export the symbol. The dilemma that arises is then that you frequently don't want those symbols to appear in the exported movie on any frame unless they were placed there with code. So placing an instance on the stage at authoring time seemingly defeats the purpose, or at least causes an obstacle. The solution is to approach the Flash project in a somewhat nonlinear fashion. Even though a timeline plays from first frame to last frame by default, there's no reason it has to do that. As you've already learned, you can use simple ActionScript commands to tell Flash to stop, play, and jump to any frame within a timeline. Therefore, you can always place the movie clip instances on a frame that is never played. For example, you can place the preloader on frame 1, the movie clip symbol instances on frame 2, and then the actual content starting on frame 3. Within the script on frame 1, you can instruct Flash to jump to frame 3 once the file has downloaded.

20.6   Creating Preloaders for Files with Components

Problem

Your movie contains components, and they prevent the preloader from appearing until the movie is almost entirely loaded.

Solution

Use the same principles as discussed in Recipe 20.5. Additionally, assign a frame other than 1 to the Export frame for classes field.

Discussion

Components are special movie clips. And by default they are set to export on the first frame. That means that in order to properly preload an SWF that uses components you must employ the same strategy as is discussed in Recipe 20.5. However, in addition to the challenges presented by exported movie clips, components present a new challenge. Unlike standard exported movie clips, components are composed not only of graphical elements, but they consist also of ActionScript code. That ActionScript code is placed in special structures called *classes*, and those classes can account for rather significant file size. For example, the Loader component is approximately 27KB, almost all of which is due to the code in classes.

Like exported movie clips, classes export on the first frame by default. That means that all the code in all the classes used by an SWF must download before the first frame can play back, during which time the the user waits at a blank screen for seconds or even minutes. However, it's remarkably simple to adjust the export frame for the classes used by a Flash file:

1. Open the Publish Settings by selecting File → Publish Settings.
2. Select the Flash tab.

3. Click on the Settings button to the immediate right of the ActionScript version menu.

4. Enter a frame number greater than 1 in the Export frame for classes field.

5. Click OK.

In order for a component to properly work, you must make sure that the classes it requires are exported on a frame before the component is used.

CHAPTER 21

Publishing Flash

After you've built your Flash animation or application, you need to publish it. Do you want to publish it to the Web? As a standalone executable? How do you want the content to scale? Does the Flash content need to communicate with the container application, such as the web browser? These are just a few of the many things you must ask when publishing Flash content. Each common scenario is discussed in this chapter.

21.1   Publishing Flash to the Browser

Problem

You want to publish an *.swf* file for playback in a web browser.

Solution

Select the HTML option in the Publish Settings, and publish from Flash. Optionally, add the <object> and <embed> tags to the HTML manually.

In either case, you must upload the *.swf* file as well as the HTML file when placing content on a web server.

Discussion

When you want Flash content to play back in a web browser, you must add the HTML code to embed the content in the HTML page. The code tells the browser to play back a specific *.swf* file in Flash Player. There are two Flash Player versions that can potentially be embedded within a web browser: the ActiveX player for Internet Explorer running on Windows and the Flash Player plug-in for the remaining browsers. Each player version requires different HTML code. For the ActiveX player, you must add an <object> tag, and for the plug-in, you must add an <embed> tag. Generally, you'll want HTML code that can work in every browser, so you'll need to add both the <object> and <embed> tags. Because there are two tags, and because of the potential number of attributes and parameters for each, it can be difficult to remember the necessary code in order to successfully embed Flash content within a web browser. However, Flash simplifies publishing Flash content to a browser by way of the Publish functionality provided by the IDE.

If you want to publish content to a web browser using the built-in Publish functionality within Flash, you need to set the correct Publish Settings. You can access the Publish Settings by way of the File → Publish Settings menu option. From the Formats tab within the Publish Settings dialog box, make sure that both Flash and HTML are selected. That step will cause the dialog box to have two additional tabs corresponding to each of the selected options. In the Flash tab, you can select the settings specific to the SWF format that you want to publish (Flash 7, Flash 8, and so on). However, the HTML tab has the settings you'll most likely want to configure to determine how the Flash content is displayed within the browser.

From the Template menu, you'll almost always want to select the default value of Flash Only. If you are deploying content to a server using HTTPS, you can select the Flash HTTPS template. The two templates are nearly identical, except that one uses the HTTP protocol to specify the location of the download if the player isn't detected, and one uses HTTPS.

By default, the dimensions of the Flash Player instance embedded in the HTML are the same as the dimensions of the Flash document. However, you can also select Pixels or Percent from the Dimensions menu, and you can specify different values.

The HTML alignment menu lets you specify how the Flash Player instance is aligned within the HTML page. You can align it to the upper-left (Left or Default) or upper-right (Right). The behavior of the settings is up to the browser. You might expect that Top and Bottom would cause the Flash Player to be placed at the top and bottom of the page, respectively; yet it seems that no popular browsers implement that behavior.

The Scale menu options can profoundly affect how your Flash content displays within Flash Player. The default setting is "Show all," which means that as Flash Player scales, so too the content scales while maintaining the same aspect ratio. When you select the "Show all" option, the entire stage always displays within Flash Player, even if it is necessary to add borders to the right and left or top and bottom. For example, if the Flash document's dimensions are 550×400 and the Flash Player dimensions are 600×400, when the scale mode is set to "Show all," there will be a 25-pixel border on the right and left sides (assuming the content is aligned center) within Flash Player. If you never want Flash Player to display a border, you can select the "No border" option. The "No border" option also causes the content to scale with Flash Player, and it also maintains the aspect ratio. However, unlike "Show all," "No border" can cause the content to be cropped if the aspect ratio of Flash Player isn't the same as the aspect ratio of the Flash document. The "Exact fit" option causes the content to scale with Flash Player without maintaining the aspect ratio.

And the "No scale" option causes the content to remain at the default dimensions regardless of whether Flash Player is scaled.

When the Flash Player and the content have the same dimensions or when the scale mode is set to "Exact fit," there's no need to control how the content aligns within Flash Player. However, when the Flash Player scales and the content either does not scale or scales in such a way that it might have added borders or be cropped, you can control how the content aligns within Flash Player. The Publish Settings dialog box enables you to select options for both horizontal and vertical alignment. By default, they are both set to Center. You can also select Left or Right for horizontal alignment and Top or Bottom for vertical alignment. If you set the scale mode to "No scale," by default the content always remains in the center of Flash Player regardless of how the player is scaled. However, the alignment options enable you to instruct the content to align differently. For example, you can apply settings of Left and Top. Then, as Flash Player scales, the content always remains aligned to the upper-left corner of the player.

From the Publish Settings dialog box, you can click the Publish button, and Flash will publish the SWF and the HTML document. Optionally, at nearly any time you can select File → Publish (Shift-F12) to publish the content.

As mentioned previously, two HTML tags are required to embed Flash content in an HTML document that will work across every browser, because there are two Flash Player versions for browsers. The <object> tag is necessary for IE on Windows, and the <embed> tag is necessary for the rest. Obviously, each page request originates from just one browser, and so for any given page request, you want to display only one Flash Player version—either the ActiveX version or the plug-in version. You could write JavaScript that determines which browser type has made the request, and you could then output only the <object> or only the <embed> tag. However, a simpler approach is possible, because each browser will effectively ignore the tag it doesn't understand if they are coded correctly. The correct way to add the <object> and <embed> tags is to nest the <embed> tag within the <object> tag. When IE makes the request, it will run the <object> tag, and because it won't understand <embed> as a valid nested tag for <object>, it will ignore it. Likewise, when a browser such as Firefox makes the page request, it will ignore the <object> tag, but it will not ignore the nested tags such as <embed>.

The HTML that Flash exports is minimal. It has the basic HTML structure (<html>, <body>, etc.) However, if you want to embed the Flash content within a more sophisticated HTML document, you have several options. You can export the default HTML from Flash, then copy and paste the <object> and <embed> tags from that HTML document to the more sophisticated HTML document. Optionally, you can write the <object> and <embed> tags by hand, or you can use an application such as Dreamweaver that has a UI that facilitates adding Flash content to HTML pages. Regardless, it is good to at least familiarize yourself with the basics of the <object> and <embed> tags.

The following example shows the basic code necessary to embed Flash Player in an HTML document:

```
<object classid="clsid:d27cdb6e-ae6d-11cf-96b8-444553540000" codebase="http://
fpdownload.macromedia.com/pub/shockwave/cabs/flash/swflash.cab#version=8,0,0,0"
width="100%" height="100%" id="example" align="middle">
  <param name="allowScriptAccess" value="sameDomain" />
  <param name="movie" value="example.swf" />
  <param name="quality" value="high" />
  <param name="scale" value="noborder" />
  <param name="bgcolor" value="#FFFFFF" />
  <embed src="example.swf" quality="high" scale="noborder" bgcolor="#ffffff"
width="100%" height="100%" name="example" align="middle"
allowScriptAccess="sameDomain" type="application/x-shockwave-flash"
pluginspage="http://www.macromedia.com/go/getflashplayer" />
</object>
```

Notice that the <object> and <embed> tags have effectively the same data. The <object> tag uses some attributes (width, height, id, align, and so on) as well as nested <param> tags, while the <embed> tag uses attributes exclusively. The <object> tag defines a classid and a codebase attribute. Both of those attributes remain the same any time you are adding Flash 8 content. Likewise, the <embed> tag uses a pluginspage attribute and a type attribute that are always the same. The remainder of the attributes and <param> tags are generally self-explanatory. Most of the values correspond to the settings from the Publish Settings dialog box. The one exception is the allowScriptAccess attribute and <param> tag. The allowScriptAccess setting is discussed in more detail in Recipe 21.5.

21.2 Making Flash Content that Works with DHTML Menus

Problem

You want to use Flash content within an HTML page that uses DHTML menus, but the menus are obscured by the Flash content.

Solution

Use the transparent wmode setting.

Discussion

By default, Flash Player uses a window mode called window. In the default mode, Flash Player appears as though it's rendered within the browser window, but it's actually rendered in its own window space above the browser. That is the most efficient way for Flash Player to work. However, it presents some obvious issues if you want to display HTML content in front of Flash Player. No matter what, when Flash Player is using the window setting, no HTML content can appear in front of it.

You can also select from opaque and transparent window modes. If you select either opaque or transparent, Flash Player runs within the browser, and it can interact with HTML elements. That means that HTML elements can appear in front of Flash Player when the window mode is either opaque or transparent. Flash Player does not run as efficiently as it would with the window setting. (On most computers there's not likely to be a noticeable difference.) The opaque mode is more efficient than transparent, because the background of Flash Player is opaque. That means that no content that is at a lower z-index on the HTML page will be visible through the Flash content. If you use transparent mode, the Flash Player background is transparent, and content at lower z-indices will be visible through the Flash content.

You can set the window mode from the Publish Settings dialog box. From the HTML tab, you can select an option from the Window Mode menu. Optionally, you can set the value directly in the HTML. For the <object> tag you need to add a nested <param> tag called wmode:

```
<param name="wmode" value="opaque" />
```

For the <embed> tag, add a wmode attribute.

21.3 Detecting Flash Player Version

Problem

You want to detect the Flash Player version so you know that the user can view the published content.

Solution

Use the Detect Flash Version option in the Publish Settings dialog box, and then publish the *.swf* and *.html* files.

Discussion

When you publish SWF and HTML content from Flash 8, add Flash Player detection by clicking the Detect Flash Version checkbox in the Publish Settings dialog box. Unlike previous versions of Flash, the Flash 8 version detection script requires no additional files and pages aside from the standard SWF and HTML page. You don't have to write (or copy) complicated scripts. You don't have to manage lots of files. Selecting the Detect Flash Version checkbox in the Publish Settings dialog box automatically adds the necessary script to the published *.html* document.

Just below the Detect Flash Version checkbox, you can specify the minimum player version that you require. The major version is always the version of the SWF that you are publishing. For example, if you are publishing the SWF to Flash Player 8, the major version is 8. You can also specify minor version and incremental revision values if you want to require later player revisions. The Flash player detection script will test that the user has the required player version. If she does, the Flash content plays normally. If not, by default the user is presented with a basic HTML page that tells the user she must download a newer version of Flash Player to view the content. If you want to customize the alternate content, you can edit the following part of the HTML/JavaScript that is published in the HTML document:

```
} else {  // flash is too old or we can't detect the plugin
  var alternateContent = 'Alternate HTML content should be placed here.'
    + 'This content requires the Macromedia Flash Player.'
    + '<a href=http://www.macromedia.com/go/getflash/>Get Flash</a>';
  document.write(alternateContent);  // insert non-flash content
}
```

The preceding code is the `else` clause of a JavaScript if statement. It runs only if the user doesn't have the required version of Flash Player. You can edit the code between the opening and closing curly braces ({}) so that it displays different content or so that it redirects to a different page.

21.4 Passing Parameters to Flash from HTML

Problem

You want to pass parameters from HTML to Flash when the Flash content loads into the player.

Solution

Use the `flashvars` parameter/attribute with the `<object>` and `<embed>` tags.

Discussion

Frequently, you may want to pass some value from the HTML document to the Flash content when it loads. For example, you may have previously prompted the user for his name from an HTML form, and you may want to pass that to the Flash content. You can pass parameters from HTML to Flash content when the Flash content loads using something called `flashvars`. The `flashvars` parameter for the `<object>` tag and the `flashvars` attribute for the `<embed>` tag enable you to pass data from HTML to the Flash content. The value of the `flashvars` parameter/attribute needs to be in URL-encoded format. That means that the value looks like the value that normally composes a query string in a URL. The value can be one or more name-value pairs in which each name and value is delimited by an equals sign, and each pair is delimited by an ampersand. The following is an example of a URL-encoded string that defines two name-value pairs:

```
first_name=Joey&last_name=Lott
```

The basic syntax of `<object>` and `<embed>` tags is discussed in Recipe 21.1, and you can review that recipe if any part of the basic syntax in the following code is unfamiliar to you. The emboldened sections of the code are an example of the additional code that defines the flashvars parameter and attribute. In the example, two parameters are being passed to the Flash content—first_name and last_name:

```
<object classid="clsid:d27cdb6e-ae6d-11cf-96b8-444553540000" codebase="http://
fpdownload.macromedia.com/pub/shockwave/cabs/flash/swflash.cab#version=8,0,0,0"
width="100%" height="100%" id="example" align="middle">
  <param name="allowScriptAccess" value="sameDomain" />
  <param name="movie" value="example.swf" />
  <param name="quality" value="high" />
  <param name="scale" value="noborder" />
  <param name="bgcolor" value="#FFFFFF" />
  <param name="flashvars" value="first_name=Joey&last_name=Lott" />
  <embed src="example.swf" quality="high" scale="noborder" bgcolor="#ffffff"
width="100%" height="100%" name="example" align="middle"
allowScriptAccess="sameDomain" flashvars="first_name=Joey&last_name=Lott"
type="application/x-shockwave-flash" pluginspage="http://www.macromedia.com/go/
getflashplayer" />
</object>
```

When the Flash content loads, the parameters are passed to the *.swf* as variables on the main timeline. For example, the *.swf* from the preceding example can reference variables called first_name and last_name on the main timeline.

21.5   Communicating Between Flash and JavaScript

Problem

You want to call a JavaScript function from Flash or an ActionScript function from JavaScript.

Solution

Use the ExternalInterface class in ActionScript.

Discussion

Prior to Flash 8, it was difficult to build Flash applications that integrated well with the container within which Flash Player was embedded. The most common example is one in which you want Flash Player to be able to communicate with the web browser. When authoring for Flash Player versions prior to 8, the optimal solution was to use the Flash/JavaScript Integration Kit (*http://weblogs.macromedia.com/flashjavascript/*). However, the ExternalInterface ActionScript class simplifies things significantly. ExternalInterface requires that you are publishing to Flash Player 8 or higher.

The ExternalInterface class enables Flash Player to make calls to functions within the container. In the case of Flash Player embedded in a web page, that means that Flash Player can call JavaScript functions. And ExternalInterface also enables the container to call ActionScript functions. That means that JavaScript can call Action-Script functions, and thus you can build integrated web applications in which Flash and the web browser are able to communicate.

The `ExternalInterface` class is in the `mx.external` package. Therefore, you'll generally want to import the class. The rest of the code in this recipe assumes that you've imported the class with the following code:

```
import flash.external.ExternalInterface;
```

When you want to call a JavaScript function from Flash, you can use the *ExternalInterface.call()* method. The *call()* method requires at least one parameter specifying the name of the JavaScript function to call. For example, if the HTML page within which Flash Player is embedded defines a function called `updateForm`, you can call that function from ActionScript using the following code:

```
ExternalInterface.call("updateForm");
```

Supposing that the function accepts parameters, you can pass those parameters to the function by adding those parameters to the parameter list of the *call()* method. For example, if `updateForm` expects four parameters (a string, a number, a Boolean, and an array), the following will pass parameters to the function:

```
ExternalInterface.call("updateForm", "a", 2, true, [1, 2, 3, 4]);
```

Additionally, *ExternalInterface.call()* works synchronously: if the JavaScript function returns a value, you can use that return value as part of an ActionScript expression. For example, if `updateForm` returns a Boolean value, the following code assigns that value to a variable within ActionScript:

```
var bFormUpdated:Boolean = ExternalInterface.call("updateForm", "a", 2, true, [1, 2,
3, 4]);
```

When you want to call an ActionScript function from JavaScript, there are a few steps you should take:

1. Register the ActionScript function as a callback using *ExternalInterface.addCallback()*.
2. Within the JavaScript, retrieve a reference to the Flash object.
3. Call the registered function from the Flash object.

The *ExternalInterface.addCallback()* method enables you to register a function so that you can call it from JavaScript. The method requires the following parameters:

methodName
> A string specifying the name by which the function is to be registered. The registered name is the name by which you can call the function from JavaScript.

instance
> The object that will be referenced by this within the function when it is called.

method

A reference to the function or method that you want to register.

The following code defines a function called *rotateClip()* that rotates a movie clip (mClip) by the number of degrees specified by the parameter:

```
function rotateClip(nDegrees:Number):Void {
  mClip._rotation = nDegrees;
}
```

Assume that the function is defined on the main timeline. Then the following code, if also placed on the main timeline, registers the function so it can be called from Java-Script. It is registered so that from JavaScript it can be called by the name rotate instead of rotateClip.

```
ExternalInterface.addCallback("rotate", this, rotateClip);
```

The second parameter says that when *rotateClip()* is called from JavaScript, it is called as a method of the main timeline.

When a function is registered, it is possible to call it from JavaScript. In order to call the function from JavaScript you first have to retrieve a reference to the Flash object. How you retrieve the reference to the Flash object depends on the browser. If the browser is IE for Windows, the Flash object is determined by window.*objectID* where *objectID* is the value of the id attribute of the <object> tag. If the browser is not IE for Windows, the Flash object is determined by document.*embedName* where *embedName* is the value of the name attribute of the <embed> tag. You can determine whether the browser is IE Windows by testing whether navigator.appName contains the value Microsoft. The following code defines a function that returns the Flash object where the <object> id attribute and the <embed> name attribute are both examples:

```
function getFlashObject() {
  if(navigator.appName.indexOf("Microsoft") != -1) {
    return window.example;
  }
  else {
    return document.example;
  }
}
```

You can then call the ActionScript function from the Flash object by the registered name. For example, the following code calls the registered rotate function. Notice that you can pass parameters to the function.

```
var exampleFlashObject = getFlashObject();
exampleFlashObject.rotate(50);
```

21.6   Integrating Flash with the Browser Back Button

Problem

You want your Flash application to work with the browser back button.

Solution

Use a frameset with a hidden SWF that uses `LocalConnection` to communicate with the main SWF.

Discussion

One of the major usability drawbacks with Flash in a web browser is that by default it doesn't integrate with the browser back button. People are used to clicking the back button on the browser to navigate back through a web site or application. However, normally when a user clicks on the back button when a Flash application is running in the browser, it causes the browser to return to the HTML page that was open prior to the Flash application. Even if the user was navigating through the Flash application for the past hour, the default behavior of the back button causes the browser to jump out of the Flash application entirely. That can cause users to feel frustrated, particularly if the application doesn't have a way of remembering the state, so that the user has to start over again when clicking the forward button to return to the Flash application.

Although there is a feature in Flash called Anchors that is supposed to correct the issue with the back button, the feature does not work with most browsers, and it appears to have been deprecated in Flash 8. However, with a little work, it is possible to build a Flash application that works with the browser back button in every browser. This approach requires the following:

- A navigator *.swf* file and the *.html* file within which the content is embedded. The navigator SWF does not need any artwork because it is hidden from the user.
- A frameset HTML page that has two frames. One frame adds the navigator SWF such that it is hidden. One frame displays the main content.
- A main *.swf* file and the *.html* file within which the content is embedded.
- The main SWF must define a `LocalConnection` object that listens for navigation commands.
- The navigation commands within the main SWF must use *getURL()* to load the navigator SWF in a hidden frame with parameters passed to indicate the navigation command.

The way it works is that the main SWF listens for navigation commands from the navigator .swf. Every time the user navigates through the main SWF, it calls *getURL()*

to load the navigation HTML page in the hidden frame, and it passes the navigator a parameter or parameters specifying the navigation commands. For example, when the user clicks on a button in the main SWF, it might call the following code:

```
getURL("navigator.html?frame=2", "navigator");
```

The preceding code tells the browser to load *navigator.html* in a frame called navigator. Presumably. the navigator frame is hidden. When *navigator.html* is loaded, it is passed a query string of frame=2. The HTML page then passes the parameters along to the navigator SWF. The navigator SWF then uses LocalConnection to call a function within the main SWF, and it passes that function the navigation commands. That way a new (hidden) page is loaded each time the user navigates through the main SWF. And when the user clicks the back button, the hidden page gets loaded again with the navigation parameters from the browser history list. That means that the back button can effectively manage the navigation of the main SWF.

Let's consider a specific example. In the following example, a main SWF has four movie clip buttons and four frames. The four movie clips are called mA, mB, mC, and mD. When the user clicks the buttons, Flash jumps to a specified frame on the main timeline. For example, when the user clicks on mA, it jumps to frame 1, and when the user clicks on mB, it jumps to frame 2. The application requires the following code on the first keyframe of the main timeline:

```
// Only run the following code once. If lcNavigator is defined then the code was
already run, so
// don't run it again.
if(lcNavigator == undefined) {

  // The LocalConnection object, lcNavigator, is the way in which the main SWF can
listen
  // for commands from the navigator SWF. In this case it's listening for messages sent
  // over a channel called _navigation. That means that the navigator SWF must send
the messages
  // using the same channel.
  var lcNavigator:LocalConnection = new LocalConnection();
  lcNavigator.connect("_navigation");

  // Define a method called navigate() that expects one parameter specifying the
frame number to
  // which to navigate. The navigate() method name is arbitrary, but the navigator
SWF must know
  // the name of the method so it can call the method in order to send the navigation
  // instructions.
  lcNavigator.navigate = function(nFrame:Number):Void {
    gotoAndStop(nFrame);
  };

  // Define event handler methods for the movie clip buttons. In each case call
getURL() such that
  // BackButtonNavigator.html gets loaded into the navigator frame with a query
string specifying
```

```
// the frame number to which to jump.
mA.onPress = function( ):Void {
  getURL("BackButtonNavigator.html?frame=1", "navigator");
};
mB.onPress = function( ):Void {
  getURL("BackButtonNavigator.html?frame=2", "navigator");
};
mC.onPress = function( ):Void {
  getURL("BackButtonNavigator.html?frame=3", "navigator");
};
mD.onPress = function( ):Void {
  getURL("BackButtonNavigator.html?frame=4", "navigator");
};

// Tell the timeline to stop.
  stop( );
}
```

For the purposes of this example, we'll assume that the main SWF is embedded in an HTML document called *BackButtonMain.html* using standard HTML <object> and <embed> tags as discussed previously in this chapter.

The navigator SWF is very simple. It simply calls the *navigate()* method of the main SWF by way of LocalConnection. It passes the method the frame number that it retrieves using flashvars. The code for the navigator Flash document is as follows:

```
var lcNavigator:LocalConnection = new LocalConnection( );
lcNavigator.send("_navigation", "navigate", frame);
```

The HTML for the navigator is slightly unconventional, because it must use JavaScript to pass the data from the query string to the SWF via flashvars. Assuming that the *.swf* file is called *BackButtonNavigator.swf*, the code for the HTML looks like the following:

```
<html>
<body bgcolor="#ffffff">
<script language="JavaScript">

// Define a variable that contains the <object> and <embed> tag text. This is
necessary because
// part of the code must be dynamically determined from the query string.
var html = '<object classid="clsid:d27cdb6e-ae6d-11cf-96b8-444553540000"
codebase="http://fpdownload.macromedia.com/pub/shockwave/cabs/flash/swflash.
cab#version=8,0,0,0" width="550" height="400" id="BackButtonNavigator"
align="middle">';
html += '<param name="allowScriptAccess" value="sameDomain" />';
html += '<param name="movie" value="BackButtonNavigator.swf" />';
html += '<param name="quality" value="high" />';
html += '<param name="bgcolor" value="#ffffff" />';

// The following adds a flashvars parameter that has a value such as frame=1 or
frame=2
html += '<param name="flashvars" value="' + location.search.substring(1) + '" />';
```

```
// The following <embed> tag string also uses location.search to retrieve the query
string value
// and assign it to the flashvars attribute.
html += '<embed src="BackButtonNavigator.swf" quality="high" bgcolor="#ffffff"
width="550" height="400" name="BackButtonNavigator" align="middle"
allowScriptAccess="sameDomain" type="application/x-shockwave-flash"
pluginspage="http://www.macromedia.com/go/getflashplayer" flashvars="' + location.
search.substring(1) + '" />';
html += '</object>';

// Write the code to the document.
document.write(html);
</script>
</body>
</html>
```

Assuming that the preceding HTML page is called *BackButtonNavigator.html*, the
frameset HTML looks like the following:

```
<html>
  <frameset rows="0,*" frameborder="0">
    <frame name="navigator" src="BackButtonNavigator.html" />
    <frame name="main" src="BackButtonMain.html" />
  <frameset>
</html>
```

Notice that the navigator frame has a height of 0, which effectively hides that frame.

21.7   Publishing Projectors

Problem

You want to publish a standalone executable version of your Flash document.

Solution

Publish a projector file.

Discussion

Flash may be most frequently associated with the Web, but there are many ways in
which Flash can be utilized. In some cases, you may want to publish Flash content as
a standalone executable. The benefit is that you can distribute the Flash content
without requiring the user to have Flash Player installed.

The simplest way to publish an executable version of your Flash content is to publish a projector. From the Publish Settings dialog box, you can select Windows Projector and/or Macintosh Projector. When you select one or both of those options,
Flash will export the projector file(s) when you publish. You can then just double-
click the projector file to launch the Flash content.

There are third-party applications that export projectors from Flash content as well. The third-party applications have additional options not normally available to standard projectors. For example, they allow you to customize the titlebar and the file icon.

- Zinc: *http://www.multidmedia.com*
- Flash Jugglor: *http://www.flashjester.com*
- SWF Studio: *http://www.northcode.com*
- mProjector: *http://www.screentime.com*

21.8 Making Fullscreen Flash Projectors

Problem

You want a projector to play in fullscreen mode.

Solution

Use the *fscommand( )* ActionScript function to tell Flash to play in fullscreen mode.

Discussion

You can tell a projector to play fullscreen using the following ActionScript code:

```
fscommand("fullscreen", true);
```

21.9 Printing Flash Content

Problem

You want to print content from Flash.

Solution

Use the PrintJob ActionScript class.

Discussion

When you want to print Flash content, you always have the option of allowing the user to select the Print option from the Flash Player context menu. However, that is neither an obvious UI action for the user, nor does it offer much control over what will print. Instead, the better way to manage printing of Flash content is to use the PrintJob class.

The PrintJob class enables you to print one or more pages of content while prompting the user with just one dialog box. The PrintJob class enables you to print content from any frame of any movie clip, and you can even specify printable regions and how to optimize the printing depending on whether the content uses bitmaps or vectors.

The first step when working with the PrintJob class is to construct a new instance, and assign that to a variable. You can construct a new instance by using the constructor method, as in the following example:

```
var pjContent:PrintJob = new PrintJob();
```

Next, call the *start()* method in order to prompt the user with the Print dialog box. Flash doesn't allow you to print unless the user clicks OK from the dialog box. The *start()* method is synchronous. That means that the ActionScript interpreter halts when the *start()* method is called until the user clicks OK or Cancel from the Print dialog box. When the user clicks one of the buttons, a Boolean value is returned to Flash. If the user clicks OK, the value is true. If the user clicks Cancel, the value is false.

```
var bOkayToPrint:Boolean = pjContent.start();
```

As previously mentioned, you can print only if the user clicks OK and the return value is true. If the user clicks Cancel, adding pages and sending them to the printer will not work. Therefore, you can use an if statement to test if the Boolean value returned from *start()* is true. Only if it is true do you want to add pages and send them to the printer.

```
if(bOkayToPrint) {
    // Code to add pages and send them to the printer.
}
```

You can use the *addPage()* method to add pages. At a minimum, the *addPage()* method requires one parameter specifying the movie clip to print. For example, if you have a movie clip called mText, the following adds that movie clip content as a page:

```
pjContent.addPage(mText);
```

Although adding a movie clip in that fashion may work in many cases, there are many cases in which additional parameters are necessary or in which you might need to scale and/or rotate the movie clip. For example, mText may need to span several pages. Or perhaps the movie clip is aligned to print in portrait mode (taller than it is wide), but the user has selected to print in landscape mode. You can manage all these settings by specifying additional parameters when calling *addPage()*. You'll also need to retrieve values from the PrintJob object that specify the user's print settings.

When you call *start()* and the user is presented with the Print dialog box, he or she has the option of selecting the paper size as well as the print orientation. When the user clicks OK, those settings are sent back to Flash and stored in properties of the PrintJob object from which you called *start()*. Specifically, you can retrieve the page dimensions from the pageWidth and pageHeight properties, and you can retrieve the orientation from the orientation property. The pageWidth and pageHeight properties return the dimensions of the printable page region in points (which are the equivalent of pixels, in this case). The orientation property will have a value of either portrait or landscape. You can then use those properties to determine how to add pages.

By default, Flash attempts to print the entire movie clip specified by the parameter to the *addPage()* method. Any content that extends beyond the printable region is cropped. Flash doesn't automatically scale the content, nor does it automatically span more than one page. If you want to scale the content to the printable region, you can set the _xscale/_yscale or _width/_height properties of the movie clip just before calling *addPage()*. For example, the following scales mArtwork to the dimensions of the printable region, then adds the page:

```
mArtwork._width = pjContent.pageWidth;
mArtwork._height = pjContent.pageHeight;
pjContent.addPage(mArtwork);
```

Note that you'll want to reset the dimensions of the movie clip after sending the pages to the printer. Because the code executes before the frame refreshes, the user will not see the movie clip scale.

In the preceding example, mArtwork doesn't necessarily maintain the aspect ratio. If you need to scale the content while maintaining the aspect ratio, you need slightly more sophisticated ActionScript. First, you can determine the ratios of the widths and heights. You want to then scale the object by the lesser of those ratios.

```
var nWidthRatio:Number = pjContent.pageWidth / mArtwork._width;
var nHeightRatio:Number = pjContent.pageHeight / mArtwork._height;
var nScale:Number = 100 * Math.min(nWidthRatio, nHeightRatio);
mArtwork._xscale = nScale;
mArtwork._yscale = nScale;
pjContent.addPage(mArtwork);
```

You may also need to rotate content depending on the page orientation the user has selected. If content is taller than it is wide and the user has selected landscape, you'll need to rotate the content by 90°.

```
if(pjContent.orientation == "landscape") {
  mArtwork._rotation = 90;
}
pjContent.addPage(mArtwork);
```

In addition to the one required parameter for *addPage()*, there are several optional parameters. You can specify a printable region, how to optimize the printing based on whether the content contains bitmaps, and what frame to print. The second parameter lets you specify the printable region by way of an object with xMin, xMax, yMin, and yMax properties. By default, Flash attempts to print the region starting at 0,0 and spanning the entire content in the lower-right quadrant of the movie clip. If you want to print content that appears above or to the left of 0,0, if you don't want to print some part of the default content, or if you want to start the page at a point that is not 0,0, you can specify the second parameter when calling *addPage()*. The following code adds the region from 100,100 as the upper-left corner and 400,400 as the lower-right corner:

```
pjContent.addPage(mArtwork, {xMin: 100, xMax: 400, yMin: 100, yMax: 400});
```

You can use the print area parameter to span a movie clip's content on several pages. For example, the following code causes mArtwork to span four pages:

```
pjContent.addPage(mArtwork, {xMin: 0, xMax: 400, yMin: 0, yMax: 400});
pjContent.addPage(mArtwork, {xMin: 0, xMax: 400, yMin: 400, yMax: 800});
pjContent.addPage(mArtwork, {xMin: 400, xMax: 800, yMin: 0, yMax: 400});
pjContent.addPage(mArtwork, {xMin: 400, xMax: 800, yMin: 400, yMax: 800});
```

By default, Flash assumes that you are printing vector content, and optimizes the printing with that setting. However, if the content contains bitmaps, you'll want to tell Flash to optimize for bitmap printing. You can accomplish that by passing a third parameter to the *addPage()* method with a value of {printAsBitmap: true}. If you want to pass a third parameter, but you want to use the default print area, you can specify null as the second parameter.

```
pjContent.addPage(mArtwork, null, {printAsBitmap: true});
```

The fourth parameter lets you specify a frame to print. By default, Flash assumes you want to print frame 1. You can optionally specify the frame number as follows:

```
pjContent.addPage(mArtwork, null, null, 5);
```

After you've added a page or pages, you can call *send()* to send to the printer.

```
pjContent.send( );
```

Then, regardless of whether the user clicked OK or Cancel, delete the PrintJob object. You should place the following code outside the if statement:

```
delete pjContent;
```

21.10 Hiding the Context Menus

Problem

You want to hide the context menu.

Solution

Use the Stage.showMenu property.

Discussion

By default, Flash movies display a context menu when the user right-clicks/Control-clicks. The default context menu contains options to zoom, change the quality, open the Flash Player settings, print, and display the About Macromedia Flash Player Web page. (The test player has slightly different context menu items.) You cannot completely hide the context menu. However, you can hide most of the items except the Settings and About Macromedia Flash Player. You can accomplish that with one line of ActionScript code:

```
Stage.showMenu = false;
```

If you want to completely hide the context menus, you'll have to export the Flash content as a projector using one of the third-party projector exporting applications that enables that sort of functionality.

 It's possible to customize the context menus by adding custom items. Doing so requires some detailed ActionScript and is primarily useful only when writing sophisticated ActionScript applications. Therefore, it is not within the scope of this book.

CHAPTER 22

Deploying Flash on Mobile Devices

We are lucky as Flash developers. The latest surveys show that more than 95% of all web users worldwide are able to view some level of Flash content. The dominance of Flash as the Web's rich media delivery platform is clear.

In the mobile arena, however, there is no one dominant technology for rich media and content delivery. Technologies utilized vary by carrier, phone manufacturer, and phone platform (I will spare you the acronyms). Macromedia hopes to change this with the introduction of Flash Lite.

Flash Lite appeared in 2003 as Flash Lite 1.0, which provided Flash developers with the opportunity to easily create compelling, rich content for mobile phones using the IDE they know and love. Flash Lite 1.1 (the current version as of the writing of this book), released in 2004, provides additional features, including the ability to communicate with web servers over HTTP.

Flash Lite 1.1 is based on the Flash 4 scripting engine and the Flash 5 object model; the next version of Macromedia's Flash Lite player (2.0) will be based on Flash Player 7 and includes support for ActionScript 2.0 and other exciting new features. Although many techniques for Flash Lite carry over directly from Flash development for the Web (including the IDE), the following solutions will help you address issues related specifically to Flash Lite development.

22.1   Creating a Flash Lite Movie

Problem

You want to create a movie for the Flash Lite Player.

Solution

Open Flash MX 2004 Professional or Flash 8 Professional and create a Flash document with "Flash Lite 1.0" or "Flash Lite 1.1" publish settings.

Discussion

In order to author content for Flash Lite, you must be using the Professional version of Flash MX 2004 or Flash 8. The Flash Lite 1.1 authoring tools are part of the standard install of Flash 8 Professional. If you are using Flash MX 2004, the Flash Lite 1.1 authoring components are automatically installed after you have installed the 7.2 updater. The Flash 7.2 updater is available at:

http://www.macromedia.com/support/flash/downloads.html

If you are using Flash MX 2004 Professional but do not want to install the 7.2 updater, you can also install the Flash Lite 1.1 authoring components manually by downloading the Flash Lite 1.1 CDK (Content Development Kit) from the Mobile and Devices Developer Center:

http://www.macromedia.com/devnet/devices/flashlite.html

If you are looking for a reason to upgrade to Flash Professional 8, the improved Device Templates interface (discussed in this recipe) and the new Mobile Emulator functionality (discussed in Recipe 22.2) are compelling features that make Flash Professional 8 a worthwhile investment if you plan on doing any significant amount of Flash Lite development.

When you have the necessary software installed, you can create a movie for the Flash Lite Player by following these steps:

1. Open a new Flash document (File → New, General tab, Flash Document) or open an existing Flash document you'd like to publish for Flash Lite.
2. Open the Publish Settings pane (File → Publish Settings...) and select the Flash tab.
3. Select Flash Lite 1.0 or Flash Lite 1.1 in the version pull-down menu.
4. Click OK to save the settings. You will notice that the Document pane now indicates Flash Lite 1.0 or Flash Lite 1.1 as the player.
5. Publish your movie (File → Publish or Shift+F12)—the resulting SWF is a Flash Lite SWF.

If you started with a new Flash document, your stage was set to its default dimensions, or 550×400 pixels. Mobile device screens, however, are significantly smaller in size. You can specify the dimensions of the device that you are targeting either manually or by utilizing Device Templates. The manual method is as follows:

1. Open the Document Properties dialog box (Modify → Document...), and set the dimensions manually. For reference, the accepted "standard" screen size for Flash Lite mobile phones is 176 pixels (width) × 208 pixels (height).

The Device Templates method is as follows:

1. Open a new document in Flash (File → New).
2. Select the Templates tab.

3. Select one of the Global Phones, Japanese Phones, or PDAs categories (Flash 8) or the Mobile Devices category (Flash MX 2004).

4. Select the template you'd like to use.

5. Click OK to bring up your new Flash document, and click off of the stage to ensure that the Document pane is active. Note that the document's settings have been preset to match the selected device's player version, content type, and display size.

6. If you are using Flash MX 2004, the top layer of your document is named "Preview (Delete this layer)." You should highlight and delete this layer, as it is used only to provide the preview image for the Templates tab of the new document window.

7. Publish your movie (File → Publish or Shift+F12)—the resulting *.swf* file's version matches the version of the player installed on the device you selected. If you explore the templates, you will see that, in addition to the phones that support Flash Lite 1.0 and 1.1, some PDAs support Flash Player 6.

22.2   Using the Mobile Emulator

Problem

You want to test a Flash Lite movie.

Solution

View the movie in the Mobile Emulator.

Discussion

Flash MX 2004 included a very simple (and often confusing) Flash Lite emulator. Flash 8 includes a new Mobile Emulator, which provides greatly enhanced Flash Lite testing capabilities. To use the Mobile Emulator:

1. Create a new Flash Lite movie (or open an existing one).

2. Test the movie (Control → Test Movie or Command-Enter).

When issuing the Test Movie command on a Flash Lite document, the Mobile Emulator is launched in place of the standard Test Movie window. If you created the movie using a device template (see Recipe 22.1 for discussion of device templates), the Test Device list is pre-populated with the appropriate devices. If you set the document's publish settings to Flash Lite manually, the Test Device list is populated with your default device list or <None Selected>.

Flash 8 initially ships with more than 90 device emulators for your testing needs. The devices are grouped by content type, manufacturer, carrier, and platform.

There are 22 different Flash Lite content types (also known as application modes). Each Flash Lite device supports a subset of this group. Some devices, for example, can support Flash animations for incoming calls. In this chapter, and in the Flash Lite development community, focus is on content for the Standalone Player and Browser content types, as these content types support the most advanced set of features. The Standalone Player is the content type we will be working with in Recipe 22.4. The Browser content type is used when you want to deploy Flash content inline to mobile web browsers that support Flash Lite content.

To select target devices for testing:

1. From the Test Device drop-down menu, select Device Settings... or on the document pane, click on the Settings... button next to the Device label. The Device Settings window is opened.

2. From the Content type drop-down menu, select a content type. For example, if you want to distribute your SWF as a standalone movie that can be played on the handset, select Standalone Player.

3. Folders that are tinted blue (Mac) or enabled (PC) in the Available Devices selection box contain devices that support your selected content type. Note that a device may be listed in multiple folders—the Nokia 7610, for example, is listed in both Manufacturers → Nokia and Symbian → Series 60, as it is a Nokia phone running the Symbian Series 60 platform.

4. As you drill down into the folder hierarchy, you will see that certain device icons are also tinted blue (Mac) or enabled (PC)—these are the devices that support your selected content type.

5. You can highlight individual device(s) and click Add to move them to your Test Devices list. You can also highlight a folder to move all devices in that folder (and subfolders) to your Test Devices list, though doing so is often undesirable, as it will move a device even if that device doesn't support your selected content type.

6. If there are certain devices that you want to use often for testing Flash Lite content, arrange those devices in the Test Devices list and click Make Default. Each time you test a Flash Lite movie in the Flash Lite emulator that was not created from a device template, these devices will appear for testing.

7. Devices supporting Flash Lite are expected to be released quite frequently in the future. The Device Settings window has a link titled "Check for new devices," which takes you to a page on Macromedia's web site that allows you to download the latest device emulators. You can also visit the web site directly at *http://www.macromedia.com/software/flash/download/device_profiles/*.

8. When you are satisfied with your selections, click OK to save these settings. Note that the settings apply to only the currently active Flash document.

The devices you have selected are now available in the Test Device menu. Each time you change your selection, the selected device loads in the right panel, and your movie loads into that device. You can test the interactivity of your movie using either the keyboard or by mousing over the buttons on the device skin.

By default, the Trace and Warnings checkboxes are enabled. The output window will warn you if, for example, an ActionScript function you have called is unsupported by the selected device. Additionally, try enabling the Information checkbox for more instruction. When the movie loads, you are presented with detailed information regarding this device's features and capabilities.

See Figure 22-1 for an example of testing a remote webcam monitoring application in the Flash Professional 8 Mobile Emulator.

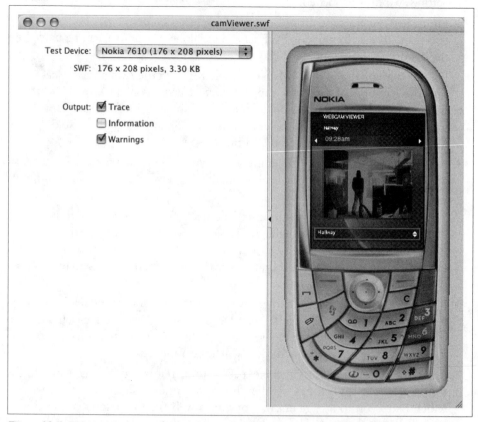

Figure 22-1. Testing a remote webcam monitoring application in the Flash Professional 8 Mobile Emulator

22.3 Finding Supported Devices

Problem

You want to determine which devices support Flash Lite.

Solution

Visit Macromedia's Mobile and Devices "Supported Devices" web site.

Discussion

The Flash Lite Player is supported on many mobile phones, and the number of supported models is increasing rapidly. Recent commitments by Nokia and Samsung to integrate the Flash Lite Player into their phones will only serve to increase the pace of penetration. There is also a Flash Player 6 version for the Pocket PC and a Flash Player 5 version for the Sony Clie.

Because the list of supported devices changes frequently, visit Macromedia Mobile and Devices "Supported Devices" web site to see which devices currently support Flash Lite:

http://www.macromedia.com/mobile/supported_devices/

You should also periodically check the "Device Profile Updates" web site at *http://www.macromedia.com/software/flash/download/device_profiles/* so you can test your movie on the latest devices with the Mobile Emulator (see Recipe 22.2).

22.4 Playing a Flash Lite Movie on a Device

Problem

You want to test the Flash Lite movie on a mobile device.

Solution

Install the Flash Lite Player on your device and use a USB cable, memory card, Bluetooth, or IR to transfer the SWF to your device.

Discussion

You have created your Flash Lite project and have run it through its paces in the mobile emulator. You are now ready to test the movie on your phone.

As of the writing of this book, the Flash Lite Player is available for sale only to developers who want to get a head start in developing content for Flash Lite. Individuals who own supported devices can purchase the software at *http://www.macromedia.com/*

software/flashlite/. It is expected that the Flash Lite Player will soon be delivered to end users preinstalled on devices and will not need to be purchased.

When you have purchased and installed the Flash Lite Player, you will need to transfer the *.swf* file to the device. Depending on the capabilities of your device, you can use a USB cable, memory card, Bluetooth, or IR to transfer the SWF to your device. If you are using a Nokia device and have access to a Windows 2000 or Windows XP machine, you can easily transfer the files using the Nokia PC Suite:

> *http://www.nokiausa.com/support/pcsuite/*

An alternative option for delivery is to store the SWF on a web server and access the SWF by its URL using a mobile web browser. Note that this method requires you to have a subscription to a data plan with your wireless carrier and to have set up your phone's GPRS settings properly. Also note that carriers typically assess charges for data access. To access your SWF using this method, follow these steps:

1. Upload your SWF file to a publicly available URL on your web server. For example, upload the file to *http://<server name>/mobileProjects/test.swf*.

2. Open a mobile browser application on your device. If you do not already have one installed, a good choice is the Opera Mobile Browser, available at *http://opera.com/products/mobile/products/*.

3. Open the URL that you specified in step 1 in your mobile browser.

4. After downloading the file, the SWF file should launch in the Flash Lite Player.

If you are having difficulty accessing data content and are using a Nokia device, Nokia offers an excellent Phone Configurator, which assists you in entering the correct data settings on your device. After you enter your phone model, wireless carrier, and phone number on their web site, Nokia sends you a series of Smart SMS text messages. When you open these messages, you receive a dialog box requesting your permission for your settings to be changed. This feature makes an otherwise tedious and confusing process quite simple. Access the application at:

> *http://www.nokiausa.com/support/settings/*

22.5   User Navigation for Flash Lite

Problem

You want to allow the user to navigate your Flash Lite movie.

Solution

Add button instances to the stage and assign actions to the press event.

Discussion

Perhaps the most complex user interface challenge you will face when designing your Flash Lite movie will be that of user navigation. When designing Flash movies for the Web, you can rely on the user having access to a mouse, trackpad, or other user input device that allows direct access to any area of the stage. When designing for Flash Lite, you cannot make such an assumption. Although PDAs and even some mobile phones (UIQ phones, such as the Sony Ericsson P910, for example) support stylus input, most phones do not.

The most basic Flash Lite 1.1 devices support three-way navigation: Up, Down, and Select. More advanced models additionally provide support for the Left and Right keys (five-way navigation). In either case, Flash Lite provides built-in key-based navigation for the movie based on button instances on the stage. An example of five-way navigation is shown in Figure 22-2.

A *button instance* is an instance of the Flash button symbol type and is used to respond to user input through various events. Note that unlike Flash movies published for the desktop Flash Player, Flash Lite 1.1 movies do not support movie clip events such as *onKeyDown()*, so you will need to use button instances extensively when responding to user input.

There are five basic steps to creating a button instance for your Flash Lite movie:

1. Insert a new symbol (Insert → New Symbol...) and select the Button behavior. The name you enter will be used to identify this button in the library.

2. Add content to the stage. This content will serve as the Up state for your button and will be displayed when the button does not have the active focus.

3. In most cases, you will want to provide alternate content for the Over state. Click on the Over frame and insert a frame (Insert → Timeline → Frame or F5). Make modifications to the content as desired. Note that the content need not be static—animated movie clips and other advanced effects can be included as well.

4. Exit the symbol-editing mode (Edit → Edit Document or click on the scene in the Edit Bar).

5. Drag the button symbol from your library to the stage to create a new instance of the button.

Initially, the Up state of the button will be displayed. After the user has navigated to the button, the Over state will be displayed.

Now that you have a button instance on the stage, you will want to define the actions that should take place when the user interacts with the button instance. To assign ActionScript to these buttons, follow these steps:

1. Select the button instance on the stage.

2. Open the Actions panel (Window → Development Panels → Actions or F9). The title bar of the Actions panel should read Actions—Button.

Figure 22-2. Nokia 7610 handset with five-way navigation keys highlighted

3. Define *on(press)*, *on(rollOver)*, and/or *on(rollOut)* handlers for the button, using the following ActionScript as a guideline:

```
on(press) {
    // press actions go here, for example
    gotoAndPlay("nextSection");
}
on(rollOver) {
    // rollOver actions goes here
}
```

```
on(rollOut) {
    // rollOut actions go here
}
```

ActionScript defined for the press (and release) events will be executed if the user presses the Enter key while the button has the active focus.

ActionScript defined for the rollOver event will be executed when the button gains focus.

ActionScript defined for the rollOut event will be executed when the button loses focus.

In the absence of a mouse, the Flash Lite player makes decisions about which button to highlight based on an internal tab order algorithm. The complete details are slightly more complex, but the tab order is essentially left to right followed by top to bottom. When the user presses up (equivalent to Shift-Tab on the keyboard for the desktop player) the focus moves to the previous button according to the tab order. When the user presses down (equivalent to Tab on the keyboard for the desktop player), the focus moves to the next button.

22.6   Overriding the Default Active Button State

Problem

You want to disable the yellow border that appears around the active button on the stage.

Solution

Give the button an empty Over frame or set the _focusrect property to false.

Discussion

By default, the Flash Lite player will draw a two-pixel yellow border around the active button, providing a visual cue as to which button is active. This behavior may be desirable for simple applications, but in many cases you will want to retain artistic control and design your own visual indicator for the active button. There are two ways to disable this automatic yellow border:

1. If you wish to disable this border only for this button symbol (and all corresponding button instances), edit the button, select the Over frame, and insert a Blank Keyframe (Insert → Timeline → Blank Keyframe).

2. If you wish to disable this border for your entire movie, enter the following ActionScript command in the Actions panel for the first frame of your movie:

    ```
    _focusrect = false;
    ```

22.7 Applying Custom Labels to the Soft Keys

Problem

You want to apply custom labels to the phone's soft keys.

Solution

Use the SetSoftKeys command.

Discussion

In addition to the three- or five-way navigation discussed in the previous section, Flash Lite offers you some level of control over the phone's left and right soft keys. The soft keys are so named because their labels and functionality change depending on the phone's state. For example, a phone might label the left soft key "PHONE BOOK" after starting up, but "EXIT" when displaying the Phone Book.

Relabeling the soft keys is achieved by executing the SetSoftKeys command of fscommand2. fscommand2 is a Flash Lite–specific ActionScript function that offers the Flash developer access to many phone-specific data and features at runtime. Among other properties, you can access the phone's battery level and signal strength, or instruct the handset to vibrate. The syntax of fscommand2 is similar to the syntax of the fscommand function you might have used in Flash development for the Flash Desktop Player, except that fscommand2 allows you to pass multiple arguments to the specified command.

As an example, you might be developing a Flash Lite game. When the game is finished, you want to allow the user to quit by pressing the left soft key or play again by pressing the right soft key. You would add the following ActionScript to the last frame of the game:

```
fscommand2("SetSoftKeys", "Quit", "Play Again");
```

Your new labels will be visible only if you have disabled FullScreen mode for your movie. FullScreen mode is set using another fscommand2 command, FullScreen. To disable FullScreen mode, issue the following command on the first frame of the movie:

```
fscommand2("FullScreen", false);
```

If you have created your Flash Lite document using the device templates method, there will already be a line of ActionScript on the first frame of your movie setting enabling FullScreen mode—in this case you will merely swap true for false in that command.

Note that even when the Soft Key labels are not visible, you still need to issue the Set-SoftKeys command if you wish to respond to the user pressing the soft keys.

22.8 Responding to the Soft Keys

Problem

You want to respond to the user pressing the phone's soft keys.

Solution

Use an offstage button instance to respond to the key press.

Discussion

In the previous section, you learned how to register and relabel the phone's soft keys. After the soft keys have been registered, you can respond to soft key presses.

The left and right soft keys are mapped to the same keycodes as the page up and page down keys on a traditional keyboard. Therefore, to detect when the user has pressed the left soft key, you will handle the keyPress event for the <PageUp> keycode. For the right key, you will handle the keyPress event for the <PageDown> keycode. In either case, the convention is to use a button placed offstage in order to handle the events. This method allows you to "listen" for the key presses regardless of whether your user interface calls for an actual button.

1. Insert a new symbol (Insert → New Symbol...) and select the Button behavior. The name you enter will be used to identify this button in the library.

2. Add a static text field to the button's stage. Enter the text "Key Catcher." This label will allow you to identify the button instance in your work area.

3. Exit the symbol editing mode (Edit → Edit Document or click on the scene in the Edit Bar).

4. Drag the button symbol from your library to your work area, off of the stage.

5. Select the button instance.

6. Open the Actions panel (Window → Development Panels → Actions or F9). The title bar of the Actions panel should read "Actions—Button."

7. Define on(press) handlers for the soft keys by entering the following Action-Script:

```
on(keyPress "<PageUp>") {
    // will be executed when left soft key is pressed
    fscommand2("Quit");
}
on(keyPress "<PageDown>") {
    // will be executed when right soft key is pressed
    gotoAndPlay("start");
}
```

22.9   Accessing External Data

Problem

You want to load external data into a Flash Lite movie.

Solution

Utilize the *loadVariables()* function in conjunction with a server-side script.

Discussion

One of the exciting features of the Flash Lite 1.1 player is its ability to access dynamic data via the Internet. You can develop Flash Lite movies that incorporate frequently changing data, such as sports scores, movie times or weather conditions. Though this technique is not appropriate for all applications, the bulk of the most popular Flash Lite applications incorporate some amount of dynamic data.

The ActionScript function *loadVariables()* is used to achieve this goal. *loadVariables()* sends a request to a specified URL, and loads the returned data into a specified movie clip as ActionScript variables that you can then reference in your movie.

Flash Lite expects the data returned via a *loadVariables()* call to be in a special format called *URL-encoded text*. Alphanumeric characters do not require special formatting; however, most punctuation and whitespace characters do. As an example, a single-space character is converted to a plus sign (+) in URL-encoded text.

Conveniently, all server-side scripting languages (ColdFusion, PHP, ASP, and so on) have built-in functions to format the text for you. For this example, I will use PHP to pass the current month, day, and year to a Flash Lite movie. The Flash Lite movie will display this information in a dynamic text field on the stage. The first step is to create the PHP script that will respond to the *loadVariables()* call.

1. Create a new text document in a text editor program (NotePad on Windows or TextEdit on Mac OS X will work fine).

2. Enter the following code into the document:

```
<?php
$date = date("F j, Y");
$dateURL = urlencode($date);
header("Content-type: application/x-www-form-urlencoded");
print "date=" . $dateURL . "&loaded=1";
?>
```

This script first stores the current date in the variable $date. It then URL-encodes the date, and stores the URL-encoded value in the variable $dateURL. The third line sends the appropriate HTTP header for URL-encoded text. Finally, it prints out two variables to be returned to the Flash Lite movie—date and loaded. Note the format of the return string. Variable name declarations are specified as `<name>=<value>` pairs and each declaration is separated by the ampersand character. This is the same format as used in URL query strings and when passing variables to a Flash movie in a web page using `FlashVars`.

3. Upload the document to your web server. Note that your web server must be configured to serve PHP files. If you do not have access to a web server, or would rather not go through the hassle, you can call this script using *http://www. rightactionscript.com/fcb/getDate.php*—I have put this script online for the purpose of this exercise.

The next step is to create the Flash Lite movie that will load this data:

1. Open a new Flash Lite document.

2. If it's not already there, create a new layer called ActionScript. Name the other layer "Content." Note that if you created the document using the device templates method in Flash 8, the new movie opens with two layers pre-initialized and named "Content" and "ActionScript."

3. Add a static text field to the first frame of the "Content" layer with the text "Loading...."

4. Insert a blank keyframe on the fourth frame of the "Content" layer (Insert → Timeline → Blank Keyframe).

5. Add a dynamic text field to the stage on the fourth frame of the "Content" layer. It should be large enough to accommodate the date information that will be passed back from the PHP script. Enter date in the Var property.

6. Select this text field and convert it to a movie clip (Modify → Convert to Symbol... or F8). Select Movie Clip as the type, and give this movie clip the instance name mcDate in the Properties pane.

7. Add the following ActionScript code to the first frame of the ActionScript layer. This code tells the Flash Player to load the data returned from the getDate PHP script into the mcDate movie clip.

```
LoadVariables("http://<your server name here>/getDate.php", "mcDate");
```

8. Insert a blank keyframe on the third frame of the Actions layer (Insert → Timeline → Blank Keyframe). We will use this keyframe to test to see whether the data has been returned from our *loadVariables()* call.

9. Add the following ActionScript code to the third frame of the Actions layer:

```
if(mcDate:loaded ne "1") {
  gotoAndPlay(2);
}
else {
  gotoAndStop(4);
}
```

This if statement checks whether the variable loaded is not equal to 1. Remember that our PHP script returns two variables: loaded (which is set to 1) and date. If loaded is not equal to 1, we know that the data has not been returned from our *loadVariables( )* call, and we tell the playhead to go to frame 2 and play. This step sets up a loop whereby the playhead will check for the loaded variable each time it reaches frame 3. When loaded is finally set to 1, the playhead will advance to frame 4 and will stop. As the mcDate clip will also have been assigned a value for the variable date, the dynamic text field we created (which has a variable name of date) will display the date value returned by the *loadVariables( )* call.

22.10 ActionScript for Flash Lite

Problem

You want to learn (or perhaps revisit) scripting techniques and syntax that are compatible with Flash Lite.

Solution

Read the "Flash 4 ActionScript Primer" in the Flash 8 Professional help panel.

Discussion

As has been discussed elsewhere, Flash Lite 1.1 is based on the Flash 4 scripting engine. Unlike the current implementation of ActionScript, which is based on the same ECMAScript standard as JavaScript, Flash 4 ActionScript syntax strays significantly from other modern programming languages. Although not all Flash Lite projects require substantial amounts of code, it is worthwhile to review the excellent "Flash 4 ActionScript Primer" that is included in the Flash 8 Professional install. To view the tutorials, follow these steps:

1. Open Flash Help (Help → Flash Help or F1).
2. Navigate to Learning Flash Lite 1.x ActionScript → Flash 4 ActionScript Primer.

22.11 Using Sound in Flash Lite

Problem

You want to incorporate sound into your Flash Lite project.

Solution

View the "Using Sound in Flash Lite 1.1" tutorial on Macromedia's Mobile and Devices Developer Center web site.

Discussion

The Flash Lite 1.1 player supports both device sounds (sounds that are passed from the Flash movie to the host device for playback) and native sounds (sounds that are played natively by the Flash Lite Player). Although the techniques for incorporating native sounds in Flash Lite are analogous to those used in Flash development for the web, the use of device sounds requires a special technique whereby you utilize a proxy sound file as a placeholder for the device sound. The reason for this technique is that Flash 8 Professional doesn't understand many of the device sound formats that can be played by the host device.

For more information, and for a discussion of the Flash Lite Sound Bundler (which allows you to bundle MIDI, MFi, and other device sound formats for use on a device) see Nader Nejat's "Using Sound in Flash Lite 1.1" tutorial on Macromedia's Mobile and Devices Developer Center web site:

http://www.macromedia.com/devnet/devices/articles/flashlite_sound.html

22.12 The Flash Lite Development Community

Problem

You want to see what other developers are creating with Flash Lite and share your Flash Lite projects with the world.

Solution

Visit the Macromedia Flash Lite Exchange.

Discussion

As of the writing of this book, the Flash Lite Player is mainly installed on handsets provided by two major Japanese carriers. Despite this fact, the global Flash developer community is preparing for the expansion of Flash Lite's reach by developing content that both highlights Flash Lite's key benefits and features and tests its capabilities. Because a handset's processor, display, and memory capabilities are far inferior to the average desktop computer, Flash Lite developers often need to implement creative workarounds and methods to achieve the effects they desire. For example, video is not supported at all in Flash Lite 1.1—one alternate method developers have used to simulate video is to break the movie into *.jpeg* images and arrange these images on the timeline.

You can keep abreast of Flash Lite development techniques and applications and even submit your own applications for QA review and then post at the Macromedia Flash Lite Exchange. Follow the "Flash Lite Exchange" link at:

http://www.macromedia.com/exchange/

Another comprehensive web resource is the Macromedia Mobile and Devices Developer center, located at

http://www.macromedia.com/devnet/devices/flashlite.html

CHAPTER 23

Making Movies Accessible

According to both professional standards, such as the Web Content Accessibility Guidelines distributed by the World Wide Web Consortium (*http://www.w3.org/TR/WCAG10*), and legal standards, including Section 508 of the U.S. Rehabilitation Act (*http://www.section508.gov*), the responsibility of ensuring that content is accessible falls on the content provider.

Accessibility refers to the potential for all users to access content electronically. Enabling electronic access to content generally requires an awareness of both the many types of disabilities that can prevent a user from accessing content and the assistive technologies that are used to overcome barriers to accessing content. Indeed, assistive technologies remove much of the burden of making content accessible.

The U.S. Census Bureau in 1997 estimated that nearly 20% of individuals in the United States have one or more disabilities. In a country with roughly 280 million citizens, that is more than 50 million people. Professional and legal frameworks have emerged to facilitate, promote, and even force content providers to meet the needs of these users. In addition to the moral and legal reasons to do so, making content accessible makes good business sense. Benefits include the following:

- Organizations extend their reach to a broader—and often underserved—audience.

- Organizations communicate to all users that they take customer needs seriously.

- By making content accessible, organizations also make it more compatible with future technologies that haven't yet emerged, thanks to the separation of content and presentation.

Collectively, these benefits outweigh the costs of making content accessible. As discussed later in this introduction and throughout the chapter, Flash has numerous accessibility features that facilitate the process of making Flash content accessible. Moreover, accessible solutions are often low-tech and easy to implement, often involving plain text or static HTML.

Several kinds of disability can affect the user's experience with electronic information. For every disability, several options exist for providing alternate means of accessing content, and in many cases, a given solution works for multiple disabilities, as shown in Table 23-1.

Table 23-1. Common disabilities and practical accessibility accommodations

Disability	Possible accessibility accommodations
Blindness	Audio alternatives, including screen readers and audio narrations
Limited vision (worse than 20/70)	Magnification, high-contrast colors, audio alternatives
Color blindness	High-contrast colors, content that doesn't rely on color (e.g., "click the red box for X, or click the blue box for Y")
Hearing impairments	Captioning, visual cues and/or feedback, ability to turn off music soundtracks that may interfere with spoken text
Motor disabilities (limited reach and strength, can't use mouse)	Keyboard-navigable movies

Although the burden of offering accessible content falls on providers, many available assistive technologies help users gain electronic access to content. *Assistive technologies* include both user agents and alternative input devices. A *user agent* is any software that enables a user to access web content, including browsers, screen readers, Braille displays, and so on. Alternative input devices include modified keyboards, touch screens, voice recognition, and head pointers.

Because assistive technologies and user agents vary so significantly in the way they provide access to content, and because all user agents—assistive or otherwise—change so frequently, it is impractical to worry about the specifics of any given one at any point in time. A more useful goal is to separate content from presentation sufficiently that all user agents can correctly interpret and present its structure and information to the user. Content that is able to be correctly interpreted and presented/rendered to the user by a user agent is said to *transform gracefully*.

Graceful transformation is both the goal and requirement of every content provider. In some cases, it can be as simple as offering an alternative version of a given piece of content. For example, the alt attribute of the HTML <img> element is used to insert a text description of the image so that users with visual impairments still can access the image's contents. HTML also offers a longdesc attribute, which enables a lengthy or detailed alternative to the image, as is beneficial for complex images, such as flowcharts.

But making content transform gracefully is often much more than simply labeling or providing a text description of an element. The purpose of accessibility is not to mechanically label every element, but rather to make the substance or meaning of the content available to all users. For example, consider a piano falling from the 12th story down to the street below, an animation that might use 12 frames in Flash. If we were to simply label the piano, the building, and the street, the words "building," "piano," and "street" would appear 12 times (because they are all in every frame). But the substance of the animation is not the repetition of these words; rather, the substance is the scene of a piano falling from a tall building and smashing into the street below. Thus, creating content that transforms gracefully is as much a soft skill as a technical skill; it is a creative process by which content developers consider how a diversity of users and user agents will attempt to access the content, and then ensure that the content is offered in such a way that the attempt is successful.

As an animated and interactive medium, Flash poses challenges to developers implementing accessibility that providers of HTML documents don't face. Assistive devices generally do well with page- or document-based content, where a finite amount of information appears in one place, and the user can dwell on it as long as she or he wants before moving on to the next document or page. HTML content usually falls in this category. But highly dynamic content, which changes quickly and constantly based on user activity—such as video games, target-based drag-and-drop, pop-up menus, live data, and exploration interactions—is harder to capture in static blocks of text. As this chapter demonstrates, solutions exist, but they often require some creativity and planning.

The Flash Player 6 and higher versions have numerous built-in accessibility features. All static text in Flash is automatically exposed in the Flash Player 6, without any work from the Flash author. Other objects, including buttons, dynamic and input text, movie clips, and the movie as a whole are also exposed by default, though several of these need additional information to be made meaningful.

You can selectively hide any of these objects as well from screen readers, with the exception of static text. Much of this work—tagging movie assets for accessibility—takes place in the Accessibility panel, which lets you name objects, provide short descriptions for them (the equivalent of giving them alt attributes), and provide long descriptions for them (the equivalent of giving them longdesc attributes).

To access an audio representation of Flash content, users must have a screen reader that uses Microsoft Active Accessibility (MSAA). At present, Window-Eyes and JAWS are the readers able to access Flash Player 6 content. Other assistive technologies, such as special input devices, are dependent on the operating system, rather than Flash, and should also work. Tab-enabling buttons and keyboard shortcuts are possible, but not automatic, in Flash.

The recipes in this chapter provide several solutions that you can implement to make movies accessible. But before you start modifying a movie, you should develop an overall strategy about how best to make content accessible. The following list summarizes three different broad approaches to making content used in a Flash movie accessible:

- Expose elements in an existing movie for accessibility. In this approach, the contents of both the regular and accessible versions of the movie come from the same source. The movie itself, and text and objects within it, are exposed to assistive technologies as the movie is played. Although the movie may be optimized in some ways for compatibility with assistive technologies, there is only one movie.

- Create one or more alternate versions of the Flash movie. Attempting to make the movie compatible with screen readers or other assistive technologies is impractical—the movie's architecture of presentation just doesn't lend itself to the transformation. Instead, a different version of the Flash movie is created, which is built from the ground up to serve these audiences.

- Don't use Flash for accessible content. Flash isn't used at all as a vehicle for accessible content. Instead, accessibility-optimized content is put in HTML or text documents, to which users are directed from the original Flash movie.

Choosing the right strategy depends on a number of factors, including the nature of the content, the user experience you are trying to create, available developer time, and concerns about maintenance. As a rule of thumb, the more the movie experience is page-based (as defined previously), the better it will transform for accessible technologies. Conversely, the more speed is a factor—for example, because the movie plays back quickly like a music video or because it demands fast user interaction, as does a video game—the less likely it will transform gracefully, no matter what you do in the Accessibility panel.

23.1 Detecting and Redirecting Users with Assistive Devices

Problem

You want to determine whether a user is accessing the movie with an assistive device so that you can redirect the user to a resource optimized for accessibility.

Solution

Use *Accessibility.isActive()* and System.capabilities.hasAccessibility to determine whether the Flash player is communicating with a screen reader.

Discussion

Testing whether the computer supports accessibility is necessary, because Flash can communicate to a screen reader only through Microsoft Active Accessibility, which is supported only in Internet Explorer for Windows. It is not presently supported in any other browser or the standalone player. You can test for this case using System.capabilities.hasAccessibility, a property that returns true when the player supports accessibility. In other words, this test always returns true in Internet Explorer for Windows and false in all other browsers.

In addition to testing whether the player supports accessibility, you also need to test whether an assistive technology (generally a screen reader) is communicating with Flash Player. You can do this using *Accessibility.isActive()*. The following Action-Script code tests whether the user appears to be using an assistive technology:

```
if (System.capabilities.hasAccessibility && Accessibility.isActive()) {
    // Flash Player is communicating with an assistive technology.
}
```

Assistive technologies take time to connect to the Flash Player—up to a second—and if the Player executes the test the moment it loads, it is likely to return false regardless of whether an assistive technology is present. Therefore, it's frequently helpful to use *setInterval()* to test for an assistive technology for a few seconds. The following script does just that:

```
var nAccessibilityInterval:Number = setInterval(this, "testAccessibility", 100);
var nStartTimer:Number = getTimer();

function testAccessibility():Void {
    if (Accessibility.isActive() && System.capabilities.hasAccessibility) {
        clearInterval(nAccessibilityInterval);
        this.gotoAndPlay("accessible"); // Or another redirection action
    }
    else if(getTimer() - nStartTimer > 2000) {
        clearInterval(nAccessibilityInterval);
        this.gotoAndPlay("standard");
    }
}
```

Although this script is likely to detect when assistive technologies are present, it is not foolproof. For example, the user could be using a technology that Flash does not detect. In addition to this script, you should consider employing an accessibility link in an obvious location in your site. When users select that link, they go directly to the accessible version, and they don't have to rely on this accessibility detection script.

23.2   Making Content Accessible

Problem

You want to make elements within a movie accessible.

Solution

Specify the name and description of each item that you want to be exposed to screen readers. If necessary, convert the item to a movie clip symbol.

Discussion

The Accessibility panel enables you to expose objects to screen readers. It also enables you to name and provide text descriptions for these objects. You can also use it to hide certain objects from screen readers. This recipe discusses how to use the panel, and more broadly, how to expose, hide, name, and describe Flash objects to maximize accessibility to the substance or meaning of the movie.

The following objects can be exposed to screen readers: movie clip instances, button instances, dynamic text, input text, and the movie as a whole. In addition, static text is automatically exposed and cannot be hidden. (If you want to hide static text, convert it to dynamic text and then hide it.)

Not all Flash content is accessible. Vector graphics drawn or imported into Flash and bitmaps imported into Flash are not accessible. Neither are graphic symbols. However, an easy workaround is to convert the content to a movie clip symbol instance and expose that.

All the objects have some or all of the following settings. To select an object to specify its accessibility, click it on the stage. The only exception is the movie as a whole: to specify its accessibility settings, deselect everything on the stage. Once the object is selected, specify the following settings, if applicable, in the Accessibility panel (Window → Accessibility).

Make Movie/Object Accessible

Available for all accessible objects. Check to expose the movie or object to screen readers, or uncheck to hide the move or object, as well as all of its children, from screen readers. This setting is checked by default for all objects.

Make Child Objects Accessible

Available only for the movie as a whole and movie clip instances. Check to expose all child objects of the selected movie or movie clip. Uncheck to hide all objects of the selected movie or movie clip. To expose some children and hide others, check Make Child Objects Accessible in the parent, and then uncheck Make Object Accessible for all children you want to hide.

Auto Label

Available only for the movie as a whole. When active, if text appears on or beside an object, Flash uses that text to name the object. For example, a button instance with the word "Home" on it would be called "Home" in a screen reader. When inactive, you must manually name all objects. In addition, any nearby text labels will still be read, which will likely be redundant. If you do not use auto labeling, you should hide nearby text labels from screen readers. However, all static text is automatically exposed; therefore, to hide text labels, first convert them to dynamic text and use the Accessibility panel to hide them.

Name

Available for the movie as a whole, movie clips, buttons, and input (but not dynamic) text. Dynamic text fields are named by their contents. The Name field is intended to hold a short, descriptive name—ideally, one under 50 characters (though the field can hold thousands), which should identify the object.

Description

Available for all objects. Use to enter a long text description for the contents.

Filling out the Accessibility panel for each object in the movie is an important first step toward making a movie accessible, but it is only a first step. Later recipes discuss some of the problems and limitations of using the Accessibility panel, as well as other accessibility concerns that go beyond screen readers.

See Also

Recipe 23.3

23.3 Making Animated, Interactive, and Visually Complex Movies Accessible

Problem

You want to make an animated, interactive, or visually complex movie accessible.

Solution

Hide animated and visually complex content from screen readers, and replace it with meaningful text alternatives. Or, create an alternative movie with an accessibility-friendly architecture. Design the movie so that users relying on assistive technologies can navigate to and control the duration of content display.

Discussion

Most assistive technologies were developed to make documents accessible. HTML, word processor, and even XML documents are static; they have a beginning, a middle, and an end, and they exist as discrete documents, distinguishable from other documents. The user loads them on the screen, accesses their content, and when finished, moves on to the next document.

This document-based user experience, and the architecture it implies, while possible in Flash, is certainly not the norm. Designed for providing rich user experiences, Flash movies are often dynamic, with the contents changing constantly, as part of a pre-designed animation or even in live response to user activity. Indeed, these constant changes are often a part of the content. Unfortunately, this content is different enough from the static page-based documents that it is not practically accessible using many assistive technologies.

One example of the kinds of problems Flash content can cause occurs in screen readers in animated movies. Screen readers start at the top of each document and read from top to bottom. Unfortunately, every time a Flash movie changes—in every frame during an animation—the screen reader starts over. At 12 frames per second, the screen reader gets trapped, indicating that the page is loading over and over again.

A similar issue occurs when users cannot control the speed at which information is presented. For example, in one popular advertising technique, two or three words of text appear at a time, fade away, and are replaced by a couple more words, and so on until the full text has been displayed. For users who can see and read the text, the animated text is usually paced well for comprehension and impact. But for users relying on assistive devices, the content may go by faster than the device can render it. The effect for users relying on these technologies is something like people with sight experience when television or movie credits scroll by so quickly that they can't read them.

Still another issue occurs with visually complex animations of relationships. For example, consider the case of a chart depicting the water cycle in which water rains, flows to rivers, empty into the ocean, and eventually evaporates into the atmosphere again. Providing alternate text descriptions for each of the graphic objects will hardly convey the meaning to a user relying on a screen reader.

The greatest challenge when making objects truly accessible is not technical—the Accessibility panel makes the process quite simple. Rather, the challenge is providing content that is actually equivalent to the content shown on the stage.

The following list summarizes some of the techniques you can use to make complex and dynamic Flash content accessible:

- Group and/or hide objects selectively to maximize meaning. For example:
  - Enclose animations in movie clip symbol instances, and provide text descriptions for the animation as a whole. Then, rather than exposing each element in the animation movie clip, hide all child elements from accessibility. With the animation movie clip instance selected, in the Description field of the Accessibility panel, enter a description of the animation as a whole unit. Describe not simply its visual details, but the relationship(s) between its components, or the progression of the animation over time.
  - Ensure that text descriptions capture the meaning or substance of the animation or interaction, not simply the names of its visible assets.
- Use descriptions to reveal the structure of the document as a whole. Users with sight see the stage and perceive the relationship between the elements—navigation, decoration, branding, main content, and so on. Use descriptions to communicate the screen's hierarchies and structural divisions, and provide cues as to how each of these divisions can be used or understood.

- Try to make your movies behave as much like documents as possible:
  — Try to divide the movie into static screens that display, unchanging, for a sufficient amount of time to enable assistive devices to render the content.
  — Give control to users. Provide a means of stopping, rewinding, and advancing through content in a self-paced way.
  — If necessary, create an optimized-for-accessibility version of the movie. Use assistive technology detection to direct the user to this optimized version, as discussed in Recipe 23.1.
- Ensure that all navigational elements are accessible via the keyboard and the mouse, as discussed in Recipe 23.5.

In many cases, the more dynamic and user-aware your Flash movie is, the harder it is to make it accessible. Whether some creativity with the Accessibility panel is sufficient, you have to create a whole new Flash movie, or you are forced to offload accessible content to an HTML page, the key is to provide meaningful, organized content, and to ensure that users can navigate to it and spend as much time with it as they need.

See Also

Recipe 23.1, Recipe 23.5

23.4   Creating Accessible Buttons

Problem

You want to design a movie with accessible buttons.

Solution

Place all meaningful content in the Up and Over frames, and focus them on the button functionality.

Discussion

When designing buttons for accessibility, it is important to bear in mind a handful of easy-to-implement best practices:

- Buttons are automatically accessible in Flash. When in focus, users need only press Enter/Return to activate them.
- Many assistive devices do not recognize Down or Hit states, so do not put vital content in these frames. This guideline also means that you should avoid using invisible buttons in accessible movies.

- Provide meaningful names, such as "Buy now," and avoid context or vision-dependent names, such as "Click here."
- Activate the Auto Label checkbox to cause Flash to name buttons based on the label that appears in the Up frame. Deactivate this feature and provide your own labels if you want custom labels. The Auto Label checkbox is found in the Accessibility panel when nothing on the stage is selected.
- Avoid animating button states.

Remember, rather than choosing between design and accessibility goals, in the event of a conflict, a third option is available, which is to create a special accessibility-friendly version of the movie, as discussed in Recipe 23.1.

Another best practice is to establish a tab order for each of the buttons as well as provide keyboard shortcuts for the buttons. These features assist both people using screen readers and people who are limited to the keyboard. Both of these techniques are discussed in Recipe 23.5.

When you use movie clips as buttons, using button events, such as onPress and onRelease, assistive technologies render these as buttons. Thus, the practices outlined in this recipe also apply to movie clips acting as buttons. For more on movie clips acting as buttons, see Recipe 9.1.

See Also

Recipe 9.1, Recipe 23.5

23.5 Making Keyboard-Navigable Movies

Problem

You want to create keyboard shortcuts that duplicate button behaviors, and you want to expose those shortcuts to assistive devices.

Solution

Create keyboard shortcuts that duplicate button actions, using *Key.isDown()*. Write code in a modular way, so that it can be accessed in more than one way. Use the Accessibility panel to inform users with assistive devices about the keyboard shortcuts. Specify a logical tab order for buttons, using tabIndex.

Discussion

Movies that rely on buttons to control playback intrinsically rely on users' ability to click on those buttons with a mouse. One way to make movies functional for those who rely on the keyboard is to create keyboard shortcuts. Buttons can be made accessible in one of two ways:

Default keyboard shortcuts

By default, users can execute button actions by setting the focus on the button and pressing Enter or Return. A disadvantage to this approach is that users must tab to the button, which could become unwieldy in a movie with many buttons. A related issue is tab order.

Custom keyboard shortcuts

The developer creates keyboard shortcuts for certain actions. For example, pressing S stops a movie, while pressing P causes it to start playing again. These require a modest amount of extra work but are generally worth it.

These two approaches to button accessibility are not exclusive, and even when you implement custom keyboard shortcuts, default keyboard shortcuts will still be in place.

If you are relying on default keyboard shortcuts—pressing Enter or Return when a button is in focus—you should specify the tab order. You can tell a button is in focus when a yellow rectangle appears on it. Though the ordering of buttons on a page may be perfectly obvious to a person with sight, Flash does not always correctly guess how the buttons should be ordered for a person tabbing through them.

You can specify button tab order (in this case, button refers to Button instances as well as MovieClip instances with button event handler methods applied to them) using the tabIndex property. Use it with the following syntax, which assumes that the stage has two buttons, with instance names of *btFirst* and *btSecond*:

```
btFirst.tabindex = 1;
btSecond.tabindex = 2;
```

When using tabIndex, be sure you specify every button that you want included in the tab order. As soon as you apply tabIndex to a button, all other buttons are excluded from tab order, unless you explicitly set their tabIndex properties as well.

Tabbing does not work as expected in Flash's test movie environment, unless Control → Disable Keyboard Shortcuts is checked. By default it is not, and pressing Tab has no effect on the movie. Regardless, tabbing does work as expected in the Flash standalone player and within browsers.

Next, if you want to make keyboard shortcuts, you need to add the ActionScript code that detects the key presses and calls the correct functions. You can read more about detecting key presses in Chapter 9.

When you add keyboard shortcuts, you typically want to call the same function whether the user presses the keyboard shortcut or selects the button while it is focused. Often the simplest way to deal with that is to call the event handler method of the corresponding button when the user presses the keyboard shortcut. The following illustrates the concept with a simple example. In the example, you can assume that btStop and btPlay are buttons and mAnimation is a movie clip with a timeline you want to control using the buttons. When the user presses the P key it plays the timeline, and when the user presses the S key, it stops the timeline.

```
btPlay.onPress = function( ):Void {
  mAnimation.play( );
};
btStop.onPress = function( ):Void {
  mAnimation.stop( );
};
var oKeyListener:Object = new Object( );
oKeyListener.onKeyDown = function( ):Void {
  if(Key.getCode( ) == new String("P").charCodeAt(0)) {
    btPlay.onPress( );
  }
  else if(Key.getCode( ) == new String("S").charCodeAt(0)) {
    btStop.onPress( );
  }
};
Key.addListener(oKeyListener);
```

After you've created keyboard alternatives, don't forget to expose them to assistive devices. Select each button in turn, and use the Accessibility panel to give the button a description and specify a keyboard shortcut. If Auto Label is active for the movie, don't specify a name for the button.

 Listing a keyboard shortcut in the Accessibility panel does not create the shortcut: it merely announces that shortcut to screen readers. You still need to create the keyboard shortcut.

See Also

Recipe 9.5, Recipe 9.15, Recipe 23.2

23.6   Providing Captions

Problem

You want to provide captions of audio content for the hearing impaired.

Solution

Create captions manually using keyframes and static text for audio placed on a timeline with the Sync option set to Stream. If you want to add captions to video, see Chapter 18.

Discussion

Captions are more than just a transcript of spoken words in a movie or video. In addition to spoken language, captions also indicate ambient noises, audible silences, and who is speaking (when the speaker is off-camera or not obvious). Captions, like text alternatives for people with vision impairments, should provide a full alternative to the audio content.

To add captions to audio that's been added to a timeline you need to set the sound's Sync setting to Stream. As noted in Chapter 17, the Stream option causes Flash to keep the timeline in sync with the sound as it plays back.

After you've selected Stream from the Sync setting for the sound, you can next add static text to keyframes whereby the text corresponds to the audio that's playing back at that moment. When you add captions, make sure that you test the playback of the text for readability as you are working. It's generally better to use longer strings of text per caption so that the reader doesn't have to deal with lots of smaller strings of text flashing by too quickly to read.

If you want to add captions to Flash video, see Chapter 18.

See Also

Recipe 8.1

Index

We'd like to hear your suggestions for improving our indexes. Send email to *index@oreilly.com*.

About the Author

Joey Lott is the author of *ActionScript Cookbook* (O'Reilly), *Learning ActionScript 2.0 in Flash MX 2004* (Lynda.com/Pearson), *Complete Flash Remoting MX* (Wiley), and is co-author of *Flash MX 2004 ActionScript Bible* (Wiley). Joey spends much of his time writing and doing consulting and project development on his own, as well as interfacing with the Flash development community (Macromedia, other experts, fans and users, media, interested corporate clients, and friends). You can learn more about Joey and follow his contributions to the Flash community by checking out his web site and his blog: *http://www.person13.com/*.

Colophon

The animal on the cover of *Flash 8 Cookbook* is a hoopoe (*Upupa epops*), an exotic-looking bird that resembles a giant butterfly in flight, its wings alternately spreading and closing to expose black-and-white barring. The hoopoe has a pinkish-brown body, a long black down-curved bill, and a distinctive crest that it raises when excited or alarmed. Although this bird is difficult to spot when it is foraging among the leaf-litter, the hoopoe is dazzling and agile in flight. It has been known to elude both the merlin and the falcon, mounting easily into the air and climbing so high that it is lost to human sight.

There is no agreement on the number of hoopoes species, but there is decidedly one genus with five subspecies, nearly all of which breed in Europe and winter in sub-Saharan Africa. The subspecies differ only slightly in color, yet the Madagascar hoopoe is vocally distinct, which gives some scientists reason to separate it from the Eurasian and African hoopoes. All hoopoes are open-country birds, preferring olive groves, orchards, vicarage gardens, and British golf courses. An average of 125 of them are spotted each year on the southern cost of England, having overshot their northern migration to continental Europe.

Perhaps because of their diet of worms and insects, or perhaps because they frequently revel in dust-baths, hoopoes are included in the Old Testament's list of unclean birds. The reason may just as likely lie, however, in the fact that these birds make their nests using copious amounts of feces. The foul odor of the tree cavities in which they live succeeds in keeping predators at a distance. Other than being dusty, worm-eating, feces-nesting Upupa, they aren't the least bit unclean.

The cover image is from *Cassell's Natural History*. The cover font is Adobe ITC Garamond. The text font is Linotype Birka; the heading font is Adobe Myriad Condensed; and the code font is LucasFont's TheSans Mono Condensed..

Better than e-books

Buy *Flash 8 Cookbook* and access the
digital edition FREE on Safari for 45 days.

Go to www.oreilly.com/go/safarienabled
and type in coupon code RZFS-2PZG-PERW-ZBGB-WKQ8

Search
thousands of
top tech books

Download
whole chapters

Cut and Paste
code examples

Find
answers fast

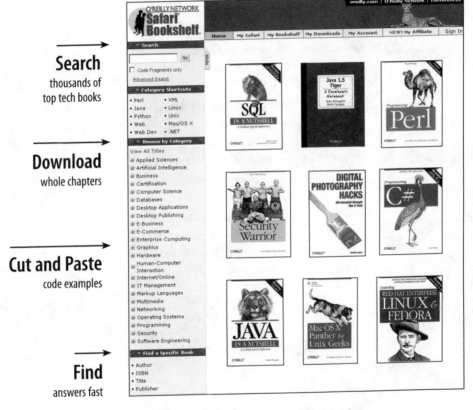

Search Safari! The premier electronic reference
library for programmers and IT professionals.

Related Titles from O'Reilly

Web Authoring and Design

Ambient Findability

Cascading Style Sheets: The Definitive Guide, *2nd Edition*

Creating Web Sites: The Missing Manual

CSS Cookbook

CSS Pocket Reference, *2nd Edition*

Dreamweaver 8: Design and Construction

Dreamweaver 8: The Missing Manual

Essential ActionScript 2.0

Flash 8: Projects for Learning Animation and Interactivity

Flash 8: The Missing Manual

Flash Hacks

Head First HTML with CSS & XHTML

Head Rush Ajax

HTML & XHTML: The Definitive Guide, *5th Edition*

HTML Pocket Reference, *2nd Edition*

Information Architecture for the World Wide Web, *2nd Edition*

Information Dashboard Design

Learning Web Design, *2nd Edition*

Programming Flash Communication Server

Web Design in a Nutshell, *3rd Edition*

Web Site Measurement Hacks